JOURNEYS THROUGH OUR WORLD

THIRD EDITION

SELECTIONS CHOSEN BY:

MICHAEL ALEXANDER

BETHANY CARSON

NANCY GRAY

SHULI LAMDEN

DIANE PINKEY

ANNIE SAHLIN

LINDA WIESEMAN

THERESE WILSON

COMPILED BY THE DEVELOPMENTAL ENGLISH DEPARTMENT
AT SANTA FE COMMUNITY COLLEGE

PEARSON
Custom
Publishing

Cover Art: "Moon Over the Sudan" by Annie Sahlin

Printed in the United States of America

10 9 8 7 6 5 4 3

ISBN 0-536-45340-3

2007240299

DA/MB

Please visit our web site at *www.pearsoncustom.com*

PEARSON CUSTOM PUBLISHING
501 Boylston Street, Suite 900, Boston, MA 02116
A Pearson Education Company

"APO 96225," by Larry Rottman, reprinted from *Expressions: Stories and Poems* (1992), Contemporary Books, Inc, a division of Random House, Inc.

"Beyond Good & Evil: Marshall Rosenberg on Creating a Non-Violent World," by Dian Killian, reprinted from *The Sun*, February 2003, by permission of the author.

"Three Wonderous Answers," by Thich Nhat Hanh, reprinted from *The Miracle of Mindfulness* (1996), by permission of Beacon Press, Boston.

"Tough Love," by Celeste Fremon, reprinted with permission from the *Los Angeles Times Magazine*, Oct. 15, 1995, by permission of the author.

"Give and Grow," by Annie Campbell, reprinted by permission of the author.

Contents

Section 4   *Making Changes*   **325**

Section 1

About Writing

From *Writing Down the Bones*

NATALIE GOLDBERG

First Thoughts

The basic unit of writing practice is the timed exercise. You may time yourself for ten minutes, twenty minutes, or an hour. It's up to you. At the beginning you may want to start small and after a week increase your time, or you may want to dive in for an hour the first time. It doesn't matter. What does matter is that whatever amount of time you choose for that session, you must commit yourself to it and for that full period:

1. *Keep your hand moving.* (Don't pause to reread the line you have just written. That's stalling and trying to get control of what you're saying.)
2. *Don't cross out.* (That is editing as you write. Even if you write something you didn't mean to write, leave it.)
3. *Don't worry about spelling, punctuation, grammar.* (Don't even care about staying within the margins and lines on the page.)
4. *Lose control.*
5. *Don't think. Don't get logical.*
6. *Go for the jugular.* (If something comes up in your writing that is scary or naked, dive right into it. It probably has lots of energy.)

These are the rules. It is important to adhere to them because the aim is to burn through to first thoughts, to the place where energy is unobstructed by social politeness or the internal censor, to the place where you are writing what your mind actually sees and feels, not what it *thinks* it should see or feel. It's a great opportunity to capture the oddities of your mind. Explore the rugged edge of thought. Like grating a carrot, give the paper the colorful coleslaw of your consciousness.

First thoughts have tremendous energy. It is the way the mind first flashes on something. The internal censor usually squelches them, so we live in the realm of second and third thoughts, thoughts on thought, twice and three times

3

removed from the direct connection of the first fresh flash. For instance, the phrase "I cut the daisy from my throat" shot through my mind. Now my second thought, carefully tutored in $1 + 1 = 2$ logic, in politeness, fear, and embarrassment at the natural, would say, "That's ridiculous. You sound suicidal. Don't show yourself cutting your throat. Someone will think you are crazy." And instead, if we give the censor its way, we write, "My throat was a little sore, so I didn't say anything." Proper and boring.

First thoughts are also unencumbered by ego, by that mechanism in us that tries to be in control, tries to prove the world is permanent and solid, enduring and logical. The world is not permanent, is ever-changing and full of human suffering. So if you express something egoless, it is also full of energy because it is expressing the truth of the way things are. You are not carrying the burden of ego in your expression, but are riding for moments the waves of human consciousness and using your personal details to express the ride.

In Zen meditation you sit on a cushion called a zafu with your legs crossed, back straight, hands at your knees or in front of you in a gesture called a mudra. You face a white wall and watch your breath. No matter what you feel—great tornadoes of anger and resistance, thunderstorms of joy and grief—you continue to sit, back straight, legs crossed, facing the wall. You learn to not be tossed away no matter how great the thought or emotion. That is the discipline: to continue to sit.

The same is true in writing. You must be a great warrior when you contact first thoughts and write from them. Especially at the beginning you may feel great emotions and energy that will sweep you away, but don't stop writing. You continue to use your pen and record the details of your life and penetrate into the heart of them. Often in a beginning class students break down crying when they read pieces they have written. That is okay. Often as they write they cry, too. However, I encourage them to continue reading or writing right through the tears so they may come out the other side and not be thrown off by the emotion. Don't stop at the tears; go through to truth. This is the discipline.

Why else are first thoughts so energizing? Because they have to do with freshness and inspiration. Inspiration means "breathing in." Breathing in God. You actually become larger than yourself, and first thoughts are present. They are not a cover-up of what is actually happening or being felt. The present is imbued with tremendous energy. It is what is. My friend who is a Buddhist said once after coming out of a meditation retreat, "The colors were so much more vibrant afterward." Her meditation teacher said, "When you are present, the world is truly alive."

A List of Topics for Writing Practice

Sometimes we sit down to write and can't think of anything to write about. The blank page can be intimidating, and it does get boring to write over and over again for ten minutes of practice, "I can't think of what to say. I can't think of what to say." It is a good idea to have a page in your notebook where you jot down, as they come to you, ideas of topics to write about. It could be a line you heard. For example, at a restaurant I complained to one waiter about another one. His response: "I know he's odd, but if they dance to a different drummer I say, 'Just let them dance.'" It could be a flash of memory: your grandfather's false teeth; how the lilacs smelled last June when you weren't there; who you were in your saddle shoes at eight years old. It could be anything. Add to the list anytime you think of something. Then when you sit down to write, you can just grab a topic from that list and begin.

Making a list is good. It makes you start noticing material for writing in your daily life, and your writing comes out of a relationship with your life and its texture. In this way, the composting process is beginning. Your body is starting to digest and turn over your material, so even when you are not actually at the desk physically writing, there are parts of you raking, fertilizing, taking in the sun's heat, and making ready for the deep green plants of writing to grow.

If you give your mind too much time to contemplate a beginning when you sit down to write, your monkey mind might meander over many topics and never quite get to putting a word on the page. So the list also helps to activate your writing quickly and cut through resistance. Naturally, once you begin writing you might be surprised where your mind takes the topic. That's good. You are not trying to control your writing. You are stepping out of the way. Keep your hand moving.

But until you get your own list, here are some writing ideas:

1. Tell about the quality of light coming in through your window. Jump in and write. Don't worry if it is night and your curtains are closed or you would rather write about the light up north—just write. Go for ten minutes, fifteen, a half hour.

2. Begin with "I remember." Write lots of small memories. If you fall into one large memory, write that. Just keep going. Don't be concerned if the memory happened five seconds ago or five years ago. Everything that isn't this moment is memory coming alive again as you write. If you get stuck, just repeat the phrase "I remember" again and keep going.

3. Take something you feel strongly about, whether it is positive or negative, and write about it as though you love it. Go as far as you can, writing as though you love it, then flip over and write about the same thing as though you hate it. Then write about it perfectly neutral.

4. Choose a color—for instance, pink—and take a fifteen-minute walk. On your walk notice wherever there is pink. Come back to your notebook and write for fifteen minutes.

5. Write in different places—for example, in a laundromat, and pick up on the rhythm of the washing machines. Write at bus stops, in cafés. Write what is going on around you.

6. Give me your morning. Breakfast, waking up, walking to the bus stop. Be as specific as possible. Slow down in your mind and go over the details of the morning.

7. Visualize a place that you really love, be there, see the details. Now write about it. It could be a corner of your bedroom, an old tree you sat under one whole summer, a table at McDonald's in your neighborhood, a place by a river. What colors are there, sounds, smells? When someone else reads it, she should know what it is like to be there. She should feel how you love it, not by your saying you love it, but by your handling of the details.

8. Write about "leaving." Approach it any way you want. Write about your divorce, leaving the house this morning, or a friend dying.

9. What is your first memory?

10. Who are the people you have loved?

11. Write about the streets of your city.

12. Describe a grandparent.

13. Write about:

    swimming
    the stars
    the most frightened you've ever been
    green places
    how you learned about sex
    your first sexual experience
    the closest you ever felt to God or nature
    reading and books that have changed your life
    physical endurance
    a teacher you had

    Don't be abstract. Write the real stuff. Be honest and detailed.

14. Take a poetry book. Open to any page, grab a line, write it down, and continue from there. A friend calls it "writing off the page." If you begin with a great line, it helps because you start right off from a lofty place. "I will die in Paris, on a rainy day. . . . It will be a Thursday," by the poet Cesar Vallejo. "I will die on Monday at eleven o'clock, on Friday at three o'clock in South Dakota riding a tractor, in Brooklyn in a delicatessen," on and on. Every time you get stuck, just rewrite your first line and keep going. Rewriting the first line gives you a whole new start and a chance for another direction—"I don't want to die and I don't care if I'm in Paris or Moscow or Youngstown, Ohio."

15. What kind of animal are you? Do you think you are really a cow, chipmunk, fox, horse underneath?

Start to generate your own writing material and topics. It is good practice.

The Power of Detail

I am in Costa's Chocolate Shop in Owatonna, Minnesota. My friend is opposite me. We've just finished Greek salads and are writing in our notebooks for a half hour among glasses of water, a half-sipped Coke, and a cup of coffee with milk. The booths are orange, and near the front counter are lines of cream candies dipped in chocolate. Across the street is the Owatonna Bank, designed by Louis Sullivan, Frank Lloyd Wright's teacher. Inside the bank is a large cow mural and beautiful stained-glass windows.

Our lives are at once ordinary and mythical. We live and die, age beautifully or full of wrinkles. We wake in the morning, buy yellow cheese, and hope we have enough money to pay for it. At the same instant we have these magnificent hearts that pump through all sorrow and all winters we are alive on the earth. We are important and our lives are important, magnificent really, and their details are worthy to be recorded. This is how writers must think, this is how we must sit down with pen in hand. We were here; we are human beings; this is how we lived. Let it be known, the earth passed before us. Our details are important. Otherwise, if they are not, we can drop a bomb and it doesn't matter.

Yad Vashem, a memorial for the Holocaust, is in Jerusalem. It has a whole library that catalogues the names of the six million martyrs. Not only did the library have their names, it also had where they lived, were born, anything that could be found out about them. These people existed and they mattered. *Yad Vashem*, as a matter of fact, actually means "memorial to the name." It was not nameless masses that were slaughtered; they were human beings.

Likewise, in Washington, D.C., there is the Vietnam memorial. There are fifty thousand names listed—middle names, too—of American soldiers killed in Vietnam. Real human beings with names were killed and their breaths moved out of this world. There was the name of Donald Miller, my second-grade friend who drew tanks, soldiers, and ships in the margins of all his math papers. Seeing names makes us remember. A name is what we carry all our life, and we respond to its call in a classroom, to its pronunciation at a graduation, or to our name whispered in the night.

It is important to say the names of who are, the names of the places we have lived, and to write the details of our lives. "I lived on Coal Street in Albuquerque next to a garage and carried paper bags of groceries down Lead Avenue. One person had planted beets early that spring, and I watched their red/green leaves grow."

We have lived; our moments are important. This is what it is to be a writer: to be the carrier of details that make up history, to care about the orange booths in the coffee shop in Owatonna.

Recording the details of our lives is a stance against bombs with their mass ability to kill, against too much speed and efficiency. A writer must say yes to life, to all of life: the water glasses, the Kemp's half-and-half, the ketchup on the counter. It is not a writer's task to say, "It is dumb to live in a small town or eat in a café when you can eat macrobiotic at home." Our task is to say a holy yes to the real things of our life as they exist—the real truth of who we are: several pounds overweight, the gray, cold street outside, the Christmas tinsel in the showcase, the Jewish writer in the orange booth across from her blond friend who has black children. We must become writers who accept things as they are, come to love the details, and step forward with a yes on our lips so there can be no more noes in the world, noes that invalidate life and stop these details from continuing.

Don't Tell, but Show

There's an old adage in writing: "Don't tell, but show." What does this actually mean? It means don't tell us about anger (or any of those big words like honesty, truth, hate, love, sorrow, life, justice, etc.); show us what made you angry. We will read it and feel angry. Don't tell readers what to feel. Show them the situation, and that feeling will awaken in them.

Writing is not psychology. We do not talk "about" feelings. Instead the writer feels and through her words awakens those feelings in the reader. The writer takes the reader's hand and guides him through the valley of sorrow and joy without ever having to mention those words.

When you are present at the birth of a child you may find yourself weeping and singing. Describe what you see: the mother's face, the rush of energy when the baby finally enters the world after many attempts, the husband breathing with his wife, applying a wet washcloth to her forehead. The reader will understand without your ever having to discuss the nature of life.

When you write, stay in direct connection with the senses and what you are writing about. If you are writing from first thoughts—the way your mind first flashes on something before second and third thoughts take over and comment, criticize, and evaluate—you won't have to worry. First thoughts are the mind reflecting experiences—as close as a human being can get in words to the sunset, the birth, the bobby pin, the crocus. We can't always stay with first thoughts, but it is good to know about them. They can easily teach us how to step out of the way and use words like a mirror to reflect the pictures.

As soon as I hear the word *about* in someone's writing, it is an automatic alarm. "This story is about life." Skip that line and go willy-nilly right into life in your writing. Naturally, when we do practice writing in our notebooks, we might write a general line. "I want to write about my grandfather" or "This is a story about success." That's fine. Don't castigate yourself for writing it; don't get critical and mix up the creator and editor. Simply write it, note it, and drop to a deeper level and enter the story and take us into it.

Some general statements are sometimes very appropriate. Just make sure to back each one with a concrete picture. Even if you are writing an essay, it makes the work so much more lively. Oh, if only Kant or Descartes had followed those instructions. "I think, therefore I am"—I think about bubble gum, horse racing, barbecue, and the stock market; therefore, I know I exist in America in the twentieth century. Go ahead, take Kant's *Prolegomena to Any Future Metaphysic* and get it to show what he is telling. We would all be a lot happier.

Several years ago I wrote down a story that someone had told me. My friends said it was boring. I couldn't understand their reaction; I loved the story. What I realize now is that I wrote "about" the story, secondhand. I didn't enter it and make friends with it. I was outside it; therefore, I couldn't take anyone else into it. This does not mean you can't write about something you did not actually experience firsthand; only make sure that you breathe life into it. Otherwise it is two times removed and you are not present.

Be Specific

Be specific. Don't say "fruit." Tell what kind of fruit—"It is a pomegranate." Give things the dignity of their names. Just as with human beings, it is rude to say. "Hey, girl, get in line." That "girl" has a name. (As a matter of fact, if she's at least twenty years old, she's a woman, not a "girl" at all.) Things, too, have names. It is much better to say "the geranium in the window" than "the flower in the window." "Geranium"—that one word give us a much more specific picture. It penetrates more deeply into the beingness of that flower. It immediately gives us the scene by the window—red petals, green circular leaves, all straining toward sunlight.

About ten years ago I decided I had to learn the names of plants and flowers in my environment. I bought a book on them and walked down the tree-lined streets of Boulder, examining leaf, bark, and seed, trying to match them up with their descriptions and names in the book. Maple, elm, oak, locust. I usually tried to cheat by asking people working in their yards the names of the flowers and trees growing there. I was amazed how few people had any idea of the names of the live beings inhabiting their little plot of land.

When we know the name of something, it brings us closer to the ground. It takes the blur out of our mind; it connects us to the earth. If I walk down the street and see "dogwood," "forsythia," I feel more friendly toward the environment. I am noticing what is around me and can name it. It makes me more awake.

If you read the poems of William Carlos Williams, you will see how specific he is about plants, trees, flowers—chicory, daisy, locust, poplar, quince, primrose, black-eyed Susan, lilacs—each has its own integrity. Williams says, "Write what's in front of your nose." It's good for us to know what is in front of our nose. Not just "daisy," but how the flower is in the season we are looking at it— "The dayseye hugging the earth/in August . . . brownedged,/green and pointed scales/armor his yellow." Continue to hone your awareness: to the name, to the month, to the day, and finally to the moment.

Williams also says: "No idea, but in things." Study what is "in front of your nose." By saying "geranium" instead of "flower," you are penetrating more

9

deeply into the present and being there. The closer we can get to what's in front of our nose, the more it can teach us everything. "To see the World in a Grain of Sand, and a heaven in a Wild Flower . . ."

In writing groups and classes too, it is good to quickly learn the names of all the other group members. It helps to ground you in the group and make you more attentive to each other's work.

Learn the names of everything: birds, cheese, tractors, cars, buildings. A writer is all at once everything—an architect, French cook, farmer—and at the same time, a writer is none of these things.

Perfectionism

ANNE LAMOTT

Perfectionism is the voice of the oppressor, the enemy of the people. It will keep you cramped and insane your whole life, and it is the main obstacle between you and a shitty first draft. I think perfectionism is based on the obsessive belief that if you run carefully enough, hitting each stepping-stone just right, you won't have to die. The truth is that you will die anyway and that a lot of people who aren't even looking at their feet are going to do a whole lot better than you, and have a lot more fun while they're doing it.

Besides, perfectionism will ruin your writing, blocking inventiveness and playfulness and life force (these are words we are allowed to use in California). Perfectionism means that you try desperately not to leave so much mess to clean up. But clutter and mess show us that life is being lived. Clutter is wonderfully fertile ground—you can still discover new treasures under all those piles, clean things up, edit things out, fix things, get a grip. Tidiness suggests that something is as good as it's going to get. Tidiness makes me think of held breath, of suspended animation, while writing needs to breathe and move.

When I was twenty-one, I had my tonsils removed. I was one of those people who got strep throat every few minutes, and my doctor finally decided that I needed to have my tonsils taken out. For the entire week afterward, swallowing hurt so much that I could barely open my mouth for a straw. I had a prescription for painkillers, though, and when they ran out but the pain hadn't, I called the nurse and said that she would really need to send another prescription over, and maybe a little mixed grill of drugs because I was also feeling somewhat anxious. But she wouldn't. I asked to speak to her supervisor. She told me her supervisor was at lunch and that I needed to buy some gum, of all things, and to chew it vigorously—the thought of which made me clutch at my throat. She explained that when we have a wound in our body, the nearby muscles cramp around it to protect it from any more violation and from infection, and that I would need to use these muscles if I wanted them to relax again. So finally my best friend Pammy went out and bought me some gum, and I began

11

to chew it, with great hostility and skepticism. The first bites caused a ripping sensation in the back of my throat, but within minutes all the pain was gone, permanently.

I think that something similar happens with our psychic muscles. They cramp around our wounds—the pain from our childhood, the losses and disappointments of adulthood, the humiliations suffered in both—to keep us from getting hurt in the same place again, to keep foreign substances out. So those wounds never have a chance to heal. Perfectionism is one way our muscles cramp. In some cases we don't even know that the wounds and the cramping are there, but both limit us. They keep us moving and writing in tight, worried ways. They keep us standing back or backing away from life, keep us from experiencing life in a naked and immediate way. So how do we break through them and get on?

It's easier if you believe in God, but not impossible if you don't. If you believe, then this God of yours might be capable of relieving you of some of this perfectionism. Still, one of the most annoying things about God is that he never just touches you with his magic wand, like Glinda the Good, and gives you what you want. Like it would be so much skin off his nose. But he might give you the courage or the stamina to write lots and lots of terrible first drafts, and then you'd learn that good second drafts can spring from these, and you'd see that big sloppy imperfect messes have value.

Now, it might be that your God is an uptight, judgmental perfectionist, sort of like Bob Dole or, for that matter, me. But a priest friend of mine has cautioned me away from the standard God of our childhoods, who loves and guides you and then, if you are bad, roasts you: God as high school principal in a gray suit who never remembered your name but is always leafing unhappily through your files. If this is your God, maybe you need to blend in the influence of someone who is ever so slightly more amused by you, someone less anal. David Byrne is good, for instance. Gracie Allen is good. Mr. Rogers will work.

If you don't believe in God, it may help to remember this great line of Geneen Roth's: that awareness is learning to keep yourself company. And then learn to be more *compassionate* company, as if you were somebody you are fond of and wish to encourage. I doubt that you would read a close friend's early efforts and, in his or her presence, roll your eyes and snicker. I doubt that you would pantomime sticking your finger down your throat. I think you might say something along the lines of, "Good for you. We can work out some of the problems later, but for now, full steam ahead!"

In any case, the bottom line is that if you want to write, you get to, but you probably won't be able to get very far if you don't start trying to get over your perfectionism. You set out to tell a story of some sort, to tell the truth as you feel it, because something is calling you to do so. It calls you like the beckoning finger of smoke in cartoons that rises off the pie cooling on the windowsill, slides under doors and into mouse holes or into the nostrils of the sleeping man or woman in the easy chair. Then the aromatic smoke crooks its finger, and the mouse or the man or woman rises and follows, nose in the air. But some days the smoke is faint and you just have to follow it as best you can, sniffing away. Still, even on those days, you might notice how great perseverance feels. And the next day the scent may seem stronger—or it may just be that you are developing a quiet doggedness. This is priceless. Perfectionism, on the other hand, will only drive you mad.

Your day's work might turn out to have been a mess. So what? Vonnegut said, "When I write, I feel like an armless legless man with a crayon in his mouth." So go ahead and make big scrawls and mistakes. Use up lots of paper. Perfectionism is a mean, frozen form of idealism, while messes are the artist's true friend. What people somehow (inadvertently, I'm sure) forgot to mention when we were children was that we need to make messes in order to find out who we are and why we are here—and, by extension, what we're supposed to be writing.

Section 2

Personal Experience

Stop! A Buddhist Is Here!

JARVIS JAY MASTERS

We had been out on the exercise yard for an hour when I noticed a new prisoner approaching the yard gate, looking like a woman. I couldn't believe it. No San Quentin exercise yard hated homosexuals more than this one. Gays came in second only to informants as candidates for stabbings and killings. I knew this was some kind of mistake, or a dirty ploy by the prison administration to get someone killed. Wondering which of these two evils it could be, I glanced up at the tower gunmen.

I'd personally never held anything against homosexuals, but I knew how many of these prisoners felt about them. Some hated them just for hate's sake. Fear motivated others—especially those who had arrived at San Quentin in the early eighties with life sentences or were on death row and had long ago been taken in by the first media reports that AIDS was exclusively a homosexual disease. Later, prison officials told us that other diseases like tuberculosis were being spread throughout the prisons by homosexuals. The men on the yard had come to believe all this.

"This guy isn't going to last one full hour out here!" I thought. I didn't have to turn around to know that there were other prisoners behind me, looking on coldly, pulling prison-made shanks out of their waistbands. I could feel it. There was silence everywhere. I wanted so badly to holler out and warn this stupid person, "Man, this isn't your damn yard. Don't bring your ass out here." But I couldn't do this. I couldn't say anything. It would have been considered snitching. So I swallowed, kept my mouth shut, and prayed.

Then came a loud clinking and whining as the motorized gate was lifted to let this person onto the yard. When the gate slammed shut, my heart dropped. He had just become a walking dead man. I had seen a few others like this throughout my many years of incarceration.

Everyone in the yard, from those on the basketball and handball courts, to the scattered groups over by the pullup bar, watched in silence as this fragile man with tiny breasts, his hair in a pony tail, Vaseline on his lips, dressed in tight state jeans, began swishing along the yard fence.

I looked up again at the gunmen hovering over the exercise yard and saw that they had already gotten in position. They both had their semiautomatic rifles hanging over the gun rail, readying themselves to fire down on the north wall. Obviously, they knew what everybody else did.

According to the laws of prison life, none of this was supposed to be any business of mine. But it was. This time it had to be. For all the life in me, I couldn't look at this gay person, sitting alone against the back wall of the exercise yard, and not see an innocent human being. Yet I could not summon up the courage to become a snitch and risk my own life to warn him off this yard. Why me, anyway? I felt crossed up.

I had to do something. I began walking along the wall. Dammit. Why were things like this happening more often since I had taken my vows? What would all those people outside these walls who call themselves Buddhists tell me to do? Would they say, "Let's all be Buddhists and just put our knives away and smile?"

I made my way around to where the homosexual was sitting. I passed him several times without stopping, so I could get a good look at him. I wanted to find out if he was aware of what was going on, aware that someone was about to stab him. The fool was not! He sat there like a tiny fish in a shark tank. I needed to think fast, because time was running out. I had to get away from this guy, quick.

I spotted Crazy Dan on the opposite side of the exercise yard. He was squatting, surreptitiously cuffing a long shank in the sleeve of his coat. "Damn!" I muttered. My head began to pound as I watched Dan, a good friend of mine, prepare to knife this innocent person. I had known Dan for more than eight years in San Quentin, and I didn't want him to end his own life trying to take someone else's with two ready gunmen watching.

Then my mind went blank. I began walking along the wall, on the opposite side of the yard from Dan. It wasn't until we both turned the corners and faced each other, with the lone gay man sitting quietly against the back wall, that I saw the shank slowly slide down Dan's coat sleeve into his right hand. I quickened my pace to get to the man before he did. I didn't have time to be scared, or even to think. I just knew I had to get there first.

Quickly, I knelt in front of the gay man and asked if he had a spare cigarette. Dan was only six feet away. I looked up and saw him stopped dead, with his right hand hiding behind his leg, gripping the long shank. He was stunned. I could sense the adrenaline coursing through his body. His eyes, like those of a ferocious beast, stared into mine. I'd never seen those eyes before—they were not the eyes of the Dan I knew. For that split second I thought my friend was going to kill me.

Then something happened. Dan blinked hard several times. He must have realized my silent plea. Maybe he remembered the time I'd stood by him when he too had been marked for death. He turned, and calmly walked away.

"Hey, Daddy, did you want this cigarette or what?" the homosexual asked in a female voice, holding one out to me.

"No, I don't smoke."

He looked around, confused.

When I realized what I had just done, I almost choked on my fear. Why had I put my life on the line for somebody I didn't know or hadn't even seen before? "Am I crazy or just plain stupid?" I wondered, looking in the face of this person who was still totally unaware of what had just happened.

I stood up and walked away, knowing that I would take a lot of heat later that day out on the exercise yard. But I figured I could make the case—which I truly believed—that all this had been one big setup, that the prison authorities had been intent on shooting and killing some of us, and that I wasn't about to let anybody that I knew, especially Crazy Dan, get killed by walking into their trap. The truth, which I would leave out, was that I did it for the gay man, too. He meant nothing to me—except that he was as human as the rest of us. He never came back to our yard after that day, but the incident left me with many questions.

Am I alone? Am I the only Buddhist out here? Does this mean that I, the Lone Buddhist Ranger, am expected to try to stop this madness by myself? I imagined myself raising my hand and yelling, "Stop! A Buddhist is here!"

I can't stop it. It isn't stopping. There are stabbings every day in this place. All I have is my spiritual practice. Every morning and night I fold my blanket under me and meditate on the floor of my cell.

Mourning Exercise

JARVIS JAY MASTERS

The day was just getting started when I went out to the exercise yard. I was one of the last prisoners to be let out, so I knew I wouldn't have a chance to play basketball. The teams would have already been picked, and they would go on playing with each other until the high-tower buzzer indicated that our three hours of exercise time were up.

It was exhilarating to be outside after three hot summer days cooped up in my single-man cell. My mood was expansive as I wandered about, talking to my fellow prisoners. Other men in the yard were lifting weights and gambling around the game table for push-ups.

An excellent day, I thought, to just hang out and take in some sun. I took off my T-shirt and leaned against the fence, watching everyone from the corner of the yard. There were the cheaters like Ace and Slick on the basketball court, and Billy and Sonny on the handball court. They were incredibly skillful. Many years of playing together had fine-tuned them like naturals. I watched them win game after game under the burning sun.

I was the first to see the prison chaplain approach the fence. The yard suddenly fell silent. I held my breath, hoping he wasn't headed my way. Most of us never saw the prison chaplain unless it was Christmas or we were about to receive some very bad news.

The chaplain walked along the fence, staring through his wire-frame glasses. He seemed like a messenger of death. I wanted to turn away and pretend I'd never seen this man of the cloth before. But like so many of my fellow prisoners I had: this very priest had brought me the news of the sudden deaths of my mother, brother, and sister.

He pressed his hands against the fence, his eyes searching intently for someone in the yard. I had nothing—no basketball to bounce, no handball to hit, no weights to lift—to distract me from my inner pleading, "Not me again!"

First relief, then sadness swept over me when I saw the chaplain trying to get Freddie's attention on the basketball court. "Hey, Freddie," he said. "Buddy, I have

21

a bit of bad news for you. I need to speak to you—just for a minute, OK?" But Freddie only played harder. I watched fear pinch his eyes as he tried to concentrate. The other players upped the pace of the game as if to shield him from the chaplain's voice. This was their way of supporting their friend for as long as he needed to deny that the chaplain's news was for him.

I had known Freddie for many years in San Quentin. We were always on the same basketball team. Like me, he was thirty-two, but six foot, bulky and powerful, stronger than I was. He was serving a fifty-year-to-life sentence and could easily bench-press the heaviest bar, 450 pounds. No one else on the yard could lift as much as he could.

The chaplain remained poised at the fence, waiting patiently. I pondered the many phone calls he had received over the years from the outside world, informing him whose mother, son, or daughter had died. He had come to know that many prisoners are capable of shedding their hardened images, to break down and cry like any other human being.

I looked at Freddie. Neither his mind nor physical skills could forestall the tragedy awaiting him. He played aggressively, like a stranger to his teammates. But even they began to acknowledge what he had to do, and finally so did Freddie.

He walked over to the fence, and he and the chaplain stood together for a minute or two. Then Freddie stepped back, a slight smile on his face, and the basketball game resumed. I was shocked. The Freddie I knew couldn't possibly take this so well. The noise level on the yard picked up again.

Several minutes later Freddie glanced up at the two guardsmen in the gun tower. I didn't make much of it, until he turned and I could see that his eyes were filled with tears, just as tears had filled my own world when members of my family had died. He was fighting hard to stay strong, to keep the pain from showing, to resist his desire to cry in front of us, whose tears he had never seen.

Freddie didn't let himself cry. Instead, rage began rolling through him like a thunder cloud about to burst. His fists tightened and his body shook violently. "Damn, he's going to explode!" I thought.

Rattler, Ace, and Slick, who were standing on the court with him, had overheard the chaplain tell him his grandmother, his only family, had died from a heart attack. They realized that he was losing it, spinning off the scales of his sanity. They approached him, like courageous swimmers, venturing into the depths of the ocean to save a drowning comrade who had begun to panic.

Rattler reached his hand out to Freddie, only to be answered with blows to his head. The tower guardsmen fired two warning shots in the air. "Freeze!" they ordered, but Freddie kept swinging violently at his friends. His rage was directed not against them, but against his own will to survive.

As his friends tried to back off, Freddie lunged at them, pulling them down hard onto the asphalt. The guardsmen yelled another warning before pointing their rifles and firing into the yard. Pow! Pow! . . . Pow! Pow! . . . Pow! The bullets punched deep holes into the asphalt, only inches away from the men scuffling on the ground. Pow! Pow!

"Don't shoot!" hollered Rattler. "Man, don't shoot! Can't you see there's something wrong with him?"

"Back away from him! Get off him!" a guard barked from the gun tower. The rifles were still pointed down; their next shots would not be aimed to miss.

"Hell, no!" shouted Rattler.

They had finally pinned Freddie to the ground and were struggling to keep him there.

"Man, can't you see something's wrong with him?" Rattler screamed, tears pouring down his face. "Can't you see he needs help? Hell, just shoot us, kill us all!"

Ace and Slick began to sob too as they held Freddie. They were suddenly holding each other, not as hardened prisoners, but simply as human beings. The entire exercise yard, all fifty or more of us, stared in amazement.

It was as humans first and men second that we all, including Freddie, returned to our cells that day.

The Moths

HELENA MARÍA VIRAMONTES

Viramontes (1954–   ) was born in East Los Angeles. She attended Immaculate Heart College. It was in college that she began writing, first poetry and then fiction. Her stories were soon published and recognized. In 1979 she was awarded the Fiction Prize for the short story "Birthday" by the University of California at Irvine in the Chicano Literary Contest. Her books include The Moths and Other Stories *(1985); another collection of stories,* Paris Rats in E.L.A. *(1993);* Under the Feet of Jesus *(1995); and* Their Dogs Came with Them *(1996). A professor at Cornell University, she has received the Dos Passos Award for Literature and an NEA Fellowship.*

I was fourteen years old when Abuelita requested my help. And it seemed only fair. Abuelita had pulled me through the rages of scarlet fever by placing, removing and replacing potato slices on the temples of my forehead; she had seen me through several whippings, an arm broken by a dare-jump off Tío Enrique's toolshed, puberty, and my first lie. Really, I told Amá, it was only fair.

Not that I was her favorite granddaughter or anything special. I wasn't even pretty or nice like my older sisters and I just couldn't do the girl things they could do. My hands were too big to handle the fineries of crocheting or embroidery and I always pricked my fingers or knotted my colored threads time and time again while my sisters laughed and called me bull hands with their cute water-like voices. So I began keeping a piece of jagged brick in my sock to bash my sisters or anyone who called me bull hands. Once, while we all sat in the bedroom, I hit Teresa on the forehead, right above her eyebrow, and she ran to Amá with her mouth open, her hand over her eye while blood seeped between her fingers. I was used to the whippings by then.

I wasn't respectful either. I even went so far as to doubt the power of Abuelita's slices, the slices she said absorbed my fever. "You're still alive, aren't you?"

Abuelita snapped back, her pasty gray eye beaming at me and burning holes in my suspicions. Regretful that I had let secret questions drop out of my mouth, I couldn't look into her eyes. My hands began to fan out, grow like a liar's nose until they hung by my side like low weights. Abuelita made a balm out of dried moth wings and Vicks and rubbed my hands, shaping them back to size. It was the strangest feeling. Like bones melting. Like sun shining through the darkness of your eyelids. I didn't mind helping Abuelita after that, so Amá would always send me over to her.

In the early afternoon Amá would push her hair back, hand me my sweater and shoes, and tell me to go to Mama Luna's. This was to avoid another fight and another whipping, I knew. I would deliver one last direct shot on Marisela's arm and jump out of our house, the slam of the screen door burying her cries of anger, and I'd gladly go help Abuelita plant her wild lilies or jasmine or heliotrope or cilantro or hierbabuena in red Hills Brothers coffee cans. Abuelita would wait for me at the top step of her porch holding a hammer and nail and empty coffee cans. And although we hardly spoke, hardly looked at each other as we worked over root transplants, I always felt her gray eye on me. It made me feel, in a strange sort of way, safe and guarded and not alone. Like God was supposed to make you feel.

On Abuelita's porch, I would puncture holes in the bottom of the coffee cans with a nail and a precise hit of a hammer. This completed, my job was to fill them with red clay mud from beneath her rose bushes, packing it softly, then making a perfect hole, four fingers round, to nest a sprouting avocado pit, or the spidery sweet potatoes that Abuelita rooted in mayonnaise jars with toothpicks and daily water, or prickly chayotes that produced vines that twisted and wound all over her porch pillars, crawling to the roof, up and over the roof, and down the other side, making her small brick house look like it was cradled within the vines that grew pear-shaped squashes ready for the pick, ready to be steamed with onions and cheese and butter. The roots would burst out of the rusted coffee cans and search for a place to connect. I would then feed the seedlings with water.

But this was a different kind of help, Amá said, because Abuelita was dying. Looking into her gray eye, then into her brown one, the doctor said it was just a matter of days. And so it seemed only fair that these hands she had melted and formed found use in rubbing her caving body with alcohol and marihuana, rubbing her arms and legs, turning her face to the window so that she could watch the Bird of Paradise blooming or smell the scent of clove in the air. I toweled her face frequently and held her hand for hours. Her gray wiry hair hung over the mattress. Since I could remember, she'd kept her long hair in braids. Her mouth was vacant and when she slept, her eyelids never closed all the way. Up close, you could see her gray eye beaming out the window, staring hard as if to remember everything. I never kissed her. I left the window open when I went to the market.

Across the street from Jay's Market there was a chapel. I never knew its denomination, but I went in just the same to search for candles. I sat down on one of

26

the pews because there were none. After I cleaned my fingernails, I looked up at the high ceiling. I had forgotten the vastness of these places, the coolness of the marble pillars and the frozen statues with blank eyes. I was alone. I knew why I had never returned.

That was one of Apá's biggest complaints. He would pound his hands on the table, rocking the sugar dish or spilling a cup of coffee and scream that if I didn't go to Mass every Sunday to save my goddamn sinning soul, then I had no reason to go out of the house, period. Punto[1] final. He would grab my arm and dig his nails into me to make sure I understood the importance of catechism. Did he make himself clear? Then he strategically directed his anger at Amá for her lousy ways of bringing up daughters, being disrespectful and unbelieving, and my older sisters would pull me aside and tell me if I didn't get to Mass right this minute, they were all going to kick the holy shit out of me. Why am I so selfish? Can't you see what it's doing to Amá, you idiot? So I would wash my feet and stuff them in my black Easter shoes that shone with Vaseline, grab a missal and veil, and wave good-bye to Amá.

I would walk slowly down Lorena to First to Evergreen, counting the cracks on the cement. On Evergreen I would turn left and walk to Abuelita's. I liked her porch because it was shielded by the vines of the chayotes[2] and I could get a good look at the people and car traffic on Evergreen without them knowing. I would jump up the porch steps, knock on the screen door as I wiped my feet and call Abuelita, mi Abuelita? As I opened the door and stuck my head in, I would catch the gagging scent of toasting chile on the placa. When I entered the sala[3] she would greet me from the kitchen, wringing her hands in her apron. I'd sit at the corner of the table to keep from being in her way. The chiles made my eyes water. Am I crying? No, Mama Luna, I'm sure not crying. I don't like going to mass, but my eyes watered anyway, the tears dropping on the tablecloth like candle wax. Abuelita lifted the burnt chiles from the fire and sprinkled water on them until the skins began to separate. Placing them in front of me, she turned to check the menudo.[4] I peeled the skins off and put the flimsy, limp-looking green and yellow chiles in the molcajete[5] and began to crush and crush and twist and crush the heart out of the tomato, the clove of garlic, the stupid chiles that made me cry, crushed them until they turned into liquid under my bull hand. With a wooden spoon, I scraped hard to destroy the guilt, and my tears were gone. I put the bowl of chile next to a vase filled with freshly cut roses. Abuelita touched my hand and pointed to the bowl of menudo that steamed in front of me. I spooned some chile into the menudo and rolled a corn tortilla thin with the palms of my hands. As I ate, a fine Sunday breeze entered the kitchen and a rose petal calmly feathered down to the table.

I left the chapel without blessing myself and walked to Jay's. Most of the time Jay didn't have much of anything. The tomatoes were always soft and the cans of Campbell soups had rusted spots on them. There was dust on the tops of cereal boxes. I picked up what I needed: rubbing alcohol, five cans of chicken broth, a big bottle of Pine Sol. At first Jay got mad because I thought I had forgotten the money. But it was there all the time, in my back pocket.

When I returned from the market, I heard Amá crying in Abuelita's kitchen. She looked up at me with puffy eyes. I placed the bags of groceries on the table and began putting the cans of soup away. Amá sobbed quietly. I never kissed her. After a while, I patted her on the back for comfort. Finally: "¿Y mi Amá!?"[6] she asked in a whisper, then choked again and cried into her apron.

Abuelita fell off the bed twice yesterday, I said, knowing that I shouldn't have said it and wondering why I wanted to say it because it only made Amá cry harder. I guess I became angry and just so tired of the quarrels and beatings and unanswered prayers and my hands just there hanging helplessly by my side. Amá looked at me again, confused, angry, and her eyes were filled with sorrow. I went outside and sat on the porch swing and watched the people pass. I sat there until she left. I dozed off repeating the words to myself like rosary prayers: when do you stop giving when do you start giving when do you . . . and when my hands fell from my lap, I awoke to catch them. The sun was setting, an orange glow, and I knew Abuelita was hungry.

There comes a time when the sun is defiant. Just about the time when moods change, inevitable seasons of a day, transitions from one color to another, that hour or minute or second when the sun is finally defeated, finally sinks into the realization that it cannot with all its power to heal or burn, exist forever, there comes an illumination where the sun and earth meet, a final burst of burning red orange fury reminding us that although endings are inevitable, they are necessary for rebirths, and when that time came, just when I switched on the light in the kitchen to open Abuelita's can of soup, it was probably then that she died.

The room smelled of Pine Sol and vomit, and Abuelita had defecated the remains of her cancerous stomach. She had turned to the window and tried to speak, but her mouth remained open and speechless. I heard you, Abuelita, I said, stroking her cheek, I heard you. I opened the windows of the house and let the soup simmer and overboil on the stove. I turned the stove off and poured the soup down the sink. From the cabinet I got a tin basin, filled it with lukewarm water and carried it carefully to the room. I went to the linen closet and took out some modest bleached white towels. With the sacredness of a priest preparing his vestments, I unfolded the towels one by one on my shoulders. I removed the sheets and blankets from her bed and peeled off her thick flannel nightgown. I toweled her puzzled face, stretching out the wrinkles, removing the coils of her neck, toweled her shoulders and breasts. Then I changed the water. I returned to towel the creases of her stretch-marked stomach, her sporadic vaginal hairs, and her sagging thighs. I removed the lint from between her toes and noticed a mapped birthmark on the fold of her buttock. The scars on her back, which were as thin as the life lines on the palms of her hands, made me realize how little I really knew of Abuelita. I covered her with a thin blanket and went into the bathroom. I washed my hands, turned on the tub faucets and watched the water pour into the tub with vitality and steam. When it was full, I turned off the water and undressed. Then I went to get Abuelita.

She was not as heavy as I thought and when I carried her in my arms, her body fell into a V. And yet my legs were tired, shaky, and I felt as if the distance between the bedroom and bathroom was miles and years away. Amá, where are you?

I stepped into the bathtub one leg first, then the other. I bent my knees slowly to descend into the water slowly so I wouldn't scald her skin. There, there, Abuelita, I said, cradling her, smoothing her as we descended. I heard you. Her hair fell back and spread across the water like eagles' wings. The water in the tub overflowed and poured onto the tile of the floor. Then the moths came. Small gray ones that came from her soul and out through her mouth fluttering to light, circling the single dull light bulb of the bathroom. Dying is lonely and I wanted to go to where the moths were, stay with her and plant chayotes whose vines would crawl up her fingers and into the clouds: I wanted to rest my head on her chest with her stroking my hair, telling me about the moths that lay within the soul and slowly eat the spirit up; I wanted to return to the waters of the womb with her so that we would never be alone again. I wanted. I wanted my Amá. I removed a few strands of hair from Abuelita's face and held her small light head within the hollow of my neck. The bathroom was filled with moths, and for the first time in a long time I cried, rocking us, crying for her, for Amá, the sobs emerging from the depths of anguish, the misery of feeling half-born, sobbing until finally the sobs rippled into circles and circles of sadness and relief. There, I said to Abuelita, rocking us gently, there, there.

Notes

1. Period (Spanish); the end, case closed.
2. A small vegetable in the pepper family that has just one seed.
3. Living room (Spanish).
4. Tripe soup (Spanish).
5. Mortar (Mexican).
6. And my Mama? (Spanish).

Blue Winds Dancing

TOM WHITECLOUD

Thomas St. Germain Whitecloud (1914–1972) was born in New York City. However, he spent much of his youth on the Lac du Flambeau Indian Reservation near Woodruff, Wisconsin, the town mentioned in paragraph 20 of "Blue Winds Dancing." After attending colleges in New Mexico and California, he received his degree in medicine from Tulane University. He lived in Louisiana and Texas throughout his medical career, and at the time of his death he was a consultant for the Texas Commission on Alcoholism and Drug Abuse for Indians. "Blue Winds Dancing," which can be considered as either a story or a fictionalized autobiographical fragment, received a prize in 1938 from both Scribner's Magazine, in which it was published, and the Phi Beta Kappa National Honor Society.

Blue Winds Dancing

There is a moon out tonight. Moon and stars and clouds tipped with moonlight. And there is a fall wind blowing in my heart. Ever since this evening, when against a fading sky I saw geese wedge southward. They were going home. . . . Now I try to study, but against the pages I see them again, driving southward. Going home.

Across the valley there are heavy mountains holding up the night sky, and beyond the mountains there is home. Home, and peace, and the beat of drums, and blue winds dancing over snowfields. The Indian lodge will fill with my people, and our gods will come and sit among them. I should be there then. I should be at home.

But home is beyond the mountains, and I am here. Here where fall hides in the valleys, and winter never comes down from the mountains. Here where all the trees grow in rows; the palms stand stiffly by the roadsides, and in the groves the orange trees line in military rows, and endlessly bear fruit. Beautiful, yes; there

31

is always beauty in order, in rows of growing things! But it is the beauty of captivity. A pine fighting for existence on a windy knoll is much more beautiful.

In my Wisconsin, the leaves change before the snows come. In the air there is the smell of wild rice and venison cooking; and when the winds come whispering through the forests, they carry the smell of rotting leaves. In the evenings, the loons call, lonely; and birds sing their last songs before leaving. Bears dig roots and eat late fall berries, fattening for their long winter sleep. Later, when the first snows fall, one awakens in the morning to find the world white and beautiful and clean. Then one can look back over his trail and see the tracks following. In the woods there are tracks of deer and snowshoe rabbits, and long streaks where partridges slide to alight. Chipmunks make tiny footprints on the limbs and one can hear squirrels busy in hollow trees, sorting acorns. Soft lake waves wash the shores, and sunsets burst each evening over the lakes, and make them look as if they were afire.

That land which is my home! Beautiful, calm—where there is no hurry to get anywhere, no driving to keep up in a race that knows no ending and no goal. No classes where men talk and talk and then stop now and then to hear their own words come back to them from the students. No constant peering into the maelstrom of one's mind; no worries about grades and honors; no hysterical preparing for life until that life is half over; no anxiety about one's place in the thing they call Society.

I hear again the ring of axes in deep woods, the crunch of snow beneath my feet. I feel again the smooth velvet of ghost-birch bark. I hear the rhythm of the drums. . . . I am tired. I am weary of trying to keep up this bluff of being civilized. Being civilized means trying to do everything you don't want to, never doing anything you want to. It means dancing to the strings of custom and tradition; it means living in houses and never knowing or caring who is next door. These civilized white men want us to be like them—always dissatisfied—getting a hill and wanting a mountain.

Then again, maybe I am not tired. Maybe I'm licked. Maybe I am just not smart enough to grasp these things that go to make up civilization. Maybe I am just too lazy to think hard enough to keep up.

Still, I know my people have many things that civilization has taken from the whites. They know how to give; how to tear one's piece of meat in two and share it with one's brother. They know how to sing—how to make each man his own songs and sing them; for their music they do not have to listen to other men singing over a radio. They know how to make things with their hands, how to shape beads into design and make a thing of beauty from a piece of birch bark.

But we are inferior. It is terrible to have to feel inferior; to have to read reports of intelligence tests, and learn that one's race is behind. It is terrible to sit in classes and hear men tell you that your people worship sticks of wood—that your gods are all false, that the Manitou forgot your people and did not write them a book.

I am tired. I want to walk again among the ghost-birches. I want to see the leaves turn in autumn, the smoke rise from the lodgehouses, and to feel the

32

blue winds. I want to hear the drums; I want to hear the drums and feel the blue whispering winds.

There is a train wailing into the night. The trains go across the mountains. It would be easy to catch a freight. They will say he has gone back to the blanket; I don't care. The dance at Christmas. . . .

A bunch of bums warming at a tiny fire talk policies and women and joke about the Relief and the WPA and smoke cigarettes. These men in caps and overcoats and dirty overalls living on the outskirts of civilization are free, but they pay the price of being free in civilization. They are outcasts. I remember a sociology professor lecturing on adjustment to society; hobos and prostitutes and criminals are individuals who never adjusted, he said. He could learn a lot if he came and listened to a bunch of bums talk. He would learn that work and a woman and a place to hang his hat are all the ordinary man wants. These are all he wants, but other men are not content to let him want only these. He must be taught to want radios and automobiles and a new suit every spring. Progress would stop if he did not want these things. I listen to hear if there is any talk of communism or socialism in the hobo jungles. There is none. At best there is a sort of disgusted philosophy about life. They seem to think there should be a better distribution of wealth, or more work, or something. But they are not rabid about it. The radicals live in the cities.

I find a fellow headed for Albuquerque, and talk road-talk with him. "It is hard to ride fruit cars. Bums break in. Better to wait for a cattle car going back to the Middle West, and ride that." We catch the next east-bound and walk the tops until we find a cattle car. Inside, we crouch near the forward wall, huddle, and try to sleep. I feel peaceful and content at last. I am going home. The cattle car rocks. I sleep.

Morning and the desert. Noon and the Salton Sea, lying more lifeless than a mirage under a somber sun in a pale sky. Skeleton mountains rearing on the skyline, thrusting out of the desert floor, all rock and shadow and edges. Desert. Good country for an Indian reservation. . . .

Yuma and the muddy Colorado. Night again, and I wait shivering for the dawn.

Phoenix. Pima country. Mountains that look like cardboard sets on a forgotten stage. Tucson, Papago country. Giant cacti that look like petrified hitchhikers along the highways. Apache country. At El Paso my road-buddy decides to go on to Houston. I leave him, and head north to the mesa country. Las Cruces and the terrible Organ Mountains, jagged peaks that instill fear and wondering. Albuquerque. Pueblos along the Rio Grande. On the boardwalk there are some Indian women in colored sashes selling bits of pottery. The stone age offering its art to the twentieth century. They hold up a piece and fix the tourist with black eyes until, embarrassed, he buys or turns away. I feel suddenly angry that my people should have to do such things for a living. . . .

Santa Fe trains are fast, and they keep them pretty clean of bums. I decide to hurry and ride passenger coaltenders. Hide in the dark, judge the speed of the train as it leaves, and then dash out, and catch it. I hug the cold steel wall of the tender and think of the roaring fire in the engine ahead, and of the passengers back in the dining car reading their papers over hot coffee. Beneath me there is a blur of rails. Death would come quick if my hands should freeze and I fall. Up over the Sangre De Cristo range, around cliffs and through canyons to Denver. Bitter cold here, and I must watch out for Denver Bob. He is a railroad bull who has thrown bums from fast freights. I miss him. It is too cold, I suppose. On north to the Sioux country.

Small towns lit for the coming Christmas. On the streets of one I see a beam-shouldered young farmer gazing into a window filled with shining silver toasters. He is tall and wears a blue shirt buttoned, with no tie. His young wife by his side looks at him hopefully. He wants decorations for his place to hang his hat to please his woman. . . .

Northward again. Minnesota, and great white fields of snow; frozen lakes, and dawn running into dusk without noon. Long forests wearing white. Bitter cold, and one night the northern lights. I am nearing home.

I reach Woodruff at midnight. Suddenly I am afraid, now that I am but twenty miles from home. Afraid of what my father will say, afraid of being looked on as a stranger by my own people. I sit by a fire and think about myself and all other young Indians. We just don't seem to fit in anywhere—certainly not among the whites, and not among the older people. I think again about the learned sociology professor and his professing. So many things seem to be clear now that I am away from school and do not have to worry about some man's opinion of my ideas. It is easy to think while looking at dancing flames.

Morning, I spend the day cleaning up, and buying some presents for my family with what is left of my money. Nothing much, but a gift is a gift, if a man buys it with his last quarter. I wait until evening, then start up the track toward home.

Christmas Eve comes in on a north wind. Snow clouds hang over the pines, and the night comes early. Walking along the railroad bed, I feel the calm peace of snowbound forests on either side of me. I take my time; I am back in a world where time does not mean so much now. I am alone; alone but not nearly so lonely as I was back on the campus at school. Those are never lonely who love the snow and the pines; never lonely when the pines are wearing white shawls and snow crunches coldly underfoot. In the woods I know there are the tracks of deer and rabbit; I know that if I leave the rails and go into the woods I shall find them. I walk along feeling glad because my legs are light and my feet seem to know that they are home. A deer comes out of the woods ahead of me, and stands silhouetted on the rails. The North, I feel, has welcomed me home. I watch him and am glad that I do not wish for a gun. He goes into the woods quietly, leaving only the design of his tracks in the snow. I walk on. Now and then I pass a field, white under the night sky, with houses at the far end. Smoke comes from the chimneys of the houses, and I try to tell what sort of wood each is burning by the smoke; some burn pine, others aspen, others tamarack. There is one from which comes black coal smoke that rises lazily and drifts out over the tops of the trees. I like to watch houses and try to imagine what might be happening in them.

Just as a light snow begins to fall I cross the reservation boundary; somehow it seems as though I have stepped into another world. Deep woods in a white-and-black winter night. A faint trail leading to the village.

The railroad on which I stand comes from a city sprawled by a lake—a city with a million people who walk around without seeing one another; a city sucking the life from all the country around; a city with stores and police and intellectuals and criminals and movies and apartment houses; a city with its politics and libraries and zoos.

Laughing, I go into the woods. As I cross a frozen lake I begin to hear the drums. Soft in the night the drums beat. It is like the pulse beat of the world. The white line of the lake ends at a black forest, and above the trees the blue winds are dancing.

I come to the outlying houses of the village. Simple box houses, etched black in the night. From one or two windows soft lamplight falls on the snow. Christmas here, too, but it does not mean much; not much in the way of parties and presents. Joe Sky will get drunk. Alex Bodidash will buy his children red mittens and a new sled. Alex is a Carlisle man, and tries to keep his home up to white standards. White standards. Funny that my people should be ever falling further behind. The more they try to imitate whites the more tragic the result. Yet they want us to be imitation white men. About all we imitate well are their vices.

The village is not a sight to instill pride, yet I am not ashamed; one can never be ashamed of his own people when he knows they have dreams as beautiful as white snow on a tall pine.

Father and my brother and sister are seated around the table as I walk in. Father stares at me for a moment, then I am in his arms, crying on his shoulder. I give them the presents I have brought, and my throat tightens as I watch my sister save carefully bits of red string from the packages. I hide my feelings by wrestling with my brother when he strikes my shoulder in token of affection. Father looks at me, and I know he has many questions, but he seems to know why I have come. He tells me to go alone to the lodge, and he will follow.

I walk along the trail to the lodge, watching the northern lights forming in the heavens. White waving ribbons that seem to pulsate with the rhythm of the drums. Clean snow creaks beneath my feet, and a soft wind sighs through the trees, singing to me. Everything seems to say, "Be happy! You are home now— you are free. You are among friends—we are your friends; we, the trees, and the snow, and the lights." I follow the trail to the lodge. My feet are light, my heart seems to sing to the music, and I hold my head high. Across white snow fields blue winds are dancing.

Before the lodge door I stop, afraid, I wonder if my people will remember me. I wonder—"Am I Indian, or am I white?" I stand before the door a long time. I hear the ice groan on the lake, and remember the story of the old woman under the ice, trying to get out, so she can punish some runaway lovers. I think to myself, "If I am white I will not believe that story; If I am Indian, I will know that there is an old woman under the ice." I listen for a while, and I know that there is an old woman under the ice. I look again at the lights, and go in.

Inside the lodge there are many Indians. Some sit on benches around the walls, others dance in the center of the floor around a drum. Nobody seems to notice me. It seems as though I were among a people I have never seen before. Heavy women with long hair. Women with children on their knees—small children that watch with intent black eyes the movements of the dancers, whose small faces are solemn and serene. The faces of the old people are serene, too, and their eyes are merry and bright. I look at the old men. Straight, dressed in dark trousers and beaded velvet vests, wearing soft moccasins. Dark, lined faces intent on the music. I wonder if I am at all like them. They dance on, lifting their feet to the rhythm of the drums swaying lightly, looking upward. I look at their eyes, and am startled at the rapt attention to the rhythm of the music.

The dance stops. The men walk back to the walls, and talk in low tones or with their hands. There is little conversation, yet everyone seems to be sharing some secret. A woman looks at a small boy wandering away, and he comes back to her.

Strange, I think and then remember. These people are not sharing words— they are sharing a mood. Everyone is happy. I am so used to white people that it seems strange so many people could be together without someone talking. These Indians are happy because they are together, and because the night is beautiful outside, and the music is beautiful. I try hard to forget school and white people, and be one of these—my people. I try to forget everything but the night, and it is a part of me that I am one with my people and we are all a part of something universal. I watch eyes, and see now that the old people are speaking to me. They nod slightly, imperceptibly, and their eyes laugh into mine. I look around the room. All the eyes are friendly; they all laugh. No one questions my being here. The drums begin to beat again, and I catch the invitation in the eyes of the old men. My feet begin to lift to the rhythm, and I look out beyond the walls into the night and see the lights. I am happy. It is beautiful. I am home.

Lullaby

LESLIE MARMON SILKO

Leslie Marmon Silko was born in Albuquerque, New Mexico, and grew up the Laguna Pueblo Reservation. She attended Bureau of Indian Affairs schools, high school in Albuquerque, the University of New Mexico, and then law school for three semesters. She has taught at Navajo Community College, the University of Arizona, and the University of New Mexico; in 1983, she received a MacArthur foundation grant. Among her writings are Laguna Woman: Poems *(1974);* Storyteller *(1981), a collection of fiction and poetry; and the novels* Ceremony *(1977) and* Almanac of the Dead *(1991).*

The sun had gone down but the snow in the wind gave off its own light. It came in thick tufts like new wool—washed before the weaver spins it. Ayah reached out for it like her own babies had, and she smiled when she remembered how she had laughed at them. She was an old woman now, and her life had become memories. She sat down with her back against the wide cottonwood tree, feeling the rough bark on her back bones; she faced east and listened to the wind and snow sing a high-pitched Yeibechei[1] song. Out of the wind she felt warmer, and she could watch the wide fluffy snow fill in her tracks, steadily, until the direction she had come from was gone. By the light of the snow she could see the dark outline of the big arroyo a few feet away. She was sitting on the edge of Cebolleta Creek, where in the springtime the thin cows would graze on grass already chewed flat to the ground. In the wide deep creek bed where only a trickle of water flowed in the summer, the skinny cows would wander, looking for new grass along winding paths splashed with manure.

Ayah pulled the old Army blanket over her head like a shawl. Jimmie's blanket—the one he had sent to her. That was a long time ago and the green wool was faded, and it was unraveling on the edges. She did not want to think about Jimmie. So she thought about the weaving and the way her mother had done it. On the tall wooden loom set into the sand under a tamarack tree for shade. She could see it clearly. She had been only a little girl when her grandma gave her the wooden combs to pull the twigs and burns from the raw, freshly washed wool. And while she combed the wool, her grandma sat beside her, spinning a silvery strand of yarn around the smooth cedar spindle. Her mother worked at the loom with yarns dyed bright yellow and red and gold. She watched them dye the yarn in boiling black pots full of beeweed petals, juniper berries, and sage. The blankets her mother made were soft and woven so tight that rain rolled off them like birds' feathers. Ayah remembered sleeping warm on cold windy nights, wrapped in her mother's blankets on the hogan's[2] sandy floor.

The snow drifted now, with the northwest wind hurling it in gusts. It drifted up around her black overshoes—old ones with little metal buckles. She smiled at the snow which was trying to cover her little by little. She could remember when they had no black rubber overshoes; only the high buckskin leggings that they wrapped over their elkhide moccasins. If the snow was dry or frozen, a person could walk all day and not get wet; and in the evenings the beams of the ceiling would hang with lengths of pale buckskin leggings, drying out slowly.

She felt peaceful remembering. She didn't feel cold any more. Jimmie's blanket seemed warmer than it had ever been. And she could remember the morning he was born. She could remember whispering to her mother, who was sleeping on the other side of the hogan, to tell her it was time now. She did not want to wake the others. The second time she called to her, her mother stood up and pulled on her shoes; she knew. They walked to the old stone hogan together, Ayah walking a step behind her mother. She waited alone, learning the rhythms of the pains while her mother went to call the old woman to help them. The morning was already warm even before dawn and Ayah smelled the bee flowers blooming and the young willow growing at the springs. She could remember that so clearly, but his birth merged into the births of the other children and to her it became all the same birth. They named him for the summer morning and in English they called him Jimmie.

It wasn't like Jimmie died. He just never came back, and one day a dark blue sedan with white writing on its doors pulled up in front of the boxcar shack where the rancher let the Indians live. A man in a khaki uniform trimmed in gold gave them a yellow piece of paper and told them that Jimmie was dead. He said the Army would try to get the body back and then it would be shipped to them; but it wasn't likely because the helicopter had burned after it crashed. All of this was told to Chato because he could understand English. She stood inside the doorway holding the baby while Chato listened. Chato spoke English like a white man and he spoke Spanish too. He was taller than the white man and he stood straighter too. Chato didn't explain why; he just told the military man they could keep the body if they found it. The white man looked bewildered; he nodded his head and he left. Then Chato looked at her and shook his head, and then he told her, "Jimmie isn't coming home anymore," and when he spoke, he used the words to speak of the dead. She didn't cry then, but she hurt inside with anger. And she mourned him as the years passed, when a horse fell with

Chato and broke his leg, and the white rancher told them he wouldn't pay Chato until he could work again. She mourned Jimmie because he would have worked for his father then; he would have saddled the big bay horse and ridden the fence lines each day, with wire cutters and heavy gloves, fixing the breaks in the barbed wire and putting the stray cattle back inside again.

She mourned him after the white doctors came to take Danny and Ella away. She was at the shack alone that day they came. It was back in the days before they hired Navajo women to go with them as interpreters. She recognized one of the doctors. She had seen him at the children's clinic at Cañoncito about a month ago. They were wearing khaki uniforms and they waved papers at her and a black ball-point pen, trying to make her understand their English words. She was frightened by the way they looked at the children, like the lizard watches the fly. Danny was swinging on the tire swing on the elm tree behind the rancher's house, and Ella was toddling around the front door, dragging the broomstick horse Chato made for her. Ayah could see they wanted her to sign the papers, and Chato had taught her to sign her name. It was something she was proud of. She only wanted them to go, and to take their eyes away from her children.

She took the pen from the man without looking at his face and she signed the papers in three different places he pointed to. She stared at the ground by their feet and waited for them to leave. But they stood there and began to point and gesture at the children. Danny stopped swinging. Ayah could see his fear. She moved suddenly and grabbed Ella into her arms; the child squirmed, trying to get back to her toys. Ayah ran with the baby toward Danny; she screamed for him to run and then she grabbed him around his chest and carried him too. She ran south into the foothills of juniper trees and black lava rock. Behind her she heard the doctors running, but they had been taken by surprise, and as the hills became steeper and the cholla cactus were thicker, they stopped. When she reached the top of the hill, she stopped to listen in case they were circling around her. But in a few minutes she heard a car engine start and they drove away. The children had been too surprised to cry while she ran with them. Danny was shaking and Ella's little fingers were gripping Ayah's blouse.

She stayed up in the hills for the rest of the day, sitting on a black lava boulder in the sunshine where she could see for miles all around her. The sky was light blue and cloudless, and it was warm for late April. The sun warmth relaxed her and took the fear and anger away. She lay back on the rock and watched the sky. It seemed to her that she could walk into the sky, stepping through clouds endlessly. Danny played with little pebbles and stones, pretending they were birds eggs and then little rabbits. Ella sat at her feet and dropped fistfuls of dirt into the breeze, watching the dust and particles of sand intently. Ayah watched a hawk soar high above them, dark wings gliding; hunting or only watching, she did not know. The hawk was patient and he circled all afternoon before he disappeared around the high volcanic peak the Mexicans called Guadalupe.

Late in the afternoon, Ayah looked down at the gray boxcar shack with the paint all peeled from the wood; the stove pipe on the roof was rusted and crooked. The fire she had built that morning in the oil drum stove had burned out. Ella was asleep in her lap now and Danny sat close to her, complaining that he was hungry; he asked when they would go to the house. "We will stay up here until your father comes," she told him, "because those white men were chasing us." The boy remembered then and he nodded at her silently.

If Jimmie had been there he could have read those papers and explained to her what they said. Ayah would have known then, never to sign them. The doctors came back the next day and they brought a BIA[3] policeman with them. They told Chato they had her signature and that was all they needed. Except for the kids. She listened to Chato sullenly; she hated him when he told her it was the old woman who died in the winter, spitting blood; it was her old grandma who had given the children this disease. "They don't spit blood," she said coldly. "The whites lie." She held Ella and Danny close to her, ready to run to the hills again. "I want a medicine man first," she said to Chato, not looking at him. He shook his head. "It's too late now. The policeman is with them. You signed the paper." His voice was gentle.

It was worse than if they had died: to lose the children and to know that somewhere, in a place called Colorado, in a place full of sick and dying strangers, her children were without her. There had been babies that died soon after they were born, and one that died before he could walk. She had carried them herself, up to the boulders and great pieces of the cliff that long ago crashed down from Long Mesa; she laid them in the crevices of sandstone and buried them in fine brown sand with round quartz pebbles that washed down the hills in the rain. She had endured it because they had been with her. But she could not bear this pain. She did not sleep for a long time after they took her children. She stayed on the hill where they had fled the first time, and she slept rolled up in the blanket Jimmie had sent her. She carried the pain in her belly and it was fed by everything she saw: the blue sky of their last day together and the dust and pebbles they played with; the swing in the elm tree and broomstick horse choked life from her. The pain filled her stomach and there was no room for food or for her lungs to fill with air. The air and the food would have been theirs.

She hated Chato, not because he let the policeman and doctors put the screaming children in the government car, but because he had taught her to sign her name. Because it was like the old ones always told her about learning their language or any of their ways: it endangered you. She slept alone on the hill until the middle of November when the first snows came. Then she made a bed for herself where the children had slept. She did not lie down beside Chato again until many years later, when he was sick and shivering and only her body could keep him warm. The illness came after the white rancher told Chato he was too old to work for him anymore, and Chato and his old woman should be out of the shack by the next afternoon because the rancher had hired new people to work there. That had satisfied her. To see how the white man repaid Chato's years of loyalty and work. All of Chato's fine-sounding English talk didn't change things.

❧

It snowed steadily and the luminous light from the snow gradually diminished into the darkness. Somewhere in Cebolleta a dog barked and other village dogs joined with it. Ayah looked in the direction she had come, from the bar where Chato was buying the wine. Sometimes he told her to go on ahead and wait; and then he never came. And when she finally went back looking for him, she would find him passed out at the bottom of the wooden steps to Azzie's Bar. All the wine would be gone and most of the money too, from the pale blue check that came to them once a month in a government envelope. It was then that she would look at his face and his hands, scarred by ropes and the barbed wire of all those years, and she would think, this man is a stranger; for forty years she had smiled at him and cooked his food, but he remained a stranger. She stood up again, with the snow almost to her knees, and she walked back to find Chato.

It was hard to walk in the deep snow and she felt the air burn in her lungs. She stopped a short distance from the bar to rest and readjust the blanket. But this time he wasn't waiting for her on the bottom step with his old Stetson hat pulled down and his shoulders hunched up in his long wool overcoat.

She was careful not to slip on the wooden steps. When she pushed the door open, warm air and cigarette smoke hit her face. She looked around slowly and deliberately, in every corner, in every dark place that the old man might find to sleep. The bar owner didn't like Indians in there, especially Navajos, but he let Chato come in because he could talk Spanish like he was one of them. The men at the bar stared at her, and the bartender saw that she left the door open wide. Snowflakes were flying inside like moths and melting into a puddle on the oiled wood floor. He motioned to her to close the door, but she did not see him. She held herself straight and walked across the room slowly, searching the room with every step. The snow in her hair melted and she could feel it on her forehead. At the far corner of the room, she saw red flames at the mica window of the old stove door; she looked behind the stove just to make sure. The bar got quiet except for the Spanish polka music playing on the jukebox. She stood by the stove and shook the snow from her blanket and held it near the stove to dry. The wet wool smell reminded her of new-born goats in early March, brought inside to warm near the fire. She felt calm.

In past years they would have told her to get out. But her hair was white now and her face was wrinkled. They looked at her like she was a spider crawling slowly across the room. They were afraid; she could feel the fear. She looked at their faces steadily. They reminded her of the first time the white people brought her children back to her that winter. Danny had been shy and hid behind the thin white woman who brought them. And the baby had not known her until Ayah took her into her arms, and then Ella had nuzzled close to her as she had when she was nursing. The blonde woman was nervous and kept looking at a dainty gold watch on her wrist. She sat on the bench near the small window and watched the dark snow clouds gather around the mountains; she was worrying about the unpaved road. She was frightened by what she saw inside too: the strips of venison drying on a rope across the ceiling and the children jabbering excitedly in a language she did not know. So they stayed for only a few hours. Ayah watched the government car disappear down the road and she knew they were already being weaned from these lava hills and from this sky. The last time they came was in early June, and Ella stared at her the way the men in the bar were now staring. Ayah did not try to pick her up; she smiled at her instead and spoke cheerfully to Danny. When he tried to answer her, he could not seem to remember and he spoke English words with the Navajo. But he gave her a scrap of paper that he had found somewhere and carried in his pocket; it was folded in half, and he shyly looked up at her and said it was a bird. She asked Chato if they were home for good this time. He spoke to the white woman and she shook her head. "How much longer?" he asked, and she said she didn't know; but Chato saw how she stared at the boxcar shack. Ayah turned away then. She did not say good-bye.

She felt satisfied that the men in the bar feared her. Maybe it was her face and the way she held her mouth with teeth clenched tight, like there was nothing anyone could do to her now. She walked north down the road, searching for the old man. She did this because she had the blanket, and there would be no place for him except with her and the blanket in the old adobe barn near the arroyo. They always slept there when they came to Cebolleta. If the money and the wine were gone, she would be relieved because then they could go home again; back to the old hogan with a dirt roof and rock walls where she herself had been born. And the next day the old man could go back to the few sheep they still had, to follow along behind them, guiding them, into dry sandy arroyos where sparse grass grew. She knew he did not like walking behind old ewes when for so many years he rode big quarter horses and worked with cattle. But she wasn't sorry for him; he should have known all along what would happen.

There had not been enough rain for their garden in five years; and that was when Chato finally hitched a ride into the town and brought back brown boxes of rice and sugar and big tin cans of welfare peaches. After that, at the first of the month they went to Cebolleta to ask the postmaster for the check; and then Chato would go to the bar and cash it. They did this as they planted the garden every May, not because anything would survive the summer dust, but because it was time to do this. The journey passed the days that smelled silent and dry like the caves above the canyon with yellow painted buffaloes on their walls.

He was walking along the pavement when she found him. He did not stop or turn around when he heard her behind him. She walked beside him and she noticed how slowly he moved now. He smelled strong of woodsmoke and urine. Lately he had been forgetting. Sometimes he called her by his sister's name and she had been gone for a long time. Once she had found him wandering on the road to the white man's ranch, and she asked him why he was going that way; he laughed at her and said, "You know they can't run that ranch without me," and he walked on determined, limping on the leg that had been crushed many years before. Now he looked at her curiously, as if for the first time, but he kept shuffling along, moving slowly along the side of the highway. His gray hair had grown long and spread out on the shoulders of the long overcoat. He wore the old felt hat pulled down over his ears. His boots were worn out at the toes and he had stuffed pieces of an old red shirt in the holes. The rags made his feet look like little animals up to their ears in snow. She laughed at his feet; the snow muffled the sound of her laugh. He stopped and looked at her again. The wind had quit blowing and the snow was falling straight down; the southeast sky was beginning to clear and Ayah could see a star.

"Let's rest awhile," she said to him. They walked away from the road and up the slope to the giant boulders that had tumbled down from the red sandrock mesa throughout the centuries of rainstorms and earth tremors. In a place where the boulders shut out the wind, they sat down with their backs against the rock. She offered half of the blanket to him and they sat wrapped together.

The storm passed swiftly. The clouds moved east. They were massive and full, crowding together across the sky. She watched them with the feeling of horses—steely blue-gray horses startled across the sky. The powerful haunches pushed into the distances and the tail hairs streamed white mist behind them. The sky cleared. Ayah saw that there was nothing between her and the stars. The light was crystalline. There was no shimmer, no distortion through earth haze. She breathed the clarity of the night sky; she smelled the purity of the half moon and the stars. He was lying on his side with his knees pulled up near his belly for warmth. His eyes were closed now, and in the light from the stars and the moon, he looked young again.

She could see it descend out of the night sky: an icy stillness from the edge of the thin moon. She recognized the freezing. It came gradually, sinking snowflake by snowflake until the crust was heavy and deep. It had the strength of the stars in Orion, and its journey was endless. Ayah knew that with the wine he would sleep. He would not feel it. She tucked the blanket around him, remembering how it was when Ella had been with her; and she felt the rush so big inside her heart for the babies. And she sang the only song she knew to sing for babies. She could not remember if she had ever sung it to her children, but she knew that her grandmother had sung it and her mother had sung it:

> The earth is your mother,
>> she holds you.
> The sky is your father,
>> he protects you.
>
> Sleep,
> sleep.
> Rainbow is your sister,
>> she loves you.

43

The winds are your brothers,
          they sing to you.

Sleep,
sleep.
We are together always
We are together always
There never was a time
when this
was not so.

Notes

1. Navajo chant for healing.
2. Traditional Navajo dwelling.
3. Bureau of Indian Affairs.

My Papa's Waltz

THEODORE ROETHKE

The whiskey on your breath
Could make a small boy dizzy;
But I hung on like death:
Such waltzing was not easy.

We romped until the pans
Slid from the kitchen shelf;
My mother's countenance
Could not unfrown itself.

The hand that held my wrist
Was battered on one knuckle;
At every step you missed
My right ear scraped a buckle.

You beat time on my head
With a palm caked hard by dirt,
Then waltzed me off to bed
Still clinging to your shirt.

Careful What You Ask For

JACK McCARTHY

I was just old enough
to be out on the sidewalk by myself,
and every day I would come home crying,
beaten up by the same little girl.

I was Jackie, the firstborn,
the apple of every eye,
gratuitous meanness bewildered me,
and as soon as she'd hit me,
I'd bawl like a baby.

I knew that boys were not supposed to cry,
but they weren't supposed to hit girls either,
and I was shocked when my father said,
"Hit her back."

I thought it sounded like a great idea,
but the only thing I remember
about that girl today
is the look that came over her face
after I did hit her back.

She didn't cry; instead
her eyes got narrow and I thought,
"Jackie, you just made a terrible mistake,"
and she really beat the crap out of me.
It was years before I trusted my father's advice again.

I eventually learned to fight—
enough to protect myself—
from girls—

but the real issue was the crying,
and that hasn't gone away.

Oh, I don't cry any more,
I don't sob, I don't make noise,
I just have hair-trigger tear ducts, and always
at all the wrong things: supermarket openings;
the mayor cutting the ribbon on the bridge.

In movies I despise the easy manipulation
that never even bothers to engage my feelings,
it just comes straight for my eyes,
but there's not a damn thing I can do about it,
and I hate myself for it.

The surreptitious nose blow a discreet
four minutes after the operative scene;
my daughters are on to me, my wife;
they all know exactly when to give me that quick,
sidelong glance. What must they think of me?

In real life I don't cry anymore
when things hurt. Never a tear at seventeen
when my mother died, my father.
I never cried for my first marriage.

But today I often cry when things turn out well:
an unexpected act of simple human decency;
new evidence, against all odds,
of how much someone loves me.

I think all this is why I never wanted a son.
I always supposed my son would be like me,
and that when he'd cry it would bring back
every indelible humiliation of my own life,

and in some word or gesture
I'd betray what I was feeling,
and he'd mistake, and think I was ashamed of him.
He'd carry that the rest of his life.

Daughters are easy: you pick them up,
you hug them, you say, "There, there.
Everything is going to be all right."
And for that moment you really believe
that you can make enough of it right

enough. The unskilled labor of love.
And if you cry a little with them for all

48

the inevitable gratuitous meanness of life,
that crying is not to be ashamed of.

But for years my great fear was the moment
I might have to deal with a crying son.
But I don't have one.
We came close once, between Megan and Kathleen;
the doctors warned us there was something wrong,

and when Joan went into labor they said
the baby would be born dead.
But he wasn't: very briefly,
before he died, I heard him cry.

Ancestor

JIMMY SANTIAGO BACA

It was a time when they were afraid of him.
My father, a bare man, a gypsy, a horse
with broken knees no one would shoot.
Then again, he was like the orange tree,
and young women plucked from him sweet fruit.
To meet him, you must be in the right place,
even his sons and daughter, we wondered
where was papa now and what was he doing.
He held the mystique of travelers
that pass your backyard and disappear into the trees.
Then, when you follow, you find nothing,
not a stir, not a twig displaced from its bough.
And then he would appear one night.
Half covered in shadows and half in light,
his voice quiet, absorbing our unspoken thoughts.
When his hands lay on the table at breakfast,
they were hands that had not fixed our crumbling home,
hands that had not taken us into them
and the fingers did not gently rub along our lips.
They were hands of a gypsy that filled our home
with love and safety, for a moment;
with all the shambles of boards and empty stomachs,
they filled us because of the love in them.
Beyond the ordinary love, beyond the coordinated life,
beyond the sponging of broken hearts,
came the untimely word, the fallen smile, the quiet tear,
that made us grow up quick and romantic.
Papa gave us something: when we paused from work,
my sister fourteen years old working the cotton fields,

my brother and I running like deer,
we would pause, because we had a papa no one could catch,
who spoke when he spoke and bragged and drank,
he bragged about us: he did not say we were smart,
nor did he say we were strong and were going to be rich someday.
He said we were good. He held us up to the world for it to see,
three children that were good,
       who understood love in a quiet way,
who owned nothing but calloused hands and true freedom,
and that is how he made us: he offered us to the wind,
to the mountains, to the skies of autumn and spring.
He said, "Here are my children! Care for them!"
And he left again, going somewhere like a child
with a warrior's heart, nothing could stop him.
My grandmother would look at him for a long time,
and then she would say nothing.
She chose to remain silent, praying each night,
guiding down like a root in the heart of earth,
clutching sunlight and rains to her ancient breast.
And I am the blossom of many nights.
A threefold blossom: my sister is as she is,
my brother is as he is, and I am as I am.
Through sacred ceremony of living, daily living,
arose three distinct hopes, three loves,
out of the long felt nights and days of yesterday.

For Jim and Meghan from *Working in the Dark* Reflections of a Poet of the Barrio

JIMMY SANTIAGO BACA

1/13/89
BIG SUR
FOR JIM AND MEGHAN

> I can't imagine a life without crying, she said,
> and quoted, "Eyes that have not cried
>   are like a soul that has not seen a
>   rainbow."

I climb up the paved road from their house,
over a mound, top the mountain,
then heel down a sharp steep curving road.
Cross the road.
I couldn't find a path down—
barred by thorned brush, scented peppermint.
Turn back
and sit now on the boulder, looking out over the vast blue
                                                    sea.

I wonder if the ocean feels pain,
in its constant thrashing and whispering roar-capped
slings—
        so wide and broad blue
        foiling waves upon
        a thorny rock crop.

        The sun is warm here.
        Grit sprays over my face.

53

Does it feel pain of not seeing or knowing the desert?

It does.
Everything is change.
It has been the desert in after-ages,
and I will see my tears
beat against the black rock someday
the door of stone
that lies on my heart
whose red roots slowly crack through
the crevices.

"A few times in my life I have felt a powerful
surge in me rise, from stomach to chest, and
I breathed it back down," I said.

Looking at the ocean now,
I wonder when I weep,
will I sit on the
rocky precipice of my old life,
wondering in awe at the marvel
of what tears have cleared away
for me to see?
Will tears bring in to me
old shipwrecked debris of journeys
I have taken and never finished,
of dreams I went after
but never found,

will salty tears,
tears,
do this?
Will there be two continents
roughly divided if I cry,
one where I have been,
trekked the deep tread of pain
endlessly,

the other offering where I have not been,
open water to follow
where I will?

On an endless course
of exploring
my being, my poor being?

I pity a man like myself,
who has depended so much on not crying
to survive in this life—
        and yet,
        each memory is an oar
        that only needs me
        to push off from shore
        steering myself back down
        the shady river
        my life is. Only me.
        Coming back to where I started—
        that clearing full of dead trees
        where I left my last cry
        like a cairn of burnt stones
        that warmed me when the night was
        long, and I lost myself
        and didn't know how to find my way
        out.

           Startle myself with the oceans
           that have formed here.

My blood beats against the black door
    of *no cry,*
and every time I needed a word to
describe the pain,
    I cried *no cry*
no cry to describe the fear,
no cry to pain,
until the words
    no cry
    built themselves up
    to a steep cliff,
    no way down
    but to fall
        fall
           fall
    back down

    to cry.

Trips from There to Here

MARJORIE SIMMINS

Marjorie Simmins holds a BA in English literature from the University of British Columbia and is a full-time freelance writer. Her areas of special interest and expertise include the British Columbia commercial fishing industry and horses.

When I think about Karin, I remember bacon and marmalade sandwiches and chocolate milk, the kind that comes out of the carton thick and sweet. And fried pork chops and baked potatoes with sour cream, her favourite dinner, back in the days when she was allowed to eat with us. I don't remember who banished her from the dinner table or when, but I remember why.

Throwing up. Anything that went down when she was stoned came flying back up within minutes. We tolerated this vomiting, even accommodated it: we always made sure she had the outside chair in our kitchen nook. That way, when she felt sick, she could run to the bathroom without tripping all over us. Sometimes she wasn't fast enough to make it to the bathroom. The back door would smash open and we'd hear food splatter onto the cement walkway below the veranda. We kept a garden hose coiled at the side of the house.

First memories of my sister always come from the sound of raised voices and the feeling of dread in my stomach. I used to run to the bathroom upstairs, the farthest corner away from the noise. I'd turn on the tap and hum as I brushed my teeth trying to block out the yells from downstairs. I knew she wouldn't hurt me—I was too young to have anything she wanted—but she hurt the others with a bewildering and relentless accuracy. I couldn't stand watching the fights and I couldn't prevent them, so I created my own territory with her, the safest one I could think of: sister as shadow. I decided to be friends with her, to move beside her, where I could keep her in my peripheral vision.

Karin went through a magician phase; maybe sorceress is a better word. She used to put on performances in her incense-sweet bedroom in the basement. She had special clothes for these occasions, harem pants and gauzy scarfs that she wrapped around her red-gold hair. Sometimes she would make things disappear and other times she'd open cupboard doors just by looking at them. A neighbour who watched one of these shows couldn't resist trying to destroy Karin's illusions.

"Look," she said, "she's using a string to pull the door open! I can see it, can't you?"

Karin's eyes searched the darkened room, looking for mine. Speak up, guard the magic.

"Mrs. Williams, you're wrong. There's no string. This is real magic." I glared at her. The show concluded to loud applause.

Cats loved Karin, loved the way she rubbed their wet noses and hypnotized them with soft words and fishy treats. Some days I felt like a cat, gut-happy and mind-stroked with gentle words and promises. As long as I protected her—accepted her choices and her rules—the anger never came my way. I didn't know how else to protect myself.

We used to play horses out in the back yard. We'd take our horse collection—plastic and china figures—and set up a farm in the rock garden. Usually we chose the spot where the water faucet was hidden by a low, thick azalea bush. There were flat rocks beneath the faucet. When it rained, or when the faucet was left on a steady drip, the rocks held a shallow pool of water. We called this the pond and took the horses to swim there. I could play for hours, but Karin eventually got bored and the game would end with a ritualistic drowning of the horses. Hands that had moments earlier created bridles out of elastic bands and gently braided silky manes and tails would now seize the small animals and shove their heads under the water, making them gurgle and scream. I could sense the mood change, could see impatience in the movement of her fingers—but the vibrancy of her imagination was irresistible. In the garden of our make-believe world, death was a temporary condition; I knew I would play with her again the next day, when the sorceress pulled us up from the chill waters to start a new game.

Karin's eyes were dark blue, with a silver star around the iris. She plucked her eyebrows thin and wore heavy eyeliner. Pale skin, with a few freckles scattered over a finely shaped nose. Her stride was short, almost bouncy. In nearly all of her photographs she has her head tilted to one side—her expression a strange blend of coyness and misery.

I don't remember when her blue eyes started going grey every day. Around the same time she started taking her meals in the TV room. It was a relief to eat quiet dinners; I even started enjoying spaghetti again. But I was uneasy with the separation—and disliked cutting her off from the rest of the family. The nonoffenders would exchange news of the day, pass the butter, salt, and pepper around the table, and I'd be worrying if she wanted more food, or if she'd nodded out over her plate. As soon as I could I'd join her in the den.

We'd watch TV together, sprawled out on the couch, me leaning on her side with a pillow underneath my elbow. Her cigarette ash would burn longer and longer and without thinking I'd reach over and bump her arm over the ashtray.

"Karin, watch your smoke."

We started to find burn holes everywhere. The couch, the pillowcases, the bed sheets. She always seemed to wake up just before the smoke turned to flames.

Karin kept her methadone bottles in the refrigerator. She lined them up tidily, on the right-hand side of the door, nestled in with the Velveeta cheese. The methadone was mixed with orange juice, which masked the bitter taste a little bit. Karin told me never to touch them. But I did. I was curious about those white-capped bottles, even jealous of their daily importance. After everyone was asleep I'd sneak down to the kitchen and pull a bottle out. Sometimes I'd just smell the stuff, and wonder what she felt like when she drank it. One night I took a tiny slurp, then, terrified she'd know I had tried it I filled the missing half-inch with water and ran back to bed. I lay awake a long time, wondering when I'd get smashed. I fell asleep with a trace of orange-sweet drug juice on my lips.

The year we bought Coqeyn, I recorded the event in my journal: "Over the weekend we bought a horse. He is an Arabian and Karin and I are going to look after it." Every twelve-year-old girl's dream come true. A living, breathing horse, to ride and love.

Coqeyn scared me. Mostly because I was sure we'd lose him, the moment our reflection in his purple-brown eyes became steady. Vet bills, board bills, and my mother teaching day school and night school to provide for us. I'd watch Mum disappear into her bedroom for a twenty-minute rest before dinner and hate the horse for filling the house with dragging steps and exhaustion. But Coqeyn was going to save the day: he was going to make Karin permanently straight and functioning. Like magic.

Karin's all-time straight record in seven years was three months. Straight from heroin and barbiturates. She drank the methadone every day, although at one point she weaned herself down to a quarter of a bottle, selling the other three-quarters to buy things for the horse. The endless supply of methadone came from the Narcotic Addiction Foundation, on Broadway at Oak, where we went each day after school. On the bus down there Karin would drink Coke, to fill her bladder for the sample she had to give to the doctors. Some days her bladder wouldn't cooperate. She'd park herself by the water fountain in the foundation's foyer and drink until the twinge in her gut felt certain.

"Okay, I'm ready." I'd watch her disappear into the bathroom, followed by a woman in a white lab coat. Minutes later, she'd return, smiling and giggling, jerking her thumb at the full sample bottle carried by the nurse: "Success!" Then she'd line up with the other junkies to get her methadone for the week. They always made her drink a cup of methadone before she left. She'd throw back her head, toss the liquid down, and make a major production of swallowing it. Actually, she didn't swallow any, but kept it in her mouth until we left the building from the back entrance. If I felt like teasing her, I'd poke her in the ribs, trying to make her laugh and spit the liquid out of her chipmunk cheeks. She'd shake her head, look furious, but I knew it was like the horses in the pond—no permanent damage done.

In the lane behind the foundation she'd take out one of her bottles and spit the methadone into it. She spat it out fast, discreet; you'd think she was stopping to cough and delicately wipe her mouth. We'd walk another half-block and sell the topped-up bottle to the first junkie with cash.

Karin loved Coqeyn as much as she loved smack. We groomed our horse, one on either side, until our arms ached. We read horse magazines and made plans to truck Coqeyn into the Interior, where we could go for long rides into the mountains. He would be an endurance horse, a jumper, a hunter—he was going to do it all and we were going to have a roomful of ribbons and trophies to gloat over. We took riding lessons, sold methadone, and bought expensive tack. Summer 1972: Jethro Tull (*Thick as a Brick*), paisley T-shirts, Export "A" cigarettes, and the barn, every day, all day.

There were triumphs in those years. The first time we won a ribbon at a recognized show I cried so hard I could hardly see where I was going as I ran over the bumpy hogfuel to meet Karin coming out of the ring.

"It's only a sixth place, Marjorie," she protested as I grabbed onto her gloved hand and squeezed it hard.

"But a ribbon, Karin! A rosette!"

She dismounted, leaned against Coqeyn's sweat-darkened shoulder. "Next time we'll do better."

Doing better. The words throbbed under our skins as the boundaries between us blurred. Doing better this week, only lied once about no bombers in the house. Found a rainbow assortment in her jewellery box, flushed them down the toilet. Doing better, though, no clouds in her eyes for three days. Relax, play the twin game: Levi jeans, blue ski jackets, black boots, velvet hunt caps, long hair in braids. Walk close, shoulders touching, steps synchronized. No one can tell us apart. You protect me and I'll protect you.

These periods—the quiet, symbiotic ones—vanished. One week we were inseparable; the next I was a Siamese twin, slowly ripping my body away from hers. We all tried to keep out of her way, to hide from the cruel taunts, the thievery, the broken dishes. My brother hid by going out with his friends; he spent nearly all his time at parties or in bars and pool halls. I used to ask him, as he was leaving, where he was going. The fringes on his leather jacket would swing as he shrugged his shoulders. "Out," he'd say, "going out." The door would slam behind him and I'd be left standing in the hallway, wondering where I could go. In six more months I would seek out all of Geoffrey's haunts and claim them as my own, but before then I spent many evenings walking around the back lanes behind our house.

Sometimes she'd still be up when I returned.

"Where have you been? I'm making a milkshake, would you like some?" Maybe she felt guilty or ashamed; maybe she just wanted to keep me on her side. I'd watch her pour the milkshake and accept the glass timidly. We'd go to the TV room and before I had a sip from my glass I'd wait, knowing she'd either spill hers or demand the rest of mine.

Her eyes and her moods were dead giveaways. Easy to know when she was high. When she got really affectionate, I knew it would be a back-lane night.

"Oh, Marjorie, I feel so good today. I'm so glad we're friends, aren't you? I love you, little sister, I love you so much." Words like those coiled every muscle in my body for flight. Karin's love always careened into anger.

Eventually even the horse wasn't safe. When Karin started coming to the barn stoned, I knew that I had to complete my separation from her. If I didn't, I'd find myself explaining not just a broken dish, or a missing wallet, but a death.

The final break came. I was in the feed room, mixing up a steaming bran mash. Karin burst in the door, eyes as wide as they could be when she was that high. Her face was white and sweaty, her words so slurred that at first I couldn't make out what she was saying.

"Come quick. It's in his stall, the cigarette, right by the door, I can't find it, hurry, hurry—come!"

He's gonna burn. He's gonna rear up in a box of flames and cook like a pig in a bonfire. Fear for Coqeyn made my heart lurch, but stronger than the fear was the pattern of hiding Karin's mistakes. No one would know what had happened, not if I moved quickly. I wanted to hit that pasty, out-of-focus face, but I just told her to get a wheelbarrow and start shovelling out the stall. I led Coqeyn out, tied him to a post. Stepped back inside the stall and glanced back over my shoulder to see who could see me. No one around. I tipped over the three-foot-high water bucket in the corner where she said she'd dropped the cigarette. All this time Karin was babbling and weaving, getting in my way. My hands, sticky with warm molasses, shook so much I could barely hold the shovel.

"Get out of my way. Get the fuck out of here." New and raw words I hurled at her, words that had nothing to do with the cigarette and a lot to do with the twin feeling its air supply being choked off. Breathe, little sister, breathe hard and fast.

Her expression was terrifying—dead straight and stoned to the limit. Of all her unusual abilities, this was the one that frightened me most. While anyone else would have fallen flat with the amount of chemicals she pumped into her body, small Karin staggered on, even casting aside, for a few minutes, the total effect of the drugs she had taken. "Thought I was a goner, sister/brother dear?" she'd sneer at Geoffrey and me, when we'd crouch beside her, deciding whether or not to call an ambulance. "Not yet, motherfuckers."

I concentrated on cleaning out the stall. By now I wasn't even scared about the cigarette. More was coming. Every hair standing up on my arms was preparing me for it.

When I came back from soaking the chips with water I found Karin tightening the girth on Coqeyn's saddle. The bridle was already on.

"What are you doing?" I kept my voice low and prayed she couldn't hear the pleading note beneath it.

"Gonna ride in the ring." As she spoke she lost her balance and caught at the bridle to steady herself. Coqeyn, jabbed in the mouth from this motion, threw up his head and took several quick steps backwards.

"Stand still, you bastard." She kneed him hard under the girth.

"Stop it!" I was shouting now, didn't care who heard me. "Leave him alone."

"Why? This bother you?" she asked, eyes for one instant clear and sober. "Watch, it gets better."

She took the bridle in both hands and jerked it down with all her weight. I could feel that iron cut down as though the bit were in my own mouth. I sucked in cold night air and howled. Coqeyn lunged, I lunged, Karin laughed. I pushed her down onto the tarmac and felt her rise up against my arm strong as a tidal wave. Fluid strength, like water all around us, and me twisting, kicking, punching to keep my head from going under.

I lost the fight. And I never walked shoulder to shoulder with Karin again.

That autumn I started grade nine. School was something that passed between hours of wondering whether Karin had died that day. Her eyes looked like grey cauliflowers now, with hardly any colour in them at all. She overdosed so many times that I got used to seeing her face blue. I distanced myself from my hands when they slapped the breath into her. She hurt herself, horribly, when she was stoned—gashes, bruises—but I didn't help her anymore. I ate my meals in the kitchen with the rest of the family and afterwards I retreated to my room.

One morning I came downstairs and found her passed out, with her eyes open, in the chair beside the front door. I stepped close to her, to see if she was breathing. It was a quarter to nine; if I didn't hurry, I'd be late for school. I couldn't bring myself to touch her. I imagined that she was a corpse that would suddenly reach out and crush my body into the deathland behind those unblinking eyes. Geoffrey walked into the hall, saw me staring at her slumped figure.

"She alive?"

"I can't tell. I think so. Wouldn't her eyes be closed if she was dead?"

"Maybe, don't know. Let's get out of here."

We walked up Dunbar Street towards the bus stop. Geoffrey's strides were long and fast; I took two for each one of his. Suddenly aware of our mismatched steps, he slowed down, until our shoulders brushed together. He reached into his jacket pocket and took out a Bar Six chocolate bar.

"Want some?"

"Yeah, sure."

Karin died a year later, in a room at the Blue Boy hotel. On Christmas Day. Unlike the china and plastic horses, she would stay dead.

I didn't ride for about eight years. Barns, with their cold cement floors and draughty corridors, felt like tombs. The smell of molasses made me sick. And when I saw young women with long hair and blue ski jackets walking close together, I'd stretch out my arms and feel oceans of empty air on either side of my body.

My hair is short now. I wear a purple and black Gore-Tex jacket when I ride in the rain. Black leather chaps, too; Karin would have loved them. Since my sister died, I have travelled in Europe, Canada, the United States, and the West Indies. I have lived on boats, in downtown high-rises. I went to university and worked, as a waitress, a driver, an editor. Men, for days and daze, and two, loved unconditionally. I kissed/kiss them, remembering Karin's precise explanation of the perfect kiss.

Last year I even dated a brother of one of her lovers. I met him, in one of those small-world situations, and wanted to be near him, because his brother had loved Karin. A tall and strange order to fill, and he only five feet eight inches, and a mind more focused on gains and losses.

"Yeah," he said, "Kevin did heroin, but he's been clean for years. Your sister didn't make it, eh?"

"Where was your brother when Karin died?" (First date, the Holiday Inn on Broadway, him figuring out my income-tax return, me scanning his face for one flicker of shared memory.)

"I don't know. Maybe they weren't friends any more. Besides, drugs weren't really a problem for Kevin. He hasn't used in years. He's married now, has a kid, and works as an actor—very talented. Why are you so hung up on the past?"

"He wasn't at her memorial service." (Only saw Lana, ward-of-the-state Lana, crying and gibbering with fear because Karin was the smart one and why were her ashes in an urn when all the dummies were still living?)

"Really? I wouldn't know. Now listen, do you want to get some money back—or a lot of money back?"

I wanted to sleep beside him, reach out for a dream fragment of his brother, my sister. I wanted to remember, for a moment, soft rubber tied around my fourteen-year-old arm and the sharp press of an empty needle against a blue, untravelled vein. Karin? Where do I stick this thing? Right in the vein? Or beside it, or under it, or in any part of my arm that is willing? Does the needle have to have heroin in it, or will water from the basement sink give me a rush?

Couldn't do it—needles belonged to Karin. I watched her, though, and tied her arm when I couldn't stand her bad moods any more. She wore a lingering perfume called Omar's Delight, which she bought from a store on 4th Avenue. She smelled sweet, as I leaned close to watch her perfect aim with the needle.

Section 3A

Our World—
Close to Home

Monk without a Robe

MIKE McINTYRE

In fine old mendicant tradition, the author
hits the road without a dime.

I'm sitting in my car, parked in a condo complex down the road from my office near San Francisco. It's lunchtime, but the turkey sandwich rests untouched on the passenger seat. I barely notice a doe and her fawn step by the window. It is a golden California day, and I am crying.

I turned 37 this week. I've been a newspaper reporter for a decade. The pay and perks are good. I've traveled all over the world. I live in a nice apartment with a beautiful girlfriend. There are people who love me.

But all of that is little consolation when you know you're a coward.

If I were told I was going to die today, I'd have to say I never took a gamble. I played life too close to the vest. I was never up and I was never down—the perfect shill.

Wiping tears from my eyes, I know it's time to bet or fold. Just this once I want to know what it feels like to shove all my chips in the pot and go for broke.

When I get back to the office, I corner my boss before I lose my nerve.

"I'm a long yo-yo on a short string," I say. "I'm ready to snap."

"Do you need some time?" he says.

"Yeah, all I got left."

I drive up to Lake Tahoe to say good-bye to my family and tell them the logic behind chucking a perfectly good job in the middle of a recession.

It's a spiritual sojourn, I say. I'm making a leap of faith a continent wide. I'll go from the Pacific to the Atlantic without a penny. A cashless journey through the land of the almighty dollar. If I'm offered money, I'll refuse it. If I see a coin in the road, I'll step over it. I'll accept only rides, food, and a place to rest my head. Wait and see, it'll work.

My relatives line up to attack the plan like children going after a piñata.

"I hate being broke and having to scrounge," says my younger brother, Pat, who has struggled financially most of his adult life. "Why would you want to deliberately put yourself in that position?"

"You'll get rousted by the cops," says my dad.

"We'll see how far he gets," says my stepmother.

And this encouraging note from my grandma: "You're going to get *raped* out there."

My final destination is Cape Fear, North Carolina, chosen as a symbol for all the fears I know I'll have to conquer if I'm to go the distance. If I make it to Cape Fear, it will be as a different man from the one who starts the journey.

I'm afraid.

I've been afraid my whole life.

I was born scared.

I grew up afraid of the baby-sitter, the mailman, the birds in the trees, the next-door neighbors' cat.

I'm afraid of the dark. I'm afraid of the ocean. I'm afraid of flying.

I'm afraid of the city and I'm afraid of the wilderness. I'm afraid of crowds and I'm afraid to be alone. I'm afraid of failure and afraid of success.

I'm afraid of fire, lightning, earthquakes.

I'm afraid of snakes. I'm afraid of bats. I'm afraid of bears.

I'm afraid of losing an arm. I'm afraid of losing a leg. I'm afraid of losing my mind.

Yes, and I'm afraid of dying, too. But what really scares the hell out of me is living.

I'm afraid.

❧

Toyota pickup with a camper shell pulls over, and I have to squint to make sure it's not a mirage. I hoist my pack onto one shoulder and will my legs to carry me swiftly to the truck before the driver changes his mind. The cab is littered with McDonald's bags, burger wrappers, coffee cups, stir sticks, and hash brown containers. The guy, Randy is his name, was down near Los Angeles, checking on some property in the desert. He's heading home to Humboldt County.

"I've got a small nursery up there," says Randy, who has red hair and a wispy mustache. "I make seventy-five dollars a week off it at the farmers' market. My wife's got a good job. I used to grow pot, but I got busted, so I can't do that anymore."

Humboldt County is famous for two things: giant redwood trees and some of the finest marijuana to have ever graced a bong. The growers were mostly hippies, content to make a quiet living. Then pot hit $6,000 a pound, and everybody got in on the act, even redneck ranchers and grandmothers. A cult of greed descended on a region long known for its counter-culture values. Volkswagen buses were traded in for Jeep Cherokees. Grocers openly sold the number one cash crop at checkout stands. The government answered with Operation Green

Sweep, a crackdown with whirlybirds, paramilitary troops, and German shepherds. A neighbor snitched on Randy. He got 90 days, plus probation. But the feds never found the fifty grand buried on his land. . . .

He pulls off at the McDonald's in a small lumber town, and my stomach growls with anticipation. But at the drive-thru intercom, Randy barks, "Gimme a large vanilla milkshake," and reaches for his wallet. There's a long, sad moment before he turns to me and says, "Do you want something? Do you want a hamburger?" I say, great, and sit a little higher in the seat. Randy leans over to the squawk box and says, "And gimme two cheeseburgers and a glass of water."

Randy sets the bag of burgers on the seat between us and pulls back onto the highway. The bag just sits there, like a third passenger. I know one of those burgers is mine, but I don't want to be rude. Finally, Randy reaches in and tosses a burger on my lap. "There you go," he says. "It isn't much."

Oh, but it is. At long last, meat! I take small bites and chew long after the food has been broken down into mush. Randy harps more on the government. I nod a lot, and say "yeah" and "hmm" and "it's insane." But I'm not hearing much. I'm transfixed by the burger wrapper in my hands. I study the yellow and red sheet of paper, carefully reading every word of it, as if it were literature.

We reach Garberville, in southern Humboldt, late in the afternoon. Randy has to go west, so he stops to let me out. Dark clouds roll over the ridge. I know what's coming.

"Does your nursery have a roof on it?"

"Yeah," Randy says cautiously.

"Do you think I could crash there tonight?"

"It's way out in the woods."

"How far?"

"Twenty-six, twenty-seven miles."

I take that as a "no" and thank Randy for the burger and the ride. I get out of the truck and almost step in a cardboard box sitting in the dirt. It's funny how quickly perceptions can change. Three days ago, I would have said the box at my feet contained spoiled produce. Now, all I see is food. Sure, that rotten tomato and shriveled celery aren't fit for pigs. But the head of cauliflower looks like it might be edible after some salvage work. I carry the vegetable to a gas station and hose off an army of ants. The black fungus won't wash away, though, so I crack open the head and eat it inside out. All in all, a tasty snack.

Things are looking up.

I ask a local merchant if there's a safe place I can lay out my sleeping bag tonight. He tells me the nearby Humboldt Redwood State Park has 155,000 acres. "It's probably illegal, though," he adds.

"Yeah, but is it safe? I mean, are there wild animals out there?"

"We have some bears, and there are some mountain lions."

Enough said.

I walk down the main drag. A woman with hairy legs appears from behind my pack and says, "Hi, do you need any help finding anything?"

I ask if she knows a spot to camp.

She says, "The best thing is to make friends with somebody." I'm about to say, "Do you want to be my friend?" but she skips ahead. "I'm in a hurry now," she calls back. "I've got to coach a soccer game, but I'll look for you later." I know that's the last I'll see of her.

It hasn't rained since spring, but the sky doesn't look like it has forgotten how. I spot an outdoor restaurant with covered picnic tables and figure I can sit out there tonight after it closes. At least I'd stay dry. I walk on, hoping for something better.

I hit the edge of town and turn back. A man stops me. He's in his 50s, wearing jeans and a baseball cap that reads, "Beef."

"You look like you need some directions."

"No, not really. I'm just kind of wandering."

"How far you wandering?"

"All the way to the Atlantic Ocean," I say. Then I add, "Without a penny."

A smile fills his face. "Say no more. Follow me."

Next thing I know, I'm standing in the studio of the local radio station, KMUD. The man, Roger, is a rancher who hosts a talk show twice a month called "Life in the Country." He's in a bind. One of tonight's guests has canceled. Could I pinch hit? I tell Roger I'm always happy to do my part for public radio.

"I'm gonna have you on the air with a local fire fighter who's just back from fighting two fires in the Tahoe National Forest," he says. "We'll have sort of an over-the-back-fence talk."

I'm still reeling from the sudden turn of events when I see what appears to be a man dressed as a woman stroll across the parking lot and enter the studio. His long blond hair is held in place by a white bow, and he's wearing a pink tank top and red lipstick. Beard stubble pokes through caked makeup. What really gives him away are his arms. They're the size of howitzers. I'm six-foot-four, and we stand eye to eye. He grips my hand and pumps it hard. He says his name is Diana. He's tonight's other guest.

"Roger, I'd like to keep the conversation more on fire fighting," Diana says, "rather than the cowboy logger turned cowgirl logger."

"Okey-dokey."

In the few minutes before we go on the air, I learn that Diana used to be called Dennis, and he's not what he seems. He really is a she. The sex change—"gender reassignment," in the parlance of transsexuals—was done years ago. All that remains is some electrolysis. Diana tells me that's the worst part, but I can't imagine anything more painful than losing the family jewels.

The three of us squeeze into the tiny sound booth. As Roger greets his listeners, I steal glances at Diana. I've never met a transsexual, not that I know of, anyway. Fatigue, anxiety, and hunger combine with the surrealism of the moment to leave me giddy. I fear I may laugh like a hyena. I consider gagging myself with a handful of foam from the soundproof wall. But Roger asks the first question, and I settle down. Though penniless, I am, after all, a professional.

Roger proves an able interviewer. He pulls my whole story from me, and then some. Callers ask about my travels to 35 countries, most of them as a journalist. I tell them how I went skiing in Bosnia during the war. How I witnessed the return of the condor to the Colombian Andes. How I found Romanian orphans living in the sewers of Bucharest. I hear myself talking and think, *How could you quit such a fascinating job?* But one thing I've always found frustrating about being a reporter: you're never able to fully enter the world of your subjects. When your notepad fills up, they go back to their lives, and you return to your hotel to order room service and watch TV. On this trek, there won't be an expense account standing between me and a fuller version of the truth.

By the end of the show, KMUD listeners have concluded that my trip is nothing short of a pilgrimage, a spiritual journey. I'm heartened by their enthusiasm, as I sometimes think of this adventure in similar terms. Then again, it's an easy audience. This is Humboldt County, where welfare recipients are called gurus. I'll have to wait to see how my enlightened poverty trip plays in Peoria.

Diana hasn't said boo. With Roger's encouragement, I've hogged the whole hour. It's too bad. There's a lot I'd like to have learned about her.

So it's a pleasant surprise when Garberville's only transsexual fire fighter leans over and says, "Mike, if you don't have any other plans, I'd like to take you to dinner."

We go to an Italian-Mexican restaurant where a football game plays on a giant video screen. Roger and the producer, Mitch, join us at the table. There's also Linda, from nearby Redway, and her eight-year-old daughter, Iona. Linda heard me on the radio and rushed to town to buy me dinner. Now that Diana's springing, Linda insists I spend the night at her house. I happily accept, with one regret: I'll never know how Diana intended our evening to end.

I'm glad to see I still know how to read a menu. I order lasagna, garlic bread, and the salad bar. The ache camped out in my head the last three days will soon be folding its tent.

In her previous life as a man, Diana was known as a fearless fire fighter and one of the region's top loggers. As a woman, not much has changed.

"I dropped a tree the other day that was seven-foot-four at the butt," she says. "I'm still a redneck, I'm just a little different now."

Diana's taco salad arrives, and she takes a bite, smearing her red lipstick. "I've always been maternal. My crew called me Mom, even before I was a woman."

Linda asks how her family reacted to her sex change. Diana's relatives have raised cattle in the area for several generations.

"My dad said it'd be easier if I was dead," she says softly. "With ranchers, you always want to breed up. You want your next calf to be better than the last. He looked at me and figured that I was a throwback."

The table falls silent.

"People come up to me now and say, 'Hey, I like to wear dresses sometimes.' And I say, '*Eeoo*, how weird,' They think I'm gay. I'm not. I've known I was this way since I was four. The thing is, when you go through your inner change, I can't see it. When I go through my change, it's there for everybody to see."

Diana spent last winter in the San Francisco area, in group counseling with other recent transsexuals. She worked a construction job to pay the bills. One day, she was remodeling the kitchen of a wealthy family's house. The couple saw how well she got along with their kids and invited her to move in as the nanny. She became the auntie for the whole upper-crust block, a real-life Mrs. Doubtfire, and no one was ever the wiser, not even her employers. On nights off, she went out with her six-foot-eight boyfriend.

"I could wear heels everywhere," she says.

We all erupt with laughter.

The check arrives, and Diana snaps it up with her sausage fingers. I've planned this journey in my mind for a year, but I never came close to imagining who would be buying my first dinner.

I look at Diana and think, *Kindness is strange, but never long a stranger.*

I load my pack into Linda's minivan, and we head for her house. She stops at the supermarket in Redway and asks if I want anything. I'm too shy to say, so she fills a plastic bag with trail mix. Perfect. At the checkout, we see Diana come in and grab a cart. She waves. The whole scene now seems normal.

Linda is forty-two and twice divorced. Besides Iona, she has two other daughters: Fauna, aged ten, and Sequoia, sixteen. Iona and Fauna split time between Linda and their father, who lives in the same neighborhood. They attend one of Humboldt's many self-styled alternative schools. Sequoia, who studies dance, lives with Linda's first husband, in Santa Cruz. Linda and her second ex founded two hugely successful mail-order record companies, specializing in children's and world music. They've just been bought out by a Hollywood entertainment conglomerate. Linda is a rich hippie.

She grew up poor in San Francisco, the only child of an Irish merchant seaman and a Swedish maid. Her mother was an alcoholic who died in an insane asylum. When Linda last saw her, she was strapped in a straitjacket, her head shaved for electroshock therapy. She swore at Linda in Swedish, blaming her daughter for her wretched life.

Ashamed of her background, Linda compensated by entering the glamorous world of high fashion. She became the buyer for an upscale San Francisco department store. A blond woman with stunning Scandinavian features, she was squired about town by wealthy men. When that lifestyle rang hollow, Linda dropped out to study herbal medicine. She arrived in Redway in the '70s, part of the second back-to-earth wave of hippies to invade Humboldt County. She delved into yoga, astrology, Eastern religions, quantum physics, and Indian mysticism. She set about repairing her soul.

Linda owns one of the area's original hippie mansions, a two-story octagonal structure built with scraps of redwood left behind by logging companies. A skylight in the shape of a pyramid crowns the roof. The house is circled by wooden decks. The trees are so close you can reach out and touch them. It is a most unconventional home. Forty African drums fill a corner of the living room. There is no TV, no curtains in the windows, and the girls call their mother Linda.

After the girls have gone to bed, I sit with Linda on a wicker sofa, gazing out the picture window into the dark forest. The house is still. Linda says she is inspired by my journey. After a decade as a cynical journalist, I've developed a pretty accurate bullshit meter. Nothing registers on it now. Linda seems to possess an inner calm, an unshakable sense of her place in the universe. I feel like a sham in comparison. I want what she has. I confess to her that I am not brave and wise. I'm a frightened boy in the body of a man. I'm afraid of the dark, the wind in the trees, the animals in the forest.

Linda smiles kindly. "When I first came here, I lived in a cabin I found out I shared with raccoons and skunks and bats. They'd all nestled away in there. I snipped pot for a living, ten dollars an hour. I did it at night by lantern. The bats swooped all around me, and I worried. But I learned that they weren't going to hurt me. They'd fly past and swirl around in these same patterns. After a while, I saw that they recognized me. They knew who I was.

"An Indian taught me something I'll never forget. He said, 'We don't have a word for loneliness in my language.' I said 'Why, because you're always surrounded by uncles and aunts and grandparents?' He said, 'No. It's because we think of nature as our kin, so we are never alone.'

"I thought, How great. When you realize that the bears and the bats and the trees are all your relatives, you can never be lonely."

Linda looks at me and says in a solemn tone, "Reverence. You can't repair your soul until you have reverence. Don't be afraid of the dark, Mike. Don't be afraid of nature."

We talk late into the night, then Linda shows me to the guest room. A bed! With flannel sheets, no less. I drift toward sleep, feeling safe and warm and profoundly grateful. Diana bought me dinner, but Linda gave me food for thought. And sometimes that's the best meal of all.

In the morning I shave and shower, washing my hair with Linda's Irish moss shampoo. The shower is made of stone and stands in a corner of the greenhouse, butting up against a wall of glass. I bathe, naked to the world, or at least to my cousins, the redwoods.

Linda fixes French toast, with honey in the batter, as I eat sliced cantaloupe and sip grapefruit juice. Fauna and Iona turn cartwheels across the hardwood floor. I've never been a comfortable guest, even in good friends' houses. But I feel totally at ease in this stranger's home. My stomach churns, but not from hunger. I must soon leave, and I know the uncertainty of the road is about to resume.

Linda hands me the bag of trail mix, along with a mutzu apple and two lemon zucchinis from her organic garden. The load adds a good seven pounds to my pack, but it's weight I'll gladly carry. She and the girls drive me back down to the highway in Garberville. I thank Linda and tell her that if the rest of my trip goes a tenth as well as it has here, it will be a great journey.

"Well, if you settle for ten percent, that's what you'll get," she says. "On your journey, don't compromise your vision. You're on a vision quest. You're an archetype. You represent middle America, who just got fed up and wants to discover the real America. Maybe America is now spelled with a small *a*, and you're out trying to find the capital-A America."

Linda leans over and hugs me, and gives my cheek a kiss. I say good-bye to the girls and step out of the van. I'm standing in the same spot where I found the cauliflower yesterday.

"Remember," Linda says through the open window, "don't compromise your vision."

Altruism

LEWIS THOMAS

Lewis Thomas was born in Flushing, New York, in 1913, and was educated at Princeton and Harvard, where he earned an M.D. in 1937. Since
1973 he has served as president of the Sloan-Kettering Institute in New
York, a center for cancer treatment and research.

In 1971, Thomas began contributing "Notes of a Biology Watcher"
to the New England Journal of Medicine. Some of these essays
were published as The Lives of a Cell, Thomas's first book, which
brought him quick recognition as one of the most imaginative and
provocative science writers in the country.

The essay that follows comes from a more recent collection, Late
Night Thoughts on Listening to Mahler's Ninth Symphony, which was published in 1983. Thomas considers altruism as
"one of biology's deep mysteries." Why? As Thomas defines the term, is
altruism an instinct—biologically determined—or a learned behavior?
What is its purpose in the natural world? What evidence does Thomas
offer to prove "that we are born and grow up with a fondness for each other,
and we have genes for that"?

Altruism has always been one of biology's deep mysteries. Why should any
animal, off on its own, specified and labeled by all sorts of signals as its
individual self, choose to give up its life in aid of someone else? Nature, long
viewed as a wild, chaotic battlefield swarmed across by more than ten million
different species, comprising unnumbered billions of competing selves locked
in endless combat, offers only one sure measure of success: survival. Survival,
in the cool economics of biology, means simply the persistence of one's own
genes in the generations to follow.

At first glance, it seems an unnatural act, a violation of nature, to give away one's life, or even one's possessions, to another. And yet, in the face of improbability, examples of altruism abound. When a worker bee, patrolling the frontiers of the hive, senses the nearness of a human intruder, the bee's attack is pure, unqualified suicide; the sting is barbed, and in the act of pulling away the insect is fatally injured. Other varieties of social insects, most spectacularly the ants and higher termites, contain castes of soldiers for whom self-sacrifice is an everyday chore.

It is easy to dismiss the problem by saying that "altruism" is the wrong technical term for behavior of this kind. The word is a human word, pieced together to describe an unusual aspect of human behavior, and we should not be using it for the behavior of mindless automata. A honeybee has no connection to creatures like us, no brain for figuring out the future, no way of predicting the inevitable outcome of that sting.

But the meditation of the 50,000 or so connected minds of a whole hive is not so easy to dismiss. A multitude of bees can tell the time of day, calculate the geometry of the sun's position, argue about the best location for the next swarm. Bees do a lot of close observing of other bees; maybe they know what follows stinging and do it anyway.

Altruism is not restricted to the social insects, in any case. Birds risk their lives, sometimes lose them, in efforts to distract the attention of predators from the nest. Among baboons, zebras, moose, wildebeests, and wild dogs there are always stubbornly fated guardians, prepared to be done in first in order to buy time for the herd to escape.

It is genetically determined behavior, no doubt about it. Animals have genes for altruism, and those genes have been selected in the evolution of many creatures because of the advantage they confer for the continuing survival of the species. It is, looked at in this way, not the emotion-laden problem that we feel when we try to put ourselves in the animal's place; it is just another plain fact of life, perhaps not as hard a fact as some others, something rather nice, in fact, to think about.

J.B.S. Haldane, the eminent British geneticist, summarized the chilly arithmetic of the problem by announcing, "I would give up my life for two brothers or eight cousins." This calculates the requirement for ultimate self-interest: the preservation and survival of an individual's complement of genes. Trivers, Hamilton, and others have constructed mathematical models to account nicely for the altruistic behavior of social insects, quantifying the self-serving profit for the genes of the defending bee in the act of tearing its abdomen apart. The hive is filled with siblings, ready to carry the *persona* of the dying bee through all the hive's succeeding generations. Altruism is based on kinship; by preserving kin, one preserves one's self. In a sense.

Haldane's prediction has the sound of a beginning sequence: two brothers, eight (presumably) first cousins, and then another series of much larger numbers of more distant relatives. Where does the influence tail off? At what point does the sharing of the putative altruist's genes become so diluted as to be meaningless? Would the line on a graph charting altruism plummet to zero soon after those eight cousins, or is it a long, gradual slope? When the combat marine throws himself belly-down on the live grenade in order to preserve the rest of his platoon, is this the same sort of altruism, or is this an act without any technically biological meaning? Surely the marine's genes, most of them, will be blown away forever; the statistical likelihood of having two brothers or eight cousins in that platoon is extremely small. And yet there he is, belly-down as if by instinct, and the same kind of event has been recorded often enough in wartime to make it seem a natural human act, normal enough, even though rare, to warrant the stocking of medals by the armed services.

At what point do our genetic ties to each other become so remote that we feel no instinctual urge to help? I can imagine an argument about this, with two sides, but it would be a highly speculative discussion, not by any means pointless but still impossible to settle one way or the other. One side might assert, with total justification, that altruistic behavior among human beings has nothing at all to do with genetics, that there is no such thing as a gene for self-sacrifice, not even a gene for helpfulness, or concern, or even affection. These are attributes that must be learned from society acquired by cultures, taught by example. The other side could maintain, with equal justification, since the facts are not known, precisely the opposite position: we get along together in human society because we are genetically designed to be social animals, and we are obliged, by instructions from our genes, to be useful to each other. This side would argue further that when we behave badly, killing or maiming or snatching, we are acting on misleading information learned from the wrong kinds of society we put together; if our cultures were not deformed, we would be better company, paying attention to what our genes are telling us.

For the purposes of the moment I shall take the side of the sociobiologists because I wish to carry their side of the argument a certain distance afield, beyond the human realm. I have no difficulty in imagining a close enough resemblance among the genomes of all human beings, of all races and geographic origins, to warrant a biological mandate for all of us to do whatever we can to keep the rest of us, the species, alive. I maintain, despite the moment's evidence against the claim, that we are born and grow up with a fondness for each other, and we have genes for that. We can be talked out of it, for the genetic message is like a distant music and some of us are hard-of-hearing. Societies are noisy affairs, drowning out the sound of ourselves and our connection. Hard-of-hearing, we go to war. Stone-deaf, we make thermonuclear missiles. Nonetheless, the music is there, waiting for more listeners.

But the matter does not end with our species. If we are to take seriously the notion that the sharing of similar genes imposes a responsibility on the sharers to sustain each other, and if I am right in guessing that even very distant cousins carry at least traces of this responsibility and will act on it whenever they can, then the whole world becomes something to be concerned about on solidly scientific, reductionist, genetic grounds. For we have cousins more than we can count, and they are all over the place, run by genes so similar to ours that the differences are minor technicalities. All of us, men, women, children, fish, sea grass, sandworms, dolphins, hamsters, and soil bacteria, everything alive on the planet, roll ourselves along through all our generations by replicating DNA and RNA, and although the alignments of nucleotides within these molecules are different in different species, the molecules themselves are fundamentally the same substance. We make our proteins in the same old way, and many of the enzymes most needed for cellular life are everywhere identical.

This is, in fact, the way it should be. If cousins are defined by common descent, the human family is only one small and very recent addition to a much larger family in a tree extending back at least 3.5 billion years. Our common ancestor was a single cell from which all subsequent cells derived, most likely a cell resembling one of today's bacteria in today's soil. For almost three-fourths of the earth's life, cells of that first kind were the whole biosphere. It was less than a billion years ago that cells like ours appeared in the first marine invertebrates and these were somehow pieced together by the joining up and fusion of the earlier primitive cells, retaining the same blood lines. Some of the joiners, bacteria that had learned how to use oxygen, are with us still, part of our flesh, lodged inside the cells of all animals, all plants, moving us from place to place and doing our breathing for us. Now there's a set of cousins!

Even if I try to discount the other genetic similarities linking human beings to all other creatures by common descent, the existence of these beings in my cells is enough, in itself, to relate me to the chestnut tree in my backyard and to the squirrel in that tree.

There ought to be a mathematics for connections like this before claiming any kinship function, but the numbers are too big. At the same time, even if we wanted to, we cannot think the sense of obligation away. It is there, maybe in our genes for the recognition of cousins, or, if not, it ought to be there in our intellects for having learned about the matter. Altruism, in its biological sense, is required of us. We have an enormous family to look after, or perhaps that assumes too much, making us sound like official gardeners and zookeepers for the planet, responsibilities for which we are probably not yet grown-up enough. We may need new technical terms for concern, respect, affection, substitutes for altruism. But at least we should acknowledge the family ties and, with them, the obligations. If we do it wrong, scattering pollutants, clouding the atmosphere with too much carbon dioxide, extinguishing the thin carapace of ozone, burning up the forests, dropping the bombs, rampaging at large through nature as though we owned the place, there will be a lot of paying back to do and, at the end, nothing to pay back with.

What Is My Job on the Planet with a Capital J?

JON KABAT-ZINN

"What is my job on the planet?" is one question we might do well to ask ourselves over and over again. Otherwise, we may wind up doing somebody else's job and not even know it. And what's more, that somebody else might be a figment of our own imagination and maybe a prisoner of it as well.

As thinking creatures, packaged, as are all life forms, in unique organismic units we call bodies, and simultaneously totally and impersonally embedded in the warp and woof of life's ceaseless unfolding, we have a singular capacity to take responsibility for our unique piece of what it means to be alive, at least while we have our brief moment in the sun. But we also have the singular capacity of letting our thinking mind entirely cloud our transit through this world. We are at risk of never realizing our uniqueness—at least as long as we remain in the shadow cast by our thought habits and conditioning.

Buckminster Fuller, the discoverer/inventor of the geodesic dome, at age thirty-two contemplated suicide for a few hours one night at the edge of Lake Michigan, as the story goes, after a series of business failures that left him feeling he had made such a mess of his life that the best move would be for him to remove himself from the scene and make things simpler for his wife and infant daughter. Apparently everything he had touched or undertaken had turned to dust in spite of his incredible creativity and imagination, which were only recognized later. However, instead of ending his life, Fuller decided (perhaps because of his deep conviction in the underlying unity and order of the universe, of which he knew himself to be an integral part) to live from then on *as if* he had died that night.

Being dead, he wouldn't have to worry about how things worked out any longer for himself personally and would be free to devote himself to living as a representative of the universe. The rest of his life would be a gift. Instead of living for himself, he would devote himself to asking, "What is it on this planet

79

[which he referred to as Spaceship Earth] that needs doing that I know something about, that probably won't happen unless I take responsibility for it?" He decided he would just ask that question continuously and do what came to him, following his nose. In this way, working for humanity as an employee of the universe at large, you get to modify and contribute to your locale by who you are, how you are, and what you do. But it's no longer personal. It's just part of the totality of the universe expressing itself.

Rarely do we question and then contemplate with determination what our hearts are calling us to do and to be. I like to frame such efforts in question form: "What is my job on the planet with a capital J?", or, "What do I care about so much that I would pay to do it?" If I ask such a question and I don't come up with an answer, other than, "I don't know," then I just keep asking the question. If you start reflecting on such questions when you're in your twenties, by the time you are thirty-five or forty, or fifty or sixty, the inquiry itself may have led you a few places that you would not have gone had you merely followed mainstream conventions, or your parents' expectations for you, or even worse, your own unexamined self-limiting beliefs and expectations.

You can start asking this question any time, at any age. There is never a time of life when it would not have a profound effect on your view of things and the choices you make. It may not mean that you will change *what* you do, but it may mean that you may want to change how you see it or hold it, and perhaps *how* you do it. Once the universe is your employer, very interesting things start to happen, even if someone else is cutting your paycheck. But you do have to be patient. It takes time to grow this way of being in your life. The place to start of course is right here. The best time? How about now?

You never know what will come of such introspections. Fuller himself was fond of stating that what seems to be happening at the moment is never the full story of what is really going on. He liked to point out that for the honey bee, it is the honey that is important. But the bee is at the same time nature's vehicle for carrying out cross-pollination of the flowers. Interconnectedness is a fundamental principle of nature. Nothing is isolated. Each event connects with others. Things are constantly unfolding on different levels. It's for us to perceive the warp and woof of it all as best we can and learn to follow our own threads through the tapestry of life with authenticity and resolve.

Fuller believed in an underlying architecture of nature, in which form and function were inextricably linked. He believed that nature's blueprints would make sense and would have practical relevance to our lives on many levels. Before he died, X-ray crystallographic studies had demonstrated that many viruses—submicroscopic assemblies of macromolecules on the edge of life itself—are structured along the same geodesic principles as those he discovered by playing around with polyhedra.

He didn't live long enough to see it, but in addition to all his other seminal inventions and ideas, a whole new field of chemistry opened up around the unpredicted discovery of soccer ball–like carbon compounds with remarkable properties which quickly became known as Buckminsterfullerenes or buckyballs. Playing in his sandbox, following his own path, his musings led to discoveries and worlds he never dreamed of. So can yours. Fuller never thought of himself as special in any sense, just a regular person who liked to play with ideas and with forms. His motto was: "If I can understand it, anybody can understand it."

Do Kids Need Religion?

ANTHONY BRANDT

Anthony Brandt, a contributing editor at Parenting *magazine, focuses on the relationship of children to religious faith. Brandt speaks as a parent, one concerned about how best to help his children face the losses and traumas life always brings. In this essay, published in 1991 in the progressive* Utne Reader, *he describes himself as a "run-of-the-mill modern skeptic," without faith or belief and asks us to consider the uses of religion in what he terms a largely secular society. Might religion serve as a unifying cultural force, even for people who don't "believe"? Even more important, Brandt asks, "What sort of meaning does a secular society offer a child?" These questions suggest that Brandt (b. 1936) is searching for a basis on which parents can make some very hard choices about how they will (and should) raise their children.*

I admire Brandt's straightforward approach here, his willingness to consider various options, and his refusal to argue that his way to spirituality is the only or even the best way. In addition, I find that Brandt establishes some common ground for all people, regardless of differences in religious faith or creed, when he says, "The longing for meaning is something we all share."

This happened nearly 20 years ago, so I may not have all the details right. As I remember, my daughter was about 10 years old. She had spent the weekend with her grandparents, and while she was gone, a house down the road from ours burned to the ground. Three children died in the fire. One was a houseguest. The other two were my daughter's closest friends.

My wife went to see the bereaved parents. They were devout Catholics and they took their loss amazingly well. They talked to her about their two girls being angels in heaven now, and they really believed it. At the funeral, they were strong and brave, braver than many others there, including myself.

My tears were bitter. I didn't think their children were angels, I thought they were dead. I had little confidence in any sort of existence beyond that. I was not a devout Catholic or a devout anything. I was your run-of-the-mill modern skeptic who long before had stopped going to church, thought most religious doctrine absurd, and was resolved to live without the illusions of belief.

What does your run-of-the-mill modern skeptic tell his 10-year-old daughter when her closest friends have just died in a fire? My wife and I told her what had happened when she got home from her grandparents' house. I was crying and so was my wife, but my daughter just sat there, stunned, in shock. I wanted so much to console her, to find something to say that would explain, would justify these deaths and give them meaning. But I didn't think these deaths had any meaning. All I could come up with was something I didn't believe. "Maybe there is a heaven," I said, "and that's where they are." Yeah, maybe. And maybe not.

I'm old enough to know now that there's no living without illusions of some sort, that we all need to find or generate some kind of meaning for our lives if life is not to become unbearable. But what kind? It goes without saying that we are no longer a religious society in the conventional sense of the word. Religion no longer stands at the center of our culture as it did a hundred or so years ago. Rather, we are a thoroughly secularized society. The miracles we marvel at are the miracles of technology. For the answers to our questions about the meaning of things, we look not to the elders of a church, but to science.

An event like the cruel and pointless death of three little girls, however, presents a fundamental challenge. What sort of meaning does a secular society offer a child? What do parents with no religious beliefs do when their children start asking those difficult questions about where Grandpa has gone, Grandpa having just died, or why Jesus was crucified, and why people are so mean, and what will happen to them when they die?

For some parents, to be sure, questions like these present no problem. Either they have religious beliefs and are confident they can transmit them to their kids, or they have no religious beliefs at all and see no reason to raise their children to have any. I asked one father what he had done about his kids' religious education and he said, "Nothing, whatsoever." Well, I went on, how did he answer their questions about God and things like that? He didn't remember there being any. And even if there are questions, a parent can say, "Go ask your mother" or "I'm no expert on that" or simply "I don't know," and let it go at that. Western culture is so secularized that parents can evade or dismiss "religious" questions without feeling that they're merely getting themselves off the hook. No one is surprised anymore by this kind of religious indifference.

For believers, too, the problem doesn't exist. Secure in their own faith, they can confidently answer the questions of a child.

Another mother and father, not so secure in their faith, say it was actually their children who brought them back to religion. They had both been raised Roman Catholic; each had children from a previous marriage; both had lapsed from the church. But they were sending their kids to a Protestant Sunday school. One night at dinner the oldest child said, "Don't you think we should pray for this food?" This was something of a shock. It was even more so when the child said, in prayer, "And thank you, God, for bringing our whole family together." The following Sunday the parents went to church. They have been actively involved (in a Protestant congregation) ever since. "Children come up with some really interesting questions," the mother told me, "and we still have to do a lot of explaining. But we have faith. We don't feel that we're alone with these questions."

◆

For those of us without faith it's not so easy. Do we send our kids to Sunday school when we ourselves never go to church? Do we have them baptized even though we have no intention of raising them to be religious? I argued against having my son baptized. It's a meaningless ritual, I said. I didn't think he had been "born in sin," so why wash him free of it, even symbolically? Why bow to convention simply for convention's sake? I gave in, but only to keep peace in the family.

For me religious education raised the issue of honesty. I thought it would be hypocritical to make my kids attend Sunday school when I not only didn't go to church but also didn't have any religious beliefs. My parents had sent me to Sunday school when neither of them was in the least religious, and under the circumstances I came to think Sunday school was a joke. I learned a few Bible stories, but that was all. I believed I should spare my children that kind of charade. My wife took them to church from time to time, but only once or twice did they attend a Sunday school class.

I'm still wondering whether we did the right thing. In *Childhood and Society* the renowned psychoanalyst Erik Erikson makes the unsettling remark that "many are proud to be without religion whose children cannot afford their being without it." Children may not need a religious upbringing, but, says Erikson, they do need a sense of "basic trust," a feeling not only that their fundamental bodily needs will be met and that their parents love them and will take care of them, but also that they have not been abandoned to the empty haphazardness of existence.

Erikson relates this sense of trust to the psychosocial origins of religious life. "The parental faith which supports the trust emerging in the newborn," he writes, "has throughout history sought its institutional safeguard . . . in organized religion." The trust of the infant in the parents, in other words, finds its parallel—and takes its mature form—in the parents' trust in God. The implication is that if trust has no institutional reinforcement, it will tend to wither. Basic trust will become basic mistrust, and there will be more work for mental health experts such as Erikson.

The institutional form that trust has taken in America has historically remained within the Judeo-Christian tradition, and the decision to deny that tradition to a child ought at the very least to be well thought out. Children will become aware of the tradition with or without parental teaching; they'll bring it home from school or the playground, wanting to know why their friend Jimmy says they'll go to hell if they don't go to church, or why Alice is getting a beautiful white confirmation dress and they're not. A psychoanalyst, Ana-Marie Rizzuto, once pointed out that no matter what parents teach their children, "religious symbols and language are so widely present in this society that virtually no child reaches school age without having constructed—with or without religious instruction—an image or images of God."

I broached the subject with one couple who have a three-year-old daughter. The father, Pete, was raised in a fundamentalist family and rebelled against it; religion holds a kind of perverse fascination for him, but he is not what you would call a believer. His wife, Valerie, has no religious beliefs to speak of. Yet they both want their daughter to go to Sunday school. "I don't want her to grow up in a religious vacuum," says Pete. He thinks that if they don't give her a religious background they will be depriving her of a choice later on. If she has the background, she can always reject it when she gets older, he says; if she doesn't, there will be nothing to reject but nothing to affirm, either. He doesn't think she would be likely to come to that crossroads on her own. Valerie agrees with this reasoning: "I want her to know the Bible stories, the mythology," she says. "It's a major part of our culture. And I want her to have a sense of mystery, of awe." A sense, says Pete, that in our society has largely been lost.

If this approach seems paradoxical coming from parents who are not themselves believers, it also makes a certain amount of sense. No matter what we believe in, our society's Judeo-Christian tradition retains a good deal of its power. I reject organized religion, yet I cannot listen to Mozart's *Requiem Mass* without being moved. Perhaps non-practicing Jews feel the same when they hear Hebrew prayers sung. Much of Western culture springs from religious feeling; we are secular but our heritage is not, and there is no true identification with a culture without some feel for its past. To raise children in a culture without at least exposing them to its religious traditions, even if you yourself have abandoned the beliefs on which they are based, may be doing them a disservice. The children will be exposed to those traditions in any case, so why not give them some real instruction?

Pete and Valerie are not alone; among the nonbelieving parents I talked to, theirs was a common rationale for sending their children to Sunday school, and the most common solution to the problem. Several other parents, however, admitted to qualms. "Kids pick up on your real feelings about things pretty fast," one father said. "If you're making them do something you yourself don't believe in, they're going to figure it out." And a mother told me, "I think you can transmit values to your kids, but belief is different. Values—respect for other people, respect for life, not taking what doesn't belong to you, things like that—they're universal, they're everywhere. But belief is a special thing. You have to come to it on your own; nobody can impose it on you."

☙

Too, it is impossible to predict with any confidence what effect a religious education will have on children. It can be more than a little uncomfortable when your children take religious teaching more seriously than you do. It is unsettling to think that they might need religion when you have decided you do not. Do kids in fact need religion? They need "basic trust," as Erikson says, but beyond that, nobody has conclusive answers. We used to think that without religious beliefs, social behavior would come unglued. "If God is dead," wrote Dostoyevski, "then everything is permitted." It hasn't happened.

Morality can survive without religion, it appears; children can be taught the importance of right versus wrong without benefit of religious training. Jean Piaget and Lawrence Kohlberg[1] have shown that moral understanding is acquired in stages, that it is a developmental process that unfolds, to some extent, as naturally as intelligence itself.

My daughter, now age 27, who was exposed to little more than my own deep skepticism, is studying Buddhism. As I write, in fact, she is in Tibet, on a journey that I'm sure is at least partly spiritual. I have made spiritual journeys during my adult life, all of them outside the sphere of Christianity that I was raised in. I continue to distrust and dislike organized religion but find it hard, as I grow older, to live with only my vague faith that life I must have some kind of meaning, even if I don't know what it is.

To believe is to be connected, and those of us who don't believe cannot help but miss the feelings that come with belonging to something larger than ourselves. I hope my children find a straighter road than I've found. "I very much wish I had had some religion, for my kids' sake," one father told me. "My son's into tarot cards now. There's not much comfort in tarot cards."

The longing for meaning is something we all share, parent and child alike. But it may be that this is an area where a parent can't help a child much. Meaning may be something all of us have to find in our own way. I don't know. I am loath to give advice. Robert Coles[2] quotes a black woman who worked as a servant for a wealthy white Southern family: "My momma told me: Remember that you're put here only for a few seconds of God's time, and he's testing you. He doesn't want answers, though. He wants you to know how to ask the right questions." Teaching our kids how to ask the right questions may be the best we can do.

Notes

1. *Jean Piaget* (1896–1980) *and Lawrence Kohlberg* (1927–87): psychologists who studied the mental and moral development of children and young adults.

2. *Robert Coles*: an educational psychologist (b. 1929) whose work on the ethical life of children has been widely influential.

Forgiveness

ANNE LAMOTT

I somehow managed to make it into October without figuring out this little scheduling quirk.

Finally, though, one Wednesday, I stopped by Sam's classroom and found him—once again—drawing with his teacher. The teacher said gently, "Annie? Did you not know that school gets out an hour early on Wednesdays?"

"Ah," I said.

"Didn't you get the papers the school mailed to you this summer?"

I racked my brain, and finally I did remember some papers coming in the mail from school. And I remembered really meaning to read them.

Sam sat there drawing with a grim autistic stare.

Well, my enemy found out.

She showed up two days later all bundled up in a down jacket, because it was cold and she was one of the parents who was driving the kids on their first field trip. Now, this was not a crime against nature or me in and of itself. The crime was that below the down jacket, she was wearing latex bicycle shorts. She wears latex bicycle shorts nearly every day, and I will tell you why: because she can. She weighs about eighty pounds. She has gone to the gym almost every day since her divorce, and she does not have an ounce of fat on her body. I completely hate that in a person. I consider it an act of aggression against the rest of us mothers who forgot to start working out after we had our kids.

Oh, and one more thing: she still had a Ronald Reagan bumper sticker on her white Volvo, seven years after he left office.

The day of the field trip, she said sweetly, "I just want you to know, Annie, that if you have any other questions about how the classroom works, I'd really love to be there for you."

I smiled back at her. I thought such awful thoughts that I cannot even say them out loud because they would make Jesus want to drink gin straight out of the cat dish.

It drove me to my knees. I prayed about it. I prayed because my son loves her son, and my son is so kind that it makes me want to be a better person, a person who does not hate someone just because she wears latex bicycle shorts. I prayed for a miracle; I wrote her name down on a slip of paper, folded it up, and put it in the box that I use as God's In Box. "Help," I said to God.

There wasn't much noticeable progress for a while. On the last day of first grade, I was asked to bake something for the farewell party. I couldn't do it. I was behind in my work. Also, I was in a bad mood. But I at least *went* to the party, and I ate the delicious cookies my enemy made, and we mingled a little, and I thought that this was progress. Then she had to go and wreck everything by asking, "Did *you* bake anything?"

I don't bake. I baked for school once and it was a bad experience: Sam was in kindergarten at the little Christian school he attended, and I baked a dozen cupcakes for his class's Christmas party and set them out to cool. Sam and I went outside to sweep the Astroturf. (OK, OK, I also don't garden.) Suddenly Sadie came tearing outside—our dog who is so obedient and eager to please. But there was icing in the fur of her muzzle and a profoundly concerned look on her face. Oh, my God, she seemed to be saying with her eyes: Terrible news from the kitchen!

Sam looked at me with total disgust, like "You ignorant slut—you left the cupcakes out where the *dog* could get them."

The next morning I bought cupcakes at Safeway. Like I said: I don't bake.

I also don't push Sam to read. There wasn't much pressure for anyone to read in first grade, but by second grade, it was apparently critical to national security that your kid be reading. He brought home bulletins from time to time to this effect. My kid was not reading. I mean, per se.

My enemy's child was reading proficiently, like a little John Kenneth Galbraith in a Spiderman T-shirt. He is what is referred to as an "early reader." Sam is a "late reader." (Albert Einstein was a "late reader." Theodore Kaczinski was an "early reader." Not that I am at all defensive on the subject. *Pas du tout*.)

Sam and this woman's child were in the same class, and the next thing I knew, she had taken a special interest in Sam's reading.

She began the year by slipping me early first grade books that she thought maybe Sam could read. And Sam could certainly read some of the words in these books. But I resented her giving them to us with a patronizing smile, as if to say her child would not be needing them because he was reading the new Joan Didion.

I went to the God box. I got the piece of paper out with her name on it. I added an exclamation mark. I put it back.

One day not long after, she sidled up to me at school and asked me if I had an extra copy of the book I wrote about being a mother. It is black-humored and quite slanted: George Bush was president when Sam was born, and perhaps I was a little angry. I had these tiny opinions. I wrote an anti-George Bush baby book.

So when she asked for a copy, I tried to stall; I tried to interest her in my anti-Reagan, anti-Bush writing book. But she insisted.

So a few days later, filled with a certain low-grade sense of impending doom, I gave her a copy, signed, "With all good wishes."

For the next few days, she smiled obliquely whenever I saw her at school, and I grew increasingly anxious. Then one day she came up to me in the market. "I read your book," she said, and then she winked. "Maybe," she whispered, because my son was only a few feet away, "maybe it's a good thing he *doesn't* read."

I wish I could report that I had the perfect comeback, something so polite and brilliantly cutting that Dorothy Parker, overhearing it in heaven, had raised her fist in victory. But I could only gape at her, stunned. She smiled very nicely, and walked away.

I called half a dozen people when I got home and told them about how she had trashed me. And then I trashed her. And it was good.

The next time I saw her, she smiled. I sneered, just a little. I felt disgust, but I also felt disgusting. I got out my note to God. I said, Look, hon. I think we need bigger guns.

Nothing happened. No burning bush, no cereal flakes dropping from heaven, forming letters of instruction in the snow. It's just that God began to act like Sam-I-Am from *Green Eggs and Ham*. Everywhere I turned were helpful household hints on loving one's enemies, on turning the other cheek, and on how doing that makes you look in a whole new direction. There were admonitions about the self-destructiveness of not forgiving people, and reminders that this usually doesn't hurt other people so much as it hurts you. In fact, not forgiving is like drinking rat poison and then waiting for the rat to die. Fortune cookies, postcards, bumper stickers, everything but skywriting—yet I kept feeling that I could not, would not forgive her in a box, could not would not forgive her with a fox, not on a train, not in the rain.

One Sunday when I was struggling with this, the Scripture reading came from the sixth chapter of Luke: "Forgive, and ye shall be forgiven." Now, try as I might, I cannot find a loophole in that. It does not say, "Forgive everyone, unless they've said something rude about your child." And it doesn't even say, "Just try." It says, If you want to be forgiven, if you want to experience that kind of love, you have to forgive everyone in your life—everyone, even the very worst boyfriend you ever had—even, for God's sake, yourself.

Then a few days later I was picking Sam up at the house of another friend and noticed a yellowed clipping taped to the refrigerator with "FORGIVENESS" written at the top—as though God had decided to abandon all efforts at subtlety and just plain noodge. The clipping said forgiveness meant that God is for giving, and that we are here for giving too, and that to withhold love or blessings is to be completely delusional. No one knew who had written it. I copied it down and taped it to my refrigerator. Then an old friend from Texas left a message on my answering machine that said, "Don't forget, God loves us exactly the way we are, and God loves us too much to let us stay like this."

Only, I think she must have misquoted it, because she said, "God loves you too much to let you stay like this."

I looked nervously over both shoulders.

A couple of days later my enemy's boy came to play at our house, and then she came to pick him up just before dinner. And for the first time, while he gathered his things, she sat down on the couch, as if she had done this before, as if it were the most natural thing. I felt around inside my heart, and it was not so cold or hard. In fact, I even almost offered her a cup of tea because she seemed sad or maybe tired. I felt a stab of kindness inside, until her son came bounding out of Sam's room, shouting that he'd gotten 100 percent on his arithmetic test, and Sam had gotten two wrong.

"Traitor!" Sam shouted from his room, and slammed the door.

By bedtime, Sam said he forgave him but didn't want to be friends anymore. I said he didn't have to be friends, but he did have to be kind. At breakfast, Sam said he still forgave him, but when we got to school he said that it had been easier to forgive him when we were farther away.

Still, several days later, when the mother called and invited Sam to come play that afternoon, Sam desperately wanted to go. She picked him up after school. When I went over to get him, she offered *me* a cup of tea. I said no, I couldn't stay. I was in my fattest pants, she wore her bicycle shorts. The smell of something baking, sweet and yeasty, filled the house. But Sam couldn't find his knapsack, so I got up to look around. The surfaces of her house were covered with fine and expensive things. "Please let me make you a cup of tea," she said again, and I started to say no, but this thing inside me used my voice to say, "Well . . . OK." It was awkward. In the living room, I silently dared her to bring up school, math tests, or field trips; I dared her to bring up exercise, or politics. As it was, we had very little to talk about—I was having to work so hard making sure she didn't bring up much of anything, because she was so goddamn competitive— and I sat there politely sipping my lemongrass tea. Everywhere you looked was more facade, more expensive stuff—show-offy I-have-more-money-than-you stuff, plus-you're-out-of-shape stuff. Then our boys appeared, and I got up to go. Sam's shoes were on the mat by the front door, next to his friend's, and I went over to help him put them on. And as I loosened the laces on one shoe, without realizing what I was doing, I sneaked a look into the other boy's sneaker—to see what size shoe he wore. To see how my kid lined up in shoe size.

And I finally got it.

The veil dropped. I got that I am as mad as a hatter. I saw that I was the one worried that my child wasn't doing well enough in school. That I was the one who thought I was out of shape. And that I was trying to get her to carry all this for me because it hurt too much to carry it myself.

I wanted to kiss her on both cheeks, apologize for all the self-contempt I'd been spewing out into the world, all the bad juju I'd been putting on her by thinking she was the one doing harm. I felt like J. Edgar Hoover, peeking into the shoes of his nephew's seven-year-old friend to see how the Hoover feet measured up, idly wondering how the kid's parents would like to have a bug on their phone. This was *me*. *She* was the one pouring me more tea, she was the one who'd been taking care of my son. She was the one who seemed to have already forgiven me for writing a book in which I trashed her political beliefs; like God and certain parents do, forgiven me almost before I'd even done anything that I needed to be forgiven for. It's like the faucets are already flowing before you even hold out your cup to be filled. Before, giveness.

I felt so happy there in her living room that I got drunk on her tea. I read once in some magazine that in Czechoslovakia, they say an echo in the woods always returns your own call, and so I started speaking sweetly to everyone—to the mother, to the boys. And my sweet voice started getting all over me, like sunlight, like the smell of the Danish baking in the oven, two of which she put on a paper plate and covered with tin foil for me and Sam to take home. Now, obviously, the woman has a little baking disorder. And I am glad.

The Love Song of J. Alfred Prufrock

T. S. ELIOT—1917

T. S. Eliot is a twentieth-century poet who moved from America to England early in his career and later became a British citizen. In his poem "The Love Song of J. Alfred Prufrock" he creates an outwardly sophisticated narrator who speaks to us of his inability to have meaningful relationships with those in his social environment. As readers of the poem, we seem to be overhearing Prufrock's thoughts as he encounters, remembers, or overhears people in his world of tea parties and other social encounters. Although Prufrock appears very much a part of his society on the surface, in many ways he discloses that he is not at all happy or comfortable with his role in it.

Have you ever experienced the frustrating inability to communicate or relate purposefully to those around you? Were there obvious reasons for the problem or were the causes unclear in your mind? As you read the poem, recall your own problematic relationships with others in a group in which you were a member.

S'io credesse che mia risposta fosse
A persona che mai tornasse al mondo,
Questa fiamma staria senza piu scosse.
Ma perciocché giammai di questo fondo
Non torno vivo alcun, s'i'odo il vero,
Senza tema d'infamia ti rispondo.[1]

Let us go then, you and I,
When the evening is spread out against the sky
Like a patient etherized upon a table;

Let us go, through certain half-deserted streets,
The muttering retreats
Of restless nights in one-night cheap hotels
And sawdust restaurants with oyster-shells:
Streets that follow like a tedious argument
Of insidious intent
To lead you to an overwhelming question . . .
Oh, do not ask, "What is it?"
Let us go and make our visit.

In the room the women come and go
Talking of Michelangelo.[2]

The yellow fog that rubs its back upon the window-panes,
The yellow smoke that rubs its muzzle on the window-panes
Licked its tongue into the corners of the evening,
Lingered upon the pools that stand in drains,
Let fall upon its back the soot that falls from chimneys,
Slipped by the terrace, made a sudden leap,
And seeing that it was a soft October night,
Curled once about the house, and fell asleep.

And indeed there will be time
For the yellow smoke that slides along the street,
Rubbing its back upon the window-panes;
There will be time, there will be time
To prepare a face to meet the faces that you meet;
There will be time to murder and create,

And time for all the works and days of hands
That lift and drop a question on your plate;
Time for you and time for me,
And time yet for a hundred indecisions,
And for a hundred visions and revisions,
Before the taking of a toast and tea.

In the room the women come and go
Talking of Michelangelo.

And indeed there will be time
To wonder, "Do I dare?" and, "Do I dare?"
Time to turn back and descend the stair,
With a bald spot in the middle of my hair—
(They will say: "How his hair is growing thin!")
My morning coat, my collar mounting firmly to the chin,
My necktie rich and modest, but asserted by a simple pin—
(They will say: "But how his arms and legs are thin!")
Do I dare

96

Disturb the universe?
In a minute there is time
For decisions and revisions which a minute will reverse.

For I have known them all already, known them all—
Have known the evenings, mornings, afternoons,
I have measured out my life with coffee spoons;
I know the voices dying with a dying fall
Beneath the music from a farther room.
So how should I presume?

And I have known the eyes already, known them all—
The eyes that fix you in a formulated phrase,
And when I am formulated, sprawling on a pin,
When I am pinned and wriggling on the wall,
Then how should I begin
To spit out all the butt-ends of my days and ways?
And how should I presume?

And I have known the arms already, known them all—
Arms that are braceleted and white and bare
(But in the lamplight, downed with light brown hair!)
Is it perfume from a dress
That makes me so digress?
Arms that lie along a table, or wrap about a shawl.
And should I then presume?
And how should I begin?

. . . . .

Shall I say, I have gone at dusk through narrow streets
And watched the smoke that rises from the pipes
Of lonely men in shirt-sleeves, leaning out of windows?

I should have been a pair of ragged claws
Scuttling across the floors of silent seas.

. . . . .

And the afternoon, the evening, sleeps so peacefully!
Smoothed by long fingers,
Asleep . . . tired . . . or it malingers,[3]
Stretched on the floor, here beside you and me.
Should I, after tea and cakes and ices,
Have the strength to force the moment to its crisis?
But though I have wept and fasted, wept and prayed,
Though I have seen my head (grown slightly bald) brought in
        upon a platter,
I am no prophet[4]—and here's no great matter;
I have seen the moment of my greatness flicker,

And I have seen the eternal Footman hold my coat, and snicker,
And in short, I was afraid.

    And would it have been worth it, after all,
After the cups, the marmalade, the tea,
Among the porcelain, among some talk of you and me,
Would it have been worth while,
To have bitten off the matter with a smile,
To have squeezed the universe into a ball
To roll it toward some overwhelming question,
To say: "I am Lazarus,[5] come from the dead
Come back to tell you all, I shall tell you all"—
If one, settling a pillow by her head,
     Should say: "That is not what I meant at all.
     That is not it, at all."

    And would it have been worth it, after all,
Would it have been worth while,
After the sunsets and the dooryards and the sprinkled streets,
After the novels, after the teacups, after the skirts that trail along
    the floor—
And this, and so much more?—
It is impossible to say just what I mean!
But as if a magic lantern threw the nerves in patterns on a
    screen:
Would it have been worth while
If one, settling a pillow or throwing off a shawl,
And turning toward the window, should say:
     "That is not it at all,
     That is not what I meant, at all."

. . . . .

No! I am not Prince Hamlet,[6] nor was meant to be;
Am an attendant lord, one that will do
To swell a progress, start a scene or two,
Advise the prince; no doubt, an easy tool,
Deferential,[7] glad to be of use,
Politic, cautious, and meticulous;
Full of high sentence, but a bit obtuse;[8]
At times, indeed, almost ridiculous—
Almost, at times, the Fool.

    I grow old . . . I grow old . . .
I shall wear the bottoms of my trousers rolled.

    Shall I part my hair behind? Do I dare to eat a peach?
I shall wear white flannel trousers, and walk upon the beach.
I have heard the mermaids singing, each to each.

I do not think that they will sing to me.

I have seen them riding seaward riding on the waves
Combing the white hair of the waves blown back
When the wind blows the water white and black.

We have lingered in the chambers of the sea
By sea-girls wreathed with seaweed red and brown
Till human voices wake us, and we drown.

Notes

1. S'io credesse . . . rispondo: From Dante's Inferno. The speaker is Guido da
   Montefeltro, one of the False Counselors, who is punished by being
   enveloped in an eternal flame. When Dante asks Guido to tell his life
   story, the spirit replies: "If I thought that my answer were to one who
   might ever return to the world, this flame would shake no more; but
   since from this depth none ever returned alive, if what I hear is true, I
   answer you without fear of infamy."

2. Michelangelo: Italian artist, architect, and poet (1475–1564)

3. malingers: to pretend illness

4. prophet: a person who speaks for God or a deity

5. Lazarus: man raised from the dead by Jesus

Cyclops

DAVID SEDARIS

The great Russian writer Leo Tolstoy opens his tragic novel Anna Karenina with a famous sentence: "Happy families are all alike; every unhappy family is unhappy in its own way." He might have added a qualification: "There are no happy families."

I'm not suggesting, of course, that home life is a perpetual sea of troubles. Still, I rather doubt that any family can totally escape the swells that give depth and character to human experience. Sometimes domestic problems are Tolstoyan in scale, sufficient to break the heart and send pain rippling across whole generations. More often, however, family troubles seem more like acne—chronic and embarrassing, but ultimately survivable. They might even build character.

David Sedaris (b. 1957) describes this off-the-rack sort of domestic strife particularly well in "Cyclops," a chapter from his autobiographical memoir Naked (1997), where the facts of his adolescence in Raleigh, North Carolina, merge happily with fertile exaggerations, even fictions. It doesn't much matter: his tales of family life still have the ring of truth. For instance, in "Cyclops, " you'll likely recognize the archetypal parent determined to scare the kids into responsible behavior. And you'll probably recall admonitions like these: Don't ever run with scissors; If you cross your eyes, they'll stay that way; If you lean back in that chair, you'll crack your head wide open! Most of us survive our dalliances with scissors and grow into adults capable of cutting paper without mishap. But not David Sedaris. And readers who need a good laugh can be grateful for his phobias.

Named Time's Humorist of the Year in 2001, David Sedaris has been a contributor to National Public Radio's Morning Edition and is currently writing plays with his sister Amy. He is also the author of Barrel Fever: Stories and Essays (1994), The SantaLand Diaries and Season's Greetings: Two Plays (1998), and Me Talk Pretty One Day (2000).

When he was young my father shot out his best friend's eye with a BB gun. That is what he told us. "One foolish moment and, Jesus, if I could take it back, I would." He winced, shaking his fist as if it held a rattle. "It eats me alive," he said. "I mean to tell you that it absolutely tears me apart."

On one of our summer visits to his hometown, my father took us to meet this guy, a shoe salesman whose milky pupil hugged the corner of his mangled socket. I watched the two men shake hands and turned away, sickened and ashamed by what my father had done.

Our next-door neighbor received a BB gun for his twelfth birthday and accepted it as a personal challenge to stalk and maim any living creature: sun-bathing cats, sparrows, slugs, and squirrels—if it moved, he shot it. I thought this was an excellent idea, but every time I raised the gun to my shoulder, I saw my father's half-blind friend stumbling forth with an armload of Capezios. What would it be like to live with that sort of guilt? How could my father look himself in the mirror without throwing up?

While watching television one afternoon my sister Tiffany stabbed me in the eye with a freshly sharpened pencil. The blood was copious, and I rode to the hospital knowing that if I was blinded, my sister would be my slave for the rest of her life. Never for one moment would I let her forget what she'd done to me. There would be no swinging cocktail parties in her future, no poolside barbeques or episodes of carefree laughter, not one moment of joy—I would make sure of that. I'd planned my vengeance so thoroughly that I was almost disappointed when the doctor announced that this was nothing but a minor puncture wound, located not on but beneath the eye.

"Take a look at your brother's face," my father said, pointing to my Band-Aid. "You could have blinded him for life! Your own brother, a Cyclops, is that what you want?" Tiffany's suffering eased my pain for an hour or two, but then I began to feel sorry for her. "Every time you reach for a pencil, I want you to think about what you've done to your brother," my father said. "I want you to get on your knees and beg him to forgive you."

There are only so many times a person can apologize before it becomes annoying. I lost interest long before the bandage was removed, but not my father. By the time he was finished, Tiffany couldn't lift a dull crayon without breaking into tears. Her pretty, suntanned face assumed the characteristics of a wrinkled, grease-stained bag. Six years old and the girl was broken.

Danger was everywhere and it was our father's lifelong duty to warn us. Attending the country club's Fourth of July celebration, we were told how one of his Navy buddies had been disfigured for life when a cherry bomb exploded in his lap. "Blew his balls right off the map," he said. "Take a second and imagine what that must have felt like!" Racing to the farthest edge of the golf course, I watched the remainder of the display with my hands between my legs.

Fireworks were hazardous, but thunderstorms were even worse. "I had a friend, used to be a very bright, good-looking guy. He was on top of the world until the day he got struck by lightning. It caught him right between the eyes while he was trout fishing and cooked his brain just like you'd roast a chicken.

Now he's got a metal plate in his forehead and can't even chew his own food; everything has to be put in a blender and taken through a straw."

If the lightning was going to get me, it would have to penetrate walls. At the first hint of a storm I ran to the basement, crouching beneath a table and covering my head with a blanket. Those who watched from their front porches were fools. "The lightning can be attracted by a wedding ring or even the fillings in your teeth," my father said. "The moment you let down your guard is guaranteed to be the day it strikes."

In junior high I signed up for shop class, and our first assignment was to build a napkin holder. "You're not going to be using a table saw, are you?" my father asked. "I knew a guy, a kid about your size, who was using a table saw when the blade came loose, flew out of the machine, and sliced his face right in half." Using his index finger, my father drew an imaginary line from his forehead to his chin. "The guy survived, but nobody wanted anything to do with him. He turned into an alcoholic and wound up marrying a Chinese woman he'd ordered through a catalog. Think about it." I did.

My napkin holder was made from found boards and, once finished, weighed in at close to seven pounds. My bookshelves were even worse. "The problem with a hammer," I was told, "is that the head can fly off at any moment and, boy, let me tell you, you've never imagined pain like that."

After a while we began to wonder if my father had any friends who could still tie their own shoes or breathe without the aid of a respirator. With the exception of the shoe salesman, we'd never seen any of these people, only heard about them whenever one of us attempted to deep-fry chicken or operate the garbage disposal. "I've got a friend who buys a set of gloves and throws one of them away. He lost his right hand doing the exact same thing you're doing. He had his arm down the drain when the cat rubbed against the switch to the garbage disposal. Now he's wearing clip-on ties and having the restaurant waiters cut up his steak. Is that the kind of life you want for yourself?"

He allowed me to mow the lawn only because he was too cheap to pay a landscaper and didn't want to do it himself. "What happened," he said, "is that the guy slipped, probably on a pile of crap, and his leg got caught up in the blade. He found his foot, carried it to the hospital, but it was too late to sew it back on. Can you imagine that? The guy drove fifteen, twenty miles with his foot in his lap."

Regardless of the heat, I mowed the lawn wearing long pants, knee-high boots, a football helmet, and a pair of goggles. Before starting, I scouted the lawn for rocks and dog feces, slowly combing the area as if it were mined. Even then I pushed the mower haltingly, always fearing that this next step might be my last.

Nothing bad ever happened, and within a few years I was mowing in shorts and sneakers, thinking of the supposed friend my father had used to illustrate his warning. I imagined this man jumping into his car and pressing on the accelerator with his bloody stump, a warm foot settled in his lap like a sleeping puppy. Why hadn't he just called an ambulance to come pick him up? How, in his shock, had he thought to search the weeds for his missing foot? It didn't add up.

I waited until my junior year of high school to sign up for driver's education. Before taking to the road, we sat in the darkened classroom, watching films that might have been written and directed by my father. *Don't do it,* I thought, watching the prom couple attempt to pass a lumbering dump truck. Every excursion ended with the young driver wrapped around a telephone pole or burned beyond recognition, the camera focusing in on a bloody corsage littering the side of the highway.

I drove a car no faster than I pushed the lawn mower, and the instructor soon lost patience.

"That license is going to be your death warrant," my father said on the day I received my learner's permit. "You're going to get out there and kill someone, and the guilt is going to tear your heart out."

The thought of killing myself had slowed me down to five miles per hour. The thought of killing someone else stopped me completely.

My mother had picked me up from a play rehearsal one rainy night when, cresting a hill, the car ran over something it shouldn't have. This was not a brick or a misplaced boot but some living creature that cried out when caught beneath the tire. "Shit," my mother whispered, tapping her forehead against the steering wheel. "Shit, shit shit." We covered our heads against the rain and searched the darkened street until we found an orange cat coughing up blood into the gutter.

"You killed me," the cat said, pointing at my mother with its flattened paw. "Here I had so much to live for, but now it's over, my whole life wiped out just like that." The cat wheezed rhythmically before closing its eyes and dying.

"Shit," my mother repeated. We walked door to door until finding the cat's owner, a kind and understanding woman whose young daughter shared none of her qualities. "You killed my cat," she screamed, sobbing into her mother's skirt. "You're mean and you're ugly and you killed my cat."

"She's at that age," the woman said, stroking the child's hair.

My mother felt bad enough without the lecture that awaited her at home. "That could have been a child!" my father shouted. "Think about that the next time you're tearing down the street searching for kicks." He made it sound as if my mother ran down cats for sport. "You think this is funny," he said, "but we'll see who's laughing when you're behind bars awaiting trial for manslaughter." I received a variation on the same speech after sideswiping a mailbox. Despite my mother's encouragement, I surrendered my permit and never drove again. My nerves just couldn't take it. It seemed much safer to hitchhike.

My father objected when I moved to Chicago, and waged a full-fledged campaign of terror when I announced I would be moving to New York. "New York! Are you out of your mind? You might as well take a razor to your throat because, let me tell you something, those New Yorkers are going to eat you alive." He spoke of friends who had been robbed and bludgeoned by packs of roving gangs and sent me newspaper clippings detailing the tragic slayings of joggers and vacationing tourists. "This could be you!" he wrote in the margins.

I'd lived in New York for several years when, traveling upstate to attend a wedding, I stopped in my father's hometown. We hadn't visited since our grandmother moved in with us, and I felt my way around with a creepy familiarity. I found my father's old apartment, but his friend's shoe store had been converted into a pool hall. When I called to tell him about it, my father said, "What shoe store? What are you talking about?"

"The place where your friend worked," I said. "You remember, the guy whose eye you shot out."

"Frank?" he said. "I didn't shoot his eye out; the guy was born that way."

My father visits me now in New York. We'll walk through Washington Square, where he'll yell, "Get a look at the ugly mug on that one!" referring to a three-hundred-pound biker with grinning skulls tattooed like a choker around his neck. A young man in Central Park is photographing his girlfriend, and my father races to throw himself into the picture. "All right, sweetheart," he says, placing his arm around the startled victim, "it's time to get comfortable." I cower as he marches into posh grocery stores, demanding to speak to the manager. "Back home I can get this exact same cantaloupe for less than half this price," he says. The managers invariably suggest that he do just that. He screams at waiters and cuts in line at tony restaurants. "I have a friend," I tell him, "who lost his right arm snapping his fingers at a waiter."

"Oh, you kids," he says. "Not a one of you has got so much as a teaspoon of gumption. I don't know where you got it from, but in the end, it's going to kill you."

I Give You Back

JOY HARJO

I release you, my beautiful and terrible
fear. I release you. You were my beloved
and hated twin, but now, I don't know you
as myself. I release you with all the
pain I would know at the death of
my daughters.

You are not my blood anymore.

I give you back to the white soldiers
who burned down my home, beheaded my children,
raped and sodomized my brothers and sisters.
I give you back to those who stole the
food from our plates when we were starving.

I release you, fear, because you hold
these scenes in front of me and I was born
with eyes that can never close.

I release you, fear, so you can no longer
keep me naked and frozen in the winter,
or smothered under blankets in the summer.

I release you
I release you
I release you
I release you

I am not afraid to be angry.
I am not afraid to rejoice.

I am not afraid to be black.
I am not afraid to be white.
I am not afraid to be hungry.
I am not afraid to be full.
I am not afraid to be hated.
I am not afraid to be loved.

to be loved, to be loved, fear.

Oh, you have choked me, but I gave you the leash.
You have gutted me but I gave you the knife.
You have devoured me, but I laid myself across the fire.
You held my mother down and raped her,
              but I gave you the heated thing.

I take myself back, fear.
You are not my shadow any longer.
I won't hold you in my hands.
You can't live in my eyes, my ears, my voice
my belly, or in my heart my heart
my heart   my heart

But come here, fear
I am alive and you are so afraid
                        of dying.

Section 3B

Our World— Culture

From *The Kite Runner*

KHALED HOSSEINI

Lore has it my father once wrestled a black bear in Baluchistan with his bare hands. If the story had been about anyone else, it would have been dismissed as *laaf*, that Afghan tendency to exaggerate—sadly, almost a national affliction; if someone bragged that his son was a doctor, chances were the kid had once passed a biology test in high school. But no one ever doubted the veracity of any story about Baba. And if they did, well, Baba did have those three parallel scars coursing a jagged path down his back. I have imagined Baba's wrestling match countless times, even dreamed about it. And in those dreams, I can never tell Baba from the bear.

It was Rahim Khan who first referred to him as what eventually became Baba's famous nickname, *Toophan agha*, or "Mr. Hurricane." It was an apt enough nickname. My father was a force of nature, a towering Pashtun specimen with a thick beard, a wayward crop of curly brown hair as unruly as the man himself, hands that looked capable of uprooting a willow tree, and a black glare that would "drop the devil to his knees begging for mercy," as Rahim Khan used to say. At parties, when all six-foot-five of him thundered into the room, attention shifted to him like sunflowers turning to the sun.

Baba was impossible to ignore, even in his sleep. I used to bury cotton wisps in my ears, pull the blanket over my head, and still the sounds of Baba's snoring—so much like a growling truck engine—penetrated the walls. And my room was across the hall from Baba's bedroom. How my mother ever managed to sleep in the same room as him is a mystery to me. It's on the long list of things I would have asked my mother if I had ever met her.

In the late 1960s, when I was five or six, Baba decided to build an orphanage. I heard the story through Rahim Khan. He told me Baba had drawn the blueprints himself despite the fact that he'd had no architectural experience at all. Skeptics had urged him to stop his foolishness and hire an architect. Of course, Baba refused, and everyone shook their heads in dismay at his obstinate ways. Then Baba succeeded and everyone shook their heads in awe at his

111

triumphant ways. Baba paid for the construction of the two-story orphanage, just off the main strip of Jadeh Maywand south of the Kabul River, with his own money. Rahim Khan told me Baba had personally funded the entire project, paying for the engineers, electricians, plumbers, and laborers, not to mention the city officials whose "mustaches needed oiling."

It took three years to build the orphanage. I was eight by then. I remember the day before the orphanage opened, Baba took me to Ghargha Lake, a few miles north of Kabul. He asked me to fetch Hassan too, but I lied and told him Hassan had the runs. I wanted Baba all to myself. And besides, one time at Ghargha Lake, Hassan and I were skimming stones and Hassan made his stone skip eight times. The most I managed was five. Baba was there, watching, and he patted Hassan on the back. Even put his arm around his shoulder.

We sat at a picnic table on the banks of the lake, just Baba and me, eating boiled eggs with *kofta* sandwiches—meatballs and pickles wrapped in *naan*. The water was a deep blue and sunlight glittered on its looking glass–clear surface. On Fridays, the lake was bustling with families out for a day in the sun. But it was mid-week and there was only Baba and me, us and a couple of long-haired, bearded tourists— "hippies," I'd heard them called. They were sitting on the dock, feet dangling in the water, fishing poles in hand. I asked Baba why they grew their hair long, but Baba grunted, didn't answer. He was preparing his speech for the next day, flipping through a havoc of handwritten pages, making notes here and there with a pencil. I bit into my egg and asked Baba if it was true what a boy in school had told me, that if you ate a piece of eggshell, you'd have to pee it out. Baba grunted again.

I took a bite of my sandwich. One of the yellow-haired tourists laughed and slapped the other one on the back. In the distance, across the lake, a truck lumbered around a corner on the hill. Sunlight twinkled in its side-view mirror.

"I think I have *saratan*," I said. Cancer. Baba lifted his head from the pages flapping in the breeze. Told me I could get the soda myself, all I had to do was look in the trunk of the car.

Outside the orphanage, the next day, they ran out of chairs. A lot of people had to stand to watch the opening ceremony. It was a windy day, and I sat behind Baba on the little podium just outside the main entrance of the new building. Baba was wearing a green suit and a caracul hat. Midway through the speech, the wind knocked his hat off and everyone laughed. He motioned to me to hold his hat for him and I was glad to, because then everyone would see that he was my father, my Baba. He turned back to the microphone and said he hoped the building was sturdier than his hat, and everyone laughed again. When Baba ended his speech, people stood up and cheered. They clapped for a long time. Afterward, people shook his hand. Some of them tousled my hair and shook my hand too. I was so proud of Baba, of us.

But despite Baba's successes, people were always doubting him. They told Baba that running a business wasn't in his blood and he should study law like his father. So Baba proved them all wrong by not only running his own business but becoming one of the richest merchants in Kabul. Baba and Rahim Khan built a wildly successful carpet-exporting business, two pharmacies, and a restaurant.

When people scoffed that Baba would never marry well—after all, he was not of royal blood—he wedded my mother, Sofia Akrami, a highly educated woman universally regarded as one of Kabul's most respected, beautiful, and virtuous ladies. And not only did she teach classic Farsi literature at the university, she was a descendant of the royal family, a fact that my father playfully rubbed in the skeptics' faces by referring to her as "my princess."

With me as the glaring exception, my father molded the world around him to his liking. The problem, of course, was that Baba saw the world in black and white. And he got to decide what was black and what was white. You can't love a person who lives that way without fearing him too. Maybe even hating him a little.

When I was in fifth grade, we had a mullah who taught us about Islam. His name was Mullah Fatiullah Khan, a short, stubby man with a face full of acne scars and a gruff voice. He lectured us about the virtues of *zakat* and the duty of *hadj*; he taught us the intricacies of performing the five daily *namaz* prayers, and made us memorize verses from the Koran—and though he never translated the words for us, he did stress, sometimes with the help of a stripped willow branch, that we had to pronounce the Arabic words correctly so God would hear us better. He told us one day that Islam considered drinking a terrible sin; those who drank would answer for their sin on the day of Qiyamat, Judgment Day. In those days, drinking was fairly common in Kabul. No one gave you a public lashing for it, but those Afghans who did drink did so in private, out of respect. People bought their scotch as "medicine" in brown paper bags from selected "pharmacies." They would leave with the bag tucked out of sight, sometimes drawing furtive, disapproving glances from those who knew about the store's reputation for such transactions.

We were upstairs in Baba's study, the smoking room, when I told him what Mullah Fatiullah Khan had taught us in class. Baba was pouring himself a whiskey from the bar he had built in the corner of the room. He listened, nodded, took a sip from his drink. Then he lowered himself into the leather sofa, put down his drink, and propped me up on his lap. I felt as if I were sitting on a pair of tree trunks. He took a deep breath and exhaled through his nose, the air hissing through his mustache for what seemed an eternity. I couldn't decide whether I wanted to hug him or leap from his lap in mortal fear.

"I see you've confused what you're learning in school with actual education," he said in his thick voice.

"But if what he said is true then does it make you a sinner, Baba?"

"Hmm." Baba crushed an ice cube between his teeth. "Do you want to know what your father thinks about sin?"

"Yes."

"Then I'll tell you," Baba said, "but first understand this and understand it now, Amir: You'll never learn anything of value from those bearded idiots."

113

"You mean Mullah Fatiullah Khan?"

Baba gestured with his glass. The ice clinked. "I mean all of them. Piss on the beards of all those self-righteous monkeys."

I began to giggle. The image of Baba pissing on the beard of any monkey, self-righteous or otherwise, was too much.

"They do nothing but thumb their prayer beads and recite a book written in a tongue they don't even understand." He took a sip. "God help us all if Afghanistan ever falls into their hands."

"But Mullah Fatiullah Khan seems nice," I managed between bursts of tittering.

"So did Genghis Khan," Baba said. "But enough about that. You asked about sin and I want to tell you. Are you listening?"

"Yes," I said, pressing my lips together. But a chortle escaped through my nose and made a snorting sound. That got me giggling again.

Baba's stony eyes bore into mine and, just like that, I wasn't laughing anymore. "I mean to speak to you man to man. Do you think you can handle that for once?"

"Yes, Baba jan," I muttered, marveling, not for the first time, at how badly Baba could sting me with so few words. We'd had a fleeting good moment—it wasn't often Baba talked to me, let alone on his lap—and I'd been a fool to waste it.

"Good," Baba said, but his eyes wondered. "Now, no matter what the mullah teaches, there is only one sin, only one. And that is theft. Every other sin is a variation of theft. Do you understand that?"

"No, Baba jan," I said, desperately wishing I did. I didn't want to disappoint him again.

Baba heaved a sigh of impatience. That stung too, because he was not an impatient man. I remembered all the times he didn't come home until after dark, all the times I ate dinner alone. I'd ask Ali where Baba was, when he was coming home, though I knew full well he was at the construction site, overlooking this, supervising that. Didn't that take patience? I already hated all the kids he was building the orphanage for; sometimes I wished they'd all died along with their parents.

"When you kill a man, you steal a life," Baba said. "You steal his wife's right to a husband, rob his children of a father. When you tell a lie, you steal someone's right to the truth. When you cheat, you steal the right to fairness. Do you see?"

I did. When Baba was six, a thief walked into my grandfather's house in the middle of the night. My grandfather, a respected judge, confronted him, but the thief stabbed him in the throat, killing him instantly—and robbing Baba of a father. The townspeople caught the killer just before noon the next day; he turned out to be a wanderer from the Kunduz region. They hanged him from the branch of an oak tree with still two hours to go before afternoon prayer. It was Rahim Khan, not Baba, who had told me that story. I was always learning things about Baba from other people.

"There is no act more wretched than stealing, Amir," Baba said. "A man who takes what's not his to take, be it a life or a loaf of *naan* . . . I spit on such a man. And if I ever cross paths with him, God help him. Do you understand?"

I found the idea of Baba clobbering a thief both exhilarating and terribly frightening. "Yes, Baba."

"If there's a God out there, then I would hope he has more important things to attend to than my drinking scotch or eating pork. Now, hop down. All this talk about sin has made me thirsty again."

I watched him fill his glass at the bar and wondered how much time would pass before we talked again the way we just had. Because the truth of it was, I always felt like Baba hated me a little. And why not? After all, I *had* killed his beloved wife, his beautiful princess, hadn't I? The least I could have done was to have had the decency to have turned out a little more like him. But I hadn't turned out like him. Not at all.

✍

In school, we used to play a game called *Sherjangi*, or "Battle of the Poems." The Farsi teacher moderated it and it went something like this: You recited a verse from a poem and your opponent had sixty seconds to reply with a verse that began with the same letter that ended yours. Everyone in my class wanted me on their team, because by the time I was eleven, I could recite dozens of verses from Khayyám, Hãfez, or Rumi's famous *Masnawi*. One time, I took on the whole class and won. I told Baba about it later that night, but he just nodded, muttered, "Good."

That was how I escaped my father's aloofness, in my dead mother's books. That and Hassan, of course. I read everything, Rumi, Hãfez, Saadi, Victor Hugo, Jules Verne, Mark Twain, Ian Fleming. When I had finished my mother's books— not the boring history ones, I was never much into those, but the novels, the epics—I started spending my allowance on books. I bought one a week from the bookstore near Cinema Park, and stored them in cardboard boxes when I ran out of shelf room.

Of course, marrying a poet was one thing, but fathering a son who preferred burying his face in poetry books to hunting . . . well, that wasn't how Baba had envisioned it, I suppose. Real men didn't read poetry—and God forbid they should ever write it! Real men—real boys—played soccer just as Baba had when he had been young. Now *that* was something to be passionate about. In 1970, Baba took a break from the construction of the orphanage and flew to Tehran for a month to watch the World Cup games on television, since at the time Afghanistan didn't have TVs yet. He signed me up for soccer teams to stir the same passion in me. But I was pathetic, a blundering liability to my own team, always in the way of an opportune pass or unwittingly blocking an open lane. I shambled about the field on scraggy legs, squalled for passes that never came my way. And the harder I tried, waving my arms over my head frantically and screeching, "I'm open! I'm open!" the more I went ignored. But Baba wouldn't give up. When it became abundantly clear that I hadn't inherited a shred of his athletic talents, he settled for trying to turn me into a passionate spectator. Certainly I could manage that, couldn't I? I faked interest for as long as possible. I cheered with him when Kabul's team scored against Kandahar and yelped insults at the referee when he called a penalty against our team. But Baba sensed my lack of genuine interest and resigned himself to the bleak fact that his son was never going to either play or watch soccer.

I remember one time Baba took me to the yearly *Buzkashi* tournament that took place on the first day of spring, New Year's Day. Buzkashi was, and still is, Afghanistan's national passion. A *chapandaz*, a highly skilled horseman usually patronized by rich aficionados, has to snatch a goat or cattle carcass from the midst of a melee, carry that carcass with him around the stadium at full gallop, and drop it in a scoring circle while a team of other *chapandaz* chases him and does everything in its power—kick, claw, whip, punch—to snatch the carcass from him. That day, the crowd roared with excitement as the horsemen on the field bellowed their battle cries and jostled for the carcass in a cloud of dust. The earth trembled with the clatter of hooves. We watched from the upper bleachers as riders pounded past us at full gallop, yipping and yelling, foam flying from their horses' mouths.

At one point Baba pointed to someone. "Amir, do you see that man sitting up there with those other men around him?"

I did.

"That's Henry Kissinger."

"Oh," I said. I didn't know who Henry Kissinger was, and I might have asked. But at the moment, I watched with horror as one of the *chapandaz* fell off his saddle and was trampled under a score of hooves. His body was tossed and hurled in the stampede like a rag doll, finally rolling to a stop when the melee moved on. He twitched once and lay motionless, his legs bent at unnatural angles, a pool of his blood soaking through the sand.

I began to cry.

I cried all the way back home. I remember how Baba's hands clenched around the steering wheel. Clenched and unclenched. Mostly, I will never forget Baba's valiant efforts to conceal the disgusted look on his face as he drove in silence.

Later that night, I was passing by my father's study when I overheard him speaking to Rahim Khan. I pressed my ear to the closed door.

"—grateful that he's healthy," Rahim Khan was saying.

"I know, I know. But he's always buried in those books or shuffling around the house like he's lost in some dream."

"And?"

"I wasn't like that." Baba sounded frustrated, almost angry.

Rahim Khan laughed. "Children aren't coloring books. You don't get to fill them with your favorite colors."

"I'm telling you," Baba said, "I wasn't like that at all, and neither were any of the kids I grew up with."

"You know, sometimes you are the most self-centered man I know," Rahim Khan said. He was the only person I knew who could get away with saying something like that to Baba.

"It has nothing to do with that."

"Nay?"

"Nay."

"Then what?"

I heard the leather of Baba's seat creaking as he shifted on it. I closed my eyes, pressed my ear even harder against the door, wanting to hear, not wanting to hear. "Sometimes I look out this window and I see him playing on the street with the neighborhood boys. I see how they push him around, take his toys from him, give him a shove here, a whack there. And, you know, he never fights back. Never, He just . . . drops his head and . . ."

"So he's not violent," Rahim Khan said.

"That's not what I mean, Rahim, and you know it," Baba shot back. "There is something missing in that boy."

"Yes, a mean streak."

"Self-defense has nothing to do with meanness. You know what always happens when the neighborhood boys tease him? Hassan steps in and fends them off. I've seen it with my own eyes. And when they come home, I say to him, 'How did Hassan get that scrape on his face?' And he says, 'He fell down.' I'm telling you, Rahim, there is something missing in that boy."

"You just need to let him find his way," Rahim Khan said.

"And where is he headed?" Baba said. "A boy who won't stand up for himself becomes a man who can't stand up to anything."

"As usual you're oversimplifying."

"I don't think so."

"You're angry because you're afraid he'll never take over the business for you."

"Now who's oversimplifying?" Baba said. "Look, I know there's a fondness between you and him and I'm happy about that. Envious, but happy. I mean that. He needs someone who . . . understands him, because God knows I don't. But something about Amir troubles me in a way that I can't express. It's like . . ." I could see him searching, reaching for the right words. He lowered his voice, but I heard him anyway. "If I hadn't seen the doctor pull him out of my wife with my own eyes, I'd never believe he's my son."

The next morning, as he was preparing my breakfast, Hassan asked if something was bothering me. I snapped at him, told him to mind his own business. Rahim Khan had been wrong about the mean streak thing.

Healing in all Times and Places from *The Middle of Everywhere*

MARY PIPHER

The most interesting thing about the world is its fantastic and unpsy-choanalyzed character, its wretched and gallant personality, its horrible idiocy and its magnificent intelligence, its unbelievable cruelty and its equally unbelievable kindness, its gorilla stupor, its canary cheerfulness, its thundering divinity, and its whimpering commonness.

—William Saroyan

On Lake Como in Northern Italy there is a beautiful villa whose gardens stretch down to the lake. About one hundred feet out from these gardens, in the lake, stands a brick tower with a terra-cotta roof. This tower has a small window facing the lake and inside the window is a statue.

About two hundred years ago, a wealthy young couple lived in this beautiful villa. They had a five-year-old daughter who played in the garden every afternoon. One day, when they called her to dinner, she didn't answer. They looked everywhere but never found her body. They presumed she fell into Lake Como and drowned.

The little statue is of the mother with her hand on her brow, shielding her eyes as she looks over the water, searching for the body of her daughter. That is what the real mother did for the rest of her life, and what the statue mother has done for almost two centuries.

We all suffer. Pain and sorrow find a niche in every household. Most of us do not carry the burdens of Bintu or Joseph, but our lives are not easy. All of us have lost people we love. We have been betrayed or abandoned. We have made serious mistakes and have needed to forgive ourselves. As Wynton Marsalis's grandmother said, "Life has a board for every behind."

In all places and times, people have needed to know how to heal. Ten thousand years ago, a woman whose husband was killed in a hunt for wild game

119

must have wondered, "How can I go on?" Parents who buried their children must have asked themselves, "Will we ever feel happy again?" Perhaps the oldest and most universal question is, How do I get over this?

Just as suffering is universal, so are systems of healing. All cultures have wisdom to offer their own members and the rest of us. This chapter will examine ideas about healing from all over the world and discuss what enables some people, but not others, to heal. It will ask, Why, with tragedy, do some people break like glass while others are tempered into steel? And, Why does suffering brutalize and coarsen some people and ennoble others?

Thrive

I started the Thrive Project with a group of mental health professionals. We trained mentors from different cultures to be cultural brokers on mental health issues. The project began with ten classes that included everything from explaining the difference between a psychiatrist and a psychologist to discussing when Americans toilet train their children to describing how to deal with a suicidal person. Mentors educated professionals as well, teaching us how other cultures deal with emotional pain. The mentors then worked with people from their own countries, easing them into our system or helping them in more traditional ways. Therapists supervised and supported their work. The lessons of Thrive pervade this book.

The value of the project was not what we taught the Bosnian, Vietnamese, Kurdish, Russian, and Caribbean mentors, but what they taught us. They spoke honestly about how their cultures perceived our mental health system. They told us about the psychological problems that people from their countries experienced, and they listened to our advice. Often, they politely told us why our advice wouldn't apply.

The mentors defined their roles broadly. They were action-oriented and they didn't wear watches. If their clients were stressed by hungry children, rather than discussing stress management theory, the mentors drove them to the grocery store. A traditional supervisor might say that these mentors didn't have good boundaries. But I came to see it differently. The mentors were not compartmentalized the way we Americans are. They didn't make distinctions between clients and friends, between professional and nonprofessional relationships. By their behavior they said, all of us humans need each other's help.

Early on, I noticed that the Thrive mentors who were the least like mental health professionals were the most popular with their own people. The ones who acted the most like us were not in great demand. What the busiest mentors had in common was that they were holistic. For example, once when I chided a Sudanese caseworker for taking calls at night, he said to me, "You don't understand. All the Sudanese people are my family. I will help them all day and all night. It is not a job to me. It is my life."

When our Vietnamese mentor had a client who needed emergency shelter, he invited her home to sleep in his daughter's bedroom. His wife fixed her a big Vietnamese meal and his family temporarily adopted her.

When our Bosnian mentor met people from her country, she gave them her heart. She had a client who had lost twenty-two male family members in Srebrenica. The woman said to the mentor, "My pain has killed my soul." The mentor listened to the woman's stories, then she invited her to the circus, which she told me later "was a big hit."

This Bosnian mentor had another client who had suffered many previous losses. All she wanted was a child and she feared she couldn't get pregnant. The mentor took her to a women's clinic where the doctor reassured the woman she could have another child. Then the mentor invited the woman and her husband to her home. The two families stayed up all night drinking plum brandy and singing.

The Bosnian mentor was my most creative mentor. She was warmhearted, helpful, and good-natured. She had common sense and intelligence. When she heard I was writing a book on refugees, she said, "Tell families to get a kitten. We were very lonely and sad until we got our little kitty. Now we have reason to laugh. My daughter jumps out of the bed every morning to check on her kitty. It is the best thing."

At first, the goal of Thrive had been to train mentors to use our system and to encourage their people to use it. As the group proceeded, I found myself wondering why had I assumed that our system was better.

Refugees and Psychotherapy

Refugees don't seek therapy for a variety of reasons, some practical and some cultural. First, they often don't know that such a thing exists. They have no transportation to appointments, or they work all the time and cannot schedule sessions, or they have immediate concerns that take precedence over dealing with past pain. Usually therapy is lower on their priority lists than work, housing, or transportation.

Refugees resist therapy because of language and trust issues as well as a lack of understanding about our mental health system. Many refugees come from cultures with no cultural analogue for talking about problems outside the family. Certain things cannot be discussed even within the family. Domestic violence and rape are taboo subjects. In many cultures, the expression of certain emotions, such as anger, is not tolerated.

Often refugees label what we call mental health problems as spiritual problems, physical problems, or the result of a curse or the evil eye. Depending on the labeling process, different kinds of healers are required. A Vietnamese Catholic might talk to a priest. A Kurdish person might consult a tribal elder or visit a sacred shrine. Others might go to a shaman, a curandero, or a medicine man.

Even if refugees come from a culture that acknowledges mental health problems, these problems often are seen as shameful. Many people believe that only crazy people see therapists. Often times, mental health professionals are not trusted. The Vietnamese have a saying: You have to be crazy to understand crazy people.

Beyond these reasons there is another universal reason for avoiding therapy. Talking about trauma is not easy. To remember pain is to reexperience it. Many people just try to blot it out and pretend things didn't happen.

When I first worked with refugees, I thought that, with access and understanding, many would want our services. They were traumatized people who could use therapy to work through their past tragedies and current stresses. Of course, there were refugees who wanted our mental health services. However, I now realize that many refugees choose not to be in therapy. Even when it's affordable, accessible, and user-friendly, and even when they truly understand what therapy entails, they turn down our offers of help.

Refugees are able to partake of the services they truly want in our communities. Because newcomers quickly see their value, they find our schools, job counselors, libraries, doctors' offices, and cultural centers. But in spite of our efforts to make therapy more available, we can't lure many people in. Most refugees don't want to sit in a room with a perfect stranger and talk over their traumas. Many listen to descriptions of what therapists do and then decide, "I'll help distribute clothes at the Asian Center," or "I want to watch movies," or "I'd rather go fishing."

And if refugees do show up in our offices, they are likely to come for practical advice, not help processing the past. They are likely to bring a form they need help filling out, or they'll come in with the classified ads and ask for advice on buying a washing machine. They bring up problems with a supervisor or a landlord, or they ask for help finding a used car.

Problems in Psychology

Psychology was founded in the late Victorian era by middle-class white men. There was no concept of cultural relativity. For example, at Ellis Island, the IQ tests were given only in English. In 1917 psychologists announced that 83 percent of Jews, 80 percent of Hungarians, 79 percent of Italians, and 80 percent of Russians were morons. About this time, Margaret Mead entered graduate school in psychology. She administered the Otis IQ test to foreigners and found that their scores were related to their English ability. However, her findings weren't accepted. She was out-maneuvered in a sea of powerful male psychologists and she left psychology because of its racism and sexism.

Fortunately, since then our field has worked to become less sexist, racist, and ethnocentric. While there is still resistance to dealing with culture in therapy and also a lack of sophistication about cross-cultural issues, many psychologists have devoted their careers to understanding diversity and increasing tolerance.

However, in this time of transition to a multicultural society, psychologists often rely on models dusty with age. The field tries to fit people from all over the world into models developed for a very different time and place.

Psychologists ask, What does Gestalt theory or Jungian theory have to say about the Kurds or the Sudanese or the Vietnamese? These are the wrong questions. Better questions are, What models could we develop from our experience with refugees that would allow us to expand our knowledge of the human race? What are the universal components of healing? What are the aspects of resilience?

Sometimes psychologists have proselytized like missionaries. We have taught "Follow Sigmund Freud and Carl Rogers and you will be saved." We have said, "Our system is better than yours. Trust us to know you better than you know yourselves." But we have had an abysmal conversion rate. Our Western mental health system is dependent on verbal expressiveness, self-disclosure, and a belief in individualism. It splits the personal and the professional, the sacred and profane, and the mind and the body. Our system is also expensive, hard to schedule, and involves sitting in small rooms baring one's deepest secrets to perfect strangers.

Our ideas about how to deal with pain do not seem relevant to many newcomers. Catharsis and self-analysis are by no means universally respected as ways to heal. Not many refugees can be persuaded they will feel better if they talk about trauma. Psychologists have a metaphor for healing—a wound must be washed, cleaned to heal. It may be painful but it is necessary. The Vietnamese also employ the wound metaphor for healing. But they say, "A wound will only heal if it is left alone."

Common Reactions to Loss

In his introductory psychology text, David G. Myers writes, "Most political dissidents who survive dozens of episodes of torture do not later exhibit post-traumatic stress disorder (Mineka and Zinbarg, 1996). And, although suffering some lingering stress symptoms, most American Jews who survived the Holocaust trauma, experiencing starvation, beatings, lost freedom, and the murders of loved ones, went on to live productive lives. In fact, compared to other American Jews of the same age, these survivors have been less likely to have seen a psychotherapist (18 percent vs. 31 percent) and more likely to have had stable marriages (83 percent vs. 62 percent). Moreover, virtually none has committed a criminal act."

These statistics suggest we should be extremely cautious about assuming that traumatized people are necessarily suffering clinical syndromes. Yet extreme situations induce extreme reactions. People who suffer terrible things have a time when they are sadder, angrier, more agitated, more withdrawn, and more passive. They are temporarily disorganized by grief and permanently changed by the tragic events.

One of the most common changes is a shifting of priorities. With tragedy, what is most and least important changes. Often people value family and friends more and care less about property and money. Spiritual concerns become more salient. Many Americans experience this change of priorities after a cancer scare or heart attack. They stop worrying about unfinished housework or job promotions. They spend more time with their grandchildren, travel, and watch sunsets.

Depression is certainly one of the most common reactions to trauma. Almost all the Afghani women I met were severely depressed. However, depression is a confusing word in this context. Who wouldn't be depressed after suffering these experiences? Depression implies pathology whereas reacting to trauma is normal, even healthy. Perhaps a better phrase for what we have called depression would be bone-deep sadness.

Avoidance is also common. A Kurdish woman could hardly bear to think of her past. And, most likely, her ability to push aside her memories was adaptive during her years on the run. Now, however, she had a therapy appointment once a week that she always forgot. After many weeks of no-shows, her kind therapist sent a car for her. Every Tuesday the Kurdish woman was shocked when the car pulled up. Her memory was generally excellent, but she'd blocked out her appointment. She wanted to avoid reliving those terrible years. Slowly, in her sessions, she talked about events that had once been too painful to recall.

Guilt is a big problem. Some of this guilt is survivor guilt, or the irrational feeling that one is somehow to blame for having stayed alive while loved ones died. Some guilt comes from situations in which people were forced to make terrible choices. Other people genuinely behaved badly. They took food from hungry people or killed others so that they might escape. Under abnormal conditions, normal people do very abnormal things. Human beings, afraid for their lives, don't always function at their best.

Anxiety and restlessness are common reactions to severe stress. People are startled at the smallest of events—a door slamming, a car backfiring, or a shadow on their floor. Many newcomers cannot fall asleep. Or, they wake easily, have nightmares and night sweats.

Paradoxically, torpor and lassitude are also common reactions. People just don't see any reason to get out of bed in the morning. They don't have the energy to cope with the complex new situations they are in. They don't have the energy to brush their teeth.

One common, and generally not very adaptive, way refugees deal with their pain and difficulties in America is to move. Moves are common among refugees as they find one town difficult and hear rumors that the grass is greener in other places. Generally these moves don't make things better; they are expensive, disruptive of the family's relationships with schools and community resources, and they don't solve the original problems. Still, it's understandable that geographical moves would appeal to refugees. After all, they have moved before to solve problems.

Refugees also are at risk to become hooked on drugs, alcohol, and nicotine as ways to cope with stress. They desperately want to forget reality and drugs help with that, at least in the short term. Many refugees come from places where they had limited access to alcohol and other mind-altering drugs. They also come from places where there were no traditions for helping people learn to drink responsibly and where there was no education about drugs and nicotine. It is tragic to see a person who has endured terrible things and escaped from a dangerous place become enslaved by gin or heroin, surely as cruel a jailer as any in the old country.

Reactions to trauma depend on many things. In general, one discrete traumatic incident is more easily handled than years of chronic stress. The Kakuma refugees and Bintu and Mohamed, who had long periods of great stress, had more trouble healing than refugees who had one terrible experience.

Whether a person is singled out for victimization is also important. It is easier to deal with abuse that is random or the result of membership in a group than with abuse that feels personal. Torture is a great injury to the human spirit. No matter how serious the physical wounds, the spiritual wounds are worse.

Attributes of Resilience

Psychology has documented with great precision all human inadequacies. We have the *Diagnostic and Statistical Manual* to catalog our problems, but we have no equivalent inventory of human strengths. Writing this book, I discovered certain qualities in resilient people from all over the world, and I labeled them the attributes of resilience. Few refugees had all the attributes, but the ones who were successful at adapting to America had many of them. Those refugees with few or none of the attributes were in a great deal of trouble in America.

All of us can benefit from the attributes of resilience. As we cope with loss or adjust to new situations, we will do better if we have a sense of humor, if we are hardworking and honest, and if we know how to stay calm. On airplanes, we hear, "If needed, an oxygen mask will appear automatically." In times of crisis, these attributes are our oxygen masks. This list of attributes of resilience, while neither perfect nor exhaustive, summarizes what it takes to adjust to new and difficult environments.

Attributes of Resilience

1. Future Orientation

Future orientation is about letting go and moving on. It is about newcomer zest. All refugees must put their hearts into America if they are to succeed in our country. Bintu is a good example of someone who has experienced great sorrow, but who looks toward the future. She began computer classes right away and made plans for bringing her "kids" from Ghana over to America.

Having a future orientation doesn't mean repression of memory or silence about the past. On the contrary, dealing honestly with pain often allows refugees to leave the past behind. Nor does it mean leaving loved ones behind. Many of the most successful refugees are deeply tied to their homeland, and often much of their motivation to succeed is because they want to help people in their old country. However, having a future orientation does mean that refugees have plans and purpose. They do not live only in the past; they can envision a better future.

2. Energy and Good Health

Adjusting to America and recovering from loss requires an enormous amount of energy. Just facing each day, with difficult jobs and coworkers who are hard to understand, is exhausting. Life is hard enough for the healthiest refugees, but it is almost impossible for refugees who are in chronic pain from injuries, who cannot work because of disabilities, or who have previous histories of mental illness. The children at Sycamore School, filled with life and wriggly with energy, exemplify energy and good health. I think of Khoa and Ly, so lively they could barely sit in their chairs. Youth is a great advantage in a new culture.

3. The Ability to Pay Attention

Paying attention means being aware of subtle cues, knowing whom to trust, and accurately sensing danger. It means catching on to patterns and rules, picking up on how things work, and not repeating mistakes. Paying attention includes being empathic, remembering, and detecting small changes in tone and nuance.

The Kurdish sisters had survived by paying attention. All of them could expertly read other people and respond quickly and sensitively to the slightest needs in others. I was struck by how rapidly they responded to changes in my face or mood. The Kurdish sisters didn't miss anything and they learned things the first time. We joked that they remembered my life better than I did. I said, "Don't move away or I won't know who to ask what I did last year."

4. Ambition and Initiative

Being a hard worker requires motivation and stamina. It requires time-management skills, the ability to work with others, and the ability to do what one is told and more.

Mohamed exemplifies these attributes. Within a few weeks of his arrival, he'd signed up for GED classes and was going to a mosque, working two jobs, and sending money to Africa. His employers respected him because he always offered to do more than his share of work. He was on time and never called in sick. He was taking driving lessons and computer classes in his spare time.

5. Verbal Expressiveness

One of the most important attributes is simply being able to express one's needs clearly and appropriately. Being able to communicate thoughts and feelings, to ask good questions, and to articulate problems are all aspects of this attribute.

Walat at Sycamore School was able to communicate clearly. He knew what he knew and what he didn't know. He asked for help when he needed it. In contrast, Trinh and Abdul were silent about their needs and feelings and hence were much harder to help. Knowing one needs information and knowing how to ask for it are critical survival skills.

6. Positive Mental Health

Many people have "a talent for happiness." Long ago La Rochefoucauld seemed to know this when he wrote, "Happiness and misery depend as much on temperament as on fortune." Positive mental health requires an optimistic nature, a sense of humor, and the ability to appreciate and enjoy what one can in the midst of sorrow.

Bintu is a good example of this. In spite of all her misfortune she is a joker and a seeker of fun. The Even Start mothers also exemplify this attribute. They worked all day in factories, then cared for their families and came to class. Many had lost children, husbands, and homes. However, I have rarely been with a happier group of women, all jokes, smiles, and high hopes and kindness to the teacher and one another.

7. The Ability to Calm Down

These skills, which include deep breathing, putting things into perspective, and optimistic thinking, allow people to stay calm and positive, to forgive themselves and others, to sleep nights, to avoid addictions or impulsive behaviors, and to control feelings in the face of great sadness and trauma. These are the skills Martin Seligman teaches in his work on "learned optimism" and Daniel Goleman teaches as "emotional intelligence," a concept pioneered by Peter Salovey and John Mayer.

Many people get into trouble because they cannot tolerate pain. They run from it, try to drink it away, or inflict their pain on others. Stoicism, or being able to endure pain, is an important attribute of resilience. Wendy Kaminer defined stoicism as "the strength to tolerate sorrow."

Because refugees have experienced pain and chaos, many of them have had a chance to develop good coping skills. Tharaya and Velida could tolerate the pain of their pasts. Velida even coped with her brain tumor in a stoic and heroic way. Even as the Afghani women struggled with great sadness, they did what they needed to do to take good care of their children.

Nithal was a high school student from the Nuba Mountains in Sudan. She helped her mother with many younger siblings, made A's at high school in her fourth language, and gave talks about her people to raise money for supplies. Nithal was shy, but she spoke clearly as she told of the tragedy of war in her country. One quarter million of her people had died and the attacks on them continued. Nithal's father was Yousif Kowa, leader of the Nuba people. He stayed in the Nuba Mountains to fight for his people, but he sent his family to America to be safe. While I wrote this book, Yousif died. Nithal said of her father's death, "He has been gone so much. It's easy to think of him as on a journey. I like to think that this trip is a safe one. We will be together when it is over."

8. Flexibility

Flexibility means simply that one can behave differently in new situations. One can assess the situation and act accordingly. It's being adept at cultural switching. Flexibility also involves understanding the concept of point of view, that is, knowing that different people have different perspectives and that all behavior is contextual.

The high school students come to mind as moving between worlds, being traditional at home and American at school. Liem is an example of someone adept at cultural switching. He adopted Vietnamese ways at home and mostly American behaviors at school. He managed to stay out of trouble and work toward his goals in a very complicated environment.

Anton was having more trouble. He was in a safe place now, but his behavior remained that of a person in a war zone. His mother also had trouble being flexible. She and Anton would have had an easier time if they had been able to change a little and trust others in a new, more trustworthy place.

9. Intentionality, or Being Thoughtful about Choices

In the United States, where there are so many choices, it's imperative to make careful decisions, to choose wisely what to do and not do. It's also important to be able to pick wholesome friends who will help with adjustment and to make good choices about work, housing, schools, time, and money. It's necessary to rapidly develop consumer skills and some sophistication about media and advertising. One of the most useful skills is knowing the difference between what one wants and what one needs.

Mohamed was an intentional person. He realized cars were expensive and decided to bike as long as he could, at least until his first Nebraska winter. He knew to stay away from credit cards, nicotine, alcohol, and useless products. He was a good judge of people and soon had solid, intelligent friends around him.

10. Lovability

Lovability is a complex attribute that includes many qualities from other attributes. Certainly energy, verbal expressiveness, empathy, and good character are all part of being lovable. It's an elusive quality, but we all know it when we see it. Lovable people make us feel good. We want to be with them and we want to make them happy.

There were no refugees more lovable then the Kurdish sisters. With their bright eyes and hearty laughter, their jokes and eager curiosity about the world, and their enthusiasm for parties, for dressing up, for camping trips and adventures, they were easy to love. I never was with them without enjoying myself, without feeling cared for and appreciated, and without learning something new about the world.

11. The Ability to Love New People

Originally I thought lovability might be the most important attribute of resilience. People who are loved are granted favors, given advice and privileges. They are invited to events and awarded scholarships. But I now realize that even more important than being loved is being able to love.

Caring for others is what motivates humans to get out of bed in the morning. It gives life purpose and meaning. Especially if one has had great losses, the best cure is to find new people to love. Zahra, the bereft Afghani grandmother, was saved when she became interested in Ritu's children. Bintu befriended needy refugee families here and worked for the children in her refugee camp in Ghana. With all that had happened to Bintu, if she did not have this skill, she could not have survived psychically. She cared for herself by caring for others. And there was Ly, the Vietnamese schoolgirl who thought I, a very ordinary fifty-four-year-old woman, was beautiful.

A man in our town lost his wife in the same time period that one of his daughters had triplets and the other had twins. He alternated nights at his daughters' homes, getting up to help feed and change the babies. Mercifully, he had five new people to love as he dealt with the loss of his wife.

A friend of mine lost her daughter to cancer. Shortly after this untimely death, her first grandchild was born. This new baby came into her life at a time of great need and gave my friend a reason to keep on living. My friend said, "I can see my daughter's smile in the baby's smile, my daughter's eyes in her eyes." When we lose people, as we all do, we must be able to find new people to love. They cannot replace those who were lost, but they can give us joy, hope, and a sense of purpose.

12. Good Moral Character

Good character is vital to success. Honesty, responsibility, and loyalty all help newcomers succeed. One of the joys of writing this book was that I met many heroes. Joseph worked to support his siblings and studied bleary-eyed for his GED. Often I could hear his stomach rumbling with hunger. Leda commuted hours to a job that made her cry, then on weekends she cooked meals of nourishing Iraqi food and cleaned the house. Deena from Sycamore School helped her overwhelmed family cope with their first year in America. She found time to pull Trinh, a withdrawn Vietnamese girl, into the life of the school.

Cross-Cultural Healing

Freya Stark wrote that "People who have gone through sorrow are more sympathetic, not so much because of what they know about sorrow but because they know more about happiness—they appreciate its value and fragility and welcome it wherever it may be."

Laughter, music, prayer, touch, truth telling, and forgiveness are universal methods of healing. Talking to friends, sharing food, enjoying children, and watching the stars have soothed us humans for thousands of years. Many cultures have healing ceremonies, purification and forgiveness rituals, often with a spiritual component. Karl Marx called religion the opium of the people. Described more kindly, religion is the healing balm for all people. Faith is an important aspect of healing, faith that one's suffering has not been in vain and that the future will be better.

Traditional healers and customs work because they are believed to work. Almost all mental health cures are about placebo effects. Placebo effects aren't negligible. They are about hope and faith. Langston Hughes wrote, "Hold on to dreams for when dreams go / Life is a barren field frozen with snow."

In the Middle East, troubled people often visit "saint's houses." Usually these are peaceful retreats with kind people to assist the travelers. The guests visit with food to share. They pray, cry, talk to others, and rest. Most return home feeling much better.

Buddhism has an ancient and sophisticated set of practices for calming and healing. Breathing properly, meditating, and focusing on the impermanence of all things are healing activities. In fact, some of our most successful psychotherapy incorporates aspects of Buddhism.

Praying works whether or not people believe in God. Prayer is a more active, trusting process than worrying. It is more calming and hopeful. Talking to God is generally more satisfying to people than talking to Freud. Also, with prayer, there is no need for diagnosis, treatment, or authorization from managed-care representatives.

Rituals are often part of healing. They vary in their depth and intensity. Sometimes they reflect deep cultural values, sometimes they merely allow people to go on with their lives. They mark transitions and allow the next step. They acknowledge that something has happened and allow people to say what needs to be said. The flower ceremony at Sycamore School was a simple ritual that helped the children heal from loss.

Art is also a great connector. Art and music don't require a common language, they are a language. They allow people to express pain they may not be able to communicate in any other way. Sometimes art allows people to transcend pain, to turn pain into meaning and beauty.

Refugees seem to understand the value of positive emotions and joyful events. There is an Iraqi saying, Three things are calming—the color of grass, water, and the face of a beautiful woman. Latinos have all-night fiestas. The Vietnamese are masters of potlucks. All cultures like food, dance, music, and parties. The Africans came from places where whole villages of people had been slaughtered and children had been stolen from their parents. We offered them therapy and doctors, but the first thing they wanted was to get all their people together and have a celebration. And they wanted a community center so that they could be together and plan more festivals. They knew that before housing, jobs, medical care, or money, community is what heals. It is good to share pain, but what is really healing is to share joy.

Social activism provides meaning and assuages survivor guilt. Documenting the abuses of an authoritarian regime or working for human rights is what saves many victims of a repressive government. Bringing family over from the old country is profoundly healing. Toni Morrison put it well when she said, "The purpose of freedom is to free someone else."

Refugees are great role models for resilience. They don't fit our theories. With all their stress and sadness they should be the most miserable of people. Still, for most, healing occurs with the tincture of time. Slowly most people learn to relax and trust again. And after trauma, instead of being bitter, many people become more loving and more appreciative of life. They often describe their characters as greatly improved by their experiences. They see the world in a more layered, complex, and empathic way.

After a few years, refugees find themselves humming as they walk to work or smiling as they hang clothes on a spring morning. They have babies, learn how to e-mail their friends, and form neighborhood support systems. In fact, refugee communities are often our most vibrant, bustling, and hopeful communities, filled with people who believe in the American dream.

Healing Packages

Sara Alexander, a psychologist from Boston, talked about her collaborative work with refugees to create "healing packages." She helped refugees design healing packages from a smorgasbord of activities that included reading to children, exercising, finding a mosque, taking a class in English, looking for a better job, or going out to eat. Healing packages were about joy, contentment, recreation, physical pleasure, rest, and social connection. Not all refugees included psychotherapy in their healing packages.

This lack of interest in therapy is quite consistent with the findings from Thrive. Refugees chose circuses and dances, GED classes and job fairs, over opportunities to talk to mental health professionals. Thrive mentors demonstrated that refugees could only be helped when they were seen as whole people with physical, spiritual, social, intellectual, and vocational needs. They also showed us the importance of love, work, fun, and community in healing.

However, therapists can be part of healing packages, especially if we take a problem-solving or psycho-educational approach. An educational approach involves sharing information or teaching skills such as stress management, assertiveness, or relaxation techniques. Many newcomers resist psychotherapy, but most people like to learn. Education carries no stigma, no shame, and no hierarchy.

Psycho-education can help people look at the circumstances at the time of their trauma and understand that they were powerless to stop certain events. Just because they felt vulnerable and frightened doesn't mean they were weak. A mother whose baby starved needs to hear, "You did all you could. There was nothing to eat." A father whose son washed away in a river needs to hear, "You could not help how swiftly the current flowed."

Therapists' best work emphasizes empowerment and control. Identifying strengths and celebrating victories build trust and pride. It is good to ask, "How did you survive all this? What helped you stay sane?" Or, "Are there things you did that you feel proud of?" It's good to find out what people do well and encourage them to do more.

Therapists will be more useful to refugees if we broaden our roles and become cultural brokers, college advisers, drivers, teachers, case managers, advocates, or cooks. We can help with life planning, mediation, money and time management, and strength building. We can ask people to elaborate on their strengths, although this can be overdone. I complimented one man on not going crazy and he asked me, "How do you know I am not crazy?" Our specialty areas can be dealing with emotions and resolving conflicts. We can empower with information. If what we offer is useful, newcomers will want to come see us. They won't need to be coaxed, they'll beat down our doors.

Therapy can happen anywhere—in homes, schools, community centers, churches, cars, parks, and cafés. I'm reminded of a story about Willie Sutton, the famous bank robber. He was asked, "Why do you rob banks?" Sutton answered, "That's where the money is." If the question is "Where should therapists do therapy?" The answer is, "Where refugees are."

Not too long ago, I listened to a roomful of professionals discuss how to help traumatized people. People suggested various forms of therapy, all of which involved facing pain. Fair enough. In many cases, pain needs to be faced, but no one in the room suggested anything pleasant such as music, art, parties, pets, or walks in the countryside. This serious discussion seemed a metaphor for our blind spots as a field. We have focused on narrow, and not necessarily the most palatable, of treatments. We have ignored some of the oldest, most useful, and most universal healing procedures.

After thirty years of being a therapist and several years of working with refugees, I have found certain constants in the healing experience, certain experiences that help people in all times and places. These constants include some things we've seen with the Thrive mentors—fun, useful work, the support of community and family, and religious beliefs. And the constants include some of the essential elements in psychotherapy—safe, calm places; caring relationships; finding hope and meaning in painful events. In the future, good therapists will use elements from healing from all over the world.

Safe Space

Calmness is a language that the deaf can hear and the blind can read.
—MARK TWAIN

A calm, safe environment begins the healing process. The best treatment facilities for refugees know this. The Center for Victims of Torture is housed in an old home near the University of Minnesota. There is a fountain in the lobby that makes splashy, soothing water sounds. The house has lots of skylights and windows and no small rectangular rooms. Artifacts from many cultures remind visitors of their homelands. The Universal Declaration of Human Rights is translated into many languages and framed on the walls. Offices are homey and noninstitutional, with easy chairs, couches, and soft light. Classical music plays, flowers decorate desks and tables, and outside a garden flourishes.

The best treatment programs for refugees are user-friendly systems. Paperwork is kept to a minimum. Greeters and gifts, such as pizza and free TB tests, draw people in. The best treatment is holistic and incorporates school, family, and community resources. Dr. Keller at the Bellevue/NYU Program for Survivors of Torture put it this way, "Whatever problem a person has, we try to find the nicest person we can to solve it."

Therapy is very much about the construction of a space for people to think, talk, and work out their problems. But the ideas about a quiet space are much older than psychology. Almost all of the great religious leaders found enlightenment when they were alone in the wilderness. Many tribes encourage their members to go away from the community and be alone to seek knowledge and to heal. Healing rituals from all over the world involve isolating people from others and decreasing the amount of stimulation they receive so that they can calm down and think.

Time alone outdoors is an ancient and a modern remedy. Some of our most cutting-edge therapy recommends wilderness experience. A local social worker, who was one of the wisest people I knew, walked on our prairie for hours every day to heal from the death of her husband.

Healing Relationships

The first casualty of trauma is trust. After being tortured or witnessing murders, people lose their protective shields of invulnerability. They have no illusions that they are safe. They know what humans will do to each other. This puts them in a difficult bind. They cannot heal without relationships, but relationships seem dangerous.

Earlier we discussed the importance of family, friends, and community in the healing process. Just knowing that someone cares is therapeutic. Healing occurs when a real person connects to another real person, that is, when people are comfortable enough with each other to be who they truly are.

People who have been betrayed by the human race most need a person who asks, "What is your experience?" then listens closely to their answers. This person can be a family member, a friend, a cultural broker, or a religious leader. It can be a shaman, a curandero, or a therapist. The important thing isn't the label, but the relationship, which is nurturing, consistent, and respectful.

This healing relationship often relies on what psychologist Celia Jaes Falicov calls "the power of small gestures." When I visit Bintu, I take her flowers. In fact, whenever I visit people who have suffered, I try to take a small gift. When grief-stricken people visited my aunt Grace, she offered them pie. Sometimes what heals is as simple as a touch of the hand, a smile, or the expression of sympathy.

Relationships reintroduce people who have suffered to the community of love. If they have been dehumanized, caring can rehumanize them. Warmth and respect can rebuild a person who has been systematically humiliated and degraded by torturers. Many people have been pulled back from the precipice of despair by one person who let them know they mattered.

Linda Simon wrote of William James, one of our best psychologists, "He was a birthright member of the great society of encouragers." We can all be in that great society of encouragers. We can ask people about their feelings and allow them to cry and rage. And we can be what Donald Meichenbaum called "purveyors of hope."

Love and hope are necessary to keep people's heads above water when they are in dire straits. A truly good listener manages to convey, "You have lost a lot, but you have not lost everything." In the end, healing relationships are about finding dignity adequate to the sorrow. I think of the three Iraqi men from the prison camp in Saudi Arabia. The most important thing for them was to find meaning in their experiences, to understand what happened to them in a way that allowed them to see themselves as men, worthy of respect.

Healing Stories

All sorrows can be borne if they can be put into a story.
—Isak Dinesen

People survive because they partake of the alchemy of healing. They turn their pain into a deeper understanding of themselves and of what it means to be human. As Pico Iyer wrote, "The final destination of any journey is not after all the last item on the agenda but rather some understanding, however simple and provisional, of what one has seen."

To say that people can grow and learn from any experience is not to justify their experience or even to say that they couldn't have learned from an easier life, but it is to say that healthy people learn and grow from everything, even trauma.

Almost all who become wiser and stronger after trauma do so because they develop a sense of purpose that transcends their immediate survival needs and allows them to focus on the future. They survive so that their children can become citizens and go to college, or so that they can become doctors or teachers and help others from their country, or so that they can bring their grandparents to America or write the truth about a bloody regime. This sense of purpose, as necessary to life as oxygen, propels refugees into the future

A woman from Colombia saw her husband shot by drug dealers. He was an honest judge who was unlucky enough to live in the wrong place and time. She was an educated woman who wrote books and worked all over the world. Afterward she spent her life writing and speaking about the problems of her country. She said, "I honor his memory by fighting for justice."

Healing stories might be about courage or generosity under fire, wresting victory from the jaws of defeat, or hard lessons learned. Stories should focus on what can be remembered with pride. Healing stories help people cast their lives in epic terms. Often just a slight spin can turn a story of misery into an epic of danger, heroism, sacrifice, and reward. Joseph's story can be told as one of victimization or as one in which he is a hero who saves his younger siblings. All of us need to see our lives as a quest for something more enticing then mere survival. All of us need to be a superhero to someone. The best question to elicit healing stories is, "What did you learn from your experience?"

Talking to the Sudanese and Kosovar refugees, I found that no matter what they had suffered they all said they had gained from their experiences. Many mentioned increased self-awareness, stronger love for family, closeness to other refugees, and witnessing acts of heroism or great generosity. One woman, who had been about to be shot, told of a stranger who placed his body between her body and the executioners. Another woman talked of people who gave away their only food.

Suffering is redemptive when it leads us to a deeper, more nuanced understanding of ourselves and other humans. For countless generations humans have used their pain to grow souls. Through tragedy many people realize they are capable of much better behavior than they thought possible. Or perhaps they realize how much they are loved. After she had broken her ankle, a woman from Azerbaijan was carried across a war zone by her husband. She said, "I never realized how much he cared for me." A Croatian boy said of his sister, "She was starving, but she handed me her last piece of bread."

Perhaps refugees have been heroes, much braver, more competent, or kinder than they ever suspected they could be. Through suffering, people learn the importance of kindness. They learn that love is all that matters. They develop a sense of perspective and scale. They learn tolerance and empathy. After much is lost, they learn appreciation for what remains.

I spoke to my aunt Grace the day she lost her only son. He had lived nearby all sixty years of his life and died of a heart attack mowing Grace's lawn. My aunt sounded old and tired on the phone. At the end of the call, she told me, "We'll just have to love and take care of the ones who are left."

My aunt was very wise. Her simple statement of purpose really sums up the nature of healing. After great loss, we must find who is left to love and resolve to care for them. That is all we can do. In most cases, the great miracle is that it is enough.

Samuel Beckett wrote, "Ever tried, Ever failed. No matter. Try again. Fail again. Fail better." We tend to underestimate our own resilience. Striving and overcoming obstacles can bring joy and focus to life. One of the great ironies is that stressful lives often provoke positive emotions, while easier lives can induce laziness and apathy. Who is happier, a mountain climber or a person who sits around and watches television all weekend?

135

The psychologist who has most understood healing and the relationship between pain and meaning is Viktor Frankl. In *Man's Search for Meaning*, he wrote that while he was in a concentration camp, he discovered that everything can be taken from a person but one thing—the ability to choose one's attitude to any given set of circumstances.

Nelson Mandela discovered the same great truth. He was locked up for twenty-seven years. At a certain point, he realized that, "My enemies could take it all, everything but my mind and heart. I decided not to give them away." This insight helped him reestablish his dignity and personal integrity.

Human life is not freedom from conditions, but freedom to take a stand on conditions. To live is to suffer. To survive is to find meaning in suffering. Working for the welfare of others is the best antidote to despair. Working to help extended family left in the old country, testifying about human rights abuses, working for democracy—all these activities give life meaning and help refugees heal. No one comes out of a holocaust to sell sausages. To truly recover, one must find a deep sense of purpose and meaning.

Americans who have suffered find similar ways to cope. They work for worthy causes, reconnect with friends, recommit themselves to their religious faith. They decide to spend more time with family, to read all of Shakespeare, or to visit the national parks they always wanted to see. They give their money to the needy.

Resilient people tell themselves a story that gives their lives meaning and purpose. The African American and Native American communities are especially good at using proverbs and stories to build meaning. Throughout their histories, these cultures have created stories that allowed them to laugh, to learn, and to find dignity in situations of oppression and despair.

In an ideal world we would learn about healing from one another. We would draw on the wisdom from all times and places. We would be intentional in our healing. That is, we would select from all cultures that which might work for us. In an ideal world we would all be able to pray, to dance and to feast, to watch sunsets and moonrises, and to talk to each other about our pain. We would use both laughter and tears and that great antidote to despair, being useful.

We would create healing ceremonies. We would find symbols that gave meaning to our grief. We would teach each other to endure, that greatest of human strengths. I remember an old saying my mother taught me: There are three cures for all human pain and all involve salt—the salt of tears, the salt of sweat from hard work, and the salt of the great open seas. Years ago when my mother told me this, I was a teenager and I believed the reference to open seas was about the escape one could make on the open seas, the escape from family or memory. Now I believe it is about the healing power of the natural world. After my time with refugees, I appreciate even more the truth of this saying about salt.

On the eve of January 1, 2000, National Public Radio commentator Daniel Schorr named Anne Frank Person of the Century. He praised her for keeping her humanity and faith in humankind in the face of all the horrors of the Nazi experience. I was touched and pleased by his choice. Ever since I read Anne's journal when I was thirteen years old, she has been a moral beacon for me.

She had all the attributes of resilience. However, she wasn't a disembodied saint, but a real person, capable of anger, self-doubt, tears, and joy. All through her last years, up until the end, she managed to remain awake, aware, and profoundly human. Even at the end of her life, in the concentration camp she was capable of grief when the gypsy girls were led to their deaths. Patricia Hampl wrote of our yearning for this girl who embodies resilience, "We seek her still, this sane person that we long for at the end of our terrible century that tried so desperately to erase her."

Elephant Ballad

KUKI GALLMANN

For HRH Prince Bernhard of the Netherlands

Recognizing that a creature of another species is in danger from one's own kind; going to the aid of that creature . . . imply the exercise of true compassion and also other most sensitive emotions.

> IVAN T. SANDERSON: The Dynasty of Abu:
> A History and Natural History of Elephant
> and Their Relatives, Past and Present

Its breath is said to be a cure for headaches in man.

> Cassiodorus, *Variae*, X, 30

The man limped towards my car holding on to rudimentary crutches made of cut branches. Below his loose turban, feverish eyes peered at me above gaunt cheeks.

'Jambo!' he addressed me shakily. '*Mimi ni ile ulikufa mwaka hi. Unakumbuka mimi? Ulitembelea musijana yako na ngamia.*' 'I am the one who has died this year. Do you still know me? I used to bring your young girl riding with my camels.'

Of course I remembered him. His name was Borau, a camel handler of the Boran tribe, whom we had employed in Laikipia for years. He herded camels day after day, and often came up to Kuti to hold the bridle of Sveva's camel when, at four or five, she had developed a passion for camel riding. He spoke constantly to his camels in the ancient camel language developed over generations and generations of close relationship with these extraordinary creatures, the noblest of African livestock and essential to the survival of his tribe and the related Somalis.

'*Toh-toh galla.*' The camel sat, crashing down on its knees.

'*Oh. Ohohoh oh galla.*' And the camel went.

'*Ahiaeh ellahereh.*' And the camel drank.

'*Kir-kir-kir.*' The camel trotted faster and faster . . . and so on.

Day after day, off went Borau at sunrise to guide his herd to the grazing grounds. Until one day he met the elephant.

A morning like all September mornings; a sky of deep rose and the stillness of dawn; the profile of the horizon black, with sculpted acacia trees; birds chattering from the *lelechwa* shrubs; and a yellow sun, round and flaming, rising in a glow of promised heat.

The camels had waited patiently, chewing their cud with a crusty noise of long worn teeth, sitting on knobbly knees and surveying through sad eyelashes the morning preparations in the *boma*. A hot mug of spiced tea to wash away sleep; a bowl of sour camel milk; incitations, calls, and they were on their way. His camel stick firm across his shoulders, today Borau headed towards Marati Mbili.

He liked his job. He knew nothing else but walking in front of the camels, timing his agile step to their rhythm, curiously similar to them in his long ambling steps and his thin legs with heavy joints, built to march without pause. Or walking behind the camels, following their large soft feet that raised no dust, and left only neat rounded prints, like the shadows of a leaf.

He knew their favourite browse, and interpreted their needs like all herdsmen who match their lives to those of the animals they tend. His very existence was camels.

Today was drinking day for the camels, and Borau decided to wash in the *marati*. The camels drank first, extending their necks to the troughs, stimulated by the Song of Water, a triumphant biblical lament as ancient as the need to drink.

'*Hayee helleree, oho helleheree.*'

Immediately after drinking, the camels started grazing, nibbling with prehensile lips on nearby bushes and filling their discerning mouths with *carissa* leaves. The sun was higher now, and Borau slid off his *shuka* and his head-scarf to wash.

It was then that a big young male camel, who had been mauled by a lion, started a courting skirmish with one of the females, but was intercepted instantly by the dominant rutting male. The old camel came behind the suitor with frightening gurgles, and chased him off furiously. The younger one crashed away through the bushes with alarming speed, and was instantly lost to sight.

It is extraordinary how suddenly and completely the African bush can swallow animals. A shiver runs through the leaves, as the shrubs recompose themselves like ripples settling after a plunging stone. A cloud of dust suspended in the air; a whiff of rank smell; a sudden intake of our breath; perhaps the impression of a shadow, darting too quickly to let us focus on what we think we have seen. Only the prints of feet running on the track remain to prove that a herd of animals has just passed.

Borau sped after his camel, dressing while he ran. He tracked its rounded foot marks, but soon lost them in a mess of fresh elephant prints round a muddy water-hole. He looked and looked in vain; not only did the abundant elephant spoor confuse any other marks, but it announced the presence of a large invisible herd. It was wiser to go back to the camels, and make sure they did not become frightened and scatter in all directions.

Now, from the signs he saw, he knew the elephants were ahead of him. Not that it mattered. Borau was used to this. He just ought to be on guard, make sure he remained downwind, so that his scent would not alarm them, and move on light feet, hardly touching the soil, like the impala.

Soon he sighted the backsides of two elephants emerging from the sage just a few steps in front of him. He moved behind them carefully, all his senses alert so as not to disturb them.

He never heard the cow elephant which followed silently. He never saw her, until it was too late.

An instinctive glance over his shoulder. A large hovering shadow obscuring the sun for an instant, the pungent smell of ripe dung and hay, a hot breath fanning his neck and shoulders. The look of a yellow eye fixed on him, from a few feet above. Large grey ears flattened against grey temples. Extended trunk curled up to expose long tusks. The horrible recognition that the elephant was after him, and that he could not escape.

Blind terror squeezed his heart and Borau ran.

In total silence, the elephant ran after him. She was a heavily pregnant female, young enough to be quick, agile, and gain deadly speed; old enough to remember that man is the only danger to elephant. Old enough also to have been part of a group caught in a poaching ambush, when the screams of pain and the smell of the blood of her fallen companions left an indelible mark in her memory. And female elephants are known to become overprotective, often touchy and aggressive in the time immediately before and after they give birth.

Borau ran and ran, mindless of thorns and sticks tearing his clothes apart, blinded by the sweat filling his eyes, and while he ran, he knew that he was going to die.

The thought of a slender girl, her velvet eyes laughing below her head-shawl; a bowl of camel milk steaming in the chill of dawn; the call of a child running towards him; the familiar hollow sound of the wooden camel bell. The simple things of his lost life now beyond his reach.

The earth vibrated, shaken by the elephant's feet, and by the thumping noise of his heart.

He wildly looked around for somewhere to hide, for a tree to climb. But there are no trees, in thick lelechwa country. Then the impenetrable, impassable lelechwa gave way to an open mbogani, littered with roots and boughs. One caught his foot, and he tripped, face down, onto the hardened soil, his nose squashed into the dust. With a jerk he turned and looked up.

The elephant was on him.

In perfect silence she went down on her knees at his side, and in one movement lifted her tusks high and plunged them down into his leg. The tusks were butter-coloured but hard as spears, and like spears they penetrated his thigh like butter. The snap of fractured bone sounded like the snap of a broken branch. No pain. A spreading numbness.

The elephant stood, towering over him, looking down at his squirming body, as if to make sure he could hurt her no more. Slowly, deliberately, she lifted her foot above him. He screamed.

Startled by the strange noise, she stiffened, her foot hesitated and, in this pause, Borau instantly saw his chance and started pleading. If his camels understood, why not the elephant?

'*Hapana. Hapana, ndovu. Wacha. Kwenda. Akuue mimi, tafadhali akuue rafiki yako.*' 'No. No, elephant. Leave me. Go. Do not kill me, please do not kill your friend.'

Had the elephant cow ever heard a human voice before? The new sound pierced her open ears, puzzling them with a new note. She seemed to listen. Her large ears flapped once, twice. Her foot came down onto the exposed face, but not to hurt. It stopped almost in mid-air, then descended to touch him.

Borau was too shocked to protect his face with his hands, and the elephant's nail caught his turban, and undid it. The material came loose, covering his eyes. The foot hovered over him slowly, deliberately, brushing down the length of his whimpering body, but pausing to feel his head and chest. He could see now the furrows dug into the sole of the elephant's foot by walking thousand and thousand miles over thorns and rocks. She probed him with surprising gentleness, as if the sound of pain and fear in his moaning voice was one she could understand.

After a while she stood back, and, more confident now, Borau agitated his hands and began calling out loud with all his remaining strength, the camel's command to run: 'Kir-kir, kir-kir.' 'Go fast. Go fast.' He screamed louder and louder.

The elephant shook her head from side to side a few times, as if to chase that sound away stamping round him in the dust. Then she turned, and crashed away trumpeting. Only the cicadas remained, to fill the sudden silence with their eager songs.

The pain began to pulsate. Borau's mouth was parched and dry, his leg wet with blood and urine. He tried to move, to crawl towards the direction of the track, but he could not.

Perhaps the people back at the camp would notice that he was missing; when night came they would come and look for him and find him. But when night came so would the hyenas, and the lion, and the little silver-back jackals with their greedy mouths. If a sheep or a steer were lost, he knew it would never survive a night outside the *boma*.

The smell of blood, the smell of fear would attract all the scavengers. It was strange that there were no vultures yet; only the formidable presence of the elephant could have discouraged them, but he knew they would not be long in coming. In Africa there was always a vulture circling high, close to the sun, looking down with its telescopic eye for a dying animal on the plains.

The vultures would come from the sky, free-falling fast like bombs, and land on a branch, gathering their wings about them—first one, then another and another, until all the trees would be black with them. While the air filled with the sinister sounds of their presence, the vultures would sit and wait with undertakers' patience, and they would not have to wait long. Then one would come close, with awkward leaps, flapping his wings with raucous chortles of anticipation—the grotesque vulture that goes for the eyes first.

Visions of death and carnage filled Borau's mind—a sense of his own total vulnerability, crushed, unable to move, dying alone in the bush, an easy prey to any animal of the African night. He wondered at his own destiny, he who so many times had escaped malaria and the grip of high fevers, and infections and wild animals. Was it the wish of Allah that his road had reached its end in such a way?

The sun was setting now, he knew by the changed sounds of the bush; the sun he saluted every morning and to which he prayed every night. He tried to talk to Allah. Was God too remote from this *lelechwa* country?

He prayed for company, for any company. And he soon realized that God had listened.

He was not alone.

Slowly, through the fog of his total misery, Borau became aware of presences round him. They were gathering quietly, betrayed only by a noise of a broken branch, by a stomach gurgle, a shuffle, a deep breath, a rustle of leaves. They were extraordinarily quiet, and they were coming towards him. Their large feet did not hammer the ground. They waded through the bush with great ease and the calm of creatures who are unafraid. Soon their vast grey shapes cast vast shadows over him.

And Borau knew, without fear, that the herd of elephant had come back.

Earlier they had stopped feeding to watch what was happening. Now they came curious and unfrightened, to see what it was, this small trembling animal on the ground. First, came the young ones, tended by the matriarchs; they ran to him with open ears and stopped a few feet away, to observe him with attentive eyes. Then, one by one, the entire herd approached until they all stood round him, watching.

With feverish eyes, Boran looked up at the elephants as they looked down at him. He gazed into their yellow eyes, which examined him with benevolent attention, and he could feel that they would not harm him. In a weird way, he knew that, on the contrary, they would shelter him from the nocturnal dangers, and that for as long as they were there to guard him, no predator would dare to approach.

For a very long time, they stood in silence, as if studying him, and during that time, Borau talked to them. Heads lowered towards him, ears wide open, while they appeared to listen to the universal language of pain and surrender.

A trunk lifted, stretched, reached out and then another. Tentatively, smelling him and feeling him as gently as the caring hand of a nursing friend, they all touched him with their trunks. Quietly, they inspected him, carefully, unhurriedly, as if to reassure him.

Night had now fallen, with calls of guinea-fowl, grass-crickets, tree-frogs and nightjars. The elephant began to feed around him, like silent guardians. Now and again they each came back to stroke him. They ate, and then they came and checked, as if to reassure themselves that he was still there and fine, as if to reassure him that they were there to protect him.

Time drew on; Borau curled up on the cool spiky grass, trembling now with fever and shock, almost unconscious, but feeling utterly safe in their mighty protection.

They waited there around him while night approached. And who knows for how long they might have stayed. Even when the sound of an engine broke the silence, they still waited, alert now, with heads held high to smell the wind, ready to flee from the only animal of which they were scared. Car lights pierced the night and human voices; the engine droned closer now, advancing wheels opening up the shrubs.

Only then, like a school of dolphins going back to their ocean, leaving the shipwrecked sailor they have brought ashore to the care of a rescuing boat, did the elephant disappear, noiselessly, into the dark.

Malignant Sadness

KALLE LASN AND BRUCE GRIERSON

Kalle Lasn is the author of Culture Jam: The Uncooling of America *(HarperCollins, 1999). Bruce Grierson is a Vancouver-based writer and editor. From* Adbusters *(June/July 2000).*
Chat with author Kalle Lasn at Cafe Utne: cafe.utne.com

The United States is probably too independent-minded a country ever to trust a therapist telling it that it's sick. That's understandable: The paradox of mental health is that those who need help most are often least likely to recognize it.

America is the opposite of a hypochondriac: It underestimates how bad it's hurting—even with the evidence staring it in the face. What would you say about a friend, who showed the following behavior?

- Always, always on the go, seldom if ever taking a quiet moment to reflect.
- Willing to plunge deeper and deeper into debt to finance shopping sprees for nonessentials.
- Unshakable conviction that happiness is as close as the next stock split, breast augmentation, or Mazatlan vacation.

Martin Seligman, University of Pennsylvania psychology professor and head of the American Psychological Association, believes that the United States is in the throes of an "epidemic" of clinical depression. An American today, he says, is significantly more likely to suffer clinical depression at some point in his or her life than at any other time in the past hundred years.

Other modernized nations are not far behind us. A nine-nation study by epidemiologist Myrna Weissman of Columbia University and a cross-cultural group of international scholars found that people born after 1945 are three times more likely to experience depression than people born before. Clinical depression may, however, simply be the tip of the iceberg of America's mental distress. Skeptics will scoff—*Crisis? What crisis?*—but strip away the denial, the vested interest in the myth of sunny, can-do Americanism, and it begins to feel that something is awry at a fundamental level in many people's lives. It's not so much what's happening to us as what isn't. Something is missing. Something essential and meaningful has been displaced by something . . . hollow. The possibility that forces outside our control might be overwhelming us—changing us—is so frightening that most of us busily hunt down safe responses to our escalating anxiety. We rely in record numbers on prescription drugs. We escape into the media/entertainment pleasureplex. We pile on the amusements only to find (as Leonard Cohen sings) that "you are locked into your suffering, and your pleasures are the seal."

Situationism, an aesthetic and political movement that influenced young radicals of the 1968 Paris uprising, identified the beginnings of all of this more than 30 years ago. "A mental illness has swept the planet," wrote Gilles Ivain, an early leader in the Situationist Movement. The symptoms: "Banalization: no more laughter, no more dreams. Just the endless traffic, the blank eyes that pass you by, the nightmarish junk we're all dying for. Everyone hypnotized by work and comfort."

No one credibly claims to have identified the precise cause of the malaise. Psychologists, sociologists, epidemiologists speculate: Is it something in the environment—electromagnetism or microwaves in the air: a chemical in our food or water? Are cultural and economic factors creating stress that's opening us up to other kinds of problems? Answers to these questions may elude us until well into the future. But for each of us living in America, a Faustian, personal, almost religious question presents itself right now: What's the point of living in the most dynamic and affluent nation on earth if you're feeling sad and anxious a lot of the time? Have we, and the rest of the industrialized world, gained power and wealth at the price of—let's just say it—a piece of our soul? The moment you confront these questions-head-on, the cool, commercial facade of modern life suddenly dissolves. Behind it is a web of psycho-, socio-, and cybercultural threads. Why am I sad? Why am I anxious? Why can't I love? The answer, perhaps, lies deep in our collective subconscious. The route to the surface passes through the postmodern hall of mirrors. The trip looks forbidding.

And yet it is a worthwhile excursion. Think of it as trying to solve the tantalizing psychothriller of your own life—the ultimate existential whodunit.

Is It a Disease of Modernity?

The paradox is painfully clear: America is enjoying unprecedented levels of prosperity, life expectancy, health care breakthroughs, food supply, and peace. Life has never been more rich or stimulating, yet there are similarly unprecedented rates of melancholy and anxiety.

Perhaps the puzzle is itself the answer: The modern world that brought these advances is responsible for this epidemic of sadness.

Depression in China is three to five times less common than in the West. Worldwide, depression is increasing most quickly among the young and the well-off.

Psychologists Bernardo Carducci and Philip Zimbardo claim, based on their research, that hypercommercialized contemporary life, with its speed and complications, alters the nature of day-to-day interactions: "As we approach the limits of our ability to deal with the complexities of our lives, we begin to experience a state of anxiety. We either approach or avoid. And indeed, we are seeing both—a polarization of behavior in which we see increases both in aggression, marked by a general loss of manners, and in withdrawal."

Is It Social Isolation?

America is still a nation of lonely wanderers—folks who are achingly anonymous in the crowd. This is the downside of fierce American "individualism."

The U.S. Census Bureau tells us that more than 26 million Americans now live alone. And that figure is expected to rise by 5 million over the next 10 years. It's doubtful that any society in human history has experienced this kind of fundamental isolation. Living alone is hard on us. According to the National Institute for Healthcare Research (NIHR), "depression is significantly more common among people living by themselves than among those residing in families." It's more common still among the utter loners—folks living without any support or affinity group at all. Researchers believe that's partly why, in Western societies—where the young are increasingly cut off from the influence of families and other support systems, and left to forge a unique identity on their own—depression rates are far higher than in countries where solid social networks are the norm.

Is It the Electronic Environment?

Now, into this American culture of loners drops the Internet. We are the most cyberliterate nation in the world. Whether the Net will ultimately build more connections than it severs is a question that is still very much up in the air, but early returns suggest that it diminishes actual social participation. The authors of a Stanford University study released this year found that the Internet steals time normally spent with other human beings.

Even the online magazine *Slate*, which has an obvious interest in promoting Net culture, admitted that while it's true that you can "stay 'in touch' with thousands of people," the interaction is necessarily limited. You laser in by subject, interacting with people "along a slender strand of common vocational interests." Where once the few people in our lives fulfilled many roles, now we have effectively surrounded ourselves with specialists, whom we call on briefly for one thing only.

Our species has just made a sudden leap from a natural to an electronic environment. For 3,000 generations, human beings got their cues from each other and from nature. Now we're getting them from computer and video game screens.

"Reality" is disappearing as our navigable star. A predictable but nonetheless key culprit remains television. For 50 years, television has been the great anodyne. It lifts the mood, calms the nerves, fills the void. Like most things, it's probably harmless enough in judicious moderation. But TV-philic America is neither judicious nor moderate, and we now have overwhelming evidence that heavy TV watching is doing harm—to kids in particular.

In a study published this year, a team of Harvard researchers added even more damning evidence to the heap. Chronic TV watching was linked to low public engagement and lack of sociability. It "even correlates positively with 'giving the finger' to people," said David Campbell, a member of the research team.

Television has been around long enough now that some of the most interesting writing about it no longer concerns its effects, but rather the effects of its absence. A fair number of self-experimenters have managed to give it up, and they overwhelmingly report an increase in quality of life. They speak with the passion of those who didn't know they couldn't see until they got glasses.

Of course, television is just one ingredient in the postmodern media bouillabaisse. Steaming forth are sex, violence, race and gender stereotypes, and about 3,000 marketing messages a day. Pop culture fully occupies the psyche of a nation. The sole purpose of this new electronic environment is to keep us entertained. The product and purpose is the "escape."

But escape from what? Danger? Confinement? Disadvantaged circumstances? Or something deeper from a self we can no longer live with? Ironically, the more anxious we get, the more we need to be distracted; the more distracted we are, the more anxious we get. It's a closed loop. Sometimes, the way out seems to involve getting our hands on more information. If we were only more perfectly informed, all would become clear.

Yet we don't know what to do with the vast amount of useless information we ingest. We can't sweat it out, or excrete it, or trash it. It stays, imperfectly stored, somewhere, taking up space, forever. The result is a kind of low-level tension, as if we're perpetually preparing for an exam that never comes. New York University communications professor Neil Postman calls the information explosion a "cultural garbage problem": "The chief function of computers," he said in a lecture in Vancouver in February 2000, "will soon be to help people filter out unneeded information."

Postman often makes the point that when a new technology is introduced into a culture, that culture is forever and permanently changed, through and through. If you drop the Internet (or the telephone, or television) into an existing culture, you don't end up with the Internet plus that old culture; you end up with an utterly new culture.

Is It Consumer Capitalism?

In a consumerist capitalist system, author David Korten (*When Corporations Rule the World*, Kumarian, 1996) points out, we are all caught to some degree in a downward spiral of deepening alienation: Our quest for money widens the gulf between ourselves and our families and communities. Our growing alienation then creates an inner sense of social and spiritual emptiness. That's when advertisers get into the loop by assuring us that their products can make us whole again. We go out and buy their products, which requires money. And so we're back at the beginning, the quest for money.

The booming economy is minting new millionaires right and left. Staggering wealth at the top of the pyramid creates a psychological climate in which, ironically, everybody suffers. The "have-nots" lose, since they are seized by envy for a happiness they never knew they lacked, until they happened to peek through the hole in the wall and spied the elites enjoying unimaginable riches. The "haves" lose in a different way. "Sudden wealth syndrome" can afflict the newly rich with a sense of isolation and uncertainty, as if they had been teleported into an alien world. Uberprosperity drives a wedge down the middle of America, scattering seeds of guilt and insecurity on both sides of the divide.

Under consumer capitalism, corporations wield unprecedented power; they are sovereign, untouchable, far more powerful than any elected government. Could this power imbalance citizens and corporations be linked to high rates of depression?

Is It an Existential Crisis of Meaning?

Randolph Nesse, director of the evolution and human adaptation program at the University of Michigan's Institute for Social Research, believes that there are more kinds of depression than the diagnosticians have identified. Some depression may be a useful, adaptive response to situations in which a desired goal is unattainable.

"If I had to put my position in a nutshell," Nesse has explained, "I'd say that mood exists to regulate investment strategies, so that we spend more time on things that work and less time on things that don't work."

Many Americans use antidepressants to pull them back to "normal," but this may be precisely the wrong response. If, as Nesse and others theorize, depression

149

is a defensive response, one that tells us something important about ourselves or our culture, it makes no sense to clip its alarm wires with drugs.

Enter the young, urban, modern, fabulously "successful" Americans who are nonetheless disconnected from things they, at the most profound level, want: nature, intimacy, a quiet, unmediated environment. There's nowhere they can immediately go to find these things. The desired goal seems unattainable. So depression sets in as the organism adapts to the problem, searching for a way out.

Searching for Meaning

Austrian psychiatrist Victor Frankl, who died in 1997, believed that there is an existential dimension to much mental illness—as distinct from, but sometimes in addition to, psychic or social or physical dimensions.

Specifically, he identified people caught in what he called the "existential vacuum." It's not a mental affliction, but a spiritual one: Your life seems utterly devoid of purpose. No path beckons. Eventually, a kind of paralytic cynicism sets in. You believe in nothing. You accept nothing as truthful, useful, or significant. You don't value anything you're currently doing and can't imagine doing anything of value in the future.

Frankl believed that the existential vacuum he described was a modern condition. Carl Jung identified it in about a third of his patients, and he and his contemporaries noted that it was different from any neuroses they had seen before.

We pump for meaning. We hope to find it in malls. As Daniel Boorstin, retired Librarian of Congress, has pointed out, Americans shop not to get what they want (as Europeans, say, do) but to discover what they want. This may tie into modernity's new, heroic explanation about the meaning of life, which has swept aside older spiritual teachings and cosmologies. We now place our faith in a grand narrative of consumer choice, of never-ending economic growth and technological progress. But this largely excludes the spiritual dimension of human existence.

Is It Postmodernism?

And so now we find ourselves in the postmodern hall of mirrors. It's difficult to talk about postmodernism because nobody really understands it—it's elusive to the point of being impossible to articulate. But what this philosophy basically says is that we've reached an endpoint in human history, that the modernist traditions of advancement and ceaseless extension of the frontiers of innovation are now dead. Originality is dead. The avant-garde artistic tradition is dead. All religions and utopian visions are dead. And resistance to the status quo is impossible because revolution, too, is now dead. Like it or not, we humans are stuck in a permanent crisis of meaning, a dark room from which we can never escape.

Postmodernism pulls the philosophical carpet out from under us and leaves us in an existential void. And it poses an intellectual challenge to the next generation of thinkers who we hope will show the way to a post-postmodernism—a place where everything isn't relative, where all meaning isn't just a social construct, where faith means neither a sexy country singer nor slavish devotion to a monotheist myth, but a belief that there are things worth living for, and that those things are simpler and closer at hand than we imagine.

The Cure

How do Americans deal with mood disorders? We pop a pill or escape into frenzied activity that keeps us from dwelling on how we feel.

But here's the thing. No one can count on these things to restore in them what they never had in the first place. We want our problems to be solved without ever having to trouble ourselves with investigating their root causes—or, worse, having to entertain the idea that some problems simply have no solutions.

Two centuries of philosophers stand in opposition to the modern American recipe for happiness and fulfillment. You can't buy your way in. You can't amuse yourself in. You can't even expect falling in love to deliver you. The most promising way to happiness is, perhaps, through creativity, through literally creating a fulfilling life for yourself by identifying some unique talent or passion and devoting a good part of your energy to it, forever.

The trouble with being passive ticketholders in the media/entertainment pleasureplex is that we're standing in a "happiness" line that isn't moving. Receiving rather than acting, we insure that we will never feel a unique creative spark, much less nurture one. We forestall the moment of asking the big question: What am I doing here?

The way forward begins—it must begin—with voluntarily taking a step back and then looking around for clues.

There are parts of the world not yet thoroughly saturated with postmodern culture, places that still have some lush mental wilderness. Places where people still connect—not electronically, but physically and emotionally—with one another. There are intact communities where vital human juices still flow. There are countries where people do things differently than mainstream North Americans and, lo and behold, the sun still comes up in the morning.

We can learn from these places and cultures before they disappear. Their very existence challenges the American idea that there is a single right way for human beings to live—that the lone choice is either the grand narrative of consumer capitalism or the highway to benighted misery. At the very least, such places prompt questions, about their culture and ours. Can they possibly "develop" without suffering the same sort of psychological homogenization we have? Can we develop as a culture when millions of us live with minimal human interaction—when reality has become just one of many options? Has our own "progress" been worth it?

151

The 19-Inch Neighborhood

JOSHUA MEYROWITZ

I live in a small New Hampshire town, but in the last few weeks I met the Lebanese leader of Amal and I was shouted at by militant Shiite hijackers. I sat beside the families of hostages as they anxiously watched their loved ones at a news conference in Beirut and as they later rejoiced when the hostages were released.

I weighed the somber questions and comments of anchorman Dan Rather as he "negotiated" with Lebanese minister Nabih Berri. I evaluated firsthand the demeanor of the news reporters, the facial expressions of the hijackers and the public comments of President Reagan and his spokesmen.

And I participated in this drama of international scope without ever leaving New Hampshire; indeed, I shared in it fully when sitting isolated in my living room in front of my television, watching the 525-line screen of flickering specks of light and color that my brain translates into pictures of people, objects and motions. The visual liveliness—like a conglomeration of thousands of flashing neon lights—and the intensity of the drama itself kept me riveted to the screen.

In contrast, the images through my window of trees, dogs and neighbors' houses are crisp and clear—tangible, real. Yet when I think of "keeping in touch" with things each day, I, along with a hundred million others, turn to the blurry television set. Recently a house in my town was destroyed by fire, and I vaguely recall reading the story in my local paper. Was anyone hurt? Is the family that lived there homeless now? Have they, too, suddenly been taken hostage by a swirl of events not of their making? I don't know. I could find out, I suppose, but I probably won't.

Reality

For I, and most of my neighbors, no longer simply live in this town; we don't live "with" each other in quite the same way our grandparents did. We, like the

153

98 percent of American families who own a TV, have granted it the power to redefine our place and our social reality. We pay more attention to, and talk more about, fires in California, starvation in Africa and sensational trials in Rhode Island than the troubles of nearly anyone except perhaps a handful of close family, friends and colleagues.

Our widespread adoption of television and other electronic media has subtly but significantly reshaped our world. For the first time in human civilization we no longer live in physical places. And the more we rely on our video window, the less relation there is between where we are and what we know and experience, the less there's a relationship between where we are and who we are.

Such changes affect our sense of identification with our community—and role relationships within our family. Isolated at home or school, young children were once sheltered from political debates, murder trials, famines and hostage crises. Now, via TV, they are taken across the globe before we give them permission to cross the street.

Similarly, our society was once based on the assumption that there were two worlds: the public male sphere of "rational accomplishments" and brutal competitions, and the private female sphere of child rearing, of emotion and intuition. But just as public events have become dramas played out in the privacy of our living rooms and kitchens, TV close-ups reveal the emotional side of public figures. Television has exposed women to parts of the culture that were once considered exclusively male and forced men to face the emotional dimensions and consequences of public actions.

For both better and worse, TV has smashed through the old barriers between the worlds of men and women, children and adults, people of different classes, regions, and levels of education. It has given us a broader but also a shallower sense of community. With its wide reach, it has made it difficult to isolate oneself from the informational arena it creates.

To watch TV now is to enter the new American neighborhood. The average household keeps a TV set on for 50 hours a week. One may watch popular programs not merely to see the program, but to see what others are watching. One can watch not necessarily to stare into the eyes of America, but to look over the shoulders of its citizens and see what they see.

Television has become our largest shared arena where the most important things happen. When a friend sings exquisitely, we no longer say, "You should sing in our church," but rather, "You should be on television." Our funniest friends are wished an appearance on *The Tonight Show*, not a performance at the town hall. The early presidents of this country were seen by few of the voters of their day; now it is impossible to imagine a candidate who has not visited us all, on television.

Weather

Television has replaced the local street corner and market as an important place to monitor—but, as with a marketplace, we do not always identify personally with what goes on inside. We may avidly watch what is on the news and on the entertainment and talk shows even as we exclaim, "I can't believe people watch this!" or, "What's the world coming to?"

Regardless of its specific content, then, television today has a social function similar to the local weather. No one takes responsibility for it, often it is bad, but nearly everyone pays attention to it and sees it as a basis of common experience and as a source of conversation. Indeed, television has given insularity of place a bad name; it now seems bizarre to be completely unaware or cut off. The TV set is a fixture in the recreation rooms of convents; it is even something that is sometimes watched in the formerly silent halls of Trappist monks.

Paradoxically, TV is both a hijacker and a liberator, hostage and hostage taker. It frees us from the constraints of our isolated physical locations, but flies us to a place that is no place at all. And our attention is most easily held hostage when television itself becomes a hostage of terrorists, demonstrators, politicians and other self-conscious social actors who vie for the chance to become—at least for a while—our closest video neighbor.

"I'm the King": The Macho Image

RUDOLFO ANAYA

Rudolfo Anaya is the author of several novels, plays, memoirs, and collections of short stories. He is best known for his first novel, Bless Me Ultima, *which was recently reprinted in mass paperback by Warner Books. Selections from his novels, plus essays and stories, are collected in* The Rudolfo Anaya Reader, *also by Warner. His two most recent novels,* Zia Summer *and* Alburquerque, *are part of a trilogy set in New Mexico.* Alburquerque *received the 1993 Pen/Faulkner Award for Fiction. In 1992, he retired from teaching at the University of New Mexico and lives in Albuquerque.*

What Is Macho?

The word *macho* has one of the shortest definitions in the Spanish language dictionary, and yet the cult of macho behavior (machismo or the macho image) is as ambiguous and misunderstood as any aspect of Hispanic/Latino culture. To be macho is to be male, that's simple, but when the term is applied to Hispanic male behavior, then the particulars of the role are defined according to the particular culture. From Spain to Latin America, from Mexico to the Chicanos in the USA, one gets a slightly different definition of the macho image at every turn.

Being macho is essentially a learned behavior; as such it is a conditioned behavior. We males learn to act "manly" from other males around us; the "macho" that preceded us was learned from the cultures from which it evolved. Many forces impinge on the Hispanic/Latino cultures, so throughout history, machismo—or the conditioning of male behavior—has attracted all sorts of positive and negative elements.

Many cultural forces (from literature and religion to the latest musical fad, movies, MTV, or car styles) play a role in promoting the behavior of the macho, and these influences are the issue here. Still, beneath the conditioned behavior, the essence of what maleness means remains largely unchanged across time. We can describe conditioning and its effects; it is more difficult to describe the essence of maleness, especially today, when males seem to be retreating from describing, or laying claim to, a positive macho image.

Drunkenness, abusing women, raising hell (all elements of *la vida loca*) are some mistaken conceptions of what macho means. And yet the uninformed often point to such behavior and call it machismo. In fact, much of this negative behavior is aped by a new generation, because as young men they are not aware that they are being conditioned. Young men acting contrary to the good of their community have not yet learned the real essence of maleness.

Sex

One generation passes on to the next its ideals and rituals, and important behavior that has to do with our sexuality. People have always composed games about sexuality. In this respect, the macho image has a history. The cock-of-the-walk behavior is game playing. Games and sex go hand in hand.

The game can be spontaneous and fun, reflecting the courtship and mating we see in the natural world. Part of the purpose of gender games is to reflect nature's dance of life, evolution playing itself out in each new encounter. Animals, insects—high and low organisms—engage in this dance of life. We are caught up in "nature's game," this vast and beautiful dance that is part of the awe of life. We feel love in the harmonious flow of nature, the movement of birth and death, and we take meaning from our sexual natures.

But the game has taken on a manipulative aspect. The assertion of one over another is part of our conditioning. The game has turned ugly in many ways, and we are numbed by the outcome of the conditioning factors. But we can still be in charge of the game, and change the negative aspects of the game. We can choose not to play a power game that hurts and demeans women.

Macho behavior, in large part, revolves around the acting out of sex roles. The games the macho plays may be part of nature's dance, with the goal of procreation imprinted on the cells long ago, but the power to subjugate is also inherent in our relationships. When the male gets caught up in superficial power plays that have to do with sex, he is acting against his community. It's time to analyze the social forces that condition negative behavior and toss out the ones that destroy family, friendship, and community.

For the Chicano, the roots of the idea of maleness extend not only into the Mediterranean world but also into the Native-American world. We still act out patterns of male behavior emerging from those historic streams. To fully understand our behavior requires a knowledge of those literary and cultural histories. The Don Juan image and how it sets the tone for a pattern of behavior from

Mediterranean Spain to the present day is only one aspect of behavioral legacy. We need to know the role of the Native American warrior and how he cares for the community. The Chicano is a synthesis of those, and many more, streams of influence.

"I Can Piss the Farthest"

Little boys like to brag about the length of their penises, or they have contests to see who can piss the farthest. Acting out "I'm bigger, I'm better," the game begins to have its built-in power aspect. Later, boys will brag about having scored with a girl, and in the boast is contained a hint of the power they have exercised. Those who haven't yet scored have less power. They're virgins in the game. Those who don't see girls as the goal to be conquered have even less power. A hierarchy of needs and behavior begins to define the male role, and the power inherent in it. The true essence of male and female doesn't need this hierarchy, for hierarchy implies the use of power over others. And why should that which is most natural to our nature, our sexuality, require us to deal with others as objects?

Macho needs partners, not objects.

Until my father's generation, the men of the Mexican culture of the southwest U.S. could continue to speak Spanish and interact within the parameters of their history. That is, they set the code of behavior, one that was communal and focused on survival in an often harsh land. As Anglo-Americans moved into the territory, a wrenching of male relationships took place. As Anglos moved in, the language of domination shifted from English to Spanish. The Anglo-American law came to New Mexico in the mid-nineteenth century, but the rule of law in daily life in most communal enterprises remained Spanish. It was not until after World War II that the ways of my ancestors were overwhelmed. And therein lies an epic tragedy.

My father's generation *had* to adjust to the new language, the new man in town, the new laws. To be a man under Anglo domination was difficult if you didn't have the tools. I saw men broken by the new time, the new space. If they didn't adjust to the new language, they were demeaned. I now better understand my father's behavior, why he gave up. He didn't have the language, the tool with which to protect his own dignity, his own concept of macho. An excellent example of this meeting of cultures is shown in the movie *The Ballad of Gregorio Cortez*, a film that takes its story from a real legend.

In some areas the males did absorb one another's concept of maleness. For example, the New Mexican land owners, lawyers, and politicians (those generally known as *los ricos* or *los patrones*) quickly learned to work with their Anglo counterparts. The Mexican vaqueros taught the Anglo cowboys the trade, so there existed some camaraderie on a macho level in those endeavors. But overall, the power of law and language was too vast and overwhelming. The Anglos could dictate roles; they could piss the farthest, so to speak.

"I'm the King"

"*Sigo siendo el Rey*. I'm the king" are the lyrics from a popular Chicano rap song I hear on the radio. The words and rhythm are catchy. I listen to the song and find myself repeating the lines.

Macho behavior is instilled in us as children. Both father and mother want their boys to grow up to be manly. Usually, the more traditional the rules of behavior are for the macho, the stricter the behavior the child learns. When he becomes a man the child sings, "I'm the king. I rule the family, like my father before me, and what I say goes." The child is the father to the man. But fathers at home are more and more rare. The child turns to the gang in the streets. A new style of being king is learned.

My parents knew a wonderful couple, old friends, who came to visit. My mother and her *comadre* would cook up big meals, my father and his *compadre* would buy the wine. It was fiesta time. The old man would have a few glasses of wine and start acting like the king. "*Yo mando*," he would tell his wife, and the teasing about who ruled, the man or the woman, would go on. Visiting across the kitchen table and drinking wine, they were all caught up in discussing the roles of man and woman.

It has always been so. In that space of the family fiesta in the small kitchen, they could define and redefine their roles. The mask of gaiety put on for the fiesta allowed them to speak freely. But beneath the surface a real dialogue was going on, defining and refining the roles of the men and the women. Do we have that dialogue about machismo going on in our community today? Or have we accepted old roles conditioned by forces beyond our control? Are we too programmed to see the light?

The male child observes and learns to be the king, how to act as *número uno*, how to act around men and women. In a community that is poor and often oppressed there is much suffering, so he is taught *aguantar*: to grin and bear it. "*Aguántate*," the men around him say. A macho doesn't cry in front of men. A macho doesn't show weakness. Grit your teeth, take the pain, bear it alone. Be tough. You feel like letting it out? Well, then let's get drunk with our *compadres*, and with the *grito* that comes from within, we can express our emotions. Lots of essays could be written on *aguantar*. The women also learn *aguantar*: Bearing it crosses the gender boundary. How women express the floodwaters of the *aguanto* is now being documented by Chicana writers.

The macho learns many games while learning to be *número uno*. Drinking buddies who have a contest to see who can consume the most beer, or the most shots of tequila, are trying to prove their maleness. From the pissing contest to drinking, the wish to prove his manliness becomes antisocial, dangerous. The drunk macho driving home from the contest he won can become a murderer.

The car in our society has become an extension for the macho. The young male hungers for the most customized, flashiest car. It replicates him. It is power. The car is used in the mating ritual. As in our small villages generations ago the young vaqueros came into town to show off their horses and their horseman-ship, the young now parade the boulevard showing off their cars. The dance is the same; the prize is the same.

To other males, the *vato* with the best car is saying, "I'm bigger, I'm better, I'm the king." Exactly the lyrics to the rap song. "*Sigo siendo el Rey,*" he sings, "I con-tinue being the king." The song describes one goal of the macho, to be king, to be *número uno*, to answer to no one. The message is aimed not only at other males, it is also for the female of the species.

Outside Influences

But guns have entered the game. Perhaps they've always been there, because certainly the Mexican *charro* and the cowboy of the movies both carried pistols, both fought it out with the bad guys, and the fastest draw won. In the rural areas hunting is most often male behavior. The gun extends the power and the sex-uality of the young men. Now you can strike farther and deadlier.

It is time to call that behavior that is good, good. And that which is negative to the self and the community, not good. To be unkind and violent is not macho. The *vato* in the song who wants to be the king needs to find positive ways of act-ing for his community.

In my generation the "attitude" of James Dean influenced young male behav-ior, as did that of black musicians and black talk. Today, parents worry about the violent influence of the movies. The characters portrayed by Arnold Schwarzeneg-ger (and other such exaggerated macho images) and the Power Rangers have become symbols of violence in our society. Machos seem to solve problems only through violence, and quickly. Discourse and problem solving, which take time, are not honored in such movies. Parents worry about the influence such media are having on the young. Macho has really gotten out of hand; in fact, it's been perverted by those who use a false idea (ideal) of manliness to achieve their goals. We need to stand up and say, loud and clear, that violence and oppres-sion are not macho.

As more Chicano families become single-parent families, the traditional role of the father and the extended-family males will not be as influential in shap-ing the behavior of boys. The boys are being conditioned instead by the behav-ior they see on TV, in movies and music videos. Boys loose in the hood are being shaped by the gang instead of the father.

La ganga shapes behavior, provides initiation, belonging. (Life in the gang— whether it's a neighborhood group of boys; an athletic fraternity ("the jocks"); or a gang into *la vida loca*, cruising, drinking, drugs, and guns—is a subject that requires a book to itself.) In the traditional culture, we didn't practice drive-by shooting as initiation into maleness. Young Chicanos moving into the maleness of the gang now practice a more violent form of initiation.

Young Chicano males learn from the past generations (drinking is often learned from brothers or close relatives), and such behavior is greatly influenced by the mainstream society. The influence of the Anglo-American culture on the Chicano culture cannot be overlooked. We can no longer speak of a continuum of learned behavior that is solely Mexican macho, because young males are greatly influenced by the totality of the culture around them. MTV, music, movies, television, and the behavior of other cultural groups *all* influence the behavior of the young Chicano male. To truly understand himself, and his maleness, the young male *must* ask himself: Who is affecting me? What do they want of me? How can I take charge of my own life?

There is a lesson to be learned here. Let us *not* repeat the loss of the prior generation, a loss we see today in the streets. Let us *not* be "powerless" as men. Let us *not* act out negative behaviors. We have within us the power to change. We have the future of our community at stake, so macho behavior has to be used positively for the community.

Los Chucos

Each new generation becomes a new link in the group's tradition, but also transforms behavior. My adolescent years saw the advent of the *pachuco*, a radical departure in the male behavior of the small New Mexican town I knew. Who were *esos vatos locos* imitating in the forties when they invented the *pachuco* argot, the dress, sexual liberation in attitude and action, use of drugs, use of cars, etc.? Was there a continuous line of macho behavior in which the *chucos* were a link? Or was the behavior so spontaneous and new that the *pachucos* initiated a new definition of what it meant to be macho? After all, being macho does mean to defend the territory, and the *chucos* did defend their barrios against mainstream encroachment. Were the *pachucos* a reaction to the growing oppression by Anglo America? Partly, but once the warriors defined themselves, they spent as much time fighting each other as they did fighting the enemy, *el gabacho*.

The *pachuco* became a new model of behavior, breaking with the past, and yet in his role vis-à-vis *la chuca*, the male-female dance contained the same old elements embedded in the Mexicano culture. The power play was definitely at work. *La chuca*, as liberated as she was from her contemporary "square" sister, who remained a "nice" girl, was still subservient. The *pachuco* loved to show off his baby doll.

This makes us question if breaks with the past are really radical, or does only the surface dress of the macho change? Beneath the zoot suit of the *pachuco*, old cultural forces and conditioned behavior continued to define the relationship between the macho and his woman. "*Esta es mi ruca*," he said proudly, introducing the woman as property in which he was pleased.

The *pachuco* practicing *la vida loca* continued to influence the definition of macho behavior into the nineties. They were the early lowriders. They spawned the baby chooks and those Chicano males who today are acting out roles, sometimes unknowingly, with roots in the *pachuco* lifestyle. (The Chicano rapper borrows from the black rapper, but in his barrio, in his strut and talk, he is borrowing as much from the old *veteranos*.) This role of an "unconscious energy" in the community is something we can't measure, but it's there. History is passed on not only in stories and books, but by osmosis.

It makes us ask: Is behavior only learned? Or is there real maleness, a golden rule not only in the blood but in the myths? I look at the young machos parading down the street, acting out their roles, and I wonder how much of their behavior comes from that unconscious influence, something inherent in maleness itself. There is something in that dignity of maleness we don't want to give up. But what is it? We know those negative forces that condition us have to be repudiated. But we also yearn to be noble men, and to act in a noble fashion for our families.

La Familia

The *pachuco* macho behavior, while very visible in the barrio (and introduced to a larger audience by the U.S. Navy anti-*pachuco*, anti-Mexican riots during the early forties in Los Angeles, and made more visible through the Valdez "zoot suit" film), was not the only model of maleness in the community. A far greater percentage of the men of the barrios went about their work, raising families, trying to do the best they could for them. Macho means taking care of *la familia*. Perhaps this is the most important definition of macho, the real, positive meaning of the word. And yet it is often given short shrift. Critics often look at the negative behavior of the macho and forget the positive.

In the villages and barrios of New Mexico when I was growing up, being manly (*hombrote*) meant having a sense of honor. The intangible of the macho image is that sense of honor. A man must be honorable, for himself and for his family. There is honor in the family name. *Hombrote* also means providing for the family. Men of honor were able to work with the other men in communal enterprises. They took care of the politics of the village, law and order, the church, the *acequia*, and the old people.

The greatest compliment I could receive as a child when I did a job well was to be called *hombrote*. I was acting like an *hombre*, a man. This compliment came from both males and females in the family and in the extended family. By the way, this compliment is also given to the girls. They can be *hombrotas*, as well as *muy mujerotas*, "very womanly." Either way, the creation of male and female roles are created and rewarded with the appropriate language, and the language is male-centered.

Much is now written about male bonding, how the father and other males in the community shape the macho image. In Hispanic culture the role of the *compadres* is such a role. (The *compadres* are the godfathers, for lack of a more thorough definition.) The *compadres* bond at marriages, baptisms, or other family celebrations. Their goal is to ensure the welfare of the child that one of the *compadres* has baptized or confirmed. The best man at the wedding becomes a *compadre*. *Compadrazgo* has a very positive role to play. The *compadres* act "manly" toward one

163

another, and the children of the *compadres* learn male behavior through those interactions.

Still, it's not just the males that are in charge of shaping the macho image. Women play an important role.

The Woman Creates the Macho

Talking about being macho also means talking about the role of women in our lives. In a traditional setting, the Mexican mother raises the male child and has a great influence on the learned macho behavior of the child. We learn a lot about the sexual behavior from the males of the clan, but the mother, if she does the raising of the male child, is a most crucial ingredient in the evolving macho role.

Food, warmth, protection, the first sounds, and all that has to do with the tactile sense of the first years on earth are provided by the mother. In our culture the mother is the first confidante of the male child. If the Catholic Church says, Give me the child for indoctrination for the first six years of life and I will mold a lifelong Catholic, the mother has already imprinted her femininity on the child and the child's response to that feminine aura in the womb. No wonder mothers exclaim at birth, "I have created."

In her novel, *Face of an Angel*, Denise Chavez explores the role of women in the formation of macho. By exploring the lives of women in the culture, she gives us an excellent, uninhibited view of the woman's influence on the life of the male. Other Chicanas are also doing this in their writings. Ana Castillo in her essay on machismo (in *Massacre of the Dreamers: Essays on Xicanisma*, University of New Mexico Press, 1994) has much to tell us of the history of the macho image. We need to listen to the ideas of such writers as the role of the macho is transformed. By us, by them.

Oedipal complexes and fears aside, we are our mother's creation, and so early macho behavior will be shaped actively and by nuance by the mother. Perhaps this is what we recognize when we attribute great value to the family. A mother who is active in shaping the maleness of her child will produce a more integrated man; if the mother is not there or if her behavior has been conditioned by an oppressive patriarchy, a more dysfunctional child will emerge. (This role of the woman who has historically been controlled by the demands of a male-oriented society has been amply analyzed by Castillo.)

Chicano males brought up in a positive atmosphere do not hesitate to say they love their mothers. Embracing (*el abrazo*) is as common for the mother as for the father. A continuing relationship with the mother as a guide who provides warmth, love, strength, and direction is integral to the culture. Our community did not traditionally initiate a cut-off age when the young male had to leave the household, i.e., leave his mother's side. Both father and mother remain confidantes—thus a description of the closeness of the family. Only recently, as we copy Anglo-American behavior, and as the status of the culture has changed from rural to urban, do some Chicanos begin to practice readying the child to be completely independent.

As we grow we begin to leave the mother's side. I learned about the male's role in the family and society from my father and his *compadres*, men who worked and drank with him. And I was fortunate to have three brothers who were around long enough in my adolescent years to allow me to learn from them. I learned from my boyhood friends. Playing together we created and acted out the mythology of boyhood. Sexuality played an important part in those years of definition.

We learn not only how to talk, act, respond, and think like men from the intimate clan of males in which we are raised, we also learn an attitude toward life. We learn that intangible which lies beneath behavior. Part of that essence is how we carry ourselves as men, the dignity and honor we exude. Men who don't have this dignity are *sinvergüenzas*, men without shame. They have a tough time holding their heads high, a tough time being macho. We learn to carry ourselves as men in our families, in the community, and in respect to women and men. And because we are members of a different cultural group living within the boundary of Anglo America, we learn to carry ourselves in respect to the Other, in this case, other white males.

Myth and Macho: La Llorona

There are deeper currents to wade in when we speak of our maleness. For me, myths and their inherent messages are integral to a definition of our humanity. Myth and legend shine in our folklore; folklore is a reflection of myth when there is no written text. The stories of the people also define our maleness. Let me propose a few areas of interest that don't have their history in a Eurocentric past. For example, let's look at one of our most persistent legends, which I believe also describes the macho image.

Part of the underpinning of our worldview, our values, is indigenous. The indigenous myths are part of our inheritance, working most often quietly in the cells, in memory, in dreams, and appearing as stories in the folklore. Our male relationship to the female can be better understood if we understand such pervasive legends as that of *La Llorona*. Every Chicano I know has heard of *La Llorona*. Some have actual experiences of the wailing woman, i.e., they claim to have met her. (Who knows how many times we have met her in our dreams and our *pesadillas*, but contemporary psychologists have not been trained to listen to our mythology. They have not paid attention to that body of work and therefore lack interpretations intimately useful to us.)

Briefly, *La Llorona* is a young woman who is taken advantage of by a man. She has a child (generally out of wedlock) by the man. But the man does not stay home; he goes off seeking a new adventure (and usually a new woman). The young mother goes insane, or into a jealous rage. To get revenge on the man who has jilted her, she kills the child (or children) and throws the body in the river, into a pond or lake. She is returning the flesh to the primordial water, the ooze of primal creation.

This is not so much the replaying of the Medea tragedy. It has closer kinship in myth to the pre-Greek, Mediterranean world. When the Egyptian Osiris is killed by his brother, it is Isis, Osiris's sister, who wanders along the Nile, collecting the pieces of the dismembered body to "reconstitute" Osiris. (She symbolically gives birth to her brother, i.e., the virgin has delivered the male child who will be God.)

La Llorona of our legend also seeks the pieces of the (male) child she has murdered. Or sacrificed? To date, the legend has been too narrowly analyzed. Has *La Llorona* really sacrificed the child to re-create him in the waters of the river (the earth womb) and thus raise him symbolically to the status of God? Perhaps *La Llorona* realizes the child has to die to be reborn a better male. That is, the consciousness of the child has to be reshaped to fit the time. Consciousness is evolving, and in this case the mother (*La Llorona*) is a key player in that new consciousness. Put another way, *La Llorona* is creating a new humanity.

Another interpretation would question if it is *La Llorona* who really kills the child. In the Osiris myth, Osiris is killed by his brother, a male. It seems to me that feminist Chicana critics need to dig deeper into this paradigm. In my novel *Zia Summer*, my main character, Sonny Baca, a thirty-year-old understanding his maleness (and his cultural identity) more and more, is told the story of *La Llorona* by his grandmother. In the grandmother's story it is a man who kills *La Llorona*'s child.

What if it *is* the man who kills *La Llorona*'s child, a child she would raise to a new consciousness, thus defeating the father's old macho ways? The woman has the power to create the new male, not Nietzsche's Superman, but a child more closely aligned to the feminine sensibility, which is the mother's inheritance. The man kills the male child not because he fears an Oedipal ending (after all, in the legend the father is going off searching after a new woman), but because he fears the status quo and his macho role in it will be supplanted by the son.

Therein lies new hope. We can constantly re-create the child, raise the child in a new way, so the macho image of yesterday need not be a prison to us, especially its dysfunctional aspects. *La Llorona* knows this, and so like Isis she searches along the river's bank, the lake, the sacred springs of myth in search of the pieces of the child she can bring back to life. What incredible power lies in this woman of legend that we have dismissed as a bogey woman of the river. We've used her to frighten children, when we should be using her to raise them—the new children of a new era who understand that each one carries the hope of the future.

Children, both male and female, can put aside old, destructive ways of behavior and define maleness in a new way. *La Llorona*, the mother of the sacred lake, can play a role in describing the new macho. (The lake image represents the unconscious, that creative energy from whence rise new images.) In our time, the greatest change taking place in the macho image and its behavior is the influence of a new generation of liberated Chicanas. Their cry is not a cry of despair, but voices insisting that they are taking a greater role in defining male/female relationships, and so they *are* redefining macho. These contemporary *Lloronas* can be liberating mothers creating new concepts and behaviors by which to live. Or they can be shortsighted and engage in old gender accusations that don't move us toward the definition of a new paradigm. A lot rides on their thoughts, their stories, their actions.

So, *La Llorona* has pre-Greek, Egyptian, Semitic roots. Roots in ancient civilizations. Blame men, the pillars of the morality of the community, if she has been given a bad rap. Blame ourselves if we do not reinterpret the old myths and give them new meaning for our violent time. There's hope in new interpretations, a hope that will bring new understanding to our roles as men and women. We don't have to be stuck with old stereotypic roles of behavior that define dysfunctional machos.

La Virgen

La Virgen de Guadalupe is another mother figure. She is the Aztec goddess Tonantzin, the indigenous New World answer to the goddess religions that were destroyed during the Neolithic Age around the fringes of the Mediterranean world. *La Virgen de Guadalupe* exists because Quetzalcóatl (the monotheistic feathered-serpent god who can fly and is of heavens) could not erase the goddess worship in indigenous America. Perhaps the cult of Quetzalcóatl chose not to erase the goddess cult, after all, Quetzalcóatl was not like the Yahweh of the Old Testament. He was not a thundering god of vengeance, he was a god of the fields and civilization.

Quetzalcóatl and the cult of goddess worship went hand in hand. But Quetzalcóatl flew too high. One reason for his banishment is that he mated with his "sister," a heavenly sister of the starry skies. The feathered energy of his nature drew him toward the heavens, and thus separated him from the earth energy, the intuitive energy wound up in procreation and nurturing. He should have mated with the Earth goddess and thus preserved his serpent earth energy and procreative powers. Or at least he should have kept the energy of these polarities in balance, in harmony, able to wed the intuitive with the rational, the earth-creative with the aspirations to the spiritual. In a sense, Quetzalcóatl deserted the fields, the earth, and his people, and as such, except for the words of a few Chicano writers and poets, he passed out of our consciousness. In Mesoamerica he was easily replaced by the Catholic Cristo. But not the earth goddess Tonantzin. She lives on in *La Virgen de Guadalupe*.

Quetzalcóatl was banished. He traveled east to be absorbed into flames, into Venus as the morning star, into the sunlight of dawn. Tonantzin, the earth goddess, did not flee, nor was she banished from the hearts of her people. The Spanish

167

friars knew they could not destroy the adoration of the goddess. The ties to the earth were too deep in the ancient Mexicans. The church could stamp out Quetzalcóatl (after all, the god had already forsaken his people just before the arrival of the Europeans), and so Cristo did not have the competition of a strong, indigenous male god. But the natives would not let go of the goddess of the earth. She is incorporated into the pantheon of the Catholic Church as *La Virgen de Guadalupe*. The smartest move the Church ever made in the Americas was not to fight this syncretic impulse.

The female goddess was imprinted in the psyche of the people of the Americas. The goddess created, nurtured, provided. She is seen in corn, the sustenance of much of the New World. She spoke to the god of rain on behalf of the farmers. All attributes of *La Virgen*. And so the female (anima) of the human psyche remains represented as an active force in our lives. Take whatever route you like to the past, you will discover the prototypes of *La Virgen*. Her role remains the feminine sensibility with which we identify. For the male she is a living presence of the anima within, the female within.

Is being macho *only* learned behavior? Well, mostly, but what of this stream of myth? What part of this inheritance describes the history of our blood? What whispers do we hear from the collective memory, and how can it describe a new way of being macho? Perhaps the old macho image has to die when it does not engender the community. The essence of maleness doesn't have to die, it merely has to be understood and created anew. To re-create is evolution's role. We can take an active role in it, but to do so we have to know the history of false behavioral conditioning.

Nature dictates much. The chemicals, hormones, and elements in the blood and in the psyche are elements she needs for the job of procreation of the species. But she also provides a fantastic interplay of forces within the essence of the human, within the soul. The soul exists as a motivating, energizing force within. We can transform ourselves, and in that transcendent encounter, or epiphany, we become more than the humans whose feet are bogged down in the mud.

To do that we need to pay full attention to the forces within. We are not all male at any given time, nor are we all female. We need to find balance and give harmony to the deep currents of our nature. Macho need not be all male, *puro hombre*. Nothing is pure one thing or the other, especially when we speak of human nature. The old dictates of the fathers have to be transformed to create a new macho, and for that we need to listen to the feminine sensibility. To listen within.

Section 3C

Our World—
The Environment

Albuquerque Learns It Really Is a Desert Town

BRUCE SELCRAIG

For about as long as anyone can remember the good citizens of Albuquerque have been living a fantasy when it comes to water. Despite receiving only eight inches of rain a year, residents have grown up washing their cars in the street, playing golf on lush coastal grass and using some 250 gallons of water per person per day—nearly twice as much as folks in Phoenix or Tucson.

Yet, even in hindsight it's hard to blame them. Collectively, this high desert town of nearly 500,000, which gets its entire water supply from an aquifer, was led to believe by public officials that it sat atop an underground Lake Superior.

The aquifer allowed Albuquerque to provide its citizens with some of the cheapest water in urban America—over 60 percent less than what Santa Feans pay. Better still, not only was the aquifer enormous, so the conventional wisdom went, but it was perpetually replenished underground by the Rio Grande.

"Albuquerque behaved as it understood the commodity," Mayor Martin Chavez says in defense of his town's water ethic. "If you think you have an infinite resource, using all you want is not wasteful."

Civic boosters in pursuit of boundless growth delighted in the Duke City's good fortune. Housing permits were handed out like balloons at a bank, and new business was lured with the promise that water would never be a problem. Sure, there were warnings as far back as the early 1950s that alternative sources of water must be found, but there were always experts willing to sound more optimistic, and, besides, the realists couldn't be heard for all the bulldozers.

No less an expert than Steve Reynolds, the former (and now deceased) New Mexico state engineer for over 30 years, wrote in the *Albuquerque Tribune* in 1980 that the city could, comfortably, grow to a population of 1.5 million. "Albuquerque is probably better situated with respect to water," Reynolds said then, "than any large city in the Southwest."

171

If Reynolds were around today some citizens might like to serve his misguided words to him fajita-style.

Albuquerque's long-overdue wake-up call came in August 1993 when the U.S. Geological Survey released a report showing that Albuquerque was pumping out its groundwater nearly three times faster than it could be replenished.

Tests showed the underground water basin had dropped by as much as 40 feet between 1989 and 1992 and nearly 140 feet in some places over the past three decades. More important, the report shot down once and for all the notion that Albuquerque had a limitless source of water.

The Rio Grande, according to the USGS report, was not replenishing (or recharging) the city's aquifer at anything approaching a steady state. In 1993 the Albuquerque area pumped about 160,000 acre-feet of water from the aquifer, while the aquifer is being replenished by rainfall and mountain snowmelt at close to 65,000 acre-feet a year.

The landmark USGS report set into motion a predictable, but nonetheless fascinating, political dance:

The city's water experts said there was no immediate crisis, just a need for concern, and more definitive studies; the city council approved higher water rates and a voluntary conservation program; business leaders promised cooperation, but told everyone how little water their businesses used compared to homeowners; community activists predicted that conservation measures would fall hardest upon those least able to afford them; and, from a distance, a few sages surveyed the tumult and said, "We told you so."

"Albuquerque has been told for 20-plus years an approximate limit of its resource," says Tony Mayne, executive director of the Santa Fe Metropolitan Water Board. "And they have simply refused to believe it. They would have you believe the USGS told them one thing 20 years ago and a different thing last year. It ain't so. It just ain't so."

Suburbs spoke up for their water interests as did everyone from Indian pueblo leaders to car wash owners. There was some civic introspection about the city-sanctioned urban sprawl of the '80s and some wonderment that a desert town could not have had a water conservation program in place, but a great deal of the public reaction to the water "wake-up call" of 1993 focused on one very large company and its enormous thirst.

Chips in the Desert

On a mesa just northwest of Albuquerque sits a 200-acre complex of massive, square, beige-and-chocolate-colored buildings beneath a flock of gangly construction cranes. Grunting earthmovers and cement trucks plow up the mesa, as visitors churn through the temporary parking looking for office buildings named Jurassic Park and Godzilla.

Surrounding this futuristic compound is an almost perfect demographic portrait of changing New Mexico: on one side an evangelical church, cookie-cutter suburban homes, fast food outlets and shopping malls; on the other, beside the tranquil Rio Grande, a stylish bed-and-breakfast adobe mingles with horse stables, vineyards and old Impalas on cinder blocks. New immigrants from Dallas and Chicago walk their dogs past the few remaining vacant lots of sage and cholla that defiantly remind everyone they're still in the desert.

This is Intel, New Mexico.

When the world's largest independent maker of computer chips, the Intel Corporation of Santa Clara, California, came to this mesa in suburban Rio Rancho in 1980, the giant had but two dozen employees and gave hardly a clue that it would one day wield great influence in the Land of Enchantment.

Intel now employs 4,000 people in Rio Rancho, plans to hire at least another 500 next year and says it creates at least two spin-off jobs in the surrounding economy for every one inside the sprawling plant. Average plant salaries are $35,000—more than double the per capita income in New Mexico, the fifth poorest state. All of which made Rio Rancho the nation's fastest growing small city in 1993.

By far the state's largest private employer at one site—Wal-Mart ranks number 1 otherwise—Intel is a powerful constituency unto itself, rivaling most neighborhood groups or labor unions and crossing all racial, religious and political lines. New Mexico politicians would be certified fools to threaten those paychecks, and so, what Intel wants, Intel usually gets.

When Intel announced in 1993 that it wanted to build a new U.S. plant to make the new Pentium and next-generation P6 chips, New Mexico officials, longing to diversify from natural resource extraction and government jobs, unveiled the most lucrative come-hither campaign the state had ever seen. Their reward was Intel's $1.8 billion Fab 11, a project that would become the third largest industrial expansion in the world that year.

Beating Texas, California, Oregon, Arizona and Utah for Intel's affections, New Mexico laid out $57 million in property tax abatement, $36 million in waived new-equipment sales taxes and $20 million in manufacturing tax credits. Taxpayers would foot $1 million for training Intel workers, air pollution permitting would be streamlined and Sandoval County, in addition to floating a $2 billion bond issue for Intel, granted the chipmaker a lease on its mesa property you would have loved back in college: Intel may grant easements and build or raze improvements at will. It may sublease without the county's approval and it has the option to buy the Rio Rancho site for $1 at the end of the lease term.

An underlying assumption throughout this corporate courting process was that the Albuquerque area could provide all the water Intel could ever want. This is no small concern because Intel and all semiconductor companies freely admit they are, by the nature of their technology, world-class water hogs.

The six- and eight-inch-diameter silicon wafers Intel makes—they're later cut by diamond saws to yield the thumbnail-size chips that serve as the brains in personal computers—must be rinsed at least 20 times in hyper-clean water to remove impurities. Exactly how much water is used in these processes is something no company will divulge, but industry expert Graydon Larrabee, a former Texas Instruments fellow, says that among six companies he surveyed, an average of 2,840 gallons was used to produce one six-inch wafer and perhaps twice that for an eight-inch. If Intel's new chip factory makes about 30,000 eight-inch wafers a month, which Larrabee says is standard, the amount of water used could reach 6 million gallons a day. (For comparison, the daily use of a really gluttonous golf course is about 1 million gallons. Intel says it returns 85 percent of this water to the Rio Grande through Albuquerque's treatment plants; however, that water never makes it back to the aquifer.)

In April 1993—five months before the alarming USGS report—Intel applied to the New Mexico state engineer, who decides water allocation issues, for a new water-use permit that would allow it to use 4,500 acre-feet of water a year, or about 4 million gallons a day. An acre-foot is the amount of water it takes to cover an acre to a depth of one foot, or about 326,000 gallons. In addition to Intel's pumped water allotment, it would continue to use about 3.5 million gallons a day from Rio Rancho Utilities, which also pumps from the aquifer.

Intel's water request, arriving almost simultaneously with the aquifer alarm, quickly struck a nerve.

In the neighboring village of Corrales, just beneath the mesa on which Intel sits, residents had already complained of foul chemical emissions from Intel which they said caused skin rashes, nausea and headaches. (Intel installed $11 million worth of oxidizers to remove the odor.) Now the Corrales citizens, fearing that Intel's request for three new deep-water wells might affect their own shallower wells and the stately cottonwoods along the Rio Grande, joined with the Sierra Club, the New Mexico Environmental Law Center and others in formally opposing the Intel water request.

"Just a few feet of draw-down would put a lot of people's wells out of business," said village board member Lawrence Vigil. Tim Kraft, once Jimmy Carter's appointments secretary, and now a Corrales resident, said at a town meeting: "We've rolled out the red carpet, and now we're finding out our guest has bad breath and an unquenchable thirst."

Intel hydrologists say a solid layer of underground rock separates its 2,000-foot wells from the 200-foot wells of many Corrales residents, and so should not affect their flow.

The Debate Begins

In June 1994, after a year of study and a four-week hearing, State Engineer Eluid Martinez granted Intel 72 percent of its water application, but required Intel to drill monitoring wells to ensure that its pumping would not affect wells in Corrales. The Intel request became a catalyst for what Albuquerque had avoided for decades— serious discussion of water problems.

"The Intel application raised a debate about what's good for the state," Martinez later told reporters. "It was a lot of water, but not more than would be used to irrigate 2,000 acres of farmland. Drying up a golf course or two would make that water available."

Doug Wolf, attorney for the New Mexico Environmental Law Center, is not nearly so sanguine about the Intel deal. "There's a real question," says Wolf, "about whether this is the right kind of industry for an arid state that's looking to the future."

Says Wolf: "Intel argues that because it provides so many jobs they should get whatever they want. The logical extreme of that is that water should go to big business, tourism, golf courses and exclusive, gated communities which destroy what we care so much about in New Mexico and will homogenize us into Scottsdale or some kind of industrial center like Baton Rouge."

Wolf's colleague, water policy analyst Consuelo Bokum, points out that New Mexico water law requires the state engineer to consider "the public welfare" in allocating water—as does Alaska's and others—but that the standard is rarely applied and remains largely undefined by the courts. The state engineer "punted" on the issue of public welfare, Wolf says, by simply assuming that any use of water that wasn't a clear waste was beneficial.

"If ever there was an argument for taking the public welfare into account," Bokum says, "it's in Albuquerque. The highest and best use of water has historically been defined as who has the most money, and anyone else be damned."

Squeaky Clean

"Watch your head," shouts Intel's Richard Draper as he leads me under the scalp-high, finger-thick metal tubes that course for 44 miles through the windowless bowels of Intel.

We're striding briskly past boilers and air scrubbers on a classic dog-and-pony plant tour where the company P.R. man could tell the clueless reporter everything is run by gerbils on treadmills and he would be none the wiser.

Intel is a bit overwhelming for those who don't speak in gigabytes—a palace of science akin to the innards of a nuclear submarine, only much taller and wider and cleaner.

We peer through two narrow, vertical windows in the doors of a "clean" room, where workers in white, air-filtered, Gore-Tex "bunny" suits control the robots that imprint the wafers with millions of electronic circuits. How clean, you ask, is a "clean" room? Well, no particle in the air can be larger than one micron. The width of a human hair is roughly 75 microns. Intel likes to say the rooms are 10,000 times cleaner than a hospital emergency room.

"I'm still pretty awed by what goes on in there," Draper says. "It's pretty 2001 stuff."

While Intel hardly needs anyone's sympathy—Rio Rancho did half of Intel's $8.7 billion gross in 1993, and Intel plans to build similar factories every year for the next six—it's not hard to see why the giant chipmeister feels unfairly picked upon by some in Albuquerque. Like 'em or not, Intel has never hidden the fact that it uses enormous amounts of water. Knowing that, New Mexico politicians tripped over themselves to offer Intel tax breaks and never expressed doubts about the water supply. Yet, through unfortunate timing with the USGS report, Intel—rather than dairy farmers and golf courses—became the convenient whipping boy.

"The blame game kicks in early in the conservation debate," Draper tells me back in his gray-carpeted cubicle office. "You've got to put in perspective how much water we really use. Industries use only 3 percent of Albuquerque's water. Add Intel (which is not on Albuquerque's water system) and it's 6 percent. After our expansion it's 8 percent. Residential users make up 60 to 65 percent. We could stop pumping tomorrow and it would be a blip on the screen." Draper doesn't mention that Intel's presence has also created thousands of new water users and new demands on sewers, roads, schools and such.

Draper says Intel has spent $260 million on environmental safeguards at the Rio Rancho plant since the early 1980s and has contracted with New Mexico's Sandia and Los Alamos Department of Energy labs to improve its water conservation technology. Having been an Albuquerque TV reporter before coming to Intel, Draper wasn't surprised by some of the local anti-Intel attacks.

"Our expansion came at a time of debate about growth in New Mexico," he says. "We've had a rockier road in the last year than we would like. I think New Mexico is more complex than [Intel's leaders] thought. This isn't California or Arizona. There are different cultural and economic issues here."

That much is certain.

"No gracias Intel"

At a New Mexican restaurant in Albuquerque's downtown neighborhood, Jeanne Gauna, director of the South West Organizing Project (SWOP), heads for a back table and starts throwing punches at Intel before the chips and salsa can arrive. "How could they have not known about the water problems?" Gauna laughs. "All they know is chips, right? Come on, they're exploiting a poor state. That's such bullshit."

SWOP is a 13-year-old community group that has hounded Intel on chemical emissions, hiring practices and tax breaks, not to mention water. SWOP released a 60-page report on Intel's activities that suggests New Mexico's incentive package might cost taxpayers over $140 million more than expected, questions Intel's commitment to hiring New Mexicans and portrays the semi-conductor industry as one that fouls the environment, exposes workers needlessly to dangerous chemicals and breaks promises to communities. Composed of veteran activists, SWOP also crashed an Intel party at a local hotel by unfurling a 30-foot banner that read: "No gracias Intel—Super Profits, Super Toxic Pollution—Real New Mexicans Pay Taxes!"

One might think that however tempting a target Intel presents, Gauna would tread lightly on the giant because it still holds out the hope of doubling her constituents' income. But, based on recent reports that suggest Intel has always planned to rely heavily on out-of-state workers brought to Rio Rancho, Gauna has never let up.

"I'm absolutely certain," says the 48-year-old grandmother with the fiery Basque eyes, "that Intel will never be a good deal for Albuquerque. We're not anti-development or anti-growth, but Intel has yet to prove that we will benefit when almost half of the jobs are going to people from out of state. The taxpayers have underwritten their entire development, yet our communities aren't prospering."

But if not Intel, who? Ten different ways I ask Gauna if Intel is so bad, what kind of industry and which company of Intel's size would be better.

She dodges, she weaves, she trots out the line about how New Mexico should grow chilies, not (computer) chips, but suggesting a real alternative proves difficult.

"If they would pay their taxes and pay for all the infrastructure," Gauna says, "just about any industry could come in, but we should not have to pay for their profits. Intel is not sustainable growth. Their industry is famous for boom-and-bust cycles. There's no guarantee those jobs we paid so dearly for will even be there in 10 or 20 years."

Fine points, but how *should* New Mexico grow out of its dependence upon government, the military and exploiting the land? As long as states will grovel for any corporate prize it will be hard for New Mexico to turn down companies that promise thousands of jobs and at least the hope of environmental stewardship.

For the Lords of Sprawl, however, it is a laughable debate. For them, attracting and keeping Intel has been the state's greatest economic achievement in years, and they welcome all the new homes, roads, malls and fast food emporia without a second thought. They see water conservation as a worthy topic for junior high school science posters, but never as a limit to growth and profits.

Albuquerque Mayor Martin Chavez can't afford to think that way. "If we don't act now about the water problem," Chavez told me, "we will have a crisis for which our grandchildren will condemn us." Chavez says he has already rejected the overtures of a California firm that wanted to relocate in Albuquerque but wanted a guarantee of 1 million gallons of water a day.

"Three years ago Albuquerque would've been shining their shoes," Chavez says, "but their attitude wasn't one of conservation, so we basically just said, no thanks."

Chavez now heads into a city-wide water education and conservation program designed to cut water use by 30 percent in 10 years. He's already pushed through an increase to monthly water bills and is preaching the new gospel to golf courses and gardeners alike. The city is also looking into injecting treated water back into the aquifer to replenish it, as some other cities do.

177

If Chavez is smart, say conservationists, he'll seize this historic opportunity to play the role of Head Water Miser to the hilt. Maybe he should walk the town handing out low-flow shower heads. People are willing to conserve if they see it as an equitable, community-wide effort; and Albuquerqueños, especially, know they must change their wasteful ways. But if they see water hogs being lured to the desert, they will know that politics and money still control their future—and Chavez will have squandered his chance.

Are Today's Kids
Detached from Nature?

RICHARD LOUV

Last spring a friend and I went for a walk through the neighborhoods surrounding Swarthmore, Pennsylvania. We passed through a wooded area and crossed a little creek, stepping across large, flat stones. The trees in this damp countryside were still budding. I asked my friend if his son ever came down to these woods. "No, never," he said. "He's just not interested. He's interested in baseball and organized sports. I don't know if any of his friends come down here either."

I thought about this on the way home, wondering how much of people's adult relationship with nature has something to do with their childhood fantasies. As a child, I brought cowboys and Indians and Davey Crockett and war to the woods. They were pre-packaged fantasies, and often violent, but most of them did bring human beings to nature, and served as doorways into unpackaged mysteries. Sometimes, at age eight or nine or ten, I would be in the woods alone with my BB gun, intent on shooting something, and I would end up sitting beneath a tree or next to the creek, touching my finger to my tongue and wetting my nostrils so that I might be able to smell better, listening, breathing, watching for the small critters to re-emerge, the frogs' eyes to pop up once again above the water. How many children of the 1950s and before became environmentalists or otherwise deeply concerned with the fate of nature in this way? Walking silently with my friend, I wondered how the current generation of children will relate to nature in the future: What fantasies will they bring to it: what doorways will it open for them?

I had spent the last two years traveling the country, talking with and listening to parents, children, and, on occasion, experts.

What emerged from these conversations was often stunning, sometimes terrifying, and ultimately hopeful. Parents and children described a physical environment that no longer makes sense—a divorce from nature, sprawling cities

179

with no centers and few natural meeting places, residential areas that can barely be called neighborhoods—an environment that no longer nurtures children, and that drives family life deeper into itself.

The relationship between children and nature today is a puzzling one. On one hand, children's sophistication about global environmental issues is very high—and intensely felt. On the other hand, they have much less physical and unstructured contact with nature than my generation did.

In the early 1980s, an advertisement began to appear in national magazines, depicting[1] a little boy silhouetted against a cabin window, tapping at a computer terminal. Beyond the glass, trees could be seen, and a sailboat moved lazily across a pond. In Southern California, Girl Scouts can now attend a "High-Tech Computer Whiz" camp—with $50,000 worth of terminals and software. Could it be that computers are viewed as more important to a child's life than access to nature?

With the steady disappearance of farmland and woods and streams and fields adjacent to housing, the increasing programming of children's time, and the evolving high-tech fantasies and obsessions of the nation's culture, nature—for children and adults—is becoming something to wear, to watch, to consume. We sport Irresistible Sea Otter T-shirts and view "natural mood" videos (electronic images of streams flowing, to relax and distract us), while the forests are cut, the sea is despoiled, and hilltops are decapitated to make room for more malls.

Parents speak often, and sometimes defensively, of this strange divorce between children and the outdoors. At a parent meeting in San Diego a woman said, "It's all this *watching*. We've become a more sedentary[2] society as a whole. I see ads for toys, VCRs, videos: all these machines that kids just sit there and watch. When I was a kid growing up in Detroit, we were always outdoors. The kids who were indoors were always the odd ones. We didn't have any wide-open spaces, but we were outdoors on the streets, in the vacant lots, playing baseball, hopscotch. We were out there playing even after we got older."

I would have suspected, before my interviews in Kansas, that children there would still be playing in the woods and along the streams. But the middle-class parents of Overland Park, a Kansas City suburb, viewed such activities as a vanishing part of childhood.

"The only time the kids associate with nature is when it's a science project," said one mother. "They had an assignment in the seventh grade—every morning at a certain time they had to go away from the house, somewhere they could be alone with nature and write things down. And that's the only time that they really would venture off on their own to do something like that—because it was an assignment."

"No, they're not interested," another mother said. "When the kids go skiing down a beautiful mountain on a perfect, quiet day, they've got their headphones on. They can't enjoy hearing nature and being out there alone. They can't make their own entertainment. They have to bring something with them."

She added, "Of course, we discourage them from going in the woods alone. But we're trying as a family to encourage our kids to love nature. We take them camping, we try to get them to go on bike rides and walks. We even pitch the tent in the basement in the winter when it's too cold to pack or go outside."

One of the mothers was perplexed. "I don't really know what you mean," she said. "I think that my girls enjoy a full moon, a pretty sunset, and flowers. They enjoy the trees when they turn. That sort of thing. I don't know what else you mean."

I clarified the question: What I meant was being engaged with nature—free, with time to connect with it, time to bring some fantasies to nature.

"What you're talking about is something that's totally different today," said Jack, who was raised in a farming community. "Where I grew up, no matter which direction you went, you were outdoors—it was a plowed field or woods or streets. You couldn't walk a quarter mile without getting into something like that. We're not like that here. Overland Park is a metropolitan area now." The kids don't see that type of thing around here as much. They see houses being built."

The group was quiet for a moment. I was incredulous[3] at this description of the use of the surrounding countryside in Overland Park. Yes, much of the farmland and woods were being graded and built upon; yet one could see the woods from the windows of the house in which we were sitting. They were still there. Something other than a lack of access was keeping their children away from nature.

"Our kids and the neighborhood kids rush into the house, and they head straight for the video games," said one of the fathers in Overland Park. "It's almost like the house with the most kids in it is the house with the best Nintendo cartridges." Another mother added, "We can't get some of our kids' friends to come to our house because we only have kids to play with."

All these screens in children's lives can reverse the very polarity of childhood reality. One fourth-grader told me, "I like to play indoors better 'cause there's where all the electrical outlets are."

When I asked the gifted students, third- to sixth-graders, in the class at San Diego's Dewey Elementary—children who spoke at length of their relationship to computers—how many would rather be outside with nature instead of working on their computers, 12 of the 40 raised their hands. One pragmatic girl said that it all depended on the weather. "It's kind of a toss-up. But a computer will always be there as opposed to the good weather."

While children do seem to be spending less time physically in natural surroundings, they also seem to worry more about the disappearance of nature—in a global sense—than my generation did. At Kenwood Elementary in Miami, most of the fourth-graders in one class said that they would rather play in the house or on the street. I asked them if they thought that kids would play in the woods or in the fields in the future. One boy, who had said earlier that his ambition was to be an astronaut, offered: "Maybe, but not if the city keeps making these new ventures, making new buildings and tearing down all the wilderness."

I shifted the subject: You kids are going to be in charge of the environment in the future. What do you think could be done?

"If I was in charge, in one part you would have city and the other part of it would be forest, and you couldn't pollute it and if you do, you would get punished. You could live in the forest too, but you wouldn't be allowed to pollute."

"If people pull down nature, if they pull down all the trees to put up buildings, how are they going to make their living if they can't use the trees to build their furniture?"

These comments, it seemed to me, expressed some surprisingly sophisticated environmental concepts. As a boy, I was intimate with the fields and the woods behind my house, and protective of them. Yet, unlike these children, I had no sense of any ecological degradation beyond my small natural universe. Children today may be less intimately involved with nature than many of us were, but they exhibit far more global environmental awareness. Ironically, the electronic world that disrupts intimacy with nature has also been used to communicate nature's distress to these children.

One of my journey's last Midwestern stops was at Southwood Elementary in Raytown, Missouri, near Kansas City. This had been my elementary school. As the teachers herded the children in from several classrooms, second through fifth grade, I unpacked my tape recorder and glanced at the ridge of blue-green elms moving slowly in the spring breeze. How often I had dreamed of those trees . . .

I turned to the children and felt suddenly that they might have been friends from my own childhood. There were fewer slogans on the T-shirts than I remembered seeing in other schools. Many of the girls in this class wore cotton print dresses. Perhaps this sense of continuity had to do with the geography of Raytown, which still exists on the edge of farmland and woods. Developers apparently lost their interest in it and moved west, on to Johnson County and Overland Park. Whatever the reason, the school and these children seemed suspended in time.

I began by telling them that I had gone to this school, that I had lived on Ralston Street, that there had been a big woods behind my house, and that the woods were all gone now. Replaced by a housing tract—in which some of these children might now live.

I told them I wanted to know how kids felt about nature. I asked: How many kids here spend a lot of time in woods and fields? Almost all of them raised their hands. I was astonished. This was the opposite of the response in every other classroom that I had visited around the country.

"Let me ask you a specific question," I said. "When you go out into the woods and fields, what are the fantasies—the images—in your mind? What do you think about, who do you pretend to be?"

The answers came quickly. Many of them were connected to science.

"I'm some famous mad scientist out looking for some frogs or something to stick in a new chemical to make the world explode or something."

"I feel like I'm a scientist and I'm looking for cures for diseases. And like I'm finding some secret passages."

"What I imagine whenever I go in the woods and go look for stuff is I'm one of the world's great explorers and I'm exploring something else. I'm trying to look for something."

The fantasies these children took into the woods are more indirect than mine were. Rather than being associated with the cowboys, Indians, and frontiersmen of my boyhood, these fantasies were more likely to involve technology, space, and—particularly for the girls in this class—family issues.

"Well, when I'm in the woods, I play like it's just a home. I just go back to the woods and with all the trees gathered together, and some of the trees split, it sort of looks like a home."

One fifth-grader was wearing a plain print dress and an intensely serious expression. She later told me that she wanted to be a poet when she grew up. She said, "When I'm in the woods, I feel like I'm in my mother's shoes."

In addition to the sense of freedom and fantasy, access to nature also gives children a sense of privacy, a place separate from the adult world, older than the adult world:

"Whenever I'm out in the woods, it feels like that's where I should go, like it's your home, and you can do anything you want to because there's not anyone bothering you. You have the woods to yourself ."

The young poet said, "For me it's completely different there. It's more peaceful and it's like you're free when you go out there, it's your own time. When you go back in the woods, it's like if your brain's empty, you got everything back there. Sometimes, I go there when I'm mad and then just with the peacefulness I'm better. I can walk back and be happy and my mom doesn't even know why."

I asked them how their parents felt about their being in the woods. Several of the kids said their parents didn't want them going out there because of fear of strangers.

"My parents are always worrying about me. I don't know why. And I'll just go and usually I don't tell 'em where I'm going so that makes 'em mad so usually I go without them knowing 'cause I just want to go freely. I'll sit behind the tree or something, or lay in the field with all the rabbits."

Finally, I asked if any of them had had a favorite woods or favorite field replaced by a housing development.

"We had a field," said a boy. "They were going to tear it down, so we had this meeting, and we sat in this real tall grass where nobody could see us and we all discussed what we were going to do. We said we wouldn't let 'em. We moved our hideout to right on the edge of the field where they started to build and we started just sittin' there and sayin' to them that this was ours but they just said, 'Sorry kids, we already planned this out to make houses here so you're going to have to find someplace else.' That made us really mad."

It touched me deeply that these children still felt the way about the woods that I had, that this part of childhood was not lost for them, and that for others, perhaps it was only misplaced.

Listening to them, I remembered how, from third to sixth grade, I had pulled out hundreds of survey stakes—the wooden stakes with the bright orange flags attached to them. I knew what they were for. The year we moved out of that neighborhood, the woods were torn down and a new housing development went up.

I asked if any of them had ever pulled out a survey stake. More than 20 of them raised their hands. Enthusiastically. And I laughed.

I told the kids it was almost time to leave and began to ask another question, but one red-haired girl, who had not yet talked, began to wave her hand frantically.

"Behind Ralston Street!" she exclaimed. "There's still some woods back there!"

No, it was all torn down. I was sure of it.

"But some of it *is* still there, and there's a park back there. It's *your* woods!"

After the class, I found myself driving toward Ralston. I was sure that the kids and I were talking about different places. But, still, I drove back to my old neighborhood and looked for the woods.

The kids were right. There was a little park. But where most of my woods had been, now there were houses. According to a hand-made sign, the little park was called Cap Garvin Park. I got out of the rental car and walked the length of it. It was just a long field, located at the extreme end of where the woods had been. A few trees remained near the end of the field.

As I passed under one tree, I remembered walking in the snow there with my father, now dead. He had his old army coat on, and was holding an air pistol. We were looking for rabbits, and I saw a trail of ungraceful tracks across the snow through the trees.

Now this part of the field was covered with dandelions. In the branches of one of the old trees were the remnants of a treehouse built a long time ago.

The end of the park was marked off with barbed wire. Beyond the wire were more woods, as the schoolkids had said. I could barely see the old farmhouse hidden in the trees and brush. When I was a boy, an old horse had grazed near a swamp in those woods: I had to stand on a fence to mount him, and I'd ride wherever he chose to go.

From the fence on, the woods were dark and thick. Maybe the swamp was still down below where the dam had been broken out, where at dusk I had seen, in one of those blinding flashes, a great heron lift up on the air, lift up above the old barn, which stared with vacant windows out across the swamp.

No doubt the horse was gone, but maybe the swamp and the barn were still there. Maybe sometime a great heron sailed through the sky. Maybe that part of childhood still existed. If I had been a kid, I would have crossed the barbed wire and gone down there.

It was good to know that the best part of my childhood was still safe. I turned and walked back to the car, and as I passed the little sign, I thought: Here's to you, Cap Garvin, whoever you are.

Notes

1. Showing a picture of.
2. Inactive.
3. Unbelieving.

The Clan of
One-Breasted Women

TERRY TEMPEST WILLIAMS

Born (1955) in Corona, California, Terry Tempest Williams grew up in Utah, downwind of the federal government's nuclear weapons tests in Nevada. In a breach of fundamental American values, officials told residents that they were in no danger; years later, deaths from illnesses traceable to radiation numbered in the thousands. The experience shaped Williams' fundamental ambition: to celebrate and protect the environment as part of a community of friends and family. Refuge: An Unnatural History of Family and Place *(1992), Williams' most acclaimed book, is about the Great Salt Lake and the women in her family: Both suffered greatly because of environmental abuses. At the same time that she discovered ecosystem imbalances were causing the lake to rise, her mother was approaching death from ovarian cancer, which Williams believes was linked to radioactive fallout. Williams has authored many books that similarly contemplate the delicate balance of nature, such as* The Secret Language of Snow *(1984), a children's book that earned praise from* Scientific American *magazine;* Pieces of White Shell: A Journey to Navajo Land *(1984) about Native American traditions; and* An Unspoken Hunger: Stories from the Field *(1995) about anti-nuclear protesting, the African Serengeti Plain, and Utah's Great Basin. In* Leap *(2000), she explores the world of art and spirituality through Hieronymus Bosch's painting "The Garden of Earthly Delights";* Red: Passion and Patience in the Desert *(2001) is about America's Redrock Wilderness in southern Utah.*

"The Clan of One-Breasted Women," from Refuge, *portrays the women in Williams' family as stoic heroes in a battle they did not choose, but that is only the beginning. In a nightmarish sequence, her family drives through radioactive fallout from a nuclear explosion; later she witnesses*

the death of one female family member after another. Yet the nightmare turns into a myth of resistance, as she and other women join in antinuclear protests.

Epilogue

I belong to a Clan of One-Breasted Women. My mother, my grandmothers, and six aunts have all had mastectomies. Seven are dead. The two who survive have just completed rounds of chemotherapy and radiation.

I've had my own problems: two biopsies for breast cancer and a small tumor between my ribs diagnosed as a "borderline malignancy."

This is my family history.

Most statistics tell us breast cancer is genetic, hereditary, with rising percentages attached to fatty diets, childlessness, or becoming pregnant after thirty. What they don't say is living in Utah may be the greatest hazard of all.

We are a Mormon family with roots in Utah since 1847. The "word of wisdom" in my family aligned us with good foods—no coffee, no tea, tobacco, or alcohol. For the most part, our women were finished having their babies by the time they were thirty. And only one faced breast cancer prior to 1960. Traditionally, as a group of people, Mormons have a low rate of cancer.

Is our family a cultural anomaly? The truth is, we didn't think about it. Those who did, usually the men, simply said, "bad genes." The women's attitude was stoic. Cancer was part of life. On February 16, 1971, the eve of my mother's surgery, I accidentally picked up the telephone and overheard her ask my grandmother what she could expect.

"Diane, it is one of the most spiritual experiences you will ever encounter."

I quietly put down the receiver.

Two days later, my father took my brothers and me to the hospital to visit her. She met us in the lobby in a wheelchair. No bandages were visible. I'll never forget her radiance, the way she held herself in a purple velvet robe, and how she gathered us around her.

"Children, I am fine. I want you to know I felt the arms of God around me."

We believed her. My father cried. Our mother, his wife, was thirty-eight years old.

A little over a year after Mother's death, Dad and I were having dinner together. He had just returned from St. George, where the Tempest Company was completing the gas lines that would service southern Utah. He spoke of his love for the country, the sandstoned landscape, bare-boned and beautiful. He had just finished hiking the Kolob trail in Zion National Park. We got caught up in reminiscing, recalling with fondness our walk up Angel's Landing on his fiftieth birthday and the years our family had vacationed there.

Over dessert, I shared a recurring dream of mine. I told my father that for years, as long as I could remember, I saw this flash of light in the night in the desert—that this image had so permeated my being that I could not venture south without seeing it again, on the horizon, illuminating buttes and mesas.

"You did see it," he said.

"Saw what?"

"The bomb. The cloud. We were driving home from Riverside, California. You were sitting on Diane's lap. She was pregnant. In fact, I remember the day, September 7, 1957. We had just gotten out of the Service. We were driving north, past Las Vegas. It was an hour or so before dawn, when this explosion went off. We not only heard it, but felt it. I thought the oil tanker in front of us had blown up. We pulled over and suddenly, rising from the desert floor, we saw it, clearly, this golden-stemmed cloud, the mushroom. The sky seemed to vibrate with an eerie pink glow. Within a few minutes, a light ash was raining on the car."

I stared at my father.

"I thought you knew that," he said. "It was a common occurrence in the fifties."

It was at this moment that I realized the deceit I had been living under. Children growing up in the American Southwest, drinking contaminated milk from contaminated cows, even from the contaminated breasts of their mothers, my mother—members, years later, of the Clan of One-Breasted Women.

It is a well-known story in the Desert West, "The Day We Bombed Utah," or more accurately, the years we bombed Utah: above ground atomic testing in Nevada took place from January 27, 1951 through July 11, 1962. Not only were the winds blowing north covering "low-use segments of the population" with fallout and leaving sheep dead in their tracks, but the climate was right. The United States of the 1950s was red, white, and blue. The Korean War was raging. McCarthyism was rampant. Ike was it, and the cold war was hot. If you were against nuclear testing, you were for a communist regime.

Much has been written about this "American nuclear tragedy." Public health was secondary to national security. The Atomic Energy Commissioner, Thomas Murray, said, "Gentlemen, we must not let anything interfere with this series of tests, nothing."

Again and again, the American public was told by its government, in spite of burns, blisters, and nausea, "It has been found that the tests may be conducted with adequate assurance of safety under conditions prevailing at the bombing reservations." Assuaging public fears was simply a matter of public relations. "Your best action," an Atomic Energy Commission booklet read, "is not to be worried about fallout." A news release typical of the times stated, "We find no basis for concluding that harm to any individual has resulted from radioactive fallout."

On August 30, 1979, during Jimmy Carter's presidency, a suit was filed, *Irene Allen v. The United States of America*. Mrs. Allen's case was the first on an alphabetical list of twenty-four test cases, representative of nearly twelve hundred plaintiffs seeking compensation from the United States government for cancers caused by nuclear testing in Nevada.

Irene Allen lived in Hurricane, Utah. She was the mother of five children and had been widowed twice. Her first husband, with their two oldest boys, had watched the tests from the roof of the local high school. He died of leukemia in 1956. Her second husband died of pancreatic cancer in 1978.

In a town meeting conducted by Utah Senator Orrin Hatch, shortly before the suit was filed, Mrs. Allen said, "I am not blaming the government, I want you to know that, Senator Hatch. But I thought if my testimony could help in any way so this wouldn't happen again to any of the generations coming up after us . . . I am happy to be here this day to bear testimony of this."

God-fearing people. This is just one story in an anthology of thousands.

On May 10, 1984, Judge Bruce S. Jenkins handed down his opinion. Ten of the plaintiffs were awarded damages. It was the first time a federal court had determined that nuclear tests had been the cause of cancers. For the remaining fourteen test cases, the proof of causation was not sufficient. In spite of the split decision, it was considered a landmark ruling. It was not to remain so for long.

In April 1987, the Tenth Circuit Court of Appeals overturned Judge Jenkins's ruling on the ground that the United States was protected from suit by the legal doctrine of sovereign immunity, a centuries-old idea from England in the days of absolute monarchs.

In January 1988, the Supreme Court refused to review the Appeals Court decision. To our court system it does not matter whether the United States government was irresponsible, whether it lied to its citizens, or even that citizens died from the fallout of nuclear testing. What matters is that our government is immune: "The King can do no wrong."

In Mormon culture, authority is respected, obedience is revered, and independent thinking is not. I was taught as a young girl not to "make waves" or "rock the boat."

"Just let it go," Mother would say. "You know how you feel, that's what counts."

For many years, I have done just that—listened, observed, and quietly formed my own opinions, in a culture that rarely asks questions because it has all the answers. But one by one, I have watched the women in my family die common, heroic deaths. We sat in waiting rooms hoping for good news, but always receiving the bad. I cared for them, bathed their scarred bodies, and kept their secrets. I watched beautiful women become bald as Cytoxan, cisplatin, and Adriamycin were injected into their veins. I held their foreheads as they vomited green-black bile, and I shot them with morphine when the pain became inhuman. In the end, I witnessed their last peaceful breaths, becoming a midwife to the rebirth of their souls.

The price of obedience has become too high.

The fear and inability to question authority that ultimately killed rural communities in Utah during atmospheric testing of atomic weapons is the same fear I saw in my mother's body. Sheep. Dead Sheep. The evidence is buried.

I cannot prove that my mother, Diane Dixon Tempest, or my grandmothers, Lettie Romney Dixon and Kathryn Blackett Tempest, along with my aunts developed cancer from nuclear fallout in Utah. But I can't prove they didn't.

My father's memory was correct. The September blast we drove through in 1957 was part of Operation Plumbbob, one of the most intensive series of bomb tests to be initiated. The flash of light in the night in the desert, which I had always thought was a dream, developed into a family nightmare. It took fourteen years, from 1957 to 1971, for cancer to manifest in my mother—the same time, Howard L. Andrews, an authority in radioactive fallout at the National Institutes of Health, says radiation cancer requires to become evident. The more I learn about what it means to be a "downwinder," the more questions I drown in.

What I do know, however, is that as a Mormon woman of the fifth generation of Latter-day Saints, I must question everything, even if it means losing my faith, even if it means becoming a member of a border tribe among my own people. Tolerating blind obedience in the name of patriotism or religion ultimately takes our lives.

When the Atomic Energy Commission described the country north of the Nevada Test Site as "virtually uninhabited desert terrain," my family and the birds at Great Salt Lake were some of the "virtual uninhabitants."

One night, I dreamed women from all over the world circled a blazing fire in the desert. They spoke of change, how they hold the moon in their bellies and wax and wane with its phases. They mocked the presumption of even-tempered beings and made promises that they would never fear the witch inside themselves. The women danced wildly as sparks broke away from the flames and entered the night sky as stars. And they sang a song given to them by Shoshone grand-mothers:

Ah ne nah, nah	Consider the rabbits
nin nah nah—	How gently they walk on the earth—
ah ne nah, nah	Consider the rabbits
nin nah nah—	How gently they walk on the earth—
Nyaga mutzi	We remember them
oh ne nay—	We can walk gently also—
Nyaga mutzi	We remember them
oh ne nay—	We can walk gently also—

The women danced and drummed and sang for weeks, preparing themselves for what was to come. They would reclaim the desert for the sake of their children, for the sake of the land.

A few miles downwind from the fire circle, bombs were being tested. Rabbits felt the tremors. Their soft leather pads on paws and feet recognized the shaking sands, while the roots of mesquite and sage were smoldering. Rocks were hot from the inside out and dust devils hummed unnaturally. And each time there was another nuclear test, ravens watched the desert heave. Stretch marks appeared. The land was losing its muscle.

The women couldn't bear it any longer. They were mothers. They had suffered labor pains but always under the promise of birth. The red hot pains beneath the desert promised death only, as each bomb became a stillborn. A contract had been made and broken between human beings and the land. A new contract was being drawn by the women, who understood the fate of the earth as their own.

Under the cover of darkness, ten women slipped under a barbed-wire fence and entered the contaminated country. They were trespassing. They walked toward the town of Mercury, in moonlight, taking their cues from coyote, kit fox, antelope squirrel, and quail. They moved quietly and deliberately through the maze of Joshua trees. When a hint of daylight appeared they rested, drinking tea and sharing their rations of food. The women closed their eyes. The time had come to protest with the heart, that to deny one's genealogy with the earth was to commit treason against one's soul.

At dawn, the women draped themselves in mylar, wrapping long streamers of silver plastic around their arms to blow in the breeze. They wore clear masks, that became the faces of humanity. And when they arrived at the edge of Mercury, they carried all the butterflies of a summer day in their wombs. They paused to allow their courage to settle.

The town that forbids pregnant women and children to enter because of radiation risks was asleep. The women moved through the streets as winged messengers, twirling around each other in slow motion, peeking inside homes and watching the easy sleep of men and women. They were astonished by such stillness and periodically would utter a shrill note or low cry just to verify life.

The residents finally awoke to these strange apparitions. Some simply stared. Others called authorities, and in time, the women were apprehended by wary soldiers dressed in desert fatigues. They were taken to a white, square building on the other edge of Mercury. When asked who they were and why they were there, the women replied, "We are mothers and we have come to reclaim the desert for our children."

The soldiers arrested them. As the ten women were blind-folded and hand-cuffed, they began singing:

> You can't forbid us everything
> You can't forbid us to think—
> You can't forbid our tears to flow
> And you can't stop the songs that we sing.

The women continued to sing louder and louder, until they heard the voices of their sisters moving across the mesa:

> Ah ne nah, nah
> nin nah nah—
> Ah ne nah, nah

nin nah nah—
Nyaga mutzi
oh ne nay—
Nyaga mutzi
oh ne nay—

"Call for reinforcements," one soldier said.

"We have," interrupted one woman, "we have—and you have no idea of our numbers."

I crossed the line at the Nevada Test Site and was arrested with nine other Utahns for trespassing on military lands. They are still conducting nuclear tests in the desert. Ours was an act of civil disobedience. But as I walked toward the town of Mercury, it was more than a gesture of peace. It was a gesture on behalf of the Clan of One-Breasted Women.

As one officer cinched the handcuffs around my wrists, another frisked my body. She found a pen and a pad of paper tucked inside my left boot.

"And these?" she asked sternly.

"Weapons," I replied.

Our eyes met. I smiled. She pulled the leg of my trousers back over my boot.

"Step forward, please," she said as she took my arm.

We were booked under an afternoon sun and bused to Tonopah, Nevada. It was a two-hour ride. This was familiar country. The Joshua trees standing their ground had been named by my ancestors, who believed they looked like prophets pointing west to the Promised Land. These were the same trees that bloomed each spring, flowers appearing like white flames in the Mojave. And I recalled a full moon in May, when Mother and I had walked among them, flushing out mourning doves and owls.

The bus stopped short of town. We were released.

The officials thought it was a cruel joke to leave us stranded in the desert with no way to get home. What they didn't realize was that we were home, soul-centered and strong, women who recognized the sweet smell of sage as fuel for our spirits.

Section 3D

Our World—Music

Listening to Philip Glass: The Composer Speaks with *Tricycle*

PHILIP GLASS

Philip Glass is a composer/performer who lives in New York City.

"Thus the ear is not self, sounds are not self, ear-consciousness is not self, ear-contact is not self, feeling is not self, craving is not self."
—*the Chachakka Sutta*

The problem with listening of course, is that we don't. There's too much noise going on in our heads, so we never hear anything. The inner conversation simply never stops. It can be our voice or whatever voices we want to supply, but it's a constant racket. In the same way we don't see, and in the same way we don't feel, we don't touch, we don't taste.

You have these internal organs of perception and you have these objects of perception. For example, there may be a noise; then there's my ear, which is supposed to convey the noise through the biological apparatus to the brain. The problem is that it's almost impossible for that transaction between the sound and the brain to take place because of the conceptualizing mind. It stands right in the way. There's a guardian at the door of the mind that basically turns everything into something else—into the mind that fabricates, the mind that invents, the mind that interprets. It's the compulsively interpreting and fabricating mind that hears everything the way it wants to. So we have this biological apparatus for hearing, whether it functions or not. And then we have the conceptualizing mind-editor that checks everything that comes into the brain and puts the right spin on it, makes it look the way it's supposed to look, adjusts it to our conceptions, whatever it might be. That's on the door to the brain. Then inside there's this tremendous racket going on. So we have two problems.

195

We don't listen because our internal environment is not conducive to listening, and we have this tyrannical, despotic editor who has his own ideas! Or her own ideas. We have a tyrant-censor who controls everything that comes in. So between the environment and the despot, the chance of our hearing anything becomes very remote! Somehow we manage. More or less. We can get directions to the Brooklyn Bridge; we more or less can meet our friends at dinnertime.

Cage always said that there isn't any such thing as silence. He said even if there was no sound in the environment, there would be the sounds of your own body. But there may be another perception beyond that. First we have to get to that point where we've entered a world where we can listen. Let's say that we've tied up the despot, we've got him to shut up for awhile, got him drunk or sent him home. Let's say that we've got the crowd of ninety-five lunatics in our head to stop. And then we say "OK, we have these biological noises, OK, that's just the body." Then the real activity of listening takes place. But awareness will be dormant until we provoke it, until we demand and insist that it become activated. And that awareness is something that can be cultivated and developed. Without any question that can be done. Then we come to the doorway of the world of listening. That would be awareness of what is there. Luckily for most of us, we're not completely unaware of that. I think we have those moments. And they are beacons for us.

Being a composer is about listening. Being a musician is about listening. Listening properly or performing becomes a kind of harmonizing of parts of our being— our intellectual center, our emotional center, and our moving center. So when you're performing, in the best sense you harmonize those three centers in this way. And the doorway—again the doorway—to performing is to listen. It's the activity of listening that activates these three areas, and it's in the way they work together that the performance takes place.

The essential activity of listening requires at least a minimal point of attention. And that allows us to keep the flow of attention uninterrupted. There can be other things going on—if I were playing a concert and someone shouted "Fire!" I would definitely hear it! Paying attention has a lot to do with being able to construct the detail of the attention. What may have appeared to have been, let's say, a uniform sound, may turn out to be more complex. It may embody other attributes that you may not have been aware of before, things like amplitude or pitch or depth. All those are details of the sound. Once you have attention to the sound, you can begin looking at it in terms of detail. For the performer, you can't hope to create the sound until you've heard it. That begins as an internal event and becomes perceivable as an external event. The performer hears first, and then he plays what he hears. I make it sound as if there's a period of time that elapses. In fact it may be almost no time. But it's not quite simultaneous because if it is reverses itself—if you start playing and then hearing—you run into serious interpretive problems with the music. I can tell you that from experience.

The activity of composing has to do with visualizing sound. Now we're talking about listening as a very active activity. In order to hear the music, I have to have the attention to hear it and then I have to begin to create the detail around the hearing. For both the performer and the composer, you're not listening to the outside world, you're listening to something that's a different kind of world.

How do I listen? Well, how can I listen when there's all this noise going on? Now I notice I'm not listening, then I notice that there's someone telling me what to listen to. Then I notice that this is happening all the time. Now I notice that there's a problem about listening, and now I know that I'm not listening. My own experience is that the mind—once having cleared the space—will continue to fabricate. So there is no empty place for listening. However, for the composer that's a good thing. Because having cleared the space, I may know that I'm fabricating, but the fabricating can become the work that I do. I don't imagine that it has some deeper level of authenticity, because it's closer to some crazy idea of emptiness I might have. In fact, when I stop and listen, I fabricate. When I'm fabricating from a place of greater attention to silence, I might have a better chance of holding onto the image of sound and to acquiring the detail and depth of it.

I used to ask myself the question, where does music come from? That question occupied me for about forty years. And I never found out the answer. But I did find out that I was asking the wrong question. That was an astonishing thing. I finally said, "Oh, I've been asking the wrong question my whole life!" It was like asking how to get to Jupiter. When you're on Third Street and Second Avenue, asking how to get to Jupiter is a very stupid question.

The question isn't where does music come from, but what is music to begin with? That's a much more interesting question. And I'm developing my ideas about it. It's almost too complicated to go into but it has to do with another way of experiencing music. Let me put it this way: I think that music can be experienced multidimensionally. What I suspect now is that actually music is a short-hand for something else. I mean that a piece of music is actually a code.

An architect's plan for a building is not the building. But it represents the building. I think that music may function in that way. So the hearing aspect of music, at least the aspect of music that is the heard aspect, is a code for a larger structure. That's what I meant when I said I suspect it's multidimensional. That the music is reduced from something bigger so that in a certain way it becomes the two-dimensional version of a multidimensional world. We often hear music in a much deeper way than we can communicate it to each other. We hear it in terms of this emotional depth. We hear it as physical presence. And if we think carefully about our experiencing of music, when we hear it as a sound event we're actually only hearing one layer of it.

Very roughly the same thing applies to seeing, tasting, touching. These are just doorways of our perception. That's a better word—perception—because then we're not seeing or listening or touching. We're perceiving. Cognating. So once I got over the idea of looking for the source of music, then I started asking, "Well, what is music really?" Then I began to see that what we call the stuff we listen to is only one aspect—the top of it. The despotic censor might be there, and also the crowd of fools that are babbling all the time. We can kind of shut them up a little bit. It's very hard to get rid of them. But we can still function, we can still listen, we can still see, we can still taste. It's not hopeless, but still, the sound aspect is one layer. Yet our experience of music can be quite different from that. Music is actually a kind of a symbol for a rounder, more complete reality.

On Rap, Symbolism and Fear

JON PARELES

Over the last decade rap has become the epicenter[1] of popular music and a significant influence on fashion, visual arts and language. But to much of the American mainstream, rap is an outlaw music that otherwise well-informed people vilify and fear. Rap marks a generation gap. As young people dance to it, some elders pronounce it unlistenable and others are disturbed by its messages. There's a perception gap, too, reinforced by media, both responsible and irresponsible, that reflexively connect rap and violence. The reasons generally have less to do with rap's rhetoric than with larger tensions of race and class.

Trouble at the movie "Juice"? Commentators point not just to its crime-story plot, but to its rap soundtrack. (No riots have been reported, however, at "The Addams Family," which has a theme song by Hammer.) People trampled to death at an ineptly[2] promoted, poorly policed basketball game at City College in New York? Out come the statistics about violence at rap concerts, although the rap celebrities were invited to shoot hoops, not to perform.

No one considered it odd when City College revealed it has a standing policy against presenting rap-related events; imagine the reaction if klezmer[3] or country music were prohibited. And when, shortly after the City College deaths, three times as many people gathered without arrests or major incidents for a rap concert at Madison Square Garden, at least one television correspondent played up a minor altercation as if it eclipsed the whole show. Television, tabloids and some newspaper columnists tend to present rap as one indivisible, alien morass,[4] "an increasingly sociopathic[5] form of pop music," quoth one *Washington Post* contributor.

Rap gets plenty of publicity when it turns most offensive. When Ice Cube spews racist demagoguery[6] on his album "Death Certificate," or when Public Enemy releases a video clip that sets out to honor Martin Luther King Jr. by killing a fictitious senator and governor of Arizona, shows like "Nightline" pay attention.

But too many people leap from a handful of lyrics to blanket denunciations. The bulk of rap lyrics, in fact, completely ignore whites, to concentrate on boasting and lately, lectures on black self-help. While rap-haters focus on the racism of Ice Cube and the sex-and-guns fantasies of N.W.A., they tend to ignore the many rappers who plead for an end to violence, and who find a wide audience. Chubb Rock, for instance, had a No. 1 single on Billboard's rap chart with "Treat 'Em Right," which urges fellow rappers to bring "decency" back to lyrics and tells would-be gang warriors, "Leave the knife and gun in the store and ignore temptation."

Hip-hop culture, which also includes dancing, fashion and visual arts, has been widely available for at least 13 years—longer in the right neighborhood. As early as 1974, disk jockeys in the South Bronx were chopping up and recombining music on multiple turntables, and they were soon joined by rhyming rappers. In 1979, the Sugar Hill Gang released "Rapper's Delight," the single that announced the arrival of a new genre. Kurtis Blow took rap further up the pop charts with "The Breaks" in 1980; Blondie's "Rapture," the first white rap hit, followed in 1981.

In pop terms, that ought to be ancient history. By the time rock-and-roll was 13 years old, in the mid-1960's only the most lunatic of fringes still denounced the entire genre as a threat to public morals and safety. Rap hasn't had it so easy. There are still some people proclaiming that it's not music, and more who are convinced that rap exists only to incite violence, corrupt children and destroy all that is good and decent.

Why hasn't rap's success, with performers ranging from Run-D.M.C. to Hammer to P.M. Dawn, made it just another branch of entertainment, taken for granted? Obviously, rap has become a symbol in a United States obsessed with race.

Representative Barney Frank, the Massachusetts Democrat, wrote in *The New York Times* that contemporary political campaigns use crime as "a marker for race." Rap is an even more precise marker; despite the growing number of rappers who are white, female, suburban or all three, rap is still overwhelmingly made by young, black, urban males—a demographic segment that many Americans consider threatening. Hating rap, a purportedly esthetic judgment, can be a synonym for hating and fearing young black men.

Yet clear-cut racism is only part of the anti-rap sentiment. As a matter of taste, hip-hop does challenge older pop esthetics. Unless a rap song lifts a whole melodic hook from an older song, as Hammer does, it's likely to be atonal or tuneless, building its catchiness on a slogan, a rhythm or a sound effect—closer to non-Western music than to Tin Pan Alley. In that, however, it is part of a larger trend in popular music; other styles like speed-metal and industrial rock also downplay melody in favor of rhythm, texture and impact. To listeners weaned on the jolting jump-cuts and assertive self-promotion of television and the electronic soundscape of video games, rap sounds familiar. If it annoys parents, all the better.

Rap is also foreground music, abrasive and insistent, perfect for blasting from a club sound system or a portable boom box or a car stereo; people who use

Bach or Bon Jovi as congenial background music are irritated by the noise. But opera also shrieks for attention, and it doesn't trigger the kind of self-righteous response that rap does.

Some reactions against rap involve historic friction among races and classes. In "Popular Musics of the Non-Western World" (Oxford University Press, 1988), Peter Manuel writes that new kinds of music usually arise from "an unassimilated,[7] disenfranchised, impoverished, socially marginalized class." Styles as far flung as Greek rebetika, Jamaican reggae, Argentine tango and American jazz have all trickled up from outcast or gangster netherworlds, eventually to be embraced by middle and upper classes (some seeking vicarious thrills) while drawing widespread denunciations on the way up. In that, hip-hop is true to form.

But when suburbia embraced hip-hop during the 1980's, the alarmist reactions only increased. For one thing rap remains defiantly unassimilated, profane[8] and disdainful[9] of middle-class proprieties. In the mainstream American imagination, blacks have historically been considered the Other, the opposite of the mainstream's genteel self-image. That mysterious, imagined Other is considered uncivilized, sex-crazed, irrational, angry.

Hip-hop, many commentators have inveighed, is intended solely to spur violence, race hatred and general lawlessness. Not so coincidentally, that's what those commentators fear from an urban black population whose prospects deteriorated steadily through the 1980's.

It's not hard to detect signs of a guilty conscience projected onto the Other. Rap often sounds like a young black man shouting; what else would he be shouting about, thinks a listener who can't understand all the words, but how angry he is at people like me? And how he's going to hurt us?

Rap is not so single-minded. Hundreds of thousands of words have been rapped on recordings in the last decade, on innumerable subjects: Egyptology, sex, sneakers, gang vendettas, the recession. Chuck D. of Public Enemy has compared rap to a black cable-news network, but rap also has something in common with citizens'-band radio and computer bulletin boards. Rap mixes public messages and private references, distress calls and jokes, information and fiction, retorts and pontifications. Sensationalism and images of violence appear, along with occasional glints of racism.

Rappers, of course, are not philosopher-kings. Like rock musicians, many rappers are immature or stupid or wildly egotistical, and they don't always hang out with the nicest people. Some rappers use criminal records as proof of authenticity, as Leadbelly did in the 1930's. And some, recognizing that outlaw images sell, set out to shock and titillate, claiming the same artistic license as the makers of, say, "A Nightmare on Elm Street." If young black men are to be stereotyped, their raps suggest, then they'll exaggerate the stereotype as far as it will go.

To be "hard"—to please a hypothetical "street" audience that will only accept the most brutal scenarios—too many rappers confuse manliness with misogyny and homophobia. Gangster rap, rap's equivalent of action-adventure films, offers frightening messages in abundance, for those who want to find them.

Many political rappers are followers of the Rev. Louis Farrakhan's Nation of Islam, whose message of black self-reliance has been widely criticized for invoking anti-white and anti-Semitic racism. Farrakhan-ite rappers tend to be more circumspect, saying "devils" instead of "white devils" and usually condemning the system rather than the race of the people who run it. Lately, Public Enemy and other rappers have denounced self-destructive elements among blacks—drug dealers, gangsters, alcoholics—as much as they've attacked outsiders. But Public Enemy gets far more attention for its blunders, like the video clip for "By the Time I Get to Arizona," which ignores Martin Luther King Jr.'s philosophy and chooses revenge (and machismo) over persuasion.

Even at its rare racist extremes, rap simply picks up demagogic ideas that have long been heard on ghetto streets, allowing them to be monitored—and answered—and reminding a wider public that racism can cut two ways. Sensible or virulent, rap also continues to be a voice of the disenfranchised; unlike David Duke, no rapper has yet been a serious contender for public office.

David Samuels, writing in *The New Republic* (Nov. 11), contended that gangster raps and racist raps (which he conflates with all of rap) foster a "voyeurism and tolerance or racism in which black and white are both complicit," particularly when whites treat gangster raps as a window into ghetto life. But only a naive listener would fail to distinguish between tall tales and reportage.

As a business, hip-hop has problems akin to early jazz and early rock-and-roll: a mixture of honest and fly-by-night entrepreneurs, some of whom exploit both performers and fans. And yes, rap audiences, with some members from poor, crime-wracked communities, can include troublemakers. But the vast majority of concert goers are happy to see metal detectors and extensive security, and rappers on stage invariably urge audiences to stay peaceful. The sensationalist image of rappers inciting slavering hordes to acts of mayhem has no basis in reality.

Rap's internal troubles reflect the poverty, violence, lack of education, frustration and rage of the ghetto. Yet in the end, rap is not a way of exporting those troubles, but a way of transcending them.

People who can't afford musical instruments or lessons—and who aren't getting much music education in the wake of school budget cuts—have made their own music with turntables, changing the passive act of playing records into the active creation of new songs. People who might be proving their toughness in street fights are, instead, proving themselves with elaborate boasts and taunts, trading physical threat for verbal dexterity.[10] Rap has also provided new, legitimate avenues for entrepreneurs and technicians—it testifies to the spirit of free enterprise.

It's time to recognize what rap is: a huge, varied symbolic realm, too big to be stereotyped. There are smart rappers and idiotic ones, positive forces and nasty ones, rappers who want to teach and rappers who want to pander and rappers who just want to make people laugh. Until rap is treated as something other than a terrifying monolith,[11] people within hip-hop may well be justified in thinking that, to the outside world, they all look alike.

Notes

1. Focal point.
2. Inefficiently.
3. Jewish musicians once banned in Europe from playing at Christian festivals or even Jewish weddings.
4. Swamp.
5. Hostile to society.
6. Appeals to the masses.
7. Left out; rejected.
8. Unholy.
9. Scornful.
10. Skill.
11. Single entity.

Because My Father Always Said He Was the Only Indian Who Saw Jimi Hendrix Play "The Star-Spangled Banner" at Woodstock

SHERMAN ALEXIE

During the sixties, my father was the perfect hippie, since all the hippies were trying to be Indians. Because of that, how could anyone recognize that my father was trying to make a social statement?

But there is evidence, a photograph of my father demonstrating in Spokane, Washington, during the Vietnam war. The photograph made it onto the wire service and was reprinted in newspapers throughout the country. In fact, it was on the cover of *Time*.

In the photograph, my father is dressed in bell-bottoms and flowered shirt, his hair in braids, with red peace symbols splashed across his face like war paint. In his hands my father holds a rifle above his head, captured in that moment just before he proceeded to beat the shit out of the National Guard private lying prone on the ground. A fellow demonstrator holds a sign that is just barely visible over my father's left shoulder. It read MAKE LOVE NOT WAR.

The photographer won a Pulitzer Prize, and editors across the country had a lot of fun creating captions and headlines. I've read many of them collected in my father's scrapbook, and my favorite was run in the *Seattle Times*. The caption under the photograph read DEMONSTRATOR GOES TO WAR FOR PEACE. The editors capitalized on my father's Native American identity with other headlines like ONE WARRIOR AGAINST WAR and PEACEFUL GATHERING TURNS INTO NATIVE UPRISING.

Anyway, my father was arrested, charged with attempted murder, which was reduced to assault with a deadly weapon. It was a high-profile case so my father was used as an example. Convicted and sentenced quickly, he spent two years in Walla Walla State Penitentiary. Although his prison sentence effectively kept him out of the war, my father went through a different kind of war behind bars.

"There was Indian gangs and white gangs and black gangs and Mexican gangs," he told me once. "And there was somebody new killed every day. We'd hear about somebody getting it in the shower or wherever and the word would go down the line. Just one word. Just the color of his skin. Red, white, black, or brown. Then we'd chalk it up on the mental scoreboard and wait for the next broadcast."

My father made it through all that, never got into any serious trouble, somehow avoided rape, and got out of prison just in time to hitchhike to Woodstock to watch Jimi Hendrix play "The Star-Spangled Banner."

"After all the shit I'd been through," my father said, "I figured Jimi must have known I was there in the crowd to play something like that. It was exactly how I felt."

Twenty years later, my father played his Jimi Hendrix tape until it wore down. Over and over, the house filled with the rockets' red glare and the bombs bursting in air. He'd sit by the stereo with a cooler of beer beside him and cry, laugh, call me over and hold me tight in his arms, his bad breath and body odor covering me like a blanket.

Jimi Hendrix and my father became drinking buddies. Jimi Hendrix waited for my father to come home after a long night of drinking. Here's how the ceremony worked:

1. I would lie awake all night and listen for the sounds of my father's pickup.
2. When I heard my father's pickup, I would run upstairs and throw Jimi's tape into the stereo.
3. Jimi would bend his guitar into the first note of "The Star-Spangled Banner" just as my father walked inside.
4. My father would weep, attempt to hum along with Jimi, and then pass out with his head on the kitchen table.
5. I would fall asleep under the table with my head near my father's feet.
6. We'd dream together until the sun came up.

The days after, my father would feel so guilty that he would tell me stories as a means of apology.

One night my father and I were driving home in a near-blizzard after a basketball game, listening to the radio. We didn't talk much. One, because my father didn't talk much when he was sober, and two, because Indians don't need to talk to communicate.

"Hello out there, folks, this is Big Bill Baggins, with the late-night classics show on KROC, 97.2 on your FM dial. We have a request from Betty in Tekoa. She wants to hear Jimi Hendrix's version of 'The Star-Spangled Banner' recorded live at Woodstock."

My father smiled, turned the volume up, and we rode down the highway while Jimi led the way like a snowplow. Until that night, I'd always been neutral about Jimi Hendrix. But, in that near-blizzard with my father at the wheel, with the nervous silence caused by the dangerous roads and Jimi's guitar, there seemed to be more to all that music. The reverberation came to mean something, took form and function.

That song made me want to learn to play guitar, not because I wanted to be Jimi Hendrix and not because I thought I'd ever play for anyone. I just wanted to touch the strings, to hold the guitar tight against my body, invent a chord, and come closer to what Jimi knew, to what my father knew.

"You know," I said to my father after the song was over, "my generation of Indian boys ain't ever had no real war to fight. The first Indians had Custer to fight. My great-grandfather had World War I, my grandfather had World War II, you had Vietnam. All I have is video games."

My father laughed for a long time, nearly drove off the road into the snowy fields.

"Shit," he said. "I don't know why you're feeling sorry for yourself because you ain't had to fight a war. You're lucky. Shit, all you had was that damn Desert Storm. Should have called it Dessert Storm because it just made the fat cats get fatter. It was all sugar and whipped cream with a cherry on top. And besides that, you didn't even have to fight it. All you lost during that war was sleep because you stayed up all night watching CNN."

We kept driving through the snow, talked about war and peace.

"That's all there is," my father said. "War and peace with nothing in between. It's always one or the other."

"You sound like a book," I said.

"Yeah, well, that's how it is. Just because it's in a book doesn't make it not true. And besides, why the hell would you want to fight a war for this country? It's been trying to kill Indians since the very beginning. Indians are pretty much born soldiers anyway. Don't need a uniform to prove it."

Those were the kinds of conversations that Jimi Hendrix forced us to have. I guess every song has a special meaning for someone somewhere. Elvis Presley is still showing up in 7–11 stores across the country, even though he's been dead for years, so I figure music just might be the most important thing there is. Music turned my father into a reservation philosopher. Music had powerful medicine.

"I remember the first time your mother and I danced," my father told me once. "We were in this cowboy bar. We were the only real cowboys there despite the fact that we're Indians. We danced to a Hank Williams song. Danced to that real sad one, you know. 'I'm So Lonesome I Could Cry.' Except your mother and I weren't lonesome or crying. We just shuffled along and fell right goddamn down into love."

"Hank Williams and Jimi Hendrix don't have much in common," I said.

"Hell, yes, they do. They knew all about broken hearts," my father said.

"You sound like a bad movie."

"Yeah, well, that's how it is. You kids today don't know shit about romance. Don't know shit about music either. Especially you Indian kids. You all have been spoiled by those drums. Been hearing them beat so long, you think that's all you need. Hell, son, even an Indian needs a piano or guitar or saxophone now and again."

My father played in a band in high school. He was the drummer. I guess he'd burned out on those. Now, he was like the universal defender of the guitar.

"I remember when your father would haul that old guitar out and play me songs," my mother said. "He couldn't play all that well but he tried. You could see him thinking about what chord he was going to play next. His eyes got all squeezed up and his face turned all red. He kind of looked that way when he kissed me, too. But don't tell him I said that."

Some nights I lay awake and listened to my parents' lovemaking. I know white people keep it quiet, pretend they don't ever make love. My white friends tell me they can't even imagine their own parents getting it on. I know exactly what it sounds like when my parents are touching each other. It makes up for knowing exactly what they sound like when they're fighting. Plus and minus. Add and subtract. It comes out just about even.

Some nights I would fall asleep to the sounds of my parent's lovemaking. I would dream—Jimi Hendrix. I could see my father standing in the front row in the dark at Woodstock as Jimi Hendrix played "The Star-Spangled Banner." My mother was at home with me, both of us waiting for my father to find his way back home to the reservation. It's amazing to realize I was alive, breathing and wetting my bed, when Jimi was alive and breaking guitars.

I dreamed my father dancing with all these skinny hippie women, smoking a few joints, dropping acid, laughing when the rain fell. And it did rain there. I've seen actual news footage. I've seen the documentaries. It rained. People had to share food. People got sick. People got married. People cried all kinds of tears.

But as much as I dream about it, I don't have any clue about what it meant for my father to be the only Indian who saw Jimi Hendrix play at Woodstock. And maybe he wasn't the only Indian there. Most likely there were hundreds but my father thought he was the only one. He told me that a million times when he was drunk and a couple hundred times when he was sober.

"I was there," he said. "You got to remember this was near the end and there weren't as many people as before. Not nearly as many. But I waited it out. I waited for Jimi."

A few years back, my father packed up the family and the three of us drove to Seattle to visit Jimi Hendrix's grave. We had our photograph taken lying down next to the grave. There isn't a gravestone there. Just one of those flat markers.

Jimi was twenty-eight when he died. That's younger than Jesus Christ when he died. Younger than my father as we stood over the grave.

"Only the good die young," my father said.

208

"No," my mother said. "Only the crazy people choke to death on their own vomit."

"Why you talking about my hero that way?" my father asked.

"Shit," my mother said. "Old Jesse WildShoe choked to death on his own vomit and he ain't anybody's hero."

I stood back and watched my parents argue. I was used to these battles. When an Indian marriage starts to fall apart, it's even more destructive and painful than usual. A hundred years ago, an Indian marriage was broken easily. The woman or man just packed up all their possessions and left the tipi. There were no arguments, no discussions. Now, Indians fight their way to the end, holding onto the last good thing, because our whole lives have to do with survival.

After a while, after too much fighting and too many angry words had been exchanged, my father went out and bought a motorcycle. A big bike. He left the house often to ride that thing for hours, sometimes for days. He even strapped an old cassette player to the gas tank so he could listen to music. With that bike, he learned something new about running away. He stopped talking as much, stopped drinking as much. He didn't do much of anything except ride that bike and listen to music.

Then one night my father wrecked his bike on Devil's Gap Road and ended up in the hospital for two months. He broke both his legs, cracked his ribs, and punctured a lung. He also lacerated his kidney. The doctors said he could have died easily. In fact, they were surprised he made it through surgery, let alone survived those first few hours when he lay on the road, bleeding. But I wasn't surprised. That's how my father was.

And even though my mother didn't want to be married to him anymore and his wreck didn't change her mind about that, she still came to see him every day. She sang Indian tunes under her breath, in time with the hum of the machines hooked into my father. Although my father could barely move, he tapped his finger in rhythm.

When he had the strength to finally sit up and talk, hold conversations, and tell stories, he called for me.

"Victor," he said. "Stick with four wheels."

After he began to recover, my mother stopped visiting as often. She helped him through the worst, though. When he didn't need her anymore, she went back to the life she had created. She traveled to powwows, started to dance again. She was a champion traditional dancer when she was younger.

"I remember your mother when she was the best traditional dancer in the world," my father said. "Everyone wanted to call her sweetheart. But she only danced for me. That's how it was. She told me that every other step was just for me."

"But that's only half of the dance," I said.

"Yeah," my father said. "She was keeping the rest for herself. Nobody can give everything away. It ain't healthy."

"You know," I said, "sometimes you sound like you ain't even real."

"What's real? I ain't interested in what's real. I'm interested in how things should be."

My father's mind always worked that way. If you don't like the things you remember, then all you have to do is change the memories. Instead of remembering the bad things, remember what happened immediately before. That's what I learned from my father. For me, I remember how good the first drink of that Diet Pepsi tasted instead of how my mouth felt when I swallowed a wasp with the second drink.

Because of all that, my father always remembered the second before my mother left him for good and took me with her. No. I remembered the second before my father left my mother and me. No. My mother remembered the second before my father left her to finish raising me all by herself.

But however memory actually worked, it was my father who climbed on his motorcycle, waved to me as I stood in the window, and rode away. He lived in Seattle, San Francisco, Los Angeles, before he finally ended up in Phoenix. For a while, I got postcards nearly every week. Then it was once a month. Then it was on Christmas and my birthday.

On a reservation, Indian men who abandon their children are treated worse than white fathers who do the same thing. It's because white men have been doing that forever and Indian men have just learned how. That's how assimilation can work.

My mother did her best to explain it all to me, although I understood most of what happened.

"Was it because of Jimi Hendrix?" I asked her.

"Part of it, yeah," she said. "This might be the only marriage broken up by a dead guitar player."

"There's a first time for everything, enit?"

"I guess. Your father just likes being alone more than he likes being with other people. Even me and you."

Sometimes I caught my mother digging through old photo albums or staring at the wall or out the window. She'd get that look on her face that I knew meant she missed my father. Not enough to want him back. She missed him just enough for it to hurt.

On those nights I missed him most I listened to music. Not always Jimi Hendrix. Usually I listened to the blues. Robert Johnson mostly. The first time I heard Robert Johnson sing I knew he understood what it meant to be Indian on the edge of the twenty-first century, even if he was black at the beginning of the twentieth. That must have been how my father felt when he heard Jimi Hendrix. When he stood there in the rain at Woodstock.

Then on the night I missed my father most, when I lay in bed and cried, with that photograph of him beating that National Guard private in my hands, I imagined his motorcycle pulling up outside. I knew I was dreaming it all but I let it be real for a moment.

"Victor," my father yelled. "Let's go for a ride."

"I'll be right down. I need to get my coat on."

I rushed around the house, pulled my shoes and socks on, struggled into my coat, and ran outside to find an empty driveway. It was so quiet, a reservation kind of quiet, where you can hear somebody drinking whiskey on the rocks three miles away. I stood on the porch and waited until my mother came outside.

"Come on back inside," she said. "It's cold."

"No," I said. "I know he's coming back tonight."

My mother didn't say anything. She just wrapped me in her favorite quilt and went back to sleep. I stood on the porch all night long and imagined I heard motorcycles and guitars, until the sun rose so bright that I knew it was time to go back inside to my mother. She made breakfast for both of us and we ate until we were full.

Fortunate Son

DAVE MARSH

Introduction

I

This old town is where I learned about lovin'
This old town is where I learned to hate
This town, buddy, has done its share of shoveling
This town taught me that it's never too late.
—Michael Stanley, "My Town"

When I was a boy, my family lived on East Beverly Street in Pontiac, Michigan, in a two-bedroom house with blue-white asphalt shingles that cracked at the edges when a ball was thrown against them and left a powder like talc on fingers rubbed across their shallow grooves. East Beverly ascended a slowly rising hill. At the very top, a block and a half from our place, Pontiac Motors Assembly Line 16 sprawled for a mile or so behind a fenced-in parking lot.

Rust-red dust collected on our windowsills. It piled up no matter how often the place was dusted or cleaned. Fifteen minutes after my mother was through with a room, that dust seemed thick enough for a finger to trace pointless, ashy patterns in it.

The dust came from the foundry on the other side of the assembly line, the foundry that spat angry cinders into the sky all night long. When people talked about hell, I imagined driving past the foundry at night. From the street below, you could see the fires, red-hot flames shaping glowing metal.

Pontiac was a company town, nothing less. General Motors owned most of the land, and in one way or another held mortgages on the rest. Its holdings included not only the assembly line and the foundry but also a Fisher Body plant and on the outskirts, General Motors Truck and Coach. For a while, some pieces of Frigidaires may even have been put together in our town, but that might just be a trick of my memory, which often confuses the tentacles of institutions that monstrous.

In any case, of the hundred thousand or so who lived in Pontiac, fully half must have been employed either by GM or one of the tool-and-die shops and steel warehouses and the like that supplied it. And anybody who earned his living locally in some less directly auto-related fashion was only fooling himself if he thought of independence.

My father worked without illusions, as a railroad brakeman on freight trains that shunted boxcars through the innards of the plants, hauled grain from up north, transported the finished Pontiacs on the first leg of the route to almost anywhere Bonnevilles, Catalinas, and GTOs were sold.

Our baseball and football ground lay in the shadow of another General Motors building. That building was of uncertain purpose, at least to me. What I can recall of it now is a seemingly reckless height—five or six stories is a lot in the flatlands around the Great Lakes—and endless walls of dark greenish glass that must have run from floor to ceiling in the rooms inside. Perhaps this building was an engineering facility. We didn't know anyone who worked there, at any rate.

Like most other GM facilities, the green glass building was surrounded by a chain link fence with barbed wire. If a ball happened to land on the other side of it, this fence was insurmountable. But only very strong boys could hit a ball that high, that far, anyhow.

Or maybe it just wasn't worth climbing that particular fence. Each August, a few weeks before the new models were officially presented in the press, the finished Pontiacs were set out in the assembly-line parking lot at the top of our street. They were covered by tarpaulins to keep their design changes secret—these were the years when the appearance of American cars changed radically each year. Climbing that fence was a neighborhood sport because that was how you discovered what the new cars looked like, whether fins were shrinking or growing, if the new hoods were pointed or flat, how much thinner the strips of whitewall on the tires had grown. A weird game, since everyone knew people who could have told us, given us exact descriptions, having built those cars with their own hands. But climbing that fence added a hint of danger, made us feel we shared a secret, turned gossip into information.

The main drag in our part of town was Joslyn Road. It was where the stoplight and crossing guard were stationed, where the gas station with the condom machine stood alongside a short-order restaurant, drugstore, dairy store, small groceries and a bakery. A few blocks down, past the green glass building, was a low brick building set back behind a wide, lush lawn. This building, identified by a discreet roadside sign, occupied a long block or two. It was the Administration Building for all of Pontiac Motors—a building for executives, clerks, white-collar types. This building couldn't have been more than three-quarters of a mile from my house, yet even though I lived on East Beverly Street from the time I was two until I was past fourteen, I knew only one person who worked there.

In the spring of 1964, when I was fourteen and finishing eighth grade, rumors started going around at Madison Junior High. All the buildings on our side of Joslyn Road (possibly east or west of Joslyn, but I didn't know directions then—there was only "our" side and everywhere else) were about to be bought up and torn down by GM. This was worrisome, but it seemed to me that our parents would never allow that perfectly functioning neighborhood to be broken up for no good purpose.

One sunny weekday afternoon a man came to our door. He wore a coat and tie and a white shirt, which meant something serious in our part of town. My father greeted him at the door, but I don't know whether the businessman had an appointment. Dad was working the extra board in those years, which meant he was called to work erratically—four or five times a week, when business was good—each time his nameplate came to the top of the big duty-roster board down at the yard office. (My father didn't get a regular train of his own to work until 1966; he spent almost twenty years on that extra board, which meant guessing whether it was safe to answer the phone every time he actually wanted a day off—refuse a call and your name went back to the bottom of the list.)

At any rate, the stranger was shown to the couch in our front room. He perched on that old gray davenport with its wiry fabric that bristled and stung against my cheek, and spoke quite earnestly to my parents. I recall nothing of his features or of the precise words he used or even of the tone of his speech. But the dust motes that hung in the air that day are still in my memory, and I can remember his folded hands between his spread knees as he leaned forward in a gesture of complicity. He didn't seem to be selling anything; he was simply stating facts.

He told my father that Pontiac Motors was buying up all the houses in our community from Tennyson Street, across from the green glass building, to Baldwin Avenue—exactly the boundaries of what I'd have described as our neighborhood. GM's price was more than fair; it doubled what little money my father had paid in the early fifties. The number was a little over ten thousand dollars. All the other houses were going, too; some had already been sold. The entire process of tearing our neighborhood down would take about six months, once all the details were settled.

The stranger put down his coffee cup, shook hands with my parents and left. As far as I know, he never darkened our doorstep again. In the back of my mind, I can still see him through the front window cutting across the grass to go next door.

"Well, *we're* not gonna move, right, Dad?" I said. Cheeky as I was, it didn't occur to me this wasn't really a matter for adult decision-making—or rather, that the real adults, over at the Administration Building, had already made the only decision that counted. Nor did it occur to me that GM's offer might seem to my father an opportunity to sell at a nice profit, enabling us to move some place "better."

My father did not say much. No surprise. In a good mood, he was the least taciturn man alive, but on the farm where he was raised, not many words were needed to get a serious job done. What he did say that evening indicated that we might stall awhile—perhaps there would be a slightly better offer if we did. But he exhibited no doubt that we would sell. And move.

I was shocked. There was no room in my plans for this . . . rupture. Was the demolition of our home and neighborhood—that is, my life—truly inevitable? Was there really no way we could avert it, cancel it, *delay* it? What if we just plain *refused to sell?*

Twenty years later, my mother told me that she could still remember my face on that day. It must have reflected extraordinary distress and confusion, for my folks were patient. If anyone refused to sell, they told me, GM would simply build its parking lot—for that was what would replace my world—around him. If we didn't sell, we'd have access privileges, enough space to get into our driveway and that was it. No room to play, and no one there to play with if there had been. And if you got caught in such a situation and didn't like it, then you'd really be in a fix, for the company wouldn't keep its double-your-money offer open forever. If we held out too long, who knew if the house would be worth anything at all. (I don't imagine that my parents attempted to explain to me the political process of condemnation, but if they had, I would have been outraged, for in a way, I still am.)

My dreams always pictured us as holdouts, living in a little house surrounded by asphalt and automobiles. I always imagined nighttime with the high, white-light towers that illuminated all the other GM parking lots shining down upon our house—and the little guardhouse that the company would have to build and man next door to prevent me from escaping our lot to run playfully among the parked cars of the multitudinous employees. Anyone reading this must find it absurd, or the details heavily derivative of bad concentration-camp literature or maybe too influenced by the Berlin Wall, which had been up only a short time. But it would be a mistake to dismiss its romanticism, which was for many months more real to me than the ridiculous reality—moving to accommodate a *parking lot*—which confronted my family and all my friends' families.

If this story were set in the Bronx or in the late sixties, or if it were fiction, the next scenes would be of pickets and protests, meaningful victories and defeats. But this isn't fiction—everything set out here is as unexaggerated as I know how to make it—and the time and the place were wrong for any serious uproar. In this docile midwestern company town, where Walter Reuther's trip to Russia was as inexplicable as the parting of the Red Sea (or as forgotten as the Ark of the Covenant), the idea that a neighborhood might have rights that superseded those of General Motors' Pontiac division would have been regarded as extraordinary, bizarre and subversive. Presuming anyone had had such an idea, which they didn't—none of my friends seemed particularly disturbed about moving, it was just what they would *do.*

So we moved, and what was worse, to the suburbs. This was catastrophic to me. I loved the city, its pavement and the mobility it offered even to kids too young to drive. (Some attitude for a Motor City kid, I know.) In Pontiac, feet or a bicycle could get you anywhere. Everyone had cars, but you weren't immo-

216

bilized without them, as everyone under sixteen was in the suburbs. In the suburb to which we adjourned, cars were, the fundamental of life—many of the streets in our new subdivision (not really a neighborhood) didn't even have sidewalks.

Even though I'd never been certain of fitting in, in the city I'd felt close to figuring out how to. Not that I was that weird. But I was no jock and certainly neither suave nor graceful. Still, toward the end of eighth grade, I'd managed to talk to a few girls, no small feat. The last thing I needed was new goals to fathom, new rules to learn, new friends to make.

So that summer was spent in dread. When school opened in the autumn, I was already in a sort of cocoon, confused by the Beatles with their paltry imitations of soul music and the bizarre emotions they stirred in girls.

Meeting my classmates was easy enough, but then it always is. Making new friends was another matter. For one thing, the kids in my new locale weren't the same as the kids in my classes. I was an exceptionally good student (quite by accident—I just read a lot) and my neighbors were classic underachievers. The kids in my classes were hardly creeps, but they weren't as interesting or as accessible as the people I'd known in my old neighborhood or the ones I met at the school bus stop. So I kept to myself.

In our new house, I shared a room with my brother at first. We had bunk beds, and late that August I was lying sweatily in the upper one, listening to the radio (WPON-AM, 1460) while my mother and my aunt droned away in the kitchen.

Suddenly my attention was riveted by a record. I listened for two or three minutes more intently than I have ever listened and learned something that remains all but indescribable. It wasn't a new awareness of music. I liked rock and roll already, had since I first saw Elvis when I was six, and I'd been reasonably passionate about the Ronettes, Gary Bonds, Del Shannon, the Crystals, Jackie Wilson, Sam Cooke, the Beach Boys and those first rough but sweet notes from Motown: the Miracles, the Temptations, Eddie Holland's "Jamie." I can remember a rainy night when I tuned in a faraway station and first heard the end of the Philadelphia Warriors' game in which Wilt Chamberlain scored a hundred points and then found "Let's Twist Again" on another part of the dial. And I can remember not knowing which experience was more splendid.

But the song I heard that night wasn't a new one. "You Really Got a Hold on Me" had been a hit in 1963, and I already loved Smokey Robinson's voice, the way it twined around impossibly sugary lines and made rhymes within the rhythms of ordinary conversation, within the limits of everyday vocabulary.

But if I'd heard those tricks before, I'd never understood them. And if I'd enjoyed rock and roll music previously, certainly it had never grabbed me in quite this way: as a lifeline that suggested—no, insisted—that these singers spoke for me as well as to me, and that what they felt and were able to cope with, the deep sorrow, remorse, anger, lust and compassion that bubbled beneath the music, I would also be able to feel and contain. This intimate revelation was what I gleaned from those three minutes of music, and when they were finished and I climbed out of that bunk and walked out the door, the world looked different.

No longer did I feel quite so powerless, and if I still felt cheated, I felt capable of getting my own back, some day, some way.

Trapped

II

It seems I've been playing your game way too long
And it seems the game I've played has made you strong
—Jimmy Cliff, "Trapped"

That last year in Pontiac, we listened to the radio a lot. My parents always had. One of my most shattering early memories is of the radio blasting when they got up—my mother around four-thirty, my father at five. All of my life I've hated early rising, and for years I couldn't listen to country music without being reminded almost painfully of those days.

But in 1963 and 1964, we also listened to WPON in the evening for its live coverage of city council meetings. Pontiac was beginning a decade of racial crisis, of integration pressure and white resistance, the typical scenario. From what was left of our old neighborhood came the outspokenly racist militant anti-school busing movement.

The town had a hard time keeping the shabby secret of its bigotry even in 1964. Pontiac had mushroomed as a result of massive migration during and after World War II. Some of the new residents, including my father, came from nearby rural areas where blacks were all but unknown and even the local Polish Catholics were looked upon as aliens potentially subversive to the community's Methodist piety.

Many more of the new residents of Pontiac came from the South, out of the dead ends of Appalachia and the border states. As many must have been black as white, though it was hard for me to tell that as a kid. There were lines one didn't cross in Michigan, and if I was shocked, when visiting Florida, to see separate facilities labeled "White" and "Colored," as children we never paid much mind to the segregated schools, the lily-white suburbs, the way that jobs in the plants were divided up along race lines. The ignorance and superstition about blacks in my neighborhood were as desperate and crazed in their own way as the feelings in any kudzu-covered parish of Louisiana.

As blacks began to assert their rights, the animosity was not less, either. The polarization was fueled and fanned by the fact that so many displaced Southerners, all with the poor white's investment in racism, were living in our community. But it would be foolish to pretend that the situation would have been any more civilized if only the natives had been around. In fact the Southerners were often regarded with nearly as much condescension and antipathy as blacks—race may have been one of the few areas in which my parents found themselves completely in sympathy with the "hillbillies."

Racism was the great trap of such men's lives, for almost everything could be explained by it, from unemployment to the deterioration of community itself. Casting racial blame did much more than poison these people's entire concept of humanity, which would have been plenty bad enough. It immobilized the racist, preventing folks like my father from ever realizing the real forces that kept their lives tawdry and painful and forced them to fight every day to find any meaning at all in their existence. It did this to Michigan factory workers as effectively as it ever did it to dirt farmers in Dixie.

The great psychological syndrome of American males is said to be passive aggression, and racism perfectly fit this mold. To the racist, hatred of blacks gave a great feeling of power and superiority. At the same time, it allowed him the luxury of wallowing in self-pity at the great conspiracy of rich bastards and vile niggers that enforced workaday misery and let the rest of the world go to hell. In short, racism explained everything. There was no need to look any further than the cant of redneck populism, exploited as effectively in the orange clay of the Great Lakes as in the red dirt of Georgia, to find an answer to why it was always the next generation that was going to get up and out.

Some time around 1963, a local attorney named Milton Henry, a black man, was elected to Pontiac's city council. Henry was smart and bold—he would later become an ally of Martin Luther King, Jr., of Malcolm X, a principal in the doomed Republic of New Africa. The goals for which Henry was campaigning seem extremely tame now, until you realize the extent to which they *haven't* been realized in twenty years: desegregated schools, integrated housing, a chance at decent jobs.

Remember that Martin Luther King would not take his movement for equality into the North for nearly five more years, and that when he did, Dr. King there faced the most strident and violent opposition he'd ever met, and you will understand how inflammatory the mere presence of Milton Henry on the city council was. Those council sessions, broadcast live on WPON, invested the radio with a vibrancy and vitality that television could never have had. Those hours of imprecations, shouts and clamor are unforgettable. I can't recall specific words or phrases, though, just Henry's eloquence and the pandemonium that greeted each of his speeches.

So our whole neighborhood gathered round its radios in the evenings, family by family, as if during wartime. Which in a way I guess it was—surely that's how the situation was presented to the children, and not only in the city. My Pontiac junior high school was lightly integrated, and the kids in my new suburban town had the same reaction as my Floridian cousins: shocked that I'd "gone to school with niggers," they vowed they would die—or kill—before letting the same thing happen to them.

This cycle of hatred didn't immediately elude me. Thirteen-year-olds are built to buck the system only up to a point. So even though I didn't dislike any of the blacks I met (it could hardly be said that I was given the opportunity to know any), it was taken for granted that the epithets were essentially correct. After all, anyone could see the grave poverty in which most blacks existed, and the only reason ever given for it was that they liked living that way.

But listening to the radio gave free play to one's imagination. Listening to music, that most abstract of human creations, unleashed it all the more. And not in a vacuum. Semiotics, the New Criticism, and other formalist approaches have never had much appeal to me, not because I don't recognize their validity in describing certain creative structures but because they emphasize those structural questions without much consideration of content: And that simply doesn't jibe with my experience of culture, especially popular culture.

The best example is the radio of the early 1960s. As I've noted, there was no absence of rock and roll in those years betwixt the outbreaks of Presley and Beatles. Rock and roll was a constant for me, the best music around, and I had loved it ever since I first heard it, which was about as soon as I could remember hearing anything.

In part, I just loved the sound—the great mystery one could hear welling up from "Duke of Earl," "Up on the Roof," "Party Lights"; that pit of loneliness and despair that lay barely concealed beneath the superficial bright spirits of a record like Bruce Channel's "Hey Baby"; the nonspecific terror hidden away in Del Shannon's "Runaway." But if that was all there was to it, then rock and roll records would have been as much an end in themselves—that is, as much a dead end—as TV shows like Leave It to Beaver (also mysterious, also—thanks to Eddie Haskell—a bit terrifying).

To me, however, TV was clearly an alien device, controlled by the men with shirts and ties. Nobody on television dressed or talked as the people in my neighborhood did. In rock and roll, however, the language spoken was recognizably my own. And since one of the givens of life in the outlands was that we were barbarians, who produced no culture and basically consumed only garbage and trash, the thrill of discovering depths within rock and roll, the very part that was most often and explicitly degraded by teachers and pundits, was not only marvelously refreshing and exhilarating but also in essence liberating—once you'd made the necessary connections.

It was just at this time that pop music was being revolutionized—not by the Beatles, arriving from England, a locale of certifiable cultural superiority, but by Motown, arriving from Detroit, a place without even a hint of cultural respectability. Produced by Berry Gordy, not only a young man but a black man. And in that spirit of solidarity with which hometown boys (however unalike) have always identified with one another, Motown was mine in a way that no other music up to that point had been. Surely no one spoke my language as effectively as Smokey Robinson, able to string together the most humdrum phrases and effortlessly make them sing.

That's the context in which "You Really Got a Hold on Me" created my epiphany. You can look at this coldly—structurally—and see nothing more than a naked marketing mechanism, a clear-cut case of a teenager swaddled in and swindled by pop culture. Smokey Robinson wrote and sang the song as much to make a buck as to express himself; there was nothing of the purity of the mythical artist about his endeavor. In any case, the emotion he expressed was unfashionably sentimental. In releasing the record, Berry Gordy was mercenary in both instinct and motivation. The radio station certainly hoped for nothing more from playing it than that its listeners would hang in through the succeeding block of commercials. None of these people and institutions had any intention of elevating their audience, in the way that Leonard Bernstein hoped to do in his *Young People's Concerts* on television. Cultural indoctrination was far from their minds. Indeed, it's unlikely that anyone involved in the process thought much about the kids on the other end of the line except as an amorphous mass of ears and wallets. The pride Gordy and Robinson had in the quality of their work was private pleasure, not public.

Smokey Robinson was not singing of the perils of being a black man in this world (though there were other rock and soul songs that spoke in guarded metaphors about such matters). Robinson was not expressing an experience as alien to my own as a country blues singer's would have been. Instead, he was putting his finger firmly upon a crucial feeling of vulnerability and longing. It's hard to think of two emotions that a fourteen-year-old might feel more deeply (well, there's lust . . .), and yet in my hometown expressing them was all but absolutely forbidden to men. This doubled the shock of Smokey Robinson's voice, which for years I've thought of as falsetto, even though it really isn't exceptionally high-pitched compared to the spectacular male sopranos of rock and gospel lore.

"You Really Got a Hold on Me" is not by any means the greatest song Smokey Robinson ever wrote or sang, not even the best he had done up to that point. The singing on "Who's Loving You," the lyrics of "I'll Try Something New," the yearning of "What's So Good About Goodbye" are all at least as worthy. Nor is there anything especially newfangled about the song. Its trembling blues guitar, sturdy drum pattern, walking bass and call-and-response voice arrangement are not very different from many of the other Miracles records of that period. If there is a single instant in the record which is unforgettable by itself, it's probably the opening lines: "I don't like you/But I love you . . ."

The contingency and ambiguity expressed in those two lines and Robinson's singing of them was also forbidden in the neighborhood of my youth, and forbidden as part and parcel of the same philosophy that propounded racism. Merely calling the bigot's certainty into question was revolutionary—not merely rebellious. The depth of feeling in that Miracles record, which could have been purchased for 69¢ at any K-Mart, overthrew the premise of racism, which was that blacks were not as human as we, that they could not feel—much less express their feelings—as deeply as we did.

When the veil of racism was torn from my eyes, everything else that I knew or had been told was true for fourteen years was necessarily called into question. For if racism explained everything, then without racism, not a single commonplace explanation made any sense. *Nothing* else could be taken at face value. And that meant asking every question once again, including the banal and obvious ones.

For those who've never been raised under the weight of such addled philosophy, the power inherent in having the burden lifted is barely imaginable.

Understanding that blacks weren't worthless meant that maybe the rest of the culture in which I was raised was also valuable. If you've never been told that you and your community are worthless—that a parking lot takes precedence over your needs—perhaps that moment of insight seems trivial or rather easily won. For anyone who was never led to expect a life any more difficult than one spent behind a typewriter, maybe the whole incident verges on being something too banal for repetition (though in that case, I'd like to know where the other expressions of this story can be read). But looking over my shoulder, seeing the consequences to my life had I not begun questioning not just racism but all of the other presumptions that ruled our lives, I know for certain how and how much I got over.

That doesn't make me better than those on the other side of the line. On the other hand, I won't trivialize the tale by insisting upon how fortunate I was. What was left for me was a raging passion to explain things in the hope that others would not be trapped and to keep the way clear so that others from the trashy outskirts of barbarous America still had a place to stand—if not in the culture at large, at least in rock and roll.

Of course it's not so difficult to dismiss this entire account. Great revelations and insights aren't supposed to emerge from listening to rock and roll records. They're meant to emerge only from encounters with art. (My encounters with Western art music were unavailing, of course, because every one of them was prefaced by a lecture on the insipid and worthless nature of the music that I preferred to hear.) Left with the fact that what happened to me did take place, and that it was something that was supposed to come only out of art, I reached the obvious conclusion. You are welcome to your own.

Johnny Clegg's War on Apartheid from *The Best of Rolling Stone*

SAMUEL G. FREEDMAN

One evening when Johnny Clegg was twelve years old, his mother sent him to buy a loaf of bread. Beneath the street lights outside the store stood a black man playing a guitar, and the sound from his strings halted the boy. Something in that African song reminded Johnny of the Celtic music he adored, adored because he associated it with the English father who had vanished from his life before his first birthday.

"Please teach me," Johnny asked.

The black man nodded yes.

After school the next day, with his mother still safely at her job, Johnny went to the apartment building where the musician worked as a janitor. The superintendent, an Afrikaner, asked the boy's purpose and, learning what it was, ordered him to return home. Johnny retreated out the door, then sneaked to the servants' entrance and scaled the fire escape to his new teacher's room.

His name, Johnny now learned, was Charlie Mzila. He was a Zulu. He was a warrior. He was a migrant worker, forced by laws Johnny had only begun to comprehend to live apart from his family eleven months each year. The room smelled of sweat and a paraffin stove. Pictures of saints hung on the wall. Beneath the mattress, Mzila stored what was most dear, the traditional tribal machete and fighting sticks and a photo album whose every snapshot had been bent and smudged. Mzila seated Johnny on the one chair—a cardboard box covered with newspaper—and played songs in Zulu of the itinerant's life. With their minor keys and 6/8 time signatures, they were jaunty and mournful all at once.

"It was as if some very powerful disclosure was being made to me," Clegg recalls, "and I didn't understand it. And that freaked me out. Those songs seemed to be from another place, another time. And yet they were discussing something about the world. There was a secret locked in there. And then I knew that I had to know the secret."

223

Mzila taught Johnny the Zulu language and dances. He led him into gambling dens and migrant hostels and the township bars called shebeens, all the places where racial pride refused to be crushed by the passbook laws, which rendered blacks aliens in their own land, and by the utterance a thousand times a day of "Yes, me baas." Johnny asked his mother for a Gallo-tone guitar, the cheapest brand made but the one that for its economy had become central to modern Zulu music. For three months he made the backstairs pilgrimage to Mzila's room for lessons, until one day the superintendant burst through the door, drunk.

"Out," he shouted, grabbing Johnny by the shirt. "Get out. Never come back." Mzila shoved the man away from Johnny, and the man shoved Mzila back. And then the Zulu warrior did the perilous, the almost unthinkable: He turned his fists on a white man, an Afrikaner, his baas, and drove him from the room in defeat. And in the super's wake hovered the unspoken presentiment of dismissal, arrest, exile.

"It was a terrible thing," Clegg remembers. "All I'd wanted to do was play music. And yet I was terribly moved. Because this was the first time anyone older than me had stood up for me. Just to be with me."

All he had wanted was to play music. All he had wanted was the approval of a father, who would initiate him into the mysteries of manhood. It had been that simple. It had had nothing to do with anything as abstract as politics. But Johnny Clegg was white and Charlie Mzila was black and South Africa was South Africa, where in matters of race nothing was simple and everything was political, inescapably and tortuously political. Others, to be sure, could cross the line and then withdraw behind it, withdraw into the protective laager that is the governing metaphor of white South Africa. They could love their black nannies and their black houseboys and grow up to call them "kaffirs" and march with the army through their townships. It was an emotional dynamic that tore one apart, if one happened to have both white skin and a working conscience.

Johnny Clegg, however, did not enjoy the option of rejection. By age twelve he had been sundered not only from his father but from his stepfather as well. He had lived in three countries, attended six schools. He only felt at peace camping in the bush, sighting birds in the parks and singing and dancing with Charlie Mzila and the other migrants. Then as now he considered himself a "marginal man," and in their marginality he found fellowship. He could hardly imagine where such an elemental human instinct would ultimately lead.

The police surged into the Wemmer Hostel, a brick barracks for 3000 migrants, on a routine search for stolen goods and workers without passbooks. They found thirty or forty men dancing and humming in a space cleared between the bunks and barely lit by one bulb. Only when they herded the group outdoors did the officers notice that one of its members was a white teenager, his tank top and khakis augmented by Zulu beads and sandals.

"*Wat gaan heir aan?*" one officer demanded of fourteen-year-old Johnny Clegg, incredulous. "What's going on here?"

"I'm dancing here," he began to answer before the *isango*, the dance leader, stepped forward to speak for him, according to tribal protocol. The leader proceeded to tell the officers that the white boy had been dancing with this troupe for a long time. The Zulu men, in fact, had given Johnny the nickname Madlebe, from the word for the large earrings Zulu men wear. This so incensed the police they dragged Johnny to their car. The migrants assumed he was being taken to jail, though the officers decided instead to bring him to his mother.

"This is your son," one told Muriel Pienaar when she opened her door ten minutes later. "Do you know where we found him?"

"Must've been one of the hostels."

"You mean to say you *allow* him?"

"Why, yes. He's studying Zulu dancing."

"Do you know how dangerous those places are?" the officer persisted. "There are weapons. There are drugs. We have four or five murders there every weekend. We don't go in there without a gun on."

"It's a bit different for Johnny," Pienaar explained sweetly. "He's their friend."

"Your son is crazy," the officer concluded. "You must look after him." Turning to leave, he added, "And what he's doing is illegal."

That Pienaar remained calm should have been no surprise. She and Johnny had been called worse than crazy by her own mother, a Lithuanian Jew who had settled in Rhodesia. "Oy, vay," she said on her periodic visits to Johannesburg. "What will become of him, running around barefoot with his *shwartzer* friends? What a disgrace. What sort of mother lets him grow wild?"

Yet it was largely because her own parents had discouraged her musical ambitions that Pienaar so nurtured those of her son. Before Johnny's stepfather moved away, he had filled the house with African music and contempt for apartheid. And when the family had lived in Zambia for two years in the early Sixties, just as that nation was gaining its independence, Johnny had attended an integrated school. Racial isolation was simply at odds with his most intimate and formative moments.

But the older Johnny grew, the less the authorities saw his hostel evenings as harmlessly perverse. He was arrested more than a dozen times, and Pienaar grew afraid they might both be deported. (She carried a Rhodesian passport, Johnny a British one, since he had been born in Manchester.) Short of trying to halt Johnny's visits to Wemmer, she forced him to carry a letter from the South African Folk Music Association assuring the police that his business there was strictly apolitical. The Zulus at the hostel, however, could hardly have been prouder. Going to jail was part of coming of age; jail was called *urela emadobenr*, "the place of men."

By day, it was true, Johnny was forced to inhabit segregated schools and cinemas and parks, and he was bound by his late teens for the University of the Witwatersrand, where he would receive an education available to virtually no blacks. Yet it was not in any of those settings that his political and musical enlightenment truly commenced. It was in the migrant hostel—the institution that was, paradoxically, integral to both apartheid and the vibrant urban African culture.

The hostel system was designed to supply white South Africa with a permanent pool of cheap black labor that itself would be deprived of the benefits of permanence. A family's breadwinner needed a work permit, which by law expired on a regular basis; the rest of the family remained hundreds of miles away in the tribal "homeland." So with the push of joblessness and the pull of blood, every migrant had to leave the city every year or two, uncertain whether he would be permitted to return.

At the same time, however, the hostels gave birth to a distinctively citified culture, one that subverted the apartheid ideal. The musical instruments of the hostels and townships were ones borrowed and adapted from their white rulers—a concertina with its buttons rearranged to suit African scales, a guitar restrung to carry bass and treble lines, a penny whistle turned from toy into woodwind. The choral music lately popularized by Ladysmith Black Mambazo and Paul Simon's *Graceland* grew from the encounter of African worshipers and the Christian church. So as he learned the tribal dances, Johnny also learned the urban music, the *kwela* and *mbaqanga*, and came to hear between the bars a language of perseverance and resistance.

If he had achieved Zulu manhood with his maiden arrest, then Johnny accomplished musical brotherhood the evening not long after when he first met Sipho Mehunu. Sipho was only twelve then, newly arrived in Johannesburg from Natal and serving without passbook or work permit as a white family's gardener. He had learned tales back home of a white who spoke and sang and danced like a tribesman, but he did not believe them.

Then one evening as he played guitar on a street corner, Sipho heard someone whistle in Zulu fashion. When he looked up, all he saw was a white boy on a bike. Then the boy spoke in *fanakalo*, the migrant's pidgin mix of Zulu and English, inviting him home to take tea. Once there, Johnny set up a tape recorder, the first Sipho had ever seen, and asked his guest to sing. Then he rewound the tape and played it back. "This boy has *umlingo*," Sipho thought. "This boy has magic."

Soon Sipho took on Charlie Mzila's role of musical guide, but he also became a friend in a way Mzila as a father figure necessarily could not.

In 1976 the two recorded their first single. They pieced together uniforms at the Saturday flea market, learned and arranged Zulu songs and started to write their own. One of Johnny's first was the bittersweet internal monologue of a migrant returning home after his months away. Then, in 1979, Johnny and Sipho formed a full band named Juluka, Zulu for "sweat."

Folkish in tone, painfully earnest in intent, Juluka aroused remarkable controversy solely by being the first racially mixed band in South Africa. For in 1965 the government had adopted laws protecting "cultural purity" by balkanizing the media not merely into black and white but into Afrikaans, English, Zulu, Sotho and similar sectors. At almost any white setting except the Witwatersrand campus, a stronghold of English liberalism, Juluka's shows were likely to be forcibly canceled. Their songs were barred from the government's English station for having Zulu lyrics and from its Zulu station for having English lyrics. From time to time, a spectator would grow so incensed at Clegg, the *kaffirboetjie*, that he would leap onstage to take a swing at him. Even Johnny's best white friend told him he had no right to write about the black lives, lives he could not possibly understand.

As if to contradict that friend, Juluka found a devoted audience in the townships like Soweto, Sebokeng and Alexandra. Outside of Johannesburg, the solution to censorship was simpler: drive down the dirt lanes, announce the show out of the windows of a moving van, set up in a tumbledown municipal hall and start playing. Juluka sold at least half of its early records to black listeners, and several of the albums went gold with sales exceeding 20,000. Three Zulu clans formally inducted Johnny, and when his son Jesse was born years later, Clegg was married in a Zulu ceremony to his wife, Jenny, a former dancer. (Zulu practice is not to perform a marriage until the wife has proven her fertility.) To this day men and women from the townships will hail Clegg not by his own name but with the salutation "Juluka!"

But the plight of the South African moderate is to be flayed from both flanks of the racial divide. And in the aftermath of the 1976 Soweto uprising, the inauguration of the modern era of resistance, Juluka endured enormous pressure from black intellectuals and activists. The Black Consciousness philosophy articulated by Steve Biko, like America's black nationalism, instructed sympathetic whites to work solely among those of their own color. In any racially integrated enterprise, however admirable its goals, white presence would retard black development. Only when the races could meet as equals—however many decades in the future that might be—would they meet at all.

"They talking politics all the time," Sipho Mchunu recalls. "Some people they come to me, say, 'You're wasting your time. Why you play with this white guy? You can play with your own.' I said, 'What I started I cannot give up. Johnny is a friend.'"

"There was an argument I shouldn't sing in Zulu, because English was the international language," says Clegg. "There was criticism that what we were doing was 'conservative.' But I said culture by itself isn't 'liberal' or 'conservative.' It's what you *do* with it. And I wasn't interested in struggling against anything. I was interested in establishing an African identity."

Here, then, was a new definition of marginality for a man obsessed with transcending it. The songs Clegg wrote about itinerants took on another level of metaphor amid the increasing insurrection. In context, if not in original design, they became the *cri de coeur* of all the decent South Africans whose good intentions appeared irrelevant, whose democratic dreams seemed obsolete. As Clegg put it in one 1982 composition: "They are the scatterlings of Africa/Each uprooted one/On the road to Phelamanga/ Where the world began/I love the scatterlings of Africa/Each and every one/In their hearts a burning hunger/ Beneath the copper sun."

❧

Juluka disbanded in 1985 when Sipho Mchunu, tried of the road, returned to KwaZulu to tend his family's livestock. And in some respects that was a blessing, because when State President P.W. Botha declared a state of emergency the following year, the entire idea of making music seemed pointless. By the end of the decade, some 5000 South Africans had perished, either in army assaults or internecine black violence, and another 35,000 had been detained by the authorities. The resistance, in turn, aimed to render the townships ungovernable, and any band that dared schedule a performance would find its crowd stoned and its equipment burned. There was no time for concerts, the comrades said, there was only time for the struggle.

Whatever distance Clegg as an artist had tried to maintain from politics closed with a crash. The Botha regime, adroitly exploiting tribal rivalries, used the Zulu nation that Clegg considered his own to divide, politically and physically, the black resistance. In the vicious intraracial bloodshed that followed (and that continues in Natal), Zulu migrants whom Clegg recognized from Juluka's audiences were slain by the score. Then a white social worker from Durban, whom Clegg had known since she housed him and Mchunu during the 1978 Natal Folk Festival, was seized by the Special Branch, the notorious political police.

Charged with aiding the African National Congress (ANC), the woman disappeared into a series of prisons, where she was placed in solitary confinement and interrogated without cease. Clegg joined a detainees' support committee, sent his friend letters and tapes, tried to locate her in the security labyrinth. Three months after her arrest, the friend was released without explanation. Alive and physically unscarred, she was luckier than most. But Clegg was nearly shattered.

"I had a sense of hopelessness," he says. "I felt paralyzed. Desperate. There were these two opposing factions—the securocrats and the young black militants—neither of whom gave any quarter. There's always been a hidden, invisible middle ground in South Africa of connections between people and cultures. That was being incinerated. Music was the most effective way I could work out my feelings. It was a way of trying to understand what I was experiencing."

The sidemen Clegg assembled to help him—including two Juluka alumni, percussionist Dudu Zulu and drummer Derek De Beer—evolved into Savuka. The songs Clegg wrote and recorded became the band's first record, *Third World Child*, a despairing personal history of the times.

Clegg and Savuka achieved gold or platinum designation for *Third World Child* and its successor *Shadow Man* in South Africa and several European countries. As Clegg's music metamorphosed from Juluka's folkloric stylings to a more accessible interweaving of Celtic and African influences, Clegg found himself last spring in Los Angeles recording the album intended to secure him stardom in the United States.

Several weeks into the sessions, the telephone rang in Clegg's bedroom. The voice was that of the friend who had been detained.

228

"Johnny," she said, "the most terrible thing has happened. They shot David. David Webster."

Clegg hardly needed the surname to know. Webster had been Clegg's mentor from the moment they had met eighteen years earlier at the University of the Witwatersrand. Webster was teaching an anthropology course on Zulu culture, and Clegg stuck out as the one freshman fluent in the language. With Webster's encouragement, he earned his degree in anthropology and went on to become a junior lecturer in the field.

It was impossible for Clegg to picture this man as the woman on the telephone described him—struck as he strolled home from jogging, bleeding to death in his wife's arms. No, perhaps it was all too easy to conceive and that was far more disturbing.

"I felt like I'd been axed, like a cleaver had come into my brain," Clegg recalls. "I was seized once again by this fucking paralysis, an impotence, a real fright. In a death like this, you realize the contingency of history, the reality of existing in chaos. We have a superficial web of order we place over things. This smashed my web."

For three weeks, Clegg could not write a word. "I felt lost in the world," he says. "I didn't trust the universe anymore."

Trying to salvage both the album and Clegg's spirits, producer Hilton Rosenthal hastily arranged a short European tour. The evening after the final show, Clegg flew to New York, where he was to deliver the keynote address at the New Music Seminar. As he crossed the night sky, he scribbled notes on his topic, the history of progressive music in South Africa, a history otherwise undocumented and largely forgotten.

The more Clegg wrote, the more absurd he felt. Had these events really taken place? Or did they exist only in his imagination? And even if they had occurred, what did it matter? Amid detention and emergency and sidewalk assassination, who cared?

Yet as he spoke the next afternoon, and the audience listened, Clegg felt lifted by some small catharsis. Perhaps in declaiming this history of persecution, he had made the musicians' sacrifices not less real, but more. He knew then he would be able to continue. "There's no going back," he says. "I can't stand still; I've done it. I can only move forward."

Shorn of naiveté but not an existential need to believe, Clegg renamed the album *Cruel, Crazy, BeautifulWorld*. The first song he wrote was "One (Hu)'Man, One Vote." He dedicated it to the memory of David Webster.

As the sound of a talking drum poured from the speakers at the Standard Bank Arena in Johannesburg, before the lights even rose on Johnny Clegg and Savuka, the capacity crowd shrieked with an abandon that bordered on Beatlemania. There were black and colored and Indian listeners among the 6000, but with a ticket price of seven dollars, relatively high for South Africa, most were whites in surf shirts and designer jeans. They would not have seemed alien in Orange County, except that when one looked closer, especially at those nearest the stage, one saw a banner declaring, WE ARE ONE WORLD, and a T-shirt emblazoned with the ANC Freedom Charter and another bearing a photograph of David Webster.

They burst into delirium when Clegg unstrapped his guitar and stepped back from the microphone to dance with Dudu Zulu. The men dropped to their haunches, spun on their heels, arms outstretched for balance; they stood straight and then kicked each leg high into the air; and then they fell backward as if in rapture. Theirs was a warrior dance of the Zulus, and together, black and white, they had slain the enemy.

In the crowd boys with baggy shorts and tank tops mimicked their moves. Girlfriends jumped into the air for a glimpse of the stage. And what did it mean? What did their joy mean? Their clenched fists and swaying arms? For gestures so direct, their meaning remained elusive. Were these young white inheritors simply riding in that moment the forbidden pleasure of an African beat? Or were they truly attending Clegg and his message, accepting an empowerment that meant surrendering their privilege?

"We all want change," said James Kamp, a thirty-eight-year-old supplier of engineering equipment, after the show. "But not so fast as Clegg says. It'll be a bloody blood bath. They'll run amok. They'll chase us out of our homes."

"Why not one man, one vote?" said Bernd Globisch, an eighteen-year-old high-school student. "As long as the minority isn't oppressed."

"What he says about one man, one vote is right," said Ashley Cohen, a twenty-three-year-old computer-systems manager. "But it's scary, because it's different and it's unknown."

Clegg himself has no illusions, but he does have some faith. There are, after all, only four destinations for a white in the land of apartheid—faith, racism, exile or madness. Faith has cost some their freedom, others their lives. Clegg has been fortunate enough to survive essentially unscathed and to embody finally a spirit in which others can invest their own faith.

"I've fought against being seen as a symbol, a messiah, who could never deliver the goods," Clegg says. "So I've been pragmatic. But if I'm someone's hero, that's wonderful. It's wonderful to play music that does more than give people a good time. Every time I come offstage, I feel, 'Another nail in the coffin.'"

Why I Gave Up On Hip-Hop

LONNAE O'NEAL PARKER

My 12-year-old daughter, Sydney, and I were in the car not long ago when she turned the radio to a popular urban contemporary station. An unapproved station. A station that might play rap music. "No way, Syd, you know better," I said, so Sydney changed the station, then pouted.

"Mommy, can I just say something?" she asked. "You think every time you hear a black guy's voice it's automatically going to be something bad. Are you against hip-hop?"

Her words slapped me in the face. In a sense, she was right. I haven't listened to radio hip-hop for years. I have no clue who is topping the charts and I can't name a single rap song in play.

But I swear it hasn't always been that way.

My daughter can't know that hip-hop and I have loved harder and fallen out further than I have with any man I've ever known.

That my decision to end our love affair had come only after years of disappointment and punishing abuse. After I could no longer nod my head to the misogyny or keep time to the vapid materialism of another rap song. After I could no longer sacrifice my self-esteem or that of my two daughters on an altar of dope beats and tight rhymes.

No, darling, I'm not anti-hip-hop, I told her. And it's true, I still love hip-hop. It's just that our relationship has gotten very complicated.

When those of us who grew up with rap saw signs that it was turning ugly, we turned away. We premised our denial on a sort of good-black-girl exceptionalism: They came for the skeezers but I didn't speak up because I'm no skeezer, they came for the freaks, but I said nothing because I'm not a freak. They came for the bitches and the hos and the tricks. And by the time we realized they were talking about bitches from 8 to 80, our daughters and our mommas and their own damn mommas, rap music had earned the imprimatur of MTV and Martha Stewart and even the Pillsbury Doughboy.

And sometimes it can seem like now, there is nobody left who is willing to speak up.

I remember the day hip-hop found me. The year was 1979 and although "Rapper's Delight" wasn't the first rap song, it was the first rap song to make it all the way from the South Bronx to Hazel Crest, Ill.

I was 12, the same age my oldest daughter is now, when hip-hop began to shape my politics and perceptions and aesthetics. It gave me a meter for my thoughts and bent my mind toward metaphor and rhyme. I couldn't sing a lick, but didn't hip-hop give me the beginnings of a voice. About the time that rap music hit Hazel Crest, all the black kids sat in the front of my school bus, all the white kids sat in back, and the loudest of each often argued about what we were going to listen to on the bus radio or boombox. Music was code for turf and race in the middle-class, mostly-white-but-heading-black suburbs south of Chicago.

One day, our bus driver tried to defuse tensions by disallowing both. Left without music, some of the black kids started singing "Rapper's Delight." Within a couple of lines, we all joined in:

Now what you hear is not a test
I'm rappin' to the beat.

Then the white kids started chanting: *Dis-co sucks, dis-co sucks, dis-co sucks, dis-co sucks,* repeating the white-backlash, anti-rap mantra of the era.

The white kids got louder: *DIS-CO SUCKS, DIS-CO SUCKS, DIS-CO SUCKS, DIS-CO SUCKS.*

So we got louder, too:

YA SEE, I AM WONDER MIKE AND I LIKE TO SAY HELLO
TO THE BLACK, TO THE WHITE, THE RED AND THE BROWN
THE PURPLE AND YELLOW.

Then the white kids started yelling until their faces suffused with color.

And so we started yelling rhymes that I still know to this day, some of which my kids know and, I bet, so do some of the kids of those white kids who screamed at us from the back of my junior high school bus, raging against change, raging against black people, or, who knows, maybe just not appreciating our musical stylings.

SO I RAPPED TO THE BEAT LIKE I NEVER DID BEFORE.

We rhymed and the white kids disappeared before our eyes because we were in another world—transported by the collective sound of our own raised voices, transfixed by our newfound ability to drown out their nullification.

We felt ourselves united, with the power of a language we didn't begin to understand. "Rap at its best can refashion the world—or at least the way we see it—and shape it in our own image," said Adam Bradley, a literature professor at Claremont McKenna College who is working on a book about hip-hop poetics.

It has the capacity "to give a voice that's distinctively our own and to do it with the kind of confidence and force we might not otherwise have."

I grew older, and my love affair with the music, swagger and semiotics of hip-hop continued. There was Kurtis Blow, Melle Mel and the seminal Grandmaster Flash and the Furious Five:

> Don't push me 'cause I'm close to the edge
> I'm tryin' not to lose my head.

I learned all the rhymes played on black radio, because do you remember when MTV wouldn't touch black music at all? I got to college and started getting my beats underground, which is where I stayed to find my hip-hop treasures. Public Enemy rapped "Fight the Power" and it could have been the soundtrack to CNN footage of Tiananmen Square or the fall of the Berlin Wall:

> Got to give us what we want
> Gotta give us what we need
> Our freedom of speech is freedom or death
> We got to fight the powers that be.

I was young and hungry and hip-hop was smart, and like Neneh Cherry said, we were raw like sushi back then, sensing we were onto something big, not realizing how easily it could get away from us.

⁂

Of course, the rhymes were sexy, too, part of a long black tradition starting with the post-emancipation blues. It was music that borrowed empathy and passion from exultations of the sacred, to try to score a bit of heaven in secular places.

It was college, and in the late 1980s and early 1990s, the post-civil rights, post-sexual revolution, newly grown hip-hop generation imagined that we had shed our momma's chastity-equals-black-uplift strictures anyway. So when MC Lyte rapped, "I ain't afraid of the sweat," well, you know, we *waved our hands in the air*. Besides, it was underground music, adult music, part of a wide range of expression, and it's not like we worried that it could ever show up on the radio.

Hip-hop was still largely about the break-beat and dance moves and brothers who battled solely on wax. It was Whodini, Eric B. & Rakim, Dana Dane, EPMD, A Tribe Called Quest. And always and forever, Lonnae Loves Cool James. I knew all LL Cool J's b-sides and used to sleep under a poster of him that hung on my wall. I still have a picture of the two of us that was taken one Howard homecoming weekend.

And if, gradually, we noticed a trend, more violence, more misogyny, more materialism, more hostile sexual stereotyping, a general constricting of subject matter, for a very long time we let it slide.

In 1988, EPMD rapped about a woman named Jane:

So PMD (Yo?) Why don't you do me a favor?
Chill with the bitch and I'll hook you up later
She's fly, haircut like Anita Baker
Looked up and down and said "Hmm, I'll take her."

But by last spring, it was Atlanta-based rapper T.I.:

I ain't hangin' with my niggaz
Pullin' no triggaz
I'll be back to the trap, but for now
I'm chillin' with my bitch today, I'm chillin' with my bitch today.

Nearly 20 years later and T.I. can't even be bothered to give his "bitch" a name.

We were so happy black men were speaking their truth, "we've gone too long without challenging them," as Danyel Smith, former editor of Vibe magazine, put it. And now, perhaps, hip-hop is too far gone.

At the 2003 MTV Video Music Awards, rappers Snoop Doggy Dog and 50 Cent embellished their performance of the song "P.I.M.P." by featuring black women on leashes being walked onstage. This past August, MTV2 aired an episode of the cartoon "Where My Dogs At," which had Snoop again leading two black bikini-clad women around on leashes. They squatted on their hands and knees, scratched themselves and defecated.

The president of the network, a black woman, defended this as satire.

Hip-hop had long since gone mainstream and commercial. It was Diddy, white linen suits and Cristal champagne in the Hamptons. And it was for white suburban boys as well as black club kids. And it now promoted a sexual aesthetic, a certain body type, a certain look. Southern rappers had even popularized a kind of strip-club rap making black women indistinguishable from strippers.

I don't know the day things changed for me. When the music began to seem so obviously divorced from any truth and, just as unforgivably, devoid of most creativity. I don't know when my love turned to contempt and my contempt to fury. Maybe it happened as my children got older and I longed for music that would speak to them the way hip-hop had once spoken to me.

Maybe as the coolest black boys kept getting shot on the streets while the coolest rappers droned: *AK-47 now nigga, stop that.*

Maybe as the madness made me want to holler back: *"Niggas" can't stop AK-47s, and damn you for saying so.*

Last year, talk show host Kelly Ripa gushed to 50 Cent, a former drug dealer turned rapper, about how important his movie "Get Rich or Die Tryin'" was while black women around the country were left to explain to their own black sons, *"Sometimes, darling, black boys get shot nine times and they don't live to brag about it on the mike."*

And a few weeks ago, watching the Disney Channel cartoon short "Fabulizer," I seethed when the little white character lamented that his "thug pose" wasn't working.

While the mainstream culture celebrates the pimped-out, thugged-up, cool-by-proxy mirage of commercial rap, those of us who just love black people have to be a little more discriminating. "Sometimes," writes sociologist Mary Pattillo-McCoy, "when you dress like a gangsta, talk like a gangsta and rap like a gangsta often enough, you are a gangsta."

My husband, Ralph, and I try to tell Sydney that rap music used to be fun. It used to call girls by prettier names. We were ladies and cuties, honeys and hotties, and we all just felt like one nation under the groove. Sydney, I tell her, I want you to have all the creativity, all the bite, all the rhythms of black rhyme, but I can't let you internalize toxic messages, no matter how cool some millionaire black rappers tell you they are.

Sydney nods, but I don't know if she fully understands.

❧

I was born to be the Lyte
To give the spark in the dark
Spread the truth to the youth
The ghetto Joan of Arc
    —MC Lyte

Last spring, I got together with some other moms from the first generation of hip-hop. We decided to distribute free T-shirts with words that counter some of the most violent, anti-intellectual and degrading cultural messages: *You look better without the bullet holes. Put the guns down.* Or my favorite: *You want this? Graduate!* We called it the Hip-Hop Love Project.

Others are trying their own versions of taking back the music. In Baltimore, spoken-word poet Tonya Maria Matthews, aka JaHipster, is launching her own "Groove Squad." The idea is to get together a couple dozen women to go to clubs prepared to walk off the dance floor en masse if the music is openly offensive or derogatory. "There's no party without sisters on the dance floor," she told me. In New York, hip-hop DJ and former model Beverly Bond formed Black Girls Rock! to try to change the portrayal of black women in the music and influence the women who are complicit in it. "We don't want to be hypersexualized," said Joan Morgan, a hip-hop writer and part of the group, but we don't want to be erased, either.

Finally, it feels like we've gotten back to what black women are supposed to have always known: that it is better to fight than to lie down.

My daughter says I don't like black voices and I could weep that it's come to this. But instead I listen to the most conscious hip-hop that comes my way: Common, Talib Kweli, the Roots, KOS, Kanye West, who blends the commercial with commentary. I close my eyes to listen as Mos Def says:

My Umi said shine your light on the world.

And still, always and forever, Lonnae Loves Cool James.

I keep my CD player filled with old-school tracks and I fill my kids' heads with the coolest, most conscious, most *bang-bang the boogie say up jump the boogie* songs from when hip-hop and I were young. Sydney says I don't like black voices and I say: *Ax Butta how I zone/Man, Cleopatra Jones.*

I make Sydney listen to songs from when rap said something, but my daughter is 12 and she laughs at me. Rap says something now, Mommy, she says.

Lean wit' it
Rock wit' it
Lean wit' it
Rock wit' it

She snaps her fingers and I just nod. Change is gonna come. Meanwhile, her song is catchy. And there are no bitches!

At least not in the chorus.

Section 3E

Our World—
Work

Work and Its Contents

JOSEPH EPSTEIN

Joseph Epstein was born in 1937 in Chicago, where he still makes his home. He is editor of The American Scholar *and a visiting lecturer at Northwestern University. Epstein contributes essays to his own journal and others, including* Harper's, The New Yorker, *and* The New Criterion. *His books include* Divorced in America: Marriage in an Age of Possibility *and the essay collections* Familiar Territory: Observations on American Life, The Middle of My Tether, *and* Plausible Prejudices. *Epstein's preferred genre is the familiar essay, where he comments on contemporary society and culture. Witty, erudite, and articulate, he addresses his works to readers who, he assumes, share his concerns.*

Epstein begins his essay, which reflects on the meaning of work, with six paragraphs about his early work experiences. What function do those paragraphs serve? What kind of relationship does Epstein want to establish with you, the reader? How does the information in these paragraphs help you to get a sense of Epstein as a person?

In the rest of the essay, Epstein moves between personal anecdote and references to readings. Henry James, Max Weber, and H. L. Mencken are just a few writers to whom he refers. Do these literary allusions change the relationship that Epstein established with his reader at the beginning of the essay? What assumptions about the reader are reflected by his use of allusions? What purpose do they serve in the essay?

When I was an adolescent I never had the best jobs: these included construction worker, which paid very well, built up muscles, and withal seemed very manly; or copyboy on a major metropolitan daily, which put one on the periphery of interesting events; or lifeguard, which, along with giving one an opportunity to acquire that most ephemeral of the world's possessions, a nice tan, put one in a fine position to meet girls. But neither did I have the worst jobs: these included setting pins in a bowling alley, which in those days paid ten cents a line and gave one an opportunity for so many uninteresting and extremely painful injuries; and selling shoes, especially women's shoes, which could try the patience of a glacier and often paid no commission, except one percent on polish and laces.

I had middling jobs. My last two years in high school I sold costume jewelry on Saturdays and during Christmas holidays downtown in what must have been one of the first of this country's discount stores. During the time I was there, two veterans of carnival life worked the costume jewelry concession with me. The first was Art, a man in his late forties, with pomaded black hair, who sweated heavily in all seasons. "Hold down the fort, kid," he would say, ducking out for ten or fifteen minutes, his breath, on return, areek with booze. He was a fumbling man who had confident views, particularly on contemporary sexual mores, which, though often amusing, seemed to me even then wildly erroneous. Then there was Fritz, an Englishman who referred to all other Englishmen as limeys. He had the accent of a man of some cultivation, and on the cheap cigarette lighters, lockets, and identification bracelets we sold he engraved names and initials with a grand artistic flourish. He was a fine companion, filled with stories of traveling round the world, in all a decent sort, though at the time very much down on his uppers. He would sometimes borrow a few dollars from me, which he always repaid. Fritz, too, was a boozer, not a nipper but a binger. He would miss work for two or three days, then come in as if nothing were amiss, his same good, gentle self. For reasons never known to me, and perhaps not to himself, he was not to be one of the world's winners.

By the time I had my first factory job, I was in college, which is to say that I knew for certain, if I hadn't already known it earlier, that I would not work at a labor job permanently. I was a visitor there, a tourist on the payroll. The factory made phonograph needles. It had no assembly line; instead, most of the people, the majority of them women, worked at long tables. I worked in the receiving department. My job was to unload trucks, but not enough trucks came in to merit my working full-time at this, so I put in part of my time organizing and filing boxes of labels, which was heartily boring. But I also sat around a lot, schmoozing away with the head of the receiving room, a middle-aged man named Steve, who was extremely efficient at covering over the fact that he was exceedingly lazy. We were often joined by two brothers-in-law, Italians of fine high spirits, who were the factory's maintenance crew. Both were small men, and one of them might technically have been a dwarf. Well under five-feet tall with a large head, long arms, and big hands, he was courageous in his mischief, sometimes ducking out to one of the factory's upper floors, where behind packing cases he might take a nap of two full hours' duration. The brothers-in-law appeared to use the factory as a place to hang out during the day. Their real life was elsewhere. Their true speciality was fixing up old cars, which they would sell for a few hundred bucks profit. Then they would buy another, and start fixing it up.

At the factory it was known that I was a college student, which was problematic. It was the first inkling I had of the separation between those whose lives revolve around books and those whose lives don't. I didn't want the separation made any greater than it needed to be, so instead of saying that I was studying such things as literature, history, and philosophy, I claimed I was thinking of going to medical school. This turned out to be a mistake. More than once the brothers-in-law wanted to know if I needed any dead cats for purposes of dissection, and I was sure that one day I would have to bring a dead cat home on the bus in a shopping bag. Worse still, Steve and other people round the plant came to me for medical advice, some of it, I fear, rather intimate in nature.

Many people at the factory told me to be sure to return to school, saying that they regretted not having had the opportunity to go themselves. Yet their lives did not seem to me either dreary or dreadful. On coffee breaks in the lunchroom their talk was what most talk is about: the economy, the previous day's no-hitter or the pennant race, the bowling league being formed for the fall, their kids. I recall each afternoon standing in line to punch out. The working day did some people in; others, indomitable, were not in the least done in. Not at all. Work, I thought then, is neither intrinsically dignified nor undignified; it is the people doing the work who give it its character. There are people who can make the creation of poetry or leadership of a large university or corporation seem loathsome, and then there are people who can make the job of porter or waitress seem a good and useful thing.

The most impressive man I encountered in the army was a training sergeant named Andrew Atherton, who in private life had been a soda jerk in St. Louis; the most intelligent person in many academic departments in universities is the secretary. Nothing, really, so surprising in this. Nearly a century ago, Henry James noted the common occurrence of "imbeciles in great places, people of sense in small." Although few people actually work in Henry James novels, James knew a great deal about work and its special benefits. After the rude failure of his play *Guy Domville* on the London stage, James, it will be recalled, lapsed into a dark blue funk. The only way out of it, as he himself recognized, was work. Writing to his friend William Dean Howells, James recounted his depression and its antidote:

> The sense of being utterly out of it weighed me down, and I asked myself what the future would be. All these melancholies were qualified indeed by one redeeming reflection—the sense of how little, for a good while past (for reasons very logical, by accidental and temporary), I had been producing. I *did* say to myself, "Produce again—produce; produce better than ever, and all will yet be well."

And he did. And it was.

The restorative effects of work seem to be beyond doubt. Being out of work, for so many, is the surest path to self-loathing. The loss of work isn't only the loss of wages but the loss of an organizing principle in life. Blocked writers are but one example of the phenomenon. But one needn't turn to the arts for examples. Some years ago, when I had not yet produced enough work to be allowed to consider myself a writer, I underwent roughly a five-week period of unemployment. I was married and had children, and the sense of not producing for them diminished me in my own eyes, which is, I suppose, not surprising. What did surprise me, though, was that during this time jobs I would not formerly even have considered for myself suddenly came to seem highly possible, interesting, attractive even. Driving a bus, for one, or selling men's clothes, for another. Leisure enforced, I found, was no leisure at all, so I took no pleasure in my free time. At one point, just to be doing something, I attempted to sell newspaper subscriptions over the telephone; I rarely made more at this than seven or eight dollars for three hours' work—a figure so demoralizing that after less than a week of it, I quit. I walked around envying people who had jobs to go to. Unemployment had made me feel useless, utterly hopeless. I recognize that this doesn't compare with any sort of serious tragedy, or even with any sort of serious unemployment, but I nonetheless cannot recall when I felt quite so sorry for myself. At other difficult times in my life, at least I could throw myself into my work.

For a great many people TGIF (Thank God It's Friday) is a serious slogan, but then for a great many others so is TGIM (Thank God It's Monday). As a TGIM man, I think work has gotten a bad rep—and a bum rap—in recent years. Consider the word "workaholic," whose implicit meaning is drunk on work. Or consider the term "Protestant ethic," which began as an explanation for the economic behavior of a historical people but which today exists almost solely as a pejorative term applied to people who are thought to take their work too much in earnest. Those Protestants Max Weber described in his famous essay may or may not have been welcome in heaven for their hard work, but they surely could have spent their days worse—pool-side, let us say, at Caesar's Palace or at Esalen. I am neither Protestant nor quite a workaholic, but I have known many moments when work seemed to me a more pleasurable prospect than being with very good friends. Toward the end of two or three weeks of even a splendid vacation, I have longed to read my mail, to sit at my desk, to slip into harness.

Once one has acquired skills, it seems a waste not to use them. Strike, I say, even when the iron is merely warm. A career passes so quickly. ("Careerist" is another pejorative word.) Someone once said, cleverly in my view, that every career has five stages, which may be denoted thus: (1) Who is Joseph Epstein? (2) Get me Joseph Epstein. (3) We need someone like Joseph Epstein. (4) What we need is a young Joseph Epstein. (5) Who is Joseph Epstein? Am I now at stage 3, or getting close to stage 4? When I consider these stages, and how quickly one passes from one to the next, I think perhaps it is best to strike even before the iron is plugged in.

Life is short, and work life shorter. At many jobs, age works against one. Much work is, as the sociologists have it, age-specific. Certain jobs are more than a touch unseemly beyond a certain age: lifeguard, movie reviewer, gigolo, television anchorman or anchorwoman (unless you happen to have one of those granitic Cronkitic faces). The jobs I work at—writing, editing, teaching—though one can go at them for quite a spell, nonetheless all have about them a sense of a prime period, after which one does not figure to get better. Some writers, most famously Yeats, found their true prime in their old age, but most do not get better as they get older. Editors beyond a certain period tend to lose their touch and their passion. And teachers, perhaps from having been allowed to hold the floor for so long before a captive audience, not infrequently grow spiritually gaseous and mentally gaga. When I think of these possibilities, it occurs to me to strike even without an iron.

H. L. Mencken, himself a hard and highly efficient worker, says somewhere that it is probably a fine idea for a person to change jobs every ten or so years. Without consciously setting out to do so, I seem to have been following this plan. The last time I changed jobs was when, in my late thirties, I began teaching at a university. The chance to mold minds, the opportunity for lively exchanges of ideas, the pleasures of virtuous friendships with the young, all these are doubtless among the possible rewards of teaching. But what attracted me were the spacious margins of leisure—or, to put it less grandly, the time-off seemed terrific. My view of the job then coincides with that held by my barber now. Often, in order to beat the rush of customers that gathers in his shop in the afternoon, I will go in for a haircut at nine or nine-thirty in the morning. Flapping the sheet over me, he will usually say, with a barely perceptible smile in which I think I have espied envy mingling with the faintest contempt, "Through for the day Professor?"

I still think the leisure offered by university teaching is impressive. Yet while working at it, the job often seems oddly enervating. Perhaps it has to do with the pressures of intellectual performance—of being "on," in several of the complicated senses of that simple word. Perhaps it has to do with working too exclusively among the young, which can be a sharp reminder that young is, most clearly, what one no longer is. Perhaps it is the element of repetition, for teaching is one of those jobs in which, as one grows older, one's responsibilities do not increase. Perhaps it has to do with the fact that, in teaching, the sense of intellectual progress, in one's students and in oneself, is often unclear, and teaching is never more tiring than when the sense of intellectual progress is absent.

Still, teaching has its moments, and these come in various forms: exhilaration, surprising intellectual discovery, appreciation for things one felt confident went unnoticed. Yet of the jobs I do, teaching is the one I approach with a tinge of fear. I shall hold back on a quotation from Kierkegaard here, but even after several years on the job I often walk into classrooms slightly tremulous. Colleagues have told me that they continue to do so after thirty or more years of teaching. What is there to be fearful of? Of being boring? Of seeming boobish? Of, somehow, blowing it? I do, after all, know more than my students—at least most of the time I do. Yet the touch of fear is still usually there, and the troubling thing is that I tend to teach worse when it isn't.

I imagine fear has salubrious effects on other kinds of work. The stage fright of actors is of course well enough known. So, too, are those butterflies in the stomachs of even the most fearsome athletes before games. Do trial lawyers feel fear? I should hope that airline pilots feel a bit of it. I should hope, too, that surgeons feel fear, but fear, in their case, that stops well short of trembling. I don't mean to exaggerate the benefits of fear; a little of it, I have found, goes a long way.

So, in connection with work, does play. Good work often involves play, an element of fooling around even while doing the most serious things. Fortunate are those people in a position to transform their work into play. Artists are often able to do so. But I have seen fine waitresses and businessmen do it, too. The most fortunate of all, though, are those for whom the line between work and play gets rubbed out, for whom work is pleasure and pleasure is in work. I may be one of those people. Strange. When I was a child I never dreamed of doing any particular kind of work, for none especially attracted me. I wished merely to be rich and respected, in a general way. Rich I am not, whether I am respected is not for me to say; but, because of the joy I am able to take in my work, I feel myself luckier than any child could have dreamed. Now, if only I could shake this feeling that, comes another Depression, it's guys like me they fire first.

Who Built the Pyramids?

Mike Lefevre

It is a two-flat dwelling, somewhere in Cicero, on the outskirts of Chicago. He is thirty seven. He works in a steel mill. On occasion, his wife Carol works as a waitress in a neighborhood restaurant; otherwise, she is at home, caring for their two small children, a girl and a boy.

At the time of my first visit, a sculpted statuette of Mother and Child was on the floor, head severed from body. He laughs softly as he indicated his three-year-old daughter: "She Doctor Spock'd it."

I'm a dying breed. A laborer. Strictly muscle work . . . pick it up, put it down, pick it up, put it down. We handle between forty and fifty thousand pounds of steel a day. (Laughs). I know this is hard to believe—from four hundred pounds to three- and four-pound pieces. It's dying.

You can't take pride any more. You remember when a guy could point to a house he built, how many logs he stacked. He built it and he was proud of it. I don't really think I could be proud if a contractor built a home for me. I would be tempted to get in there and kick the carpenter in the ass (laughs), and take the saw away from him. 'Cause I would have to be part of it, you know.

It's hard to take pride in a bridge you're never gonna cross, in a door you're never gonna open. You're mass-producing things and you never see the end result of it. (Muses) I worked for a trucker one time. And I got this tiny satisfaction when I loaded a truck. At least I could see the truck depart loaded. In a steel mill, forget it. You don't see where nothing goes.

I got chewed out by my foreman once. He said, "Mike, you're a good worker but you have a bad attitude." My attitude is that I don't get excited about my job. I do my work but I don't say whoopee-doo. The day I get excited about my job is the day I go to a head shrinker. How are you gonna get excited about pullin' steel? How are you gonna get excited when you're tired and want to sit down?

It's not just the work. Somebody built the pyramids. Somebody's going to build something. Pyramids, Empire State Building—these things just don't happen. There's hard work behind it. I would like to see a building, say, the Empire

State, I would like to see on one side of it a foot-wide strip from top to bottom with the name of every bricklayer, the name of every electrician, with all the names. So when a guy walked by, he could take his son and say, "See, that's me over there on the forty-fifth floor, I put the steel beam in." Picasso can point to a painting. What can I point to? A writer can point to a book. Everybody should have something to point to.

It's the not-recognition by other people. To say a woman is just a housewife is degrading, right? Okay. Just a housewife. It's also degrading to say just a laborer. The difference is that a man goes out and maybe gets smashed.

When I was single, I could quit, just split. I wandered all over the country. You worked just enough to get a poke, money in your pocket. Now I'm married and I got two kids . . . (trails off). I worked on a truck dock one time and I was single. The foreman came over and he grabbed my shoulder, kind of gave me a shove. I punched him and knocked him off the dock. I said, "Leave me alone. I'm doing my work, just stay away from me, just don't give me the with-the-hands business."

Hell, if you whip a damn mule he might kick you. Stay out of my way, that's all. Working is bad enough, don't bug me. I would rather work my ass off for eight hours a day with nobody watching me than five minutes with a guy watching me. Who you gonna sock? You can't sock General Motors, you can't sock anybody in Washington, you can't sock a system.

A mule, an old mule, that's the way I feel. Oh yeah. See (Shows black and blue marks on arms and legs, burns.) You know what I heard from more than one guy at work? "If my kid wants to work in a factory, I am going to kick the hell out of him." I want my kid to be an effete snob. Yeah, mm-hmm. (Laughs.) I want him to be able to quote Walt Whitman, to be proud of it.

If you can't improve yourself, you improve your posterity. Otherwise life isn't worth nothing. You might as well go back to the cave and stay there. I'm sure the first caveman who went over the hill to see what was on the other side—I don't think he went there wholly out of curiosity. He went there because he wanted to get his son out of the cave. Just the same way I want to send my kid to college.

I work so damn hard and want to come home and sit down and lay around. But *I gotta get it out.* I want to be able to turn around to somebody and say, "Hey, fuck you." You know? (Laughs.) The guy sitting next to me on the bus too. 'Cause all day I wanted to tell my foreman to go fuck himself, but I can't.

So I find a guy in a tavern. To tell him that. And he tells me too. I've been in brawls. He's punching me and I'm punching him, because we actually want to punch somebody else. The most that'll happen is the bartender will bar us from the tavern. But at work, you lose your job.

This one foreman I've got, he's a kid. He's a college graduate. He thinks he's better than everybody else. He was chewing me out and I was saying, "Yeah, yeah, yeah." He said, "What do you mean, yeah, yeah, yeah. Yes sir." I told him, "Who the hell are you, Hitler? What is this *"Yes, sir"* bullshit? I came here to work, I didn't come here to crawl. There's a fuckin' difference." One word led to another and I lost.

I got broke down to a lower grade and lost twenty-five cents an hour, which is a hell of a lot. It amounts to about ten dollars a week. He came over—after breaking me down. The guy comes over and smiles at me. I blew up. He didn't know it, but he was about two seconds and two feet away from a hospital. I said, "Stay the fuck away from me." He was just about to say something and was pointing his finger. I just reached my hand up and just grabbed his finger and I just put it back in his pocket. He walked away. I grabbed his finger because I'm married. If I'd a been single, I'd a grabbed his head. That's the difference.

You're doing this manual labor and you know that technology can do it. (Laughs.) Let's face it, a machine can do the work of a man; otherwise they wouldn't have space probes. Why can we send a rocket ship that's unmanned and yet send a man in a steel mill to do a mule's work?

Automation? Depends how it's applied. It frightens me if it puts me out on the street. It doesn't frighten me if it shortens my work week. You read that little thing: what are you going to do when this computer replaces you? Blow up computers. (Laughs.) Really. Blow up computers. I'll be goddamned if a computer is gonna eat before I do! I want milk for my kids and beer for me. Machines can either liberate man or enslave 'im, because they're pretty neutral. It's man who has the bias to put the thing one place or another.

If I had a twenty-hour workweek, I'd get to know my kids better, my wife better. Some kid invited me to go on a college campus. On a Saturday. It was summertime. Hell, if I had a choice of taking my wife and kids to a picnic or going to a college campus, it's gonna be the picnic. But if I worked a twenty-hour week, I could go do both. Don't you think with that many extra twenty hours people could really expand? Who's to say? There are some people in factories just by force of circumstance. I'm just like the colored people. Potential Einsteins don't have to be white. They could be in cotton fields, they could be in factories.

The twenty-hour week is a possibility today. The intellectuals, they always say there are potential Lord Byrons, Walt Whitmans, Roosevelts, Picassos working in construction or steel mills or factories. But I don't think they believe it. I think what they're afraid of is the potential Hitlers and Stalins that are there too. The people in power fear the leisure man. Not just the United States. Russia's the same way.

What do you think would happen in this country if, for one year, they experimented and gave everybody a twenty-hour week? How do they know that the guy who digs Wallace today doesn't try to resurrect Hitler tomorrow? Or the guy who is mildly disturbed at pollution doesn't decide to go to General Motors and shit on the guy's desk? You can become a fanatic if you had the time. The whole thing is time. That is, I think, one reason rich kids tend to be fanatic about politics: they have time. Time, that's the important thing.

It isn't that the average working guy is dumb. He's tired, that's all. I picked up a book on chess one time. That thing laid in the drawer for two or three weeks, you're too tired. During the weekends you want to take your kids out. You don't want to sit there and the kid comes up: "Daddy, can I go to the park?" You got your nose in a book? Forget it.

I know a guy fifty-seven years old. Know what he tells me? "Mike, I'm old and tired *all* the time." The first thing happens at work: When the arms start moving, the brain stops. I punch in about ten minutes to seven in the morning. I say hello to a couple of guys I like, I kid around with them. One guy says good morning to you and you say good morning. To another guy you say fuck you. The guy you say fuck you to is your friend.

I put on my hard hat, change into my safety shoes, put on my safety glasses, go to the bonderizer. It's the thing I work on. They rake the metal, they wash it, they dip it in a paint solution, and we take it off. Put it on, take it off, put it on, take it off, put it on, take it off . . .

I say hello to everybody but my boss. At seven it starts. My arms get tired about the first half-hour. After that, they don't get tired any more until maybe the last half-hour at the end of the day. I work from seven to three thirty. My arms are tired at seven thirty and they're tired at three o'clock. I hope to God I never get broke in, because I always want my arms to be tired at seven thirty and three o'clock. (Laughs.) 'Cause that's when I know that there's a beginning and there's an end. That I'm not brainwashed. In between, I don't even try to think.

If I were to put you in front of a dock and I pulled up a skid in front of you with fifty hundred-pound sacks of potatoes and there are fifty more skids just like it, and this is what you're gonna do all day, what would you think about—potatoes? Unless a guy's a nut, he never thinks about work or talks about it. Maybe about baseball or about getting drunk the other night or he got laid or he didn't get laid. I'd say one out of a hundred will actually get excited about work.

Why is it that the communists always say they're for the workingman, and as soon as they set up a country, you got guys singing to tractors? They're singing to tractors? They're singing about how they love the factory. That's where I couldn't buy communism. It's the intellectuals' utopia, not mine. I cannot picture myself singing to a tractor, I just can't. (Laughs.) Or singing to steel. (Singsongs.) Oh whoop-dee-doo, I'm at the bonderizer, oh how I love this heavy steel. No thanks. Never hoppen.

Oh yeah, I daydream. I fantasize about a sexy blonde in Miami who's got my union dues. (Laughs.) I think of the head of the union the way I think of the head of my company. Living it up. I think of February in Miami. Warm weather, a place to lay in. When I hear a college kid say, "I'm oppressed," I don't believe him. You know what I'd like to do for one year? Live like a college kid. Just for one year. I'd love to. Wow! (Whispers) Wow! Sports car! Marijuana! (Laughs.) Wild, sexy broads. I'd love that, hell yes, I would.

Somebody has to do this work. If my kid ever goes to college, I just want him to have a little respect, to realize that his dad is one of those somebodies. This is why even on—(muses) yeah, I guess, sure—on the black thing. . . (Sighs heavily.) I can't really hate the colored fella that's working with me all day. The black intellectual I got no respect for. The white intellectual I got no use for. I got no use for the black militant who's gonna scream three hundred years of slavery to me while I'm busting my ass. You know what I mean? (Laughs.) I have

248

one answer for that guy; go see Rockefeller. See Harriman. Don't bother me. We're in the same cotton field. So just don't bug me. (Laughs.)

After work I usually stop off at a tavern. Cold beer. Cold beer right away. When I was single, I used to go into hillbilly bars, get in a lot of brawls. Just to explode. I got a thing on my arm here (indicates scar). I got slapped with a bicycle chain. Oh, wow! (Softly) Mmm. I'm getting older. (Laughs.) I don't explode as much. You might say I'm broken in. (Quickly) No, I'll never be broken in. (Sighs.) When you get a little older, you exchange the words. When you're younger, you exchange the blows.

When I get home, I argue with my wife a little bit. Turn on TV, get mad at the news. (Laughs.) I don't even watch the news that much. I watch Jackie Gleason. I look for any alternative to the ten o'clock news. I don't want to go to bed angry. Don't hit a man with anything heavy at five o'clock. He just can't be bothered. This is his time to relax. The heaviest things he wants is what his wife has to tell him.

When I come home, know what I do for the first twenty minutes? Fake it. I put on a smile. I got a kid three years old. Sometimes she says, "Daddy, where've you been?" I say, "Work." I could have told her I'd been in Disneyland. What's work to a three-year-old kid? If I feel bad, I can't take it out on the kids. Kids are born innocent of everything but birth. You can't take it out on your wife either. This is why you go to a tavern. You want to release it there rather than do it at home. What does an actor do when he's got a bad movie? I got a bad movie every day.

I don't even need the alarm clock to get up in the morning. I can go out drinking all night, fall asleep at four, and bam! I'm up at six—no matter what I do. (Laughs.) It's a pseudo-death, more or less. Your whole system is paralyzed and you give all the appearance of death. It's an ingrown clock. It's a thing you just get used to. The hours differ. It depends. Sometimes my wife wants to do something crazy like play five hundred rummy or put a puzzle together. It could be midnight, could be ten o'clock, could be nine thirty.

What do you do weekends?

Drink beer, read a book. See that one? *Violence in America.* It's one of them studies from Washington. One of them committees they're always appointing. A thing like that I read on a weekend. But during the weekdays, gee . . . I just thought about it. I don't do that much reading from Monday through Friday. Unless it's a horny book. I'll read it at work and go home and do my homework. (Laughs.) That's what the guys at the plant call it—homework. (Laughs.) Sometimes my wife works on Saturday and I drink beer at the tavern.

I went out drinking with one guy, oh, a long time ago. A college boy. He was working where I work now. Always preaching to me about how you need violence to change the system and all that garbage. We went to a hillbilly joint. Some guy there, I didn't know him from Adam, he said, "You think you're smart." I said "What's your pleasure?" (Laughs.) He said, "My pleasure's to kick your ass." I told him I really can't be bothered. He said, "What're you, chicken?"

249

I said, "No, I just don't want to be bothered." He came over and said something to me again. I said, "I don't beat women, drunks, or fools. Now leave me alone."

The guy called his brother over. This college boy that was with me, he came nudging my arm, "Mike, let's get out of here." I said, "What are you worried about?" (Laughs.) This isn't unusual. People will bug you. You fend it off as much as you can with your mouth and when you can't, you punch the guy out.

It was close to closing time and we stayed. We could have left, but when you go into a place to have a beer and a guy challenges you—if you expect to go in that place again, you don't leave. If you have to fight the guy, you fight.

I got just outside the door and one of these guys jumped on me and grabbed me around the neck. I grabbed his arm and flung him against the wall. I grabbed him here (indicates throat), and jiggled his head against the wall quite a few times. He kind of slid down a little bit. This guy who said he was his brother took a swing at me with a garrison belt. He just missed and hit the wall. I'm looking around for my junior Stalin (laughs), who loves violence and everything. He's gone. Split. (Laughs.) Next day I see him at work. I couldn't get mad at him, he's a baby.

He saw a book in my back pocket one time and he was amazed. He walked up to me and he said, "You read?" I said, "What do you mean, I read?" He said, "All these dummies read the sports pages around here. What are you doing with a book?" I got pissed off at the kid right away. I said, "What do you mean, all these dummies? Don't knock a man who's paying somebody's else's way through college." He was a nineteen-year-old effete snob.

Yet you want your kid to be an effete snob?

Yes, I want my kid to look at me and say, "Dad, you're a nice guy, but you're a fuckin' dummy." Hell yes, I want my kid to tell me that he's not gonna be like me . . .

If I were hiring people to work, I'd try naturally to pay them a decent wage. I'd try to find out their first names, their last names, keep the company as small as possible, so I could personalize the whole thing. All I would ask a man is a handshake, see you in the morning. No applications, nothing. I wouldn't be interested in the guy's past. Nobody ever checks the pedigree on a mule, do they? But they do on a man. Can you picture walking up to a mule and saying, "I'd like to know who his granddaddy was?"

I'd like to run a combination bookstore and tavern. (Laughs.) I would like to have a place where college kids came and a steelworker could sit down and talk. Where a workingman could not be ashamed of Walt Whitman and where a college professor could not be ashamed that he painted his house over the weekend.

If a carpenter built a cabin for poets, I think the least the poets owe the carpenter is just three or four one-liners on the wall. A little plaque: Though we labor with our minds, this place we can relax in was built by someone who can work with his hands. And his work is as noble as ours. I think the poet owes something to the guy who builds the cabin for him.

I don't think of Monday. You know what I'm thinking about on Sunday night? Next Sunday. If you work real hard, you think of a perpetual[1] vacation. Not perpetual sleep . . . What do I think on a Sunday night? Lord, I wish the fuck I could do something else for a living.

I don't know who the guy is who said there is nothing sweeter than an unfinished symphony. Like an unfinished painting and an unfinished poem. If he creates this thing one day—let's say, Michelangelo's Sistine Chapel. It took him a long time to do this, this beautiful work of art. But what if he had to create this Sistine Chapel a thousand times a year? Don't you think that would even dull Michelangelo's mind? Or if da Vinci had to draw his anatomical charts thirty, forty, fifty, sixty, eighty, ninety, a hundred times a day? Don't you think that would even bore da Vinci?

Way back, you spoke of the guys who built the pyramids, not the pharaohs, the unknowns. You put yourself in their category?

Yes. I want my signature on 'em, too. Sometimes out of pure meanness, when I make something, I put a little dent in it. I like to do something to make it really unique. Hit it with a hammer. I deliberately fuck it up to see if it'll get by, just so I can say I did it. It could be anything. Let me put it this way: I think God invented the dodo bird so when we get up there we could tell Him, "Don't you ever make mistakes?" and He'd say, "Sure, look." (Laughs.) I'd like to make my imprint. My dodo bird. A mistake, *mine*. Let's say the whole building is nothing but red bricks. I'd like to have just the black one or the white one or the purple one. Deliberately fuck up.

This is gonna sound square, but my kid is my imprint. He's my freedom. There's a line in one of Hemingway's books. I think it's from *For Whom the Bell Tolls*. They're behind the enemy lines, somewhere in Spain, and she's pregnant. She wants to stay with him. He tells her no. He says, "if you die, I die," knowing he's gonna die. But if you go, I go. Know what I mean? The mystics call it the brass bowl. Continuum. You know what I mean? This is why I work. Every time I see a young guy walk by with a shirt and tie and dressed up real sharp, I'm lookin' at my kid, you know? That's it.

Note

1. Unending.

Gun Store Owner

ROB KEY

I'm one of those people that is classically unemployable and unhireable. I have a problem with authority figures. I have a problem with discipline. Most jobs I've run across, I mastered within a few weeks and got bored as shit. It's hard to go to work for anybody if that's the way you are.

In the 1970s, I was a social worker for some private institutions. Not the state. I had a bunch of positions. The last thing I did was I was a staff coordinator for a local psychiatric hospital. It ended because I had some conflicts with the administration. That was a long time ago, far, far away. I've done a lot of things in my life since then. None of them related to the gun industry except my shop. My background? What does this have to do with the gun industry? I want to talk about the gun industry.

I needed a job. Guns were a hobby. And they just grew into my livelihood. At the time I made a conscious decision to get into them as a business, I wasn't intending to open a gun shop. I wanted to be a gun manufacturer and it was my goal, essentially, to buy a couple of pieces of equipment and to make machine guns in my garage. This was 1985 and back then there was a vast market and a great demand for machine guns.

The Feds changed the law on me just as I was about to invest all of the money I'd saved up to buy two or three pieces of equipment to make my guns. It was a good thing I hadn't already done it yet. It would've been terrible. Lord knows what I would've been doing then.

Instead, when the law changed, I had just enough money to essentially buy one machine gun—just one. But that was enough. I bought it and sold it and took the money and reinvested it, and here we are. I ended up buying this shop from the guy who was my gun guru. He had a worse attitude than I do. He was a hard man to hang out with.

My inventory is primarily exotic guns, machine guns, and older guns. Quality guns. I have a core militia and anti-NRA customer base. That's my niche. I'm not gonna talk about the militias, but I will tell you straight out, I am not a supporter or a member of the NRA. The NRA is a lobbying organization, and as lobbyists, it's their job to compromise. And to compromise, you have to give something up. In 1968, we had a hundred percent of our Second Amendment rights and now thanks to the NRA, we have maybe seventy percent. In school if you were to get a seventy percent you'd barely be passing. How is it that this is acceptable to us with the Constitution? Why can't they kick a little ass and reannoint our rights as granted?

The people who come here wouldn't shop at McBride's, which is the big gun store in this town. You should go down there and check them out. They are my best advertising. It's amazing how many people don't care to get a quality product. They would rather buy a piece of cheap aluminum disposable junk over there so they don't have to deal with my attitude. They just want somebody who will sell them whatever they think they want. And I won't. They ask me for something and if I think it's a piece of shit, I won't sell it to them. If you shop with me you're pretty damned dedicated.

When somebody comes in, I talk to them, find out how much experience they have with guns, what they want a gun for. Especially if it's somebody outside of my core group, I always ask them what they want the gun for. Most people say that they are looking for self-defense. I get a lot of scared people in here. It goes in waves. But you know what? It used to be that the waves would get bigger when something happens—some murders or rapes or any kind of crime spree—you'd get something like that and you get this big rush of folks coming in to get armed and then things would die down for a while. There'd be no waves. But now it seems like there's always these smaller waves and then you have bigger waves that rise out of the smaller waves. As we grow, as America becomes more aware of bigger things to be fearful of—not just of the rapist or the local gang bangers—as people become aware of whatever the conspiracy theory is of the day, then you have to deal with that level of fear. Who do you fear? Do you fear the militia? Or do you fear the federal government? Or do you fear the UN? Or what do you fear?

People come in messed up all the time. Drunk and what have you. People who won't even look up at me come in saying, "I want a gun." It doesn't take long to figure that out. Most of them I just ignore and they go away. I don't have to wait on them. I am controlling the sale and I won't sell to them.

I'm not saying I never make a wrong judgment. We've had people come in and buy guns and go home and within fifteen minutes of buying the gun use it to kill someone. We used to keep the evening news on in here and one time we were watching and there was a guy who shot and killed his wife and they showed a close-up of the front seat of his car and sure enough sitting right on the seat was a receipt from our store. We pulled up the forms and waited for the cops to come.

We've also had instances where we found out within weeks that a gun we sold was used in a suicide. I hate to say this, but most of them are weepy women, and you can tell right off when they come into the store. You just do not sell them a gun, thank you very much.

I believe that part of the job of selling guns is to educate people about them and the responsibilities of ownership. Nobody wants to be a part of the problem. They are inanimate objects—it's the behaviors of people that are dangerous. But sad to say, most people don't want an education. Most people want to stay stupid. I have a major problem with that. I hate to see somebody buy a gun with no idea of what it means to own one or how to even use one. I'm still learning myself. I'll never know all there is to know about guns.

So if you come in and you've never had a gun before, I'm gonna sell you something simple or nothing at all. "Keep It Simple Stupid," right? It's just the way to go. You can't afford to be oblivious or shy when a gun is involved because with a gun it is all over in an instant. So if you have no experience I'll probably hand you this gun here—a Smith and Wesson .38 revolver. You've seen these before on TV or whatever and you look at it and it is very simple, you can tell if it's loaded or not just by looking at it and you can see the trigger and how it works.

It's like with kids, you start them off with a pencil, right? Then later once they've learned to write better you can move them on to a pen.

And with a gun like this Smith and Wesson—you'd buy this gun and a thousand rounds of ammo and I would send you off to one of the trainers at the firing ranges around here. You'd go to the range, once a week, and shoot maybe two hundred rounds at a time. You'd spend hours and hours doing this until you learn that gun. Until you do it so often that you could fire that gun properly in your sleep, or when you're drunk, or when you're at home and the bad guy is right there, too. Then I'll sell you a more sophisticated weapon.

It takes time, though, going to the range every week for years. To do it properly takes training. Too many people think that they know how to use a gun. They buy ammo and they think they're set. Those are the scary ones—the ones who lose hands and eyeballs and worse.

Of course, everyone has a different idea of what gun competency is. But this is my opinion on how it should be done. And it's how I run my shop. And I think it should be the opinion of anyone else who sells firearms. But most customers don't want to do it. You talk to them about shooting thousands of rounds of ammo and their eyes just glaze over. Most people are only interested in the instant gratification, they don't want the education. Well, they can go elsewhere. I'm not that kind of guy. You could go over to McBride's and they'll sell you anything you want.

I think the way I do business is the only way to "regulate" guns. Meaning through the individual businessman using common sense. The "gun control" laws make no sense. They are not logical. People ask, "Why is this this way? What do these forms mean?" And you can't give them a reasonable, responsible answer. Nothing is realistic about the laws they pass—they say they're supposed to stop crime but they have nothing to do with crime. I mean, a crime is when you see the ATF and the FBI murder dozens of people in Waco, isn't it? That ticks me off so much, the lying, the hypocrisy of it all.

Everybody wants to blame the gun business. It's unfair. I mean somebody buys a knife and stabs their wife, does the neighborhood association send a bunch of old farts over to shut down the knife store?

The thing about the gun business that no one ever asks about or realizes is that it's work. It is a business. And that's all it is, and it's not even a very good business. I am the one who cleans the toilet here. That's being in this business. Coming down to the store every day. You could take my temperature right now and it would be a hundred and one degrees. It's been that way for three days. I'm sick, but I can't not be here.

I would never advise someone to go into this to make money. In the time I've been here I've seen at least twenty-four gun shops come and go in Austin. They last a summer, maybe two, then disappear. You have to love it, you have to believe in it, believe what you're doing is right and ignore all the lies. I myself worked for years without really taking a paycheck. If my wife hadn't had a good salary and if we didn't eat the vegetables we grow and the deer we kill on our property, we wouldn't have made it. But we did make it. We didn't waste money and we didn't buy into the culture of a consumer system. And we're better off for it.

Forty-Five a Month

R. K. NARAYAN

Anticipating: Describe a personal disappointment which occurred when you were very young. For example, you might choose to write about the bicycle that didn't appear on Christmas, a friend who moved away, a visitor who didn't arrive, a grandparent's death. Or describe a disappointment which you have experienced recently. Be sure to include how you felt and why.

Shanta could not stay in her class any longer. She had done clay-modelling, music, drill, a bit of alphabets and numbers, and was now cutting coloured paper. She would have to cut till the bell rang and the teacher said, "Now you may all go home," or "Put away the scissors and take up your alphabets—" Shanta was impatient to know the time. She asked her friend sitting next to her, "Is it five now?" "Maybe," she replied. "Or is it six?" "I don't think so," her friend replied, "because night comes at six."

"Do you think it is five?"

"Yes."

"Oh, I must go. My father will be back at home now. He has asked me to be ready at five. He is taking me to the cinema this evening. I must go home." She threw down her scissors and ran up to the teacher. "Madam, I must go home."

"Why, Shanta Bai?"

"Because it is five o'clock now."

"Who told you it was five?"

"Kamala."

"It is not five now. It is—do you see the clock there? Tell me what the time is. I taught you to read the clock the other day." Shanta stood gazing at the clock in the hall, counted the figures laboriously and declared, "It is nine o'clock."

The teacher called the other girls and said, "Who will tell me the time from that clock?" Several of them concurred with Shanta and said it was nine o'clock, till the teacher said, "You are seeing only the long hand. See the short one, where is it?"

"Two and a half."

"So what is the time?"

"Two and a half."

"It is two forty-five, understand? Now you may all go to your seats—" Shanta returned to the teacher in about ten minutes and asked, "Is it five, madam, because I have to be ready at five. Otherwise my father will be very angry with me. He asked me to return home early."

"At what time?"

"Now." The teacher gave her permission to leave, and Shanta picked up her books and dashed out of the class with a cry of joy. She ran home, threw her books on the floor and shouted, "Mother, Mother," and Mother came running from the next house, where she had gone to chat with her friends.

Mother asked, "Why are you back so early?"

"Has Father come home?" Shanta asked. She would not take her coffee or tiffin but insisted on being dressed first. She opened the trunk and insisted on wearing the thinnest frock and knickers, while her mother wanted to dress her in a long skirt and thick coat for the evening. Shanta picked out a gorgeous ribbon from a cardboard soap box in which she kept pencils, ribbons and chalk bits. There was a heated argument between mother and daughter over the dress, and finally mother had to give in. Shanta put on her favourite pink frock, braided her hair and flaunted a green ribbon on her pigtail. She powdered her face and pressed a vermilion mark on her forehead. She said, "Now Father will say what a nice girl I am because I'm ready. Aren't you also coming, Mother?"

"Not today."

Shanta stood at the little gate looking down the street.

Mother said, "Father will come only after five; don't stand in the sun. It is only four o'clock."

The sun was disappearing behind the house on the opposite row, and Shanta knew that presently it would be dark. She ran in to her mother and asked, "Why hasn't Father come home yet, Mother?"

"How can I know? He is perhaps held up in the office."

Shanta made a wry face. "I don't like these people in the office. They are bad people—"

❧

She went back to the gate and stood looking out. Her mother shouted from inside, "Come in, Shanta. It is getting dark, don't stand there." But Shanta would not go in. She stood at the gate and a wild idea came into her head. Why should she not go to the office and call out Father and then go to the cinema? She wondered where his office might be. She had no notion. She had seen her father take the turn at the end of the street every day. If one went there, perhaps one went automatically to Father's office. She threw a glance about to see if Mother was anywhere and moved down the street.

It was twilight. Everyone going about looked gigantic, walls of houses appeared very high and cycles and carriages looked as though they would bear down on her. She walked on the very edge of the road. Soon the lamps were twinkling, and the passers-by looked like shadows. She had taken two turns and did not know where she was. She sat on the edge of the road biting her nails. She wondered how she was to reach home. A servant employed in the next house was passing along, and she picked herself up and stood before him.

"Oh, what are you doing her all alone?" he asked. She replied, "I don't know. I came here. Will you take me to our house?" She followed him and was soon back in her house.

Venkat Rao, Shanta's father, was about to start for his office that morning when a *jutka* passed along the street distributing cinema handbills. Shanta dashed to the street and picked up a handbill. She held it up and asked, "Father, will you take me to the cinema today?" He felt unhappy at the question. Here was the child growing up without having any of the amenities and the simple pleasures of life. He had hardly taken her twice to the cinema. He had no time for the child. While children of her age in other houses had all the dolls, dresses and outing that they wanted, this child was growing up all alone like a barbarian more or less. He felt furious with his office. For forty rupees a month they seemed to have purchased him outright.

He reproached himself for neglecting his wife and child—even the wife could have her own circle of friends and so on; she was after all a grown-up, but what about the child? What a drab, colourless existence was hers! Every day they kept him at the office till seven or eight in the evening, and when he came home the child was asleep. Even on Sundays they wanted him at the office. Why did they think he had no personal life, a life of his own? They gave him hardly any time to take the child to the park or the pictures. He was going to show them that they weren't going to toy with him. Yes, he was prepared even to quarrel with the manager if necessary.

He said with resolve, "I will take you to the cinema this evening. Be ready at five."

"Really! Mother!" Shanta shouted. Mother came out of the kitchen.

"Father is taking me to the cinema this evening."

Shanta's mother smiled cynically. "Don't make false promises to the child—" Venkat Rao glared at her. "Don't talk nonsense. You think you are the only person who keeps promises—"

He told Shanta, "Be ready at five, and I will come and take you positively. If you are not ready, I will be very angry with you."

He walked to his office full of resolve. He would do his normal work and get out at five. If they started any old tricks of theirs, he was going to tell the boss, "Here is my resignation. My child's happiness is more important to me than these horrible papers of yours."

All day the usual stream of papers flowed onto his table and off it. He scrutinized, signed and drafted. He was corrected, admonished and insulted. He had a break of only five minutes in the afternoon for his coffee.

When the office clock struck five and the other clerks were leaving, he went up to the manager and said, "May I go, sir?" The manager looked up from his paper. "You!" It was unthinkable that the cash and account section should be closing at five. "How can you go?"

"I have some urgent private business, sir," he said, smothering the lines he had been rehearsing since the morning: "Herewith my resignation." He visualized Shanta standing at the door, dressed and palpitating with eagerness.

"There shouldn't be anything more urgent than the office work; go back to your seat. You know how many hours I work?" asked the manager. The manager came to the office three hours before opening time and stayed nearly three hours after closing, even on Sundays. The clerks commented among themselves. "His wife must be whipping him whenever he is seen at home; that is why the old owl seems so fond of his office."

"Did you trace the source of that ten-eight difference?" asked the manager.

"I shall have to examine two hundred vouchers. I thought we might do it tomorrow."

ℐℬ

No, no, this won't do. You must rectify it immediately."

Venkat Rao mumbled, "Yes, sir," and slunk back to his seat.

The clock showed 5:30. Now it meant two hours of excruciating search among vouchers. All the rest of the office had gone. Only he and another clerk in his section were working, and of course, the manager was there. Venkat Rao was furious. His mind was made up. He wasn't a slave who had sold himself for forty rupees outright. He could make that money easily; and if he couldn't, it would be more honourable to die of starvation.

He took a sheet of paper and wrote: "Herewith my resignation. If you people think you have bought me body and soul for forty rupees, you are mistaken. I think it would be far better for me and my family to die of starvation than slave for this petty forty rupees on which you have kept me for years and years. I suppose you have not the slightest notion of giving me an increment. You give yourselves heavy slices frequently, and I don't see why you shouldn't think of us occasionally. In any case it doesn't interest me now, since this is my resignation. If I and my family perish of starvation, may our ghosts come and haunt you all your life—" He folded the letter, put it in an envelope, sealed the flap and addressed it to the manager. He left his seat and stood before the manager. The manager mechanically received the letter and put it on his pad.

"Venkat Rao," said the manager, "I'm sure you will be glad to hear this news. Our officer discussed the question of increments today, and I've recommended you for an increment of five rupees. Orders are not yet passed, so keep this to yourself for the present." Venkat Rao put out his hand, snatched the envelope from the pad and hastily slipped it in his pocket.

"What is that letter?"

"I have applied for a little casual leave, sir, but I think . . ."

260

"You can't get any leave for at least a fortnight to come."

"Yes, sir. I realize that. That is why I am withdrawing my application, sir."

"Very well. Have you traced that mistake?"

"I'm scrutinizing the vouchers, sir. I will find it out within an hour. . . ."

It was nine o'clock when he went home. Shanta was already asleep. Her mother said, "She wouldn't even change her frock, thinking that any moment you might be coming and taking her out. She hardly ate any food; and wouldn't lie down for fear of crumpling her dress. . . ."

Venkat Rao's heart bled when he saw his child sleeping in her pink frock, hair combed and face powdered, dressed and ready to be taken out. "Why should I not take her to the night show?" He shook her gently and called, "Shanta, Shanta." Shanta kicked her legs and cried, irritated at being disturbed. Mother whispered, "Don't wake her," and patted her back to sleep.

Venkat Rao watched the child for a moment. "I don't know if it is going to be possible for me to take her out at all—you see, they are giving me an increment—" he wailed.

Heroes of the House

LOUISE RAFKIN

But I cannot recount or name them all: the many wives and daughters of the brave.

—The Odyssey

Once I decided to do it, my foray into professional housecleaning happened quickly. It was on the very day that I pinned my cleaning flyer on the supermarket bulletin board next to the offers of free kitties that the blinking light on my answering machine presented the reality of my newfound profession. A gynecologist and his wife wanted an estimate.

The four-bedroom tri-level Cape Cod summer home was dusted with a yellow coat of spring pollen. Trailing the woman, I scrutinized the bathrooms and counted the bedrooms. I figured and calculated. Then I choked. I blew the estimate, offering my speed-demon skills at a price that I rightly figured would land me the job. As it turned out, I cleaned that home for an entire summer for about what her husband would charge for a single Pap smear.

During my first few years I made a lot of mistakes. Times were lean. I said yes when I should have said no. I cleaned for people with dogs. I cleaned for people with gaggles of kids, even babies. Actually, babies are fine. It's only after they try feeding themselves that the trouble begins. I developed this equation: If there's a toddler, there has to be a dog—the dog will surely shed but at least the food on the floor will be taken care of.

That first year I took on a woman who paid me in loose change and talked me down five dollars on my quoted price for the job, this while I stood in her new million-dollar summer home. I worked for a couple who routinely scheduled huge parties the night *before* I came to clean.

But I accepted my Cinderella role dutifully and without complaint. During most of my early years on the job, I was a wimp.

"Where's that damn prince?" I complained to my coworker A.J. one day as we were leaving the house of the "Loose-Change Lady." (Most of the time I

263

clean with A.J. or another coworker, who vacuums while I do the wet work—bathrooms and kitchens. It's important to have someone handy to complain to, plus I prefer wet work. I enjoy spraying products meant to smell like the natural world—pine, citrus—yet still smell obviously like cleaning products.)

"I'm ready for that fairy-tale ending," I said to A.J. It had been a particularly bad day. Earlier, while I was on my hands and knees in the bathroom singing along with the song on my Walkman, Loose-Change Lady had tapped me on the shoulder. Signing wildly, she gesticulated that something was wrong. I moved my earphones aside and smiled wanly. She told me, "You're off-key."

"Fairy-tale ending?" A.J. challenged. "Cinderella ends up marrying some strange guy because of her shoe size and her sisters' evil eyes are pecked out by doves! They probably ended up freeloading on her the rest of their lives."

"You're right," I said. "She probably cleaned up after the whole lot of them—with her husband insisting she wear those uncomfortable glass slippers."

☙

By accident, while reading a story to my niece, I discovered that despite his famous parentage, Hercules put in time as a cleaner. It was part of his penance for killing about six of his own kids.

As punishment, Hercules was given a set of tasks, one of which was to clean the Augean stables. They hadn't been cleaned for thirty years.

But Hercules didn't mess around with all that horse-shit. He simply diverted two nearby rivers so that they ran smack through the stables.

Waves of horse manure swamped the flood plains, polluted endangered salmon-spawning grounds, and swept downstream into the backyards of some unsuspecting peons, but soon the job was finished. Apparently Hercules had better things to do than fret about the environment.

Although I was outraged by Hercules' selfish cleaning technique, my niece remained enamored with the macho hero. She did, however, come up with a sensible response to this fable: "Why hadn't those stables been cleaned for thirty years?"

Not surprisingly, there are few role models for responsible, strong-minded cleaners. As a kid I think I was only vaguely aware of a handful of prime-time TV cleaners. Beulah, the first black character to headline a TV show, and Hazel were the front-runners, living-in at the homes of wealthy white families. Later there was the wacky Alice who worked for the Brady Bunch, and the curmudgeonly Florence at the Jefferson's.

I never paid much attention to these characters. For the most part, they seemed silly and foolish. However, I did read and reread Peggy Parish's books about the simple-minded housekeeper Amelia Bedelia. When the overly literal Amelia was told to dress the chicken, she did just that, fashioning tiny clothes for the bird.

When I first began cleaning I liked to think of myself as a somewhat hip and creative version of Amelia Bedelia. I could only pull this off for so long. Sooner or later, reality was bound to set in. My personal transformation from meek and mild scrubwoman to maid with a mind of her own occurred organically, but suddenly. It was several years into my cleaning life, at a house where the client had never even taken the time to learn my name. At the end of our shift, he'd hand me a check with the line for the name completely blank.

I was relocating a pair of his dirty underwear from the floor to a chair by means of a coathanger. A.J. watched from across the bedroom, giggling.

"I don't move dirty underwear," I said to A.J.

"No?" she said, eyebrows up. "You could have fooled me."

Right then the man sailed in from the hall. "Change the sheets, would you?" Folded sheets in hand, he seemed baffled by my fishing maneuver.

"No," I said, the offending briefs dangling from the wire hook.

For the the right person, I'd pick up dirty underwear, change sheets, and even sweep up dead rats (and I have), but this wasn't the right person.

"No," I said again, having made the decision that this was a job I no longer wanted. "We don't change sheets." Obviously angered, he tossed the bundle of sheets on the bed and left the room.

"Unless you want them really changed," I said to A.J. once he had departed. "Like shredded."

A.J. laughed, I laughed, and we never went back there again. It was my first good riddance, though I did see this guy years later in a movie theater. He was sitting in front of me, and I knew, if I didn't move, I could never enjoy the film. I was afraid I would be recognized.

And afraid I wouldn't be.

❧

Although few can imagine them, there are fairy-tale moments in a housecleaner's life, despite crabby clients and sometimes being treated as less than human. I have felt flashes of transformation along the lines of Cinderellas, and witnessed situations as dramatic as Hercules' clean sweep.

One such moment involved a sweet elderly client. An alcoholic, he was almost always tipsy. One morning he met me at the door in a panic; he had somehow misplaced $1,000 in cash.

"Forget the cleaning," he told me. (I hated cleaning this house—it was large and rambling, and the only joy was finding bottles hidden in new places, like the guest shower.)

"Just find the money!" he implored, and I didn't dare get close to him. The smell, even at a distance, was overwhelming.

Together we turned the house upside down. Eventually, I discovered the money stuffed into an empty toilet-paper roll buried in the laundry hamper. With the wad of cash in my hand, I found him on the living room couch, weeping. Sighting the green roll, he jumped up, took my arm, and insisted on leading me in a celebratory waltz. At that moment, strange as it now seems, dancing together was the only thing we could have done.

I was tipped a crisp $100 and was home before noon.

At another house, I found my prince—of sorts. I was side-by-side at the sink with a client, a Hollywood somebody, who had taken years to warm to me. Whenever I was there, he was usually absorbed in his work, a splay of legal pads covered with scribbled bits of dialogue before him on the dining room table. Often he was on the phone talking to someone I've only experienced through the pages of *People* magazine. While cleaning, I'd listen in on his conversations, imagining what I thought would be a Somebody's life—palm trees and personal trainers.

Fastidious, he hated that his stainless-steel sink was stained. So one warm, sunny morning, I showed him the secret of sink de-rusting, and there we were, shoulder-to-shoulder, our elbows bumping, our muscles churning, swabbing the twin sinks.

He was amazed! Delighted! Rust stains, the great leveler. I imagined the advertisement: "Soft Scrub—even eradicates class distinctions!" And who could have thought that we, the two of us, from such different parts of the world, would share such a moment?

Often I just can't help myself. Once while I was dusting at a one-time-only job, I found a letter taped onto the back of a picture frame. It was unsealed and addressed to a man I vaguely knew. Of course, I couldn't resist: I read a long confession of obsessive love from another man who had previously lived in this house but had long since left town. I couldn't imagine how the letter had come to be stuck to the back of the picture, or why it was there.

"I hope someone will send this," it closed. "I am not brave enough to accept my passion."

Later that day I mailed the letter. Sometimes I want my presence in a house to have an effect beyond that of a well-mopped floor.

The Job

DORIANNE LAUX

for Tobey

When my friend lost her little finger
between the rollers of a printing press,
I hadn't met her yet. It must have taken
months for the stump to heal, skin stretched
and stitched over bone, must have taken
years before she could consider it calmly,
as she does now, in an airport cafe
over a cup of black coffee.
She doesn't complain or blame the unguarded
machine, the noise of the factory, the job
with its long unbroken hours.
She simply opens her damaged hand and studies
the emptiness, the loss
of symmetry and flesh, and tells me
it was a small price to pay,
that her missing finger taught her
to take more care with her life,
with what she reaches out
to touch, to stay awake when she's awake
and listen, to pay attention
to what's turning in the world.

Why I Want a Wife

JUDY SYFERS

Judy Syfers, a free-lance writer, says that her own experience, plus discouraging advice received from male teachers, inspired her to compose the following essay, which first appeared as the "Backpage" feature in Ms. magazine in December of 1971 and has since been widely reprinted.

I belong to that classification of people known as wives. I am A Wife. And, not altogether incidentally, I am a mother.

Not too long ago a male friend of mine appeared on the scene fresh from a recent divorce. He had one child, who is, of course, with his ex-wife. He is looking for another wife. As I thought about him while I was ironing one evening, it suddenly occurred to me that I, too, would like to have a wife. Why do I want a wife?

I would like to go back to school so that I can become economically independent, support myself, and, if need be, support those dependent upon me. I want a wife who will work and send me to school. And while I am going to school I want a wife to take care of my children. I want a wife to keep track of the children's doctor and dentist appointments. And to keep track of mine, too. I want a wife to make sure my children eat properly and are kept clean. I want a wife who will wash the children's clothes and keep them mended. I want a wife who is a good nurturant attendant to my children, who arranges for their schooling, makes sure that they have an adequate social life with their peers, takes them to the park, the zoo, etc. I want a wife who takes care of the children when they are sick, a wife who arranges to be around when the children need special care, because, of course, I cannot miss classes at school. My wife must arrange to lose time at work and not lose the job. It may mean a small cut in my wife's income from time to time, but I guess I can tolerate that. Needless to say, my wife will arrange and pay for the care of the children while my wife is working.

I want a wife who will take care of my physical needs. I want a wife who will keep my house clean. A wife who will pick up after my children, a wife who

269

will pick up after me. I want a wife who will keep my clothes clean, ironed, mended, replaced when need be, and who will see to it that my personal things are kept in their proper place so that I can find what I need the minute I need it. I want a wife who cooks the meals, a wife who is a *good* cook. I want a wife who will plan the menus, do the necessary grocery shopping, prepare the meals, serve them pleasantly, and then do the cleaning up while I do my studying. I want a wife who will care for me when I am sick and sympathize with my pain and loss of time from school. I want a wife to go along when our family takes a vacation so that someone can continue to care for me and my children when I need a rest and change of scene.

I want a wife who will not bother me with rambling complaints about a wife's duties. But I want a wife who will listen to me when I feel the need to explain a rather difficult point I have come across in my course of studies. And I want a wife who will type my papers for me when I have written them.

I want a wife who will take care of the details of my social life. When my wife and I are invited out by my friends, I want a wife who will take care of the babysitting arrangements. When I meet people at school that I like and want to entertain, I want a wife who will have the house clean, will prepare a special meal, serve it to me and my friends, and not interrupt when I talk about things that interest me and my friends. I want a wife who will have arranged that the children are fed and ready for bed before my guests arrive so that the children do not bother us. I want a wife who takes care of the needs of my guests so that they feel comfortable, who makes sure that they have an ashtray, that they are passed the hors d'oeuvres, that they are offered a second helping of the food, that their wine glasses are replenished when necessary, that their coffee is served to them as they like it. And I want a wife who knows that sometimes I need a night out by myself.

I want a wife who is sensitive to my sexual needs, a wife who makes love passionately and eagerly when I feel like it, a wife who makes sure that I am satisfied. And, of course, I want a wife who will not demand sexual attention when I am not in the mood for it. I want a wife who assumes the complete responsibility for birth control, because I do not want more children. I want a wife who will remain sexually faithful to me so that I do not have to clutter up my intellectual life with jealousies. And I want a wife who understands that my sexual needs may entail more than strict adherence to monogamy. I must, after all, be able to relate to people as fully as possible.

If, by chance, I find another person more suitable as a wife than the wife I already have, I want the liberty to replace my present wife with another one. Naturally, I will expect a fresh, new life; my wife will take the children and be solely responsible for them so that I am left free.

When I am through with school and have a job, I want my wife to quit working and remain at home so that my wife can more fully and completely take care of a wife's duties.

My God, who *wouldn't* want a wife?

A Diner in California
from *Waiting*—The True Confessions
of a Waitress

DEBRA GINSBERG

Diners have a certain image in the collective imagination. Soda fountains, for example. Endless coffee. Inexpensive but filling meals. Bright Formica and stainless steel. Waitresses in pink outfits, on roller skates. Red Naugahyde booths. An innocence of the all-American variety. There is something comforting in the warm glow of a diner, a feeling of safe haven. Diners evoke nostalgia, sweet as cherry pie, of a time when some things, at least, were simpler.

There is, of course, a darker version.

I worked in one.

When I moved to California with Maya and my year-old son, the logical first step was to find a job in the new land of low-fat milk and raw honey. My parents had raved about the quality of life in California:

"People walk around in shorts in the middle of the day!"

"Everybody's on a permanent vacation—nobody works here!"

"Beaches! Sunshine! Vegetarian restaurants!"

People, it seemed, survived in style down here. Maya and I both reckoned we could get decent waitressing jobs, which would at least pay the bills until we got on our feet and began doing whatever it was that we were really meant to do. For Maya, who had been playing violin since the age of nine, that whatever involved music. For me, a small voice in my head still whispered (although not very insistently) that I should be writing something. Anything.

Our initial approach to the job search was fairly simple. We'd found an apartment to rent that was close enough to the beach to sport an ocean view (if we craned our heads in a very specific way out of the living room window) and within walking distance of a town very popular with tourists. Because we'd moved without a car, or much of anything resembling furniture, for that

271

matter, I strapped Blaze into his stroller and both Maya and I walked along the ocean from our apartment into town, stopping in at every restaurant along the way. Usually, we took turns going in. If the restaurant looked more upscale, Maya would wait outside with the baby while I filled out an application. Having only Maxman's and Peppy's to her credit, Maya felt unsure of her waitressing skills and, despite tales of my Dining Room experience, was unwilling to try to bluff her way into a fine dining situation. As a result, I filled out countless applications and Maya spent a lot of time with Blaze.

After a couple of days of this pavement pounding, we stopped in at Hoover's, an eclectic diner only steps away from the azure surf of the Pacific. The restaurant was decorated in shades of black, pink, and seafoam green down to the flecks in the Formica tabletops. There were whole wheat muffins under glass and Warholish prints on the walls. Next to an old-fashioned industrial coffee maker was a very high-tech cappuccino machine. The overall effect was Mel's Diner meets the Twin Peaks café.

Maya and I filled out applications together while I rocked Blaze in his stroller with my foot. The diner's owner, Adrian, seemed highly amused at our team approach. He was in dire need of help, he said, and had to hire someone immediately. I marveled at our good fortune and the fact that he wasn't even planning on checking our references.

"Can you girls start Sunday morning?" was all he asked.

It all seemed so easy.

Within a few weeks, however, Maya and I both discovered why, despite a steady flow of customers, Adrian had the highest staff turnover of any restaurant in town. We also learned a style of service that I have come to label "guerrilla waitressing." Within a scant couple of months, we were preparing for our shifts as if we were going to war. And Hoover's was nothing if not a battlefield.

Allow me to illustrate . . .

I wake up on Sunday morning at 5:30 A.M. and pack a bag for Blaze with toys, diapers, and bottles. He'll be spending the day with my parents until I finish work. I take a five-minute shower and hurry myself into a pink T-shirt and shorts. For the first time in my life, I've eschewed the traditional black waitress footwear for an expensive pair of cross-training athletic shoes. As I strap them on, I realize what a good choice they are. What I will be doing for the next several hours will be more of a work-out than work. I can't leave Blaze without saying good-bye to him, so I pick him up out of his crib and kiss his sleepy face before tucking him into bed with Maya.

"I'm leaving," I tell her.

"Hmmm . . . OK," she mutters. "See you there."

I walk to work while the rest of the world sleeps. My twenty-minute route takes me along the ocean, through quiet streets. It's still fairly dark outside and the salty air has a little bite. But this is California. I'll be sweating by noon, no matter that this is the middle of January.

I arrive for my shift at Hoover's at 6:30 A.M. My first task is to rouse Danny from his stupor so that he can unlock the restaurant and prepare the popovers.

I should explain. Adrian had a very successful business, which he was doing his best to run into the Indian burial ground that his restaurant was suspected of being built upon. By the time my sister and I were hired, he was about three quarters of the way to complete ruin. There were two things that kept Hoover's busy and saved Adrian from going under: a spectacular ocean view and popovers. Every single day, Adrian, or whatever hapless cook happened to be employed at the time, made dozens of popovers, which were served with every breakfast and lunch. Most mornings the popovers came out late, half burned or half raw. They were sent back regularly by customers screaming with indignation. Yet, amazingly, these same customers came back time and again, lining up for forty-five minutes on a Sunday morning in order to wait another forty-five minutes at the table with seven refills of coffee until they received an omelette that contained not what was ordered but whatever was left in the kitchen and that was garnished by a misshapen, ill-conceived attempt at a popover.

But I digress.

"Danny!" I shriek for the third time. "Get up! Danny, can you hear me?"

Danny Davidson is one of two cooks Adrian refers to as "my international staff of chefs." Danny found his way to Southern California from New Zealand and entered almost immediately into a Faustian bargain with Adrian. At twenty, Danny has been an alcoholic for more than five years. Adrian, seeing a prime opportunity, offered to pay him mostly in beer. While the arrangement suited Danny, it didn't allow him much spare cash to live on. Magnanimously, Adrian provided Danny with a room off the restaurant, which had been serving as a spare office. Thus, Danny, who had never so much as fried an egg before being hired at Hoover's, has become something of an indentured servant. He drinks steadily all day and finishes with several six-packs when his shift is over. By the time his next shift begins, he is usually deep in a bottomless blackout.

I pound on the locked door until my fists hurt and I experience a familiar flash of panic. Could Danny, whom I like but am unable to help, be comatose this time? Or worse? I bang and scream one more time. There is a muffled groaning behind the door.

"Danny! The popovers. It's getting late—please."

The door opens and I am assaulted by a wave of alcoholic fumes. Danny, half dressed, bloodshot and pasty, looks worse than a train wreck.

"Where's Adrian, the scabby prick?" Danny mutters. "It's not my shift this morning."

"He's not here," I say, desperately. "Please unlock the door for me, Danny."

Spewing barely intelligible curses, Danny stumbles down to the diner and lets me in. I have to beg him to stay vertical and start cooking. The restaurant is scheduled to open in an hour and we'll be full to capacity within a half hour afterward. Reluctantly, Danny staggers to the kitchen and begins whipping up a batch of popovers destined to reach a new low point in culinary standards.

It's seven-thirty and Sheryl, the next waitress on, is half an hour late. I'm running around frantically trying to get the coffee made, the tables wiped down, and the condiments filled and lined up. We're not going to be ready.

The phone rings and I lunge for it, hoping it's Adrian to say he's on his way. No such luck. It's Sheryl, sounding none too happy.

"I'm sorry, I don't think I'm going to make it into work today," she says.

"Sheryl, please, even if you're late, it's no big deal. But it's going to be really busy and we really need—"

"No, I'm really not going to make it."

"Are you sick?"

"Not exactly."

"Can someone come pick you up?"

"Well, I'm kind of in Mexico."

"Well, you could make it back in a couple of hours, couldn't you?"

"Not really. I'm kind of in jail. In Tijuana."

There is a long silence. My brain is refusing to process the information.

"Listen," Sheryl continues, "can you let Adrian know what happened? Tell him I'm really sorry. Also, I think you should know that Frank's with me. I mean, he's also in jail, so he probably won't be able to make it for his shift, either."

I don't want to know the details and Sheryl doesn't offer them. What I do know is that we're now two servers short. This day has all the earmarks of certain disaster.

Adrian shows up at eight. He's wearing a pink sweatshirt, black tights, and loafers with no socks. His hair is matted and his eyes are wild. He looks as if he hasn't eaten, slept, or bathed for at least a month. He barks, "Cappuccino, make it a double!" at me and heads to the kitchen. By this time my first customers have arrived, a couple of regulars who bring the Sunday papers and fold them into neat sections to read one at a time. One of them watches Adrian, smiles, and shakes his head.

"Crazy guy," he offers. I smile and fill his coffee. "It will probably be a few minutes before the popovers are ready," I tell him. "We're running a bit late today."

"So what else is new?" Mr. Regular tells me grumpily. "I'll take the omelette first, then. Bring me the popover when it's ready. And since I have to wait for it, you can bring me an extra one for free."

Thank you, thank you, Mr. Regular. I'm happy to serve you and really earn my $1.57 tip. How empty would your life be without the chance of that free popover for all your troubles? I ring up his omelette, but I'm dubious that anyone is paying attention to the order in the kitchen, where shouting is audible.

"You call this a popover?" Adrian is screaming as I approach the kitchen. "This is an abortion!" Adrian takes the first batch and throws them into the trash. "Now, make some real popovers!"

Danny is staring at his feet, taking the abuse. His misery emanates in tidal waves.

"Um, I've got an omelette on order," I begin tentatively. Adrian and Danny stare at me as if I'm speaking Greek.

"Can you believe this fucking kid?" Adrian says, pointing at Danny. "Can't even get a fucking popover together. Where the fuck is Oaxaca?"

"Oaxaca" is the other international star in Adrian's chef roster. A Mexican national with no green card, Oaxaca is illegally employed by Adrian and treated even worse than Danny, if that's possible. Sweet, timid, and unable to understand almost any English, Oaxaca regularly works twelve- to fifteen-hour days. I don't know how much Adrian pays him, but I'm sure it's criminally low. Oaxaca is not his real name, it's the region in Mexico he comes from, but he is never referred to any other way—another attempt on Adrian's part to keep him in his place. None of us know what his name is, exactly, and he's too shy to tell us.

(This type of hiring practice was a fact of SoCal kitchens I'd discovered very soon after moving to the area. Inevitably, restaurants would hire illegal, or dubiously legal, aliens to work in the kitchen for ridiculously low wages. Thus, restaurants of every nationality—Greek, French, Italian, Indian, Thai—ended up with Mexican cooks. One restaurant I worked in later carried this policy to extremes, hiring illegals and raising their wages by minuscule increments until Immigration did a sweep. At this point, the restaurant would "fire" the cooks, only to hire them back with new names at the old wages.)

"Um, Adrian? Sheryl called from Tijuana. She's in jail with Frank. They're not going to make it to work today, obviously, so I was wondering if maybe we could call somebody else?" I run from the kitchen after delivering this news, not wanting to hear its effect.

At nine the restaurant is almost full. Maya and one other waitress, Jessie, have arrived. Maya takes one look at me and reads the morning in my face.

"How bad is it?" she asks.

"Don't ask," I tell her. "I need you to take Twelve, Fourteen, and Fifteen. And Twenty's been waiting for ten minutes. How's Blaze?"

"Fine," she says, tying on her apron. "Mom and Dad have big plans for him today. They're going to the Wild Animal Park."

I raise my eyebrows. "They could just bring him here and avoid the cost of admission," I say.

Maya and I are soon waiting on at least ten tables each, while Jessie is struggling to handle two. Jessie explains that she's hung over this morning and will need a little time to ease into her shift. Adrian doesn't care about this because Jessie's father coaches a professional football team. Even though Jessie has been disowned by her father for drug and alcohol problems, Adrian figures some of the gravy will eventually drip over onto him if he employs the daughter. Oaxaca has shown up and started cooking, but Adrian is on a rampage, criticizing every plate that comes out of the kitchen, so that now we are at least ten plates behind and not a popover in sight.

"I don't know why I keep coming here," a woman says to me, waving her diamond-encrusted hand in disdain. "The service is slow and the food is terrible."

I don't know why, either. Go to another restaurant, I want to tell her. Please. Better yet, go home and cook something yourself for your bratty children. Instead, I make her a free latte and locate crayons for her two screaming kids, buying myself ten more minutes before she erupts again.

At ten, Chris and Terry arrive, replacements for the jailed Sheryl and Frank. Terry and Chris feel that since they have come in on their day off, they should be given the best tables, which are located on the patio, up a rickety flight of wooden stairs.

While the popovers were subject to the vagaries of human nature, the ocean was consistently beautiful. Since my episode at Hoover's, I have learned that people will do just about anything to secure themselves an ocean view, even if the table they are viewing it from is made of dirty white plastic, shaded with an ancient Cinzano-emblazoned umbrella, and laid with barely edible food. This was certainly the case at Hoover's, which in addition was laid out so eccentrically that it was almost impossible to give decent service to its prime tables.

Chris and Terry are arguing their point when the question of who will serve up on the patio becomes somewhat moot. We all hear a spectacular crash and a gasp of "Ooh" from the upstairs diners. On closer investigation, it seems that Jessie has fallen up the stairs with a tray full of cappuccinos.

"I think I blacked out," she says. "I think I twisted my ankle. I can't walk. I'm going to have to go home. Or maybe to the hospital."

At Adrian's command, we begin handing out free mimosas to the patio tables to assuage the trauma they've sustained watching the accident. Several tables feel they have to justify receiving freebies that they haven't yet had the chance to demand:

"You'd better make sure you get that cleaned up. If I slip on those stairs, there's going to be a lawsuit."

"Only one mimosa? Can I get another one if I don't get my breakfast in the next half hour?"

"Are you sure you use fresh-squeezed orange juice in this? Doesn't taste like it."

"I don't drink champagne. Can I get a free Bloody Mary instead?"

The downstairs tables get wind of the situation and begin complaining bitterly:

"Hey, I've been waiting thirty minutes for two eggs and toast. Where's my free drink?"

"What kind of place is this? Free drinks for half the restaurant?"

"Get that fascist Adrian out here now."

The downstairs tables get mimosas. This ploy actually works quite well. Enough diners get tipsy enough not to notice the wait or the escalating entropy. The only trouble now is that we've run out of orange juice. The juice man hasn't made a delivery for a while since Adrian is at least two months behind on payment. We are also running out of eggs, bacon, sausage, and hamburger because the meat distributor is in the same boat as the juice man. At this rate we will be out of every menu item but the tuna melt by noon.

"Tell them that this is Vegetarian Day at Hoover's," Adrian says. "This is California, isn't it?"

Despite the chaos, business continues to be brisk. I even have time to converse with some of my customers about topics other than the lateness of their orders. One man, for example, asks me: "What is this awful music?"

Adrian has two tape loops he insists on pumping through the restaurant. One is a medley of relatively current pop tunes and the other is a collection of standards that would work well in an underground French bistro. Today we are listening to the latter.

"I believe this is Eartha Kitt," I tell him.

"Eartha Kitt? You mean Catwoman? You gotta be kidding me. This place . . ."

I approach another table and offer them something to drink. "I just want you to know," one man says, "that the last time we were here, we had a terrible experience. The food was cold and we were not given any attention from our waitress."

"I'm so sorry," I say.

"Well," he continues, "we've decided to give you one more chance. Now, what do you recommend?"

"The tuna melt is excellent," I tell him and he orders it.

A couple I've waited on before comes in with their baby girl and sits down at one of my tables. There is dread in my heart. "How's it going?" they want to know. "You remember us, right? Greg and Kate? And this is our little Annalisa. Your name's Brenda, isn't it?"

"Uh-huh," I say. I don't have the energy to correct them. I've already told them what my name is at least six times before.

"Is it *crazy* today?" They are both grinning ear to ear, as if they'll be disappointed if I say no.

"A little," I say hopefully.

"We thought so. We're so glad you're waiting on us today, you're so nice. I hope the popovers aren't soggy today. Sometimes they're pretty soggy. But we don't mind because it's always so much fun to eat here."

"Like Dinner Theater?" I ask.

"Ha ha ha, you're so *funny*. She's so funny, isn't she, Greg?"

"Cute, too," Greg says. "Say, Brenda, we'd like to have a couple of omelettes, but Kate doesn't eat the yolks. Do you think you could get her an egg white omelette? If it's too much trouble, don't worry about it, we'll understand. We know things can get a little wild around here. Also, do you think you could find some kind of cereal for the baby? Maybe some polenta or something like that. Do you have polenta? If you don't, that's OK, but she does need to eat, so if you could get something soon for her, that would be great. But don't worry, we're not in a big hurry. If you could bring us a few popovers while we're waiting for our food that would be terrific. Also, can you check and see if you've got any asparagus? It would be fantastic if I could get a side order of asparagus steamed with a little olive oil. We'd like to start with some coffee drinks, if you've got time. I'll just have a double decaf latte. What would you like, Kate?"

277

"Yes, Brenda, can you make me a half-decaf low-fat cappuccino?" Kate asks. "Nonfat would be better, but I know you might not have it. If you do, I'd be so happy. I love your cappuccinos here, they're so *good*. Except the last time we were here, it was a little cold. If it's not too much trouble, could you make sure that my cappuccino is really hot? Can you do that for me, Brenda? By the way, how's your sister? What's her name? Myra, right?"

"You guys are both so cute," Greg adds.

I hate these people.

In the kitchen, a new storm is brewing. Terry rushes up to the grill and tells Adrian, "Can you fix this omelette? The woman says it's not done in the middle."

Adrian opens the omelette with his fingers and pokes at it. "It's fine," he says. "It's the best fucking omelette we've ever made. Tell her—"

"Well, she's right behind me," Terry says. Indeed, the woman in question, wearing workout clothes and a huge attitude, has waltzed right into the kitchen.

"Are you the owner?" she demands of Adrian. "I've got to tell you, this is the worst omelette I've ever had in my life. In addition"—she checks off the list on her fingers— "it came late, the coffee is cold, I couldn't get orange juice, and this bimbo"— she points at Terry—"is rude."

Time stops as we wait for Adrian's reaction. The hum of the restaurant fades against the crackling of static in the air. Calmly, Adrian walks out from behind the grill and puts an arm around the woman.

"Let's not talk about this here," he tells her softly. "Let's go outside." He opens the screen door for her, and as she exits the kitchen, he slams it at her back.

"First of all," he growls, "don't call my waitress a bimbo. Second of all, get the hell out of my restaurant. Learn some manners."

As she strides off speechless and fuming, Adrian mutters, "Ah, fuck her. In fact, fuck everything. Close the kitchen. Shut down the restaurant. I'm outta here." He throws his apron on the floor and walks out. Terry shrugs and Oaxaca grins broadly.

"You know he'll be back," Danny says hopelessly and picks up a frying pan. Oaxaca inspects the tickets, which have continued to roll in from the printer. "Garden salad," he says, "side of potatoes, two short stacks . . ."

At two there is a brief lull in the madness. I take the time to start my portion of the day's cleanup, which mostly involves trying to clean the cappuccino machine, which now looks as if several gallons of milk have exploded and then dried on its surfaces. Because I can feel someone staring at me from across the counter, I turn and see Dominic holding a couple of pink cake boxes.

Dominic is one half of Cake and More, a tiny company he runs with his partner, Ian. These two make some of the most beautiful confections I've ever seen, which is why Adrian, who can't even keep up with his juice payments, has lately decided to sell their cheesecakes. I have to smile when I see Dominic because, despite the fact that Adrian refers to him and Ian as "those pastry fags," I know that he's come all the way out to Hoover's on a Sunday afternoon mostly to see me. We've had a running flirtation going since he started bringing his cakes to Hoover's. Right now, I couldn't be happier to see him.

"Hi, how are you?" I ask him.

"Pretty good," he says. "Just thought I'd bring these by. We're working on something new and I thought maybe you'd like to try a sample." He opens one of the boxes and shows me a tiny round gâteau coated with dark chocolate and topped with a pink sugar rose.

"Wow," I tell him, "you guys are really talented."

"Maybe you can share it around," he says a bit nervously.

"Thank you," I tell him. "Cup of coffee for your troubles?" Dominic smiles and nods assent. I make him a double espresso and rummage in my apron pocket for money to pay him for the cakes. At Hoover's, we have to pay our distributors out of the day's sales. Lucky for Dominic, I've sold more than enough today to cover his bill. It won't last, I know. Sooner or later, we'll have to stop paying him. But for now, I want to keep him around, so I give him the cash and he hands me a receipt.

"Busy day?" he asks.

"This place is insane," I tell him. "Two of our servers are in jail in Tijuana."

Dominic laughs and I start telling him about my morning. For a moment, things feel almost normal. I'm just a waitress in a pretty diner, leaning over the counter I'm polishing, flirting with the good-looking cake man.

But it can't last.

A clot of hungry beachcombers, crusted with sand, stumble through the door demanding immediate service and wanting to know if they can get popovers to go.

"Sorry," I tell Dominic, "I've got to get back to work."

"Right," he says. "Thanks for the coffee." He pulls himself up from the counter and starts to head for the door. At the last minute, he stops himself and comes back, behind the counter this time, so he can speak close to my ear. "Maybe we can get together sometime?" he says.

"That would really be nice," I tell him and pause. "You know, I've got a kid," I add.

"No, I didn't know," he says, smiling. "How old?"

"One and a half."

"What's her name?"

"It's a boy. Blaze."

"Well, where's Blaze today?" he asks.

"He's with my parents." I've said everything I need to with those four words. There's no boyfriend, no husband. I'm a single mother, plain as day.

"So Blaze can come with us," Dominic says. And now he's said everything he needs to. Ah, the modern rites of courtship, I think to myself.

"Why don't you call me?" I say and scrawl my phone number on a paper napkin and hand it to him.

"OK, good," he says and, in another second, is gone. I head toward the kitchen and am immediately body-slammed by Terry, who is coming around one of Hoover's many blind corners. Terry happens to be carrying a pot of scalding hot coffee, half of which splashes across me and sinks, still steaming, into my chest.

"Oh, I'm sorry," she mumbles as I yelp in pain. "I didn't see you."

I spend the next thirty minutes trying to assuage the burning pain in my chest with icy towels. There's not much for me in the way of sympathy. Terry is claiming that I walked into *her* and has actually become indignant. I finish my cleanup and my last few tables. My enthusiasm for Dominic and his cakes translates into cash as I am able to happily sell several slices of the cherry cheesecake to the late lunch crowd.

By three-thirty, the flow of business is slow enough for me to leave. I can identify at least four different food stains on my apron and my legs threaten to fold at any moment. I have been in a state of constant movement for eight hours. I prepare my cash drop and take it upstairs to Adrian's office, where he's been hiding for the last two hours. He says nothing as I dump cash and tickets into a cardboard box near the door.

When I come back downstairs, my parents are waiting for me with Blaze.

"We thought we'd just drop him off here," my mother says, "so he can have a nice walk home." She hands me Blaze's stroller and diaper bag. "You look tired. Long day?"

"You don't even know," I tell her and tuck Blaze into his stroller. "Un un un," he says and, right now, I'm interpreting that to mean, "Hi, Mom, let's go home."

On my way out, I pass Danny sitting outside the kitchen, drinking a beer, taking his first break of the day. Oaxaca is attempting to scrape dried popovers from the kitchen floor.

"Look at the little mite," Danny says, smiling at Blaze. "He's so sweet. Hey, chum."

"Un un un," Blaze responds.

"You going home?" Danny asks me.

"Yes, if I can make it there."

"Y'know," he says, "I'd like to have a son someday."

"Why's that, Danny?"

"Well, so I could name him Harley."

"Harley? Is that a family name?"

"No, it's so his name would be Harley Davidson. Isn't that a great name for a kid?"

"Have a good night, Danny."

When I get home, I am too tired to ponder the riddles of the day. Why, for example, people keep coming back to Hoover's. Or why Danny and Oaxaca don't take a kitchen knife to Adrian. Or how much longer I can work in this restaurant without having a nervous breakdown. I am, however, sure of two things. For one, I have the day off tomorrow. I will take Blaze down to a park by the beach and push him on the swings while he watches the ocean. On the way home, I'll stop in somewhere and have a cappuccino for myself and an apple juice for Blaze. It will be warm and sunny. The taste of life will be sweet.

The other certainty is that I have a hundred and fifty dollars in cold cash tucked into my apron pocket. Whether or not the trade-off to earn those dollars has been worth it is a question that will have to be addressed tomorrow or as soon as I can lift my aching body off the couch.

Maya arrives home at 5:30 P.M. and falls onto the other couch. "I can't believe I have to go back there in the morning," she says.

"How'd it end up?" I ask her.

"Not good. When I left, Adrian was giving Danny and Oaxaca a lesson on how to make popovers properly. I think they might be there all night. Oaxaca missed his bus and Danny looked like he was on his fiftieth beer."

"How much did you make?" I ask her.

"A hundred. You?"

"One-fifty."

"Not bad," she says. "What shall we have for dinner?"

I lasted six months at Hoover's. The final weeks were grim. Adrian stopped paying everybody, including staff. Because our paychecks bounced regularly on paydays, and this was a wonderful sales incentive, we'd have to sell at least the amount on the check in order to collect any wages at all. The muffin and doughnut man was not that lucky. He stopped coming around after issuing the following edict: "Tell Adrian to pay me or I'm comin' back here to break both his legs." Because Adrian engendered such unbridled hostility among his distributors, many of us actually started fearing for his life. Maya, for example, had a real fear that one morning she would arrive at work and find Adrian's dead body stuffed in the Dumpster. As a result, she avoided going into the back of the restaurant until she saw Adrian, still alive, walk in the front door.

Poor Danny managed to scrape enough money together to go back to New Zealand. Before he left, Maya and I invited him over for dinner. He arrived with a bottle of wine and twin turquoise necklaces, one for each of us. "You girls have been so nice to me," he told us, "and I know I haven't always been easy to work with. I don't know how to thank you." I couldn't decide which was more heartbreaking, the fact that Danny had such a low opinion of himself or that, aside from our apartment, all he ever saw of the United States was the view from inside Hoover's kitchen.

Oaxaca, whose name turned out to be Francisco, worked like a galley slave for many months before finally quitting. He resurfaced years later at another restaurant where I worked, hired as a busboy. We greeted each other like survivors of a particularly nasty accident. Unfortunately, Francisco seemed permanently scarred by his experience at Hoover's. He'd lost his edge and wandered around the restaurant as if lost, spilling coffee and showing up late. He just wasn't used to being treated fairly and quit after a couple of weeks.

As I had predicted, Adrian soon canceled orders for Dominic's cakes. Dominic, however, did call me for a date. Ultimately, we ended up seeing each other for almost a year. Dominic had a few talents. He was a very hard worker and a good businessman, and he made a Linzertorte to die for. Unfortunately, he was also peculiarly old-fashioned when it came to women and believed in traditional roles for males and females, which bordered on outright sexism. This attitude also led him to assume that I had an immediate need to provide Blaze with a father. Dominic was the first man I'd dated since John and I wasn't even sure if he was the right man for me, let alone my son. At any rate, I wasn't about to let him experiment and audition for fatherhood with Blaze.

"He's two years old," Dominic would say. "He shouldn't have a bottle anymore. He needs to be potty trained. Why don't you put him in day care?" It was a rude awakening to one aspect of single motherhood and a call for me to put as much distance as possible between myself and a similar situation in the future. This, I assumed, virtually assured that I'd spend a long period outside of any other serious relationship.

Perhaps, when he first met me, Dominic mistook me for an image of some diner waitress he had in his imagination: a poor working girl struggling to raise a kid on her own and desperately in need of a man to fix everything for her. I couldn't fault him too much for this. For a brief while, I thought I was that waitress, too. In any case, though, I'd been paving my own way for much too long to become the "girl" Dominic was looking for. The end of our relationship, when it came, was not pleasant. Anything started at Hoover's, it seemed, was destined for failure.

After the local sheriff showed up for a "till tap" to make good on bad debts, Adrian managed, through witchcraft, we all assumed, to sell Hoover's. The unsuspecting buyer was unaware of the curse on the place and he eliminated popovers from the menu to boot. After accusing Adrian of falsifying the books, the buyer and Adrian actually came to blows one day when Adrian refused to renegotiate the sale. Adrian sued the buyer for assaulting him and won a settlement. He, too, showed up later in a restaurant where I worked and insisted that I wait on him.

"Hey!" he shouted drunkenly, although he wasn't drunk at all, just mad as a hatter. "See this girl?" He pointed at me. "I taught her everything she knows!"

"Do you know that guy?" my manager asked me incredulously as I hung my head in abject embarrassment.

"I used to work for him," I answered.

"That's a relief," my manager said. "By the way he was talking to you, I thought maybe you used to date him."

Hoover's itself maintained a certain aura of madness and drama that drew customers for quite some time. Without Adrian's unique brand of insanity, however, it just wasn't as much fun. Slowly, business died. Today, Hoover's is no more, having been replaced by an upscale restaurant specializing in designer salads and fresh fish.

As for me, I leaped from the sinking ship as soon as I saw the opportunity. I headed for a new Italian restaurant that arrived in town with a sterling reputation and the promise of big money. Ironically, it was Adrian himself who pointed out this restaurant while it was still under construction.

"See that?" he said one morning. "There's a big fancy Italian place coming in there. They think they're going to do so well. I've got news for them. They're never gonna make it in this fucked-up town. Not with their overhead."

Not surprisingly, he was completely wrong about this.

Desperate to escape the vortex that was Hoover's, Maya and I both climbed over construction rubble and bits of pink Italian marble to apply and interview at the new place. Once again we took the tag team approach, with one of us interviewing while the other sat with Blaze. These people, I realized, were serious. There were four separate managers conducting interviews and quizzing us on our knowledge of wines, fine dining, and Italian food. They spoke of "teams," "expansion," and "opportunity." It sounded a bit like they wanted to take over the planet rather than open a restaurant, but I didn't care, I just wanted to be hired. There was a second interview and then a third. All my references were rigorously checked. Finally, after I'd almost given up hope, I received a call inviting me to "join our team at Baciare." There would be three weeks of training and testing before the restaurant opened and could I be at the site at ten o'clock the next morning to complete the paperwork? I said I'd be there with bells on.

My sister, told that she didn't have enough experience, was not hired. She was destined to suffer through another nine months of hell at Hoover's before her release.

Despite its obvious mental tolls, I still look back on my Hoover's experience with great amusement, even fondness. There was something almost sublime in the insanity of each shift. I also learned a great deal about human psychology and crisis management working at Hoover's. These were lessons that would stand me in good stead later, in every area of my life. There were other advantages as well. Hoover's afforded me the ability to start over in a new place with a new child and a new life. Maya and I made enough money there to buy ourselves a car, some furniture, and a little peace of mind.

And there was also something quite beautiful about Hoover's. Every day I walked outside at least once and stared at the ocean, which was close enough to be practically in my lap. The crazy pink and green curves of Hoover's provided a perfect frame around the horizon whether it was sunny or stormy, blue or gray. When a smiling waitress and the smell of popovers and fresh coffee were added to this tableau, Hoover's seemed, however briefly, like a little piece of heaven. Surely, I think now, this is why Hoover's was always so busy despite the darkness behind its pastel exterior.

After all, everybody loves a diner.

Automobile Parts Specialist
from *Gig: Americans Talk*
About Their Jobs

JOHN DOVE

People are in emotional duress when they show up, that's a general rule.
There's something wrong with their car and most of them don't know crap
about cars.

I sell Honda auto parts. That's my job, and I've been working with automobiles in one way or another for twenty years, but I don't consider it my life. Not by a long shot. It keeps me alive, keeps my family fed, but it interferes with what I'd like to be doing, which is painting, drawing, sculpting, making little airplanes.

I wanted to be an artist. And I did pursue that for a while, but I became disillusioned with it in college. I was trying to follow a more traditional pathway, and I used to get into fights with my professors about that. I went to North Texas. There was a professor up there who did "sound painting." He ran around with a tape recorder, taping various noises. Set it up in the auditorium and you'd listen to all these sounds. His philosophy was, the more outrageous the better. Kinda, try to break the boundaries of tradition. Meanwhile, I'm doing these landscape paintings, you know? Trying to be the next Van Gogh. [Laughs] We'd get in awful fights. Then I saw other people who were doing well—and this one guy's project was shaving a baby pig and then tattooing it. He got an A for that. There's another guy who went around killing blackbirds, and he would snip off their wings and their feet and glue them onto a canvas. He was getting A's for this, and I was going, what the hell am I doing here? Why am I doing this?

So I gave it up and moved to Dallas, came here and got married. This was in the mid-seventies. The only experience I had was cooking—working in restaurants and bars—which landed me a job at Howard Johnson's. It was just awful. [Laughs] No money, weird hours, just hell on your domestic life. I was like, "I need to find something else to do!" [Laughs] I didn't care what. I had a friend here who worked for Continental Cars. He said it was lucrative and that was interesting to me, so he helped fix me up as a warranty clerk at a dealer for the British-Leyland Company, which made MGs, Triumphs, Jaguars, and so on.

I had no idea what a warranty clerk was. Turns out it was basically a paper-work job. When your car's under warranty, you take it to your dealer, they fix it for free, and then they get reimbursed by the mother company for perform-ing that work. The warranty clerk is the guy who files the claims to the mother company so the dealer can get paid back.

It seemed pretty straightforward, but when I got to this particular dealer, they hadn't had a warranty clerk for six months, and they had a stack of claims representing probably fifty thousand dollars' worth of money that needed to be reimbursed. And it states clearly on each claim, "Not valid after twenty-eight days." So I had to learn how to falsify claims, big time.

I falsified the whole stack. It took about a year and a half. What I did was, we figured it would be safest to file as few fake claims as possible, so I consolidated stuff. Say we had a bunch of claims, like eight hundred bucks of little widgets and things—axle seals and oil leaks and so on—well, I'd write a claim for eight hundred bucks of major engine work on a TR6. They always blew head gaskets. And I'd file this one fake claim and get the money for the dealership. And then I'd just take this big pile of little claims and throw it in the garbage. This was before everything was computerized and it was surprisingly easy to get these fake claims paid. I did it gradually, and I don't remember British-Leyland ever even challenging one dot on anything I sent them. They just paid up.

It was weird, though. You know, it made me nervous. I was just trying to have a decent job, I didn't want any trouble of any kind. And those sons-of-bitches at my dealership set up a special account that that money went into. Because this was all done on the sly, you know, and the accountants couldn't find out about it. I even had two ledgers. I had the ledger that we showed the mother company and I had the ledger that was the real one. And the money that came in, the guys who ran the place were basically just pocketing it. They were buy-ing cameras and all kinds of stuff. It was screwy.

One guy there one time introduced me to a customer by saying I had a license to steal from the company. I didn't appreciate that. I smiled nicely at the customer and got him his warranty work, then I went over and got in that guy's face and said, "If you ever say that again I'm going to take you out." I was pissed, but it was basically true—I was stealing, or helping those guys steal. And I became very disillusioned after a few years. I just couldn't take it.

So I left. I went to work selling tires and shock absorbers for an independent shop. I liked that a good bit better, but then they forced me to join the Retail Clerks Union of America—which has like the lowest pay structure of any union ever. It's just a little above minimum wage. So I went back to, strangely enough, the same company, British-Leyland, but a different dealer and this time I was in the parts department. And that was fairly straightforward. I was selling parts and there's nothing really [laughs] questionable about that. I liked it fine, and I've stuck to parts ever since. I moved over to this Honda dealership about twelve years ago to be the parts specialist.

What I do is I sit behind a counter and I sell parts, just Honda parts for Honda cars. I get a salary and a little commission on each sale. The customers fall into two types—I sell over the front counter to people who are do-it-yourselfers and I sell over the back counter to the technicians in our repair shop. If you bring your car in here to get it serviced, the technicians will have a look at it, and any parts that it needs, they'll come to me for them and I'll bill you. If your warranty covers it, that's great. If not, you pay me.

It's mostly a memory job. You know, memory of part numbers, prices, and so on. After that, it's all dealing with people, which can be kinda stressful. People are in emotional duress when they show up, that's a general rule. There's something wrong with their car and most of them don't know crap about cars. That's why they're in the service department. I can understand their situation and their being so upset, but quite frankly, I don't like dealing with the public much. It's not my strength. Some customers get pretty angry. I spend a lot of days on the phone getting harassed. "Is it done? Why isn't it done? When will it be done?" All day. It wears me down sometimes. I have exploded on occasion. Not often, but once in a while. As a general rule, I try not to argue with them. If I'm in a situation where a customer is getting into a heated discussion or something, I'll just pass it right on to my manager. I try to avoid conflicts whenever possible.

A lot of the customers think they're getting fleeced. Most are just angry people. Paranoids, you know. But I hate to say it, but a few of 'em are right—they are getting fleeced. But the fleecing is not due to malicious intent, it's due to incompetence by the technicians. They're overworked and some of 'em are just incompetent. I mean, I'll have a technician come up to me and say, for instance, "I need an interior fan motor." So I give him the part and I bill it out on the customer's repair order. And then, an hour later, the technician'll come back to me and say, "Uh, I need a twenty amp fuse—could you charge it to the shop." And I give him the fuse and charge it to the shop.

So, in effect, the customer gets charged for a hefty fan motor and it was really just the cheap fuse. But like I say, this is an example of incompetence. Of fleecing through incompetence. It's not crooked. We could go take the new fan motor out of the car, put the old one back in, doubling the time that it takes, but we wouldn't get paid for that time, so we don't. My boss would kill us if we did that. We just charge them for that motor. It ain't fair, but it doesn't happen all that often and the majority of everything that happens is on the up and up. I sleep well.

It's a good job. There's problems, but it's not a perfect world. There's problems with everything. I've done enough different things to know what works for me. And what's good about this job is, first of all, I make a good income. Second, it's honest—I know my parts and I know Honda makes 'em well. They're the best, I think. And third—and this is very important to me—I have a lot of downtime, lots of slow time that I can devote to my projects—just little things to keep my creativity alive. Lately, I've been making little airplanes. I make the wings out of the plastic from warranty bags, and I buy sticks at Hobby Lobby for the frames, and I get these little plastic propellers from model airplane kits. I build 'em, then take 'em home, and put 'em up on the cabinets and around the house. It's a lot of fun.

I have a box in my desk full of this airplane stuff. When I first showed up, my boss was like, "What do you need a box for?" I told him it was to keep my notes in and he said okay. Of course, my box has about two notes in it, and the rest is full of little toys, balls, propellers, little things to make things out of, basically. It's my little creativity box.

My boss figured out a good while ago what I'm up to and he has, on occasion, said he doesn't like it. There've been several times where he told me that he wanted me to quit it, but he didn't have a good reason, so I didn't quit. [Laughs] Thing is, my boss has got a deep knowledge in racing and engines, but that's about all. That's the best I can say for him. He has an eighth-grade education and he's had several debilitating injuries from motorcycle crashes and he misses a lot of work because his back goes out and he has these other injuries. And there's no way that he could ever live up to the standards he expects of us. I mean, there's just a basic hypocrisy to that man. He's a real stickler for being on time, but he calls out a lot. So there you go. And he's always leaving early, he's always getting in late, he's always breaking all his own rules. But these are things I've grown to accept.

We've reached a point where he doesn't usually bother me as long as I do everything I'm supposed to do, all my duties. Then I'll go work on my projects and what's he going to say? He's sitting there filling out a crossword puzzle and the other guys are sitting around reading the paper, talking about just total crap, just total bullshit, you know? I'm just making myself happy, I'm not screwing up. I read the paper at four-thirty this morning, thanks. I've already read it. People got killed, okay? We bombed some more. The paper is just—it's real good, it pisses me off.

Making the airplanes and drawings pleases me. That's all there is to it. But that's a lot. It's important to be happy with yourself. I don't regret anything. What's to regret? I tried art, it wasn't for me. There's no money in it. I decided that I wanted to live with Jane. I wanted to marry her, and she told me right up front: "I will not starve with you. I love you, but I won't starve with you." And we don't starve. I get a good income from this, good insurance benefits, profit-sharing benefits. Jane works too, and between both of us, we are doing very well. And we have a lovely daughter, Lilly. She's twelve.

There was a time when I was younger, when I first got into cars and decided I was gonna make a career out of this, I thought that going up in management was going to be the way to go. But I changed my mind. I don't like the stress. I'd just as soon stay out of everything and sell my parts and just stay as invisible as I can, just be invisible. You don't need to work yourself to death to be happy. I've got a good retirement package. I'm looking forward to that. I'll have more free time to do my projects and be myself. It'll be sweet.

To Be of Use

MARGE PIERCY

The people I love the best
jump into work head first
without dallying in the shallows
and swim off with sure strokes almost out of sight.
They seem to become natives of that element,
the black sleek heads of seals
bouncing like half submerged balls.

　　I love people who harness themselves, an ox to a heavy cart,
　　who pull like water buffalo, with massive patience,
　　who strain in the mud and the muck to move things forward,
　　who do what has to be done, again and again.

I want to be with people who submerge
in the task, who go into the fields to harvest
and work in a row and pass the bags along,
who stand in the line and haul in their places,
who are not parlor generals and field deserters
but move in a common rhythm
when the food must come in or the fire be put out.

　　The work of the world is common as mud.
　　Botched, it smears the hands, crumbles to dust.
　　But the thing worth doing well done
　　has a shape that satisfies, clean and evident.
　　Greek amphoras for wine or oil,
　　Hopi vases that held corn, are put in museums
　　but you know they were made to be used.
　　The pitcher cries for water to carry
　　and a person for work that is real.

Customer Service Alive and Well at Ordinary Kinko's Shop

SUSAN CAMPBELL

An older woman walked into the FedEx Kinko's in Hartford, Conn., last week clutching a fistful of papers. She went to a fax machine near the front door and proceeded to line up her documents.

There are 121,000 stories in the naked city—give or take—and this is one of them.

In his regulation purple apron, Matthew Grossi stood nearby. Grossi's the kind of guy they used to call a "people person," a minority these days among an army of sullen clerks. On a regular day, he rushes from station to station gathering trash and stray paper clips and liberally sprinkling "How are we doing heres?" to customers befuddled by the technology it takes to send a fax, make a copy or enlarge a picture.

But the woman—who was 70 if she was a day—caught his eye because she was struggling with the fax machine. As senior retail consultant, Grossi's job is customer service.

When he offered to help, the older woman told him she was attempting to fax her particulars to something called the Ministry of Spanish Gaming Offices, or something like that. She'd received word that she'd won a lottery, and her check could be automatically deposited into her bank account. The information she was trying to send included but was not limited to her checking account and routing numbers.

The problem with giving out your checking account and routing numbers is that not only can money go in, it can be withdrawn as well. Sharing those numbers is akin to handing over the keys to the house and then leaving for the weekend. Grossi gently asked the woman if she remembered entering the lottery. She said she'd entered something but couldn't remember if it was this one

291

or one in Australia. She was happy about winning, though. She's been retired a few years. This was the fourth time she'd been contacted by these lottery people; this time she called the number listed on the official notice and talked to a man, but she didn't get his name.

When the doors open each day for business at the FedEx Kinko's on Farmington Avenue, the employees start running. It's one of their busier stores, and people who transfer there must get used to the quick pace. Even while Grossi listened to the woman's story, a line was forming.

But this was someone's grandmother. She was "a little old gray-haired lady, right to a T," Grossi said.

Before he came to FedEx Kinko's, Grossi, 33, worked in banking, and for a while he dealt specifically with check fraud. He explained to the woman that if she shared her account information without confirmation that this was a legitimate organization, she stood a good chance of being cleaned out. He explained routing numbers and identity theft, and then he asked her to go to her local bank and talk to someone there. He told her he'd feel a lot better if she waited a few weeks before trying to collect her winnings. The old woman was disappointed, but she told Grossi she'd at least talk to her bank, and then she left.

Two years ago, the attorney general's office issued a warning about international lottery scams, often based in Europe and Africa, but these scams are like mushrooms. As soon as one company is discovered and shut down, two more pop up to take its place. Their operators have stolen untold millions, often from people who can least afford to lose it. Law-enforcement officials do what they can, but often the last defense is people like Grossi.

As corny as it sounds, Grossi tries to do a good deed every day. It's what his parents, Patrick and Edith Grossi of West Hartford, taught him. He also credits the management at his store for letting him occasionally let a free fax walk out the door. In fact, Monday a.m., he waved away eight cents from a man he'd helped to make a copy. "I'm not going to worry about eight cents," he said. And then he turned to the next customer and said, "How are we doing here?"

From Henry Ford's English Language Melting Pot from Middlesex

JEFFREY EUGENIDES

Everyone who builds a factory builds a temple.
—Calvin Coolidge

My grandfather's short employ at the Ford Motor Company marked the only time any Stephanides has ever worked in the automobile industry. Instead of cars, we would become manufacturers of hamburger platters and Greek salads, industrialists of spanikopita and grilled cheese sandwiches, technocrats of rice pudding and banana cream pie. Our assembly line was the grill; our heavy machinery, the soda fountain. Still, those twenty-five weeks gave us a personal connection to that massive, forbidding, awe-inspiring complex we saw from the highway, that controlled Vesuvius of chutes, tubes, ladders, catwalks, fire, and smoke known, like a plague or a monarch, only by a color: "the Rouge."

On his first day of work, Lefty came into the kitchen modeling his new overalls. He spread his flannel-shirted arms and snapped his fingers, dancing in work boots, and Desdemona laughed and shut the kitchen door so as not to wake up Lina. Lefty ate his breakfast of prunes and yogurt, reading a Greek newspaper a few days old. Desdemona packed his Greek lunch of feta, olives, and bread in a new American container: a brown paper bag. At the back door, when he turned to kiss her she stepped back, anxious that people might see. But then she remembered that they were married now. They lived in a place called Michigan, where the birds seemed to come in only one color, and where no one knew them. Desdemona stepped forward again to meet her husband's lips. Their first kiss in the great American outdoors, on the back porch, near a cherry tree

293

losing its leaves. A brief flare of happiness went off inside her and hung, raining sparks, until Lefty disappeared around the front of the house.

My grandfather's good mood accompanied him all the way to the trolley stop. Other workers were already waiting, loose-kneed, smoking cigarettes and joking. Lefty noticed their metal lunch pails and, embarrassed by his paper sack, held it behind him. The streetcar showed up first as a hum in the soles of his boots. Then it appeared against the rising sun, Apollo's own chariot, only electrified. Inside, men stood in groups arranged by language. Faces scrubbed for work still had soot inside the ears, deep black. The streetcar sped off again. Soon the jovial mood dissipated and the languages fell silent. Near downtown, a few blacks boarded the car, standing outside on the runners, holding on to the roof.

And then the Rouge appeared against the sky, rising out of the smoke it generated. At first all that was visible was the tops of the eight main smokestacks. Each gave birth to its own dark cloud. The clouds plumed upward and merged into a general pall that hung over the landscape, sending a shadow that ran along the trolley tracks; and Lefty understood that the men's silence was a recognition of this shadow, of its inevitable approach each morning. As it came on, the men turned their backs so that only Lefty saw the light leave the sky as the shadow enveloped the streetcar and the men's faces turned gray and one of the *mavros* on the runners spat blood onto the roadside. The smell seeped into the streetcar next, first the bearable eggs and manure, then the unbearable chemical taint, and Lefty looked at the other men to see if they registered it, but they didn't, though they continued to breathe. The doors opened and they all filed out. Through the hanging smoke, Lefty saw other streetcars letting off other workers, hundreds and hundreds of gray figures trudging across the paved courtyard toward the factory gates. Trucks were driving past, and Lefty let himself be taken along with the flow of the next shift, fifty, sixty, seventy thousand men hurrying last cigarettes or getting in final words—because as they approached the factory they'd begun to speak again, not because they had anything to say but because beyond those doors language wasn't allowed. The main building, a fortress of dark brick, was seven stories high, the smoke-stacks seventeen. Running off it were two chutes topped by water towers. These led to observation decks and to adjoining refineries studded with less impressive stacks. It was like a grove of trees, as if the Rouge's eight main smokestacks had sown seeds to the wind, and now ten or twenty or fifty smaller trunks were sprouting up in the infertile soil around the plant. Lefty could see the train tracks now, the huge silos along the river, the giant spice box of coal, coke, and iron ore, and the catwalks stretching overhead like giant spiders. Before he was sucked in the door, he glimpsed a freighter and a bit of the river French explorers named for its reddish color, long before the water turned orange from runoff or ever caught on fire.

Historical fact: people stopped being human in 1913. That was the year Henry Ford put his cars on rollers and made his workers adopt the speed of the assembly line. At first, workers rebelled. They quit in droves, unable to accustom their bodies to the new pace of the age. Since then, however, the adaptation has been passed down: we've all inherited it to some degree, so that we plug right into joy-sticks and remotes, to repetitive motions of a hundred kinds.

But in 1922 it was still a new thing to be a machine.

On the factory floor, my grandfather was trained for his job in seventeen minutes. Part of the new production method's genius was its division of labor into unskilled tasks. That way you could hire anyone. And fire anyone. The foreman showed Lefty how to take a bearing from the conveyor, grind it on a lathe, and replace it. Holding a stopwatch, he timed the new employee's attempts. Then, nodding once, he led Lefty to his position on the Line. On the left stood a man named Wierzbicki; on the right, a man named O'Malley. For a moment, they are three men, waiting together. Then the whistle blows.

Every fourteen seconds Wierzbicki reams a bearing and Stephanides grinds a bearing and O'Malley attaches a bearing to a camshaft. This camshaft travels away on a conveyor, curling around the factory, through its clouds of metal dust, its acid fogs, until another worker fifty yards on reaches up and removes the camshaft, fitting it onto the engine block (twenty seconds). Simultaneously, other men are unhooking parts from adjacent conveyors—the carburetor, the distributor, the intake manifold—and connecting them to the engine block. Above their bent heads, huge spindles pound steampowered fists. No one says a word. Wierzbicki reams a bearing and Stephanides grinds a bearing and O'Malley attaches a bearing to a camshaft. The camshaft circles around the floor until a hand reaches up to take it down and attach it to the engine block, growing increasingly eccentric now with swooshes of pipe and the plumage of fan blades. Wierzbicki reams a bearing and Stephanides grinds a bearing and O'Malley attaches a bearing to a camshaft. While other workers screw in the air filter (seventeen seconds) and attach the starter motor (twenty-six seconds) and put on the flywheel. At which point the engine is finished and the last man sends it soaring away . . .

Except that he isn't the last man. There are other men below hauling the engine in, as a chassis rolls out to meet it. These men attach the engine to the transmission (twenty-five seconds). Wierzbicki reams a bearing and Stephanides grinds a bearing and O'Malley attaches a bearing to a camshaft. My grandfather sees only the bearing in front of him, his hands removing it, grinding it, and putting it back as another appears. The conveyor over his head extends back to the men who stamp out the bearings and load ingots into the furnaces; it goes back to the Foundry where the Negroes work, goggled against the infernal light and heat. They feed iron ore into the Blast Oven and pour molten steel into core molds from ladles. They pour at just the right rate—too quickly and the molds will explode; too slowly and the steel will harden. They can't stop even to pick the burning bits of metal from their arms. Sometimes the foreman does it; sometimes not. The Foundry is the deepest recess of the Rouge, its molten core, but the Line goes back farther than that. It extends outside to the hills of coal and coke; it goes to the river where freighters dock to unload the ore, at which point the Line becomes the river itself, snaking up to the north woods until it reaches its source, which is the earth itself, the limestone and sandstone therein;

and then the Line leads back again, out of substrata to river to freighters and finally to the cranes, shovels, and furnaces where it is turned into molten steel and poured into molds, cooling and hardening into car parts—the gears, drive shafts, and fuel tanks of 1922 Model T's. Wierzbicki reams a bearing and Stephanides grinds a bearing and O'Malley attaches a bearing to a camshaft. Above and behind, at various angles, workers pack sand into core molds, or hammer plugs into molds, or put casting boxes into the cupola furnace. The Line isn't a single line but many, diverging and intersecting. Other workers stamp out body parts (fifty seconds), bump them (forty-two seconds), and weld the pieces together (one minute and ten seconds). Wierzbicki reams a bearing and Stephanides grinds a bearing and O'Malley attaches a bearing to a camshaft. The camshaft flies around the factory until a man unhooks it, attaches it to the engine block, growing eccentric now with fan blades, pipes, and spark plugs. And then the engine is finished. A man sends it dropping down onto a chassis rolling out to meet it, as three others workers remove a car body from the oven, its black finish baked to a shine in which they can see their own faces, and they recognize themselves, momentarily, before they drop the body onto the chassis rolling out to meet it. A man jumps into the front seat (three seconds), turns the ignition (two seconds), and drives the automobile away.

Section 3F

Our World— War

War

LUIGI PIRANDELLO

Pirandello (1867–1936) was born in Girgenti, Sicily. As a young man he studied at the University of Rome and in Bonn, Germany. Subsequently, he became a professor of literature but was chiefly famous for his prodigious output as a playwright and as the author of novels and short stories. In all, he wrote forty-three plays, the bulk of them elaborating the conflict between illusion and reality. The best-known and most typical of his imaginative constructions is Six Characters in Search of an Author, in which the characters of an unfinished play assert their claims to be more real than the drab existences from which they emerge. Pirandello's inversions of reality and make-believe had a strong influence on modern drama; his practices were often imitated. His extraordinary scrambling of normal expectations led to many charges that he perpetrated hoaxes. Nevertheless, he was awarded the Nobel Prize in 1934.

The passengers who had left Rome by the night express had had to stop until dawn at the small station of Fabriano in order to continue their journey by the small old-fashioned local joining the main line with Sulmona.

At dawn, in a stuffy and smoky second-class carriage in which five people had already spent the night, a bulky woman in deep mourning was hoisted in—almost like a shapeless bundle. Behind her, puffing and moaning, followed her husband—a tiny man, thin and weakly, his face death-white, his eyes small and bright and looking shy and uneasy.

Having at last taken a seat he politely thanked the passengers who had helped his wife and who had made room for her; then he turned round to the woman trying to pull down the collar of her coat, and politely inquired:

"Are you all right, dear?"

The wife, instead of answering, pulled up her collar again to her eyes, so as to hide her face.

"Nasty world," muttered the husband with a sad smile.

And he felt it his duty to explain to his traveling companions that the poor woman was to be pitied, for the war was taking away from her her only son, a boy of twenty to whom both had devoted their entire life, even breaking up their home at Sulmona to follow him to Rome, where he had to go as a student, then allowing him to volunteer for war with an assurance, however, that at least for six months he would not be sent to the front and now, all of a sudden, receiving a wire saying that he was due to leave in three days' time and asking them to go and see him off.

The woman under the big coat was twisting and wriggling, at times growling like a wild animal, feeling certain that all those explanations would not have aroused even a shadow of sympathy from those people who—most likely—were in the same plight as herself. One of them, who had been listening with particular attention, said:

"You should thank God that your son is only leaving now for the front. Mine has been sent there the first day of the war. He has already come back twice wounded and been sent back again to the front."

"What about me? I have two sons and three nephews at the front," said another passenger.

"Maybe, but in our case it is our only son," ventured the husband.

"What difference can it make? You may spoil your only son with excessive attentions, but you cannot love him more than you would all your other children if you had any. Paternal love is not like bread that can be broken into pieces and split amongst the children in equal shares. A father gives all his love to each one of his children without discrimination, whether it be one or ten, and if I am suffering now for my two sons, I am not suffering half for each of them but double . . ."

"True . . . true . . ." sighed the embarrassed husband, "but suppose (of course we all hope it will never be your case) a father has two sons at the front and he loses one of them, there is still one left to console him . . . while . . ."

"Yes," answered the other, getting cross, "a son left to console him but also a son left for whom he must survive, while in the case of the father of an only son if the son dies the father can die too and put an end to his distress. Which of the two positions is the worse? Don't you see how my case would be worse than yours?"

"Nonsense," interrupted another traveler, a fat, red-faced man with blood-shot eyes of the palest gray.

He was panting. From his bulging eyes seemed to spurt inner violence of an uncontrolled vitality which his weakened body could hardly contain.

"Nonsense," he repeated, trying to cover his mouth with his hand so as to hide the two missing front teeth. "Nonsense. Do we give life to our children for our own benefit?"

The other travelers stared at him in distress. The one who had had his son at the front since the first day of the war sighed: "You are right. Our children do not belong to us, they belong to the Country. . . ."

300

"Bosh," retorted the fat traveler. "Do we think of the Country when we give life to our children? Our sons are born because . . . well, because they must be born and when they come to life they take our own life with them. This is the truth. We belong to them but they never belong to us. And when they reach twenty they are exactly what we were at their age. We too had a father and mother, but there were so many other things as well . . . girls, cigarettes, illusions, new ties . . . and the Country, of course, whose call we would have answered—when we were twenty—even if father and mother had said no. Now at our age, the love of our Country is still great, of course, but stronger than it is the love for our children. Is there any one of us here who wouldn't gladly take his son's place at the front if he could?"

There was a silence all round, everybody nodding as to approve.

"Why then," continued the fat man, "shouldn't we consider the feelings of our children when they are twenty? Isn't it natural that at their age they should consider the love for their Country (I am speaking of decent boys, of course) even greater than the love for us? Isn't it natural that it should be so, as after all they must look upon us as upon old boys who cannot move any more and must stay at home? If Country exists, if Country is a natural necessity, like bread, of which each of us must eat in order not to die of hunger, somebody must go to defend it. And our sons go, when they are twenty, and they don't want tears, because if they die, they die inflamed and happy (I am speaking, of course, of decent boys). Now, if one dies young and happy, without having the ugly sides of life, the boredom of it, the pettiness, the bitterness of, disillusion . . . what more can we ask for him? Everyone should stop crying: everyone should laugh, as I do . . . or at least thank God—as I do—because my son, before dying, sent me a message saying that he was dying satisfied at having ended his life in the best way he could have wished. That is why, as you see, I do not even wear mourning. . . ."

He shook his light fawn coat as to show it; his livid lip over his missing teeth was trembling, his eyes were watery and motionless, and soon after he ended with a shrill laugh which might well have been a sob.

"Quite so . . . quite so . . ." agreed the others.

The woman who, bundled in a corner under her coat, had been sitting and listening had—for the last three months—tried to find in the words of her husband and her friends something to console her in her deep sorrow, something that might show her how a mother should resign herself to send her son not even to death but to a probably dangerous life. Yet not a word had she found amongst the many which had been said . . . and her grief had been greater in seeing that nobody—as she thought—could share her feelings.

But now the words of the traveler amazed and almost stunned her. She suddenly realized that it wasn't the others who were wrong and could not understand her but herself who could not rise up to the same height of those fathers and mothers willing to resign themselves, without crying, not only to the departure of their sons but even to their death.

301

She lifted her head, she bent over from her corner trying to listen with great attention to the details which the fat man was giving to his companions about the way his son had fallen as a hero, for his King and his Country, happy and without regrets. It seemed to her that she had stumbled into a world she had never dreamt of, a world so far unknown to her and she was so pleased to hear everyone joining in congratulating that brave father who could so stoically speak of his child's death.

Then suddenly, just as if she had heard nothing of what had been said and almost as if waking up from a dream, she turned to the old man, asking him:

"Then . . . is your son really dead?"

Everybody stared at her. The old man, too, turned to look at her , fixing his great, bulging, horribly watery light gray eyes, deep in her face. For some little time he tried to answer, but words failed him. He looked and looked at her, almost as if only then—at that silly, incongruous question—he had suddenly realized at last that his son was really dead—gone for ever—for ever. His face contracted, became horribly distorted, then he snatched in haste a handkerchief from his pocket and, to the amazement of everyone, broke into harrowing, heart-rending, uncontrollable sobs.

American Ignorance of War

CZESLAW MILOSZ

Czeslaw Milosz (pronounced Ches-law Mee-wosh), poet, critic, novel-ist, essayist, and translator, was born in 1911 in Lithuania. During his first forty years he lived under three repressive political systems: as a child in Czarist Russia; in Poland as a member of the underground resistance during the Nazi occupation, during which time he taught himself English in order to read William Blake. After World War II he worked in Paris as a cultural attaché representing Communist Poland. He defected to the West in 1951 ("socialist realism is nothing more than a different name for a lie") and has written ever since of the central issues of our time: the impact of history upon moral being, the search for ways to survive spir-itual ruin in a ruined world. In 1960, he accepted a professorship at the University of California, Berkeley, where he has lived ever since, becom-ing an American citizen in 1970. His wide-ranging writings include Native Realm: A Search for Self-Definition (1968), The History of Polish Literature (1983), two novels, and eighteen vol-umes of poetry. His most recent work, To Begin Where I Am (2002) contains essays that span the length of Milosz's career and the depths of his wide-ranging interests. His work was denied publication in his native land until he was awarded the Nobel Prize for Literature in 1980.

"American Ignorance of War," translated from the Polish by Jane Zielonko, is a section of Milosz's first American publication, The Cap-tive Mind (1953), in which he examines the artist's life under Com-munism and explains why he defected. The book, praised as "a brilliant and original study of the totalitarian mentality," is still fresh and relevant fifty years later. In "American Ignorance of War," Milosz warns his new fellow citizens to learn from the history of other countries. The current gen-erations of Americans, having never experienced the mammoth upheaval of full-scale war on their own shores, regard their culture, their customs,

303

their ways of thinking about life, as natural. Yet in a totalitarian regime, especially during wartime, all is utterly changed. What was once inconceivable—repression, humiliation, genocide—becomes the new norm, natural. Considering other major changes that have occurred in the past fifty years, among them two wars in the Persian Gulf, the AIDS epidemic, and the events of (and following) September 11, 2001, is it possible to deny that Milosz's bleak vision of the future might occur?

"Are Americans *really* stupid?" I was asked in Warsaw. In the voice of the man who posed the question, there was despair, as well as the hope that I would contradict him. This question reveals the attitude of the average person in the people's democracies toward the West: it is despair mixed with a residue of hope.

During the last few years, the West has given these people a number of reasons to despair politically. In the case of the intellectual, other, more complicated reasons come into play. Before the countries of Central and Eastern Europe entered the sphere of the Imperium, they lived through the Second World War. That war was much more devastating there than in the countries of Western Europe. It destroyed not only their economies, but also a great many values which had seemed till then unshakable.

Man tends to regard the order he lives in as *natural*. The houses he passes on his way to work seem more like rocks rising out of the earth than like products of human hands. He considers the work he does in his office or factory as essential to the harmonious functioning of the world. The clothes he wears are exactly what they should be, and he laughs at the idea that he might equally well be wearing a Roman toga or medieval armor. He respects and envies a minister of state or a bank director, and regards the possession of a considerable amount of money as the main guarantee of peace and security. He cannot believe that one day a rider may appear on a street he knows well, where cats sleep and children play, and start catching passersby with his lasso. He is accustomed to satisfying those of his physiological needs which are considered private as discreetly as possible, without realizing that such a pattern of behavior is not common to all human societies. In a word, he behaves a little like Charlie Chaplin in *The Gold Rush*, bustling about in a shack poised precariously on the edge of a cliff.

His first stroll along a street littered with glass from bomb-shattered windows shakes his faith in the "naturalness" of his world. The wind scatters papers from hastily evacuated offices, papers labeled "Confidential" or "Top Secret" that evoke visions of safes, keys, conferences, couriers, and secretaries. Now the wind blows them through the street for anyone to read; yet no one does, for each man is more urgently concerned with finding a loaf of bread. Strangely enough, the world goes on even though the offices and secret files have lost all meaning. Farther down the street, he stops before a house split in half by a bomb, the privacy of people's homes—the family smells, the warmth of the beehive life, the furniture preserving the memory of loves and hatreds—cut open to public view. The house itself, no longer a rock, but a scaffolding of plaster, concrete, and brick; and on the third floor, a solitary white bathtub, rain-rinsed of all recollection of those who once bathed in it. Its formerly influential and respected owners, now destitute, walk the fields in search of stray potatoes. Thus overnight money loses its value and becomes a meaningless mass of printed paper. His walk takes him past a little boy poking a stick into a heap of smoking ruins and whistling a song about the great leader who will preserve the nation against all enemies. The song remains, but the leader of yesterday is already part of an extinct past.

He finds he acquires new habits quickly. Once, had he stumbled upon a corpse on the street, he would have called the police. A crowd would have gathered, and much talk and comment would have ensued. Now he knows he must avoid the dead body lying in the gutter, and refrain from asking unnecessary questions. The man who fired the gun must have had his reasons; he might well have been executing an Underground sentence.

Nor is the average European accustomed to thinking of his native city as divided into segregated living areas, but a single decree can force him to this new pattern of life and thought. Quarter A may suddenly be designated for one race; B, for a second; C, for a third. As the resettlement deadline approaches, the streets become filled with long lines of wagons, carts, wheel barrows, and people carrying bundles, beds, chests, caldrons, and bird cages. When all the moves are effected, 2,000 people may find themselves in a building that once housed 200, but each man is at last in the proper area. Then high walls are erected around quarter C, and daily a given lot of men, women, and children are loaded into wagons that take them off to specially constructed factories where they are scientifically slaughtered and their bodies burned.

And even the rider with the lasso appears, in the form of a military van waiting at the corner of a street. A man passing that corner meets a leveled rifle, raises his hands, is pushed into the van, and from that moment is lost to his family and friends. He may be sent to a concentration camp, or he may face a firing squad, his lips sealed with plaster lest he cry out against the state; but, in any case, he serves as a warning to his fellow men. Perhaps one might escape such a fate by remaining at home. But the father of a family must go out in order to provide bread and soup for his wife and children; and every night they worry about whether or not he will return. Since these conditions last for years, everyone gradually comes to look upon the city as a jungle, and upon the fate of twentieth-century man as identical with that of a caveman living in the midst of powerful monsters.

It was once thought obvious that a man bears the same name and surname throughout his entire life; now it proves wiser for many reasons to change them and to memorize a new and fabricated biography. As a result, the records of the civilian state become completely confused. Everyone ceases to care about formalities, so that marriage, for example, comes to mean little more than living together.

Respectable citizens used to regard banditry as a crime. Today, bank robbers are heroes because the money they steal is destined for the Underground. Usually they are young boys, mothers' boys, but their appearance is deceiving. The killing of a man presents no great moral problem to them.

The nearness of death destroys shame. Men and women change as soon as they know that the date of their execution his been fixed by a fat little man with shiny boots, and a riding crop. They copulated in public on the small bit of ground surrounded by barbed wire—their last home on earth. Boys and girls in their teens, about to go off to the barricades to fight against tanks with pistols and bottles of gasoline, want to enjoy their youth and lose their respect for standards of decency.

Which world is "natural"? That which existed before, or the world of war? Both are natural, if both are within the realm of one's experience. All the concepts men live by are a product of the historic formation in which they find themselves. Fluidity and constant change are the characteristics of phenomena. And man is so plastic a being that one can even conceive of the day when a thoroughly self-respecting citizen will crawl on all fours, sporting a tail of brightly colored feathers as a sign of conformity to the order he lives in.

The man of the East cannot take Americans seriously because they have never undergone the experiences that teach men how relative their judgements and thinking habits are. Their resultant lack of imagination is appalling. Because they were born and raised in a given social order and in a given system of values, they believe that any other order must be "unnatural," and that it cannot last because it is incompatible with human nature. But even they may one day know fire, hunger, and the sword. In all probability this is what will occur; for it is hard to believe that when one half of the world is living through terrible disasters, the other half can continue a nineteenth-century mode of life, learning about the distress of its distant fellow men only from movies and newspapers. Recent examples teach us that this cannot be. An inhabitant of Warsaw or Budapest once looked at newsreels of bombed Spain or burning Shanghai, but in the end he learned how these and many other catastrophes appear in actuality. He read gloomy tales of the NKVD until one day he found he himself had to deal with it. *If something exists in one place, it will exist everywhere.* This is the conclusion he draws from his observations, and so he has no particular faith in the momentary prosperity of America. He suspects that the years 1933–1945 in Europe prefigure what will occur elsewhere. A hard school, where ignorance was punished not by bad marks but by death, has taught him to think sociologically and historically. But it has not freed him from irrational feelings. He is apt to believe in theories that foresee violent changes in the countries of the West, for he finds it unjust that they should escape the hardships he had to undergo.

"Before joining the Marine Corps . . ." from *Jarhead*

ANTHONY SWOFFORD

Before joining the Marine Corps I'd fired two weapons—a bow and arrow and a .22-caliber rifle, both at Boy Scout camp, at the age of twelve. If I hadn't requested to leave camp a week early, I would've also fired a shotgun and a larger-caliber rifle, but I missed my mother, I had no friends at camp, the food was lousy, I was afraid of showering in public—actually, in the forest, the shower not a shower but half a dozen garden hoses draped over the lowest branches of a pine—and the leader of the camp was grouchy and probably a drunk. Because I cried-out a week early, and my parents lost the nonrefundable fee, I had to repay the money for the aborted second week. My mother supported me and my sweet reasoning behind quitting camp (that I missed her), but my father insisted I repay the money—my Boy Scout camp fees came from general family vacation funds, and to be fair to the rest of the family, members of the tribe who stayed the duration at their camps of choice, I had to reimburse my parents for the lost week. I don't remember if I ever repaid this money, but I did miss the larger weapons, and for many years I felt inferior for never having fired a shotgun or large-caliber rifle.

Two years later, in 1984, I was fourteen when the marine barracks in Lebanon was bombed, killing 241 U.S. servicemen, mostly marines. The number of dead was burned into my consciousness. As I folded my newspapers each morning, staring at the front-page images of the marines, the carnage crept into my brain, and also the sense that my country had been harmed and that I was responsible for some of the healing, the revenge. My country had been attacked, and I was a part of my country. Before me my father had gone to war and also my grandfather, and because of my unalterable genetic stain I was linked to the warrior line. I knew at this early age that despite what some politicians and philosophers and human rights advocates and priests insist, war is about revenge, war is about killing others who have killed and maimed you. After war there might be peace, but not during.

In the afternoons I watched the news bulletins, this being long before the sedating nonstop news loops of the cable stations, and as the marine bodies were carried from the rubble, I stood at attention and hummed the national anthem as the rough-hewn jarheads, some in bloody skivvy shirts, carried their comrades from the rubble. The marines were all sizes and all colors, all dirty and exhausted and hurt, and they were men, and I was a boy falling in love with manhood. I understood that manhood had to do with war, and war with manhood, and to no longer be just a son, I needed someday to fight. I thought of the marines constantly; my schoolwork, normally failing, failed even more spectacularly. Yes, I thought of the marines constantly, and I was engaged by woodshop and wrestling practice, but I sat dazed through my other classes.

While delivering my paper route, I wore my father's jungle camouflage boonie cover from Vietnam. He'd given it to me. Each morning I threw my ninety papers, with expertise, using the same aiming technique that would later help me while tossing grenades, and as the papers spun through the air toward my customers' porches, I saw—in the front-page photos of the bombed marine barracks—the kaleidoscopic trajectory of my future. The two other kids whose routes adjoined mine thought I was crazy and that with my camouflage hat and talk of war and retribution I might kill someone or myself.

They were my best friends and the three of us would, on Sunday mornings, finish our routes as quickly as possible and meet at the local donut shop and buy a dozen donuts each. One of the prettier older girls from school worked there, a girl who is probably poor and trashy but looked, through my eyes, attractive. I'd offer her a donut and she'd thank me and take a French crueller or an old-fashioned from my box, and I felt that this too was part of manhood, offering a woman a piece of something you owned, however small and possibly worthless. And she obviously already knew some of the magic of womanhood, allowing the man to think he has given you something you might not otherwise acquire, or that beforehand you didn't even know you needed. She saw my inability to meet her eyes—that I would pretend to check my watch before looking at her, before stuttering out my incomplete sentences—and she often went out of her way to be friendly toward me.

The donut shop is now gone, replaced by a megasupermarket. I believe the donut girl's name was Heather—years ago I heard she'd become pregnant a few times by various men, but still I remember fondly those Sunday mornings when I offered her donuts and grieved over the dead marines in Lebanon.

Shortly after the bombing I ordered a USMC iron-on from a recruitment ad in *Sports Illustrated*. One evening my mother ironed the Eagle, Globe, and Anchor onto a white T-shirt. Our kitchen was rather long and narrow, and my mother opened her ironing board in that space, and I sat at one end of the kitchen on a step stool while at the other end she applied my future to the shirt. She carefully cut the Eagle, Globe, and Anchor from the larger sheet of material, and I watched her steady hand with wonder, my mother always an expert at matters of craft and penmanship and the like. I felt the heat from the iron radiating throughout the room. The steam rose, the old iron coughed and spit, and my mother ran the iron across the shirt in smooth strokes, with the same rhythm as one might use to rock a baby.

I wonder now if she wanted to mar the job, to blur the ink or burn the shirt, desecrate the God-holy icon of the Corps. Or if she didn't, why not? Maybe if she had, I wouldn't have gone on to join the Marines because I'd never have worn the shirt, but she prepared the iron-on perfectly. Before she removed the backing, my mother half-heartedly counseled me against joining the military, especially the Marines.

"You should go to college before you decide to run off in the military. I missed college because I married your father, and the next fall when I should've been at the university, I was in Seville. Spain was nice, but college would've been better.

"You don't want to run away to dirty foreign countries. Every marine we ever met complained about the Marine Corps. They get paid less than anyone else and the food is supposed to be the worst." She looked away from me. "And the women near the bases have diseases. And remember your uncle."

My father's brother had been a marine, an embassy guard in Denmark, and he'd died one night on duty after ingesting, with his daily half gallon of milk, an avian disease. I'd heard the story once before, told by my father one night when he might have been drunk or lonely. My mother retold the story. I wasn't sure what it had to do with the local women having diseases, but I didn't interrupt her.

My father had received the news of his brother's sickness and rushed to Denmark from Spain and stayed at his brother's side until my grandparents arrived, and my uncle was medevacked to the States—the story goes my grandfather pumped a bellows to fill my uncle's lungs the entire flight over the Atlantic, and my uncle died minutes after touching down in Maryland. *It is best to die in America if you can.* My mother was sad over Uncle Billy, my father's closest sibling, by all accounts an honest and forthright man and stellar marine. A large portrait of Billy hung on the wall in my grandparents' family room, and I grew up looking in wonder at the portrait, made from a copy of his boot camp photo, the famous dress blue photo.

Four years after the iron-on was applied to my T-shirt, my dress blue photo would be tucked into the lower left corner of Billy's portrait.

While my mother worked on my iron-on, my father paid bills or wasted time inside his study, either unwilling to take part in the historic moment occurring in the kitchen or simply disinterested in the elite future his son might grasp, the USMC iron-on considered with the same paternal irony as Boy Scout camp and trumpet lessons and Little League, money gone and time possibly wasted but what's the hurt, this is life, and life goes on and children live happily if we're lucky and raise them well.

Finally my mother peeled away the backing and steam rose from my shirt and on the shirt the glorious Eagle, Globe, and Anchor pulsed like a heart. What splendid colors, scarlet and gold! By air, land, and sea! From the halls of Montezuma! I'd first sung "The Marines' Hymn" in grade school choir and now I belted out the first verse at the top of my lungs as my mother stood back from her ironing board. I thought I saw fear in her eyes. I ripped off the shirt I'd been wearing and poured my body into the USMC shirt, and the heat from the icon warmed my chest and my chest grew and I had become one of them, the Marines! At the ripe age of fourteen I'd decided my destiny. I would war and fight and make good for those poor boys dead in Lebanon, for my poor dead uncle killed not by the enemy but poisoned milk, for all of the marines of all time killed and dead in all wars and all cheap moments of peace.

But it was not cool to want to be in the military, so I kept this desire to myself. I wore the Marines shirt only on my paper route and occasionally to school during cold weather when I knew I would never remove my sweater. I kept most of my life to myself, not willing to share what would be ridiculed and tainted by the kids smarter and hipper and better dressed, the better athletes, the better students, the kids who'd fucked already, the punk rockers and the metalheads and all of them—any of the groups to which I could never belong.

"I believed I'd enlisted in the Marine Corps . . ." from *Jarhead*

ANTHONY SWOFFORD

I believed I'd enlisted in the Marine Corps in order to claim my place in the military history of my family, the history that included my father's service in Vietnam, his brother dying in the peacetime Marine Corps, and my grandfather serving in the army air force from December 10, 1941, through the end of World War II.

This initial impulse had nothing to do with a desire for combat, for killing, or for a heroic death, but rather was based on my intense need for acceptance into the family clan of manhood. By joining the Marine Corps and excelling within the severely disciplined enlisted ranks, I would prove both my manhood and the masculinity of the line. Also, by enlisting as an infantry grunt I was outdoing my brother, who'd spent his first few years in the army learning a practical vocation, teeth cleaning. Even before I hit puberty, Jeff and I had been in competition for the dominant male role just junior to our father's.

In the midst of my parents' divorce, my brother wrote a letter to my mother's lawyer, outlining the years of cruelty and abuse the family had suffered under my father's ironfisted rule. Largely, the letter consisted of fantasy, and my brother depicted himself as the hero of the family tragedy, wanting to run away as early as age eight but sticking around to protect his mother and siblings.

I read this letter a few months before shipping to boot camp, and I wept from the first sentence through the next five pages, and when I finished, I told my mother—a confused and angry and betrayed woman—that she couldn't use this fabricated document.

After my brother's death, among his effects I discovered my father's reply to this letter. It was full of profanity and threats of violence. My father swore that he would avenge my brother's lies and false accusations.

My father and brother didn't speak for five years after my brother wrote the letter in support of my mother. Finally, the summer my father drove to Georgia to visit his ill father and my brother was attending an army school in southern Arizona, no longer cleaning teeth but studying military intelligence, they met in a Mexican border town. I do not know what was said between the two men, if my brother apologized for the egregious lies in his letter, if my father apologized for his admittedly strict but not abusive family rule, but I do know that the first night of their rendezvous, they drank together excessively and walked arm in arm through the Mexican town, looking for my father's hotel, not finding it, and finally sleeping next to one another on the dead grass in a filthy park, and I know that after this visit the two men shared a friendship until the son died.

❧

The first time I tried to join the Marines, at the age of seventeen, I needed my parents' consent. I'd arranged for a recruiter to meet my parents at the house, and the recruiter had the contract ready for them. I assumed that after a few minutes of consultation my parents would sign.

For many years my father had planned for me to go to college and become an architect and design grand houses for him to build, but the construction company he'd started after retiring from the air force never achieved the success he'd sought, and most of his jobs were simple bedroom-and-bathroom additions that he could draw the plans for, on graph paper or even a cocktail napkin. Along with any desire to sustain his marriage, my father had lost interest in building his company and furthering my architectural education.

My mother did not want to see another son join the military, but she'd never said no to her sons and even recalled fondly applying the USMC iron-on to my T-shirt many years prior, and she asked me if the shirt was still around or if it had died a slow death in the cleaning-rag barrel. I was too embarrassed to admit that I'd pinned the T-shirt, too small now for me to wear, inside my closet.

I can't recall the recruiter's name, but he was a short and sinewy staff sergeant of Asian descent, perhaps Korean or even Vietnamese. I liked the staff sergeant. He ran 10Ks with me along the American River and afterward treated me to dinner. There he gleefully talked to me about buying sex in the Philippines and Italy and Sweden and Panama—information my mother would never see in the brochures. The recruiter guaranteed me I could book a threesome for forty American dollars in Olongapo, PI. I'd just turned seventeen. I'd had sex three times and been the recipient of five blow jobs and fourteen hand jobs. I was sold.

I wanted to be a grunt, a rifleman, I didn't even need to hear what other options existed, and the recruiter supported this choice. "You'll be a fine killer," he'd say to me after our meals.

My mother made fresh coffee and arranged a cookie plate for the recruiter's visit and sent my younger sister down the street to play with a friend.

The recruiter arrived and my father welcomed him and walked him outside for a tour of the backyard, to show off the new built-in pool and recently landscaped lawn, and to introduce him to our dogs. The recruiter was wearing his modified dress blues with ribbons and badges, and our two dogs were disciplined enough not to jump on the recruiter and ruin the sharp, clean lines of his uniform. Our dogs understood uniforms.

Inside, my father offered the recruiter his own chair, and my father sat next to me on the couch while my mother sat in her chair and faced the recruiter.

The conversation flowed amicably: the recruiter offered my parents compliments on the interior of the house, the art and furniture from twenty years of traveling and living abroad. He asked my father about the places he'd been in the air force, and my father made a joke about the feeble air force and said something about all of the crazy jarheads he'd known in Vietnam, and before that his poor, sweet marine brother who'd died, and how he'd always believed the Corps was the backbone of the U.S. military. The recruiter accepted the compliment and said something positive yet tempered about the air force. Then the conversation moved to me. The recruiter congratulated my parents on what a fine young man they'd raised, a bright young man with a promising future, physically fit and a great specimen prepared to be molded into a hard piece of USMC steel, the recruiter said with a smile. And this is when my father said, "Staff Sergeant," and placed his hands together as if for prayer, and bit on the tips of his index fingers, and then said, "Staff Sergeant, I'll sign your contract if you guarantee me you won't get my son killed. Then I'll sign your contract. Otherwise, you should leave my house." And the polite staff sergeant began to speak and reach for one of his slick brochures, the brochures I knew by heart but that my parents hadn't even seen yet, but my father said, "Tell me my son will not die in your holy fucking Marine Corps." And this was the first time I heard my father curse, and the only time until I returned from war.

The recruiter said, "I'm sorry, sir. I cannot tell you that. I can tell you Tony will be a great marine, that he'll be a part of the finest fighting force on earth and he'll fight proudly all enemies of the United States, just as you did once. He will be a great killer."

I walked the staff sergeant to his car. He said, "Hey, we'll get you next time. Your dad wants something that's impossible. Keep up with the physical training. When you're seventeen and a half, you can join on your own."

I returned to my bedroom and looked over the well-thumbed recruiting brochures that showed jarheads running in tight formation, their voices warped into war cries; jarheads gathered with friends, on liberty, sharing photos from their various exotic duty stations; jarheads firing rifles and climbing fifty foot ropes and swimming the ocean.

In a matter of seconds my entire life plan had been altered. I wept. What would I do with myself? I'd already, in my heart, signed the contract and accepted the warrior lifestyle. I wanted to be a killer, to kill my country's enemies. Now I'd have to take the SATs and visit colleges, I'd have to find a part-time job. I'd never live abroad and chase prostitutes through the world's brothels, or Communists through the world's jungles. I needed the Marine Corps *now*, I needed the Marine Corps to save me from the other life I'd fail at—the life of the college boy hoping to find a girlfriend and later a job.

My father knocked on my door and entered my room before he'd stopped knocking. I tried to look angry rather than sad.

He sat on my weight bench and asked, "How many pounds are on the bar?"

"Two fifty."

"How many times can you lift it?"

"Twelve or fifteen."

"I didn't know you were so strong."

"Lots of guys are stronger than me."

"No, they aren't. As soon as you can sign that contract on your own, go ahead. Until then, I'm responsible for you. I'm not stronger than you, but I know some things about the military that they don't show you in the brochures."

Shortly after this conversation my father left my mother, and a few months later, while he continued to run his business out of the house but slept wherever he wanted, we fought. I'd used his business phone to call a girl I was pursuing. I talked in his office for the privacy it offered, away from my little sister's curious ears and my mother's sad eyes. While using his phone over the two weeks of the failed romance, I'd somehow disabled his answering machine and he'd lost several important phone messages and subsequently a few contracts. When he realized what had occurred, he confronted me, and I first attempted to lie, telling him I had thought someone was breaking into the house and so had used the phone to call 911, but he didn't believe me, and as he spoke to me, he pounded his index finger against my chest. Crying, and telling my father he had no right to touch me that way, I walked backward through the house until I backed my way into the garage, out of the sight of my mother and sister, and I threw the first punch, a solid punch that connected with his jaw and stunned him, and then he punched back, and he connected with me, and for what might have been a minute we exchanged blows, to the face and body, until I fell slowly to the ground, of my own volition, and he continued to hit me, though I curled my body up and covered my face with my arms so his blows connected only with my muscular arms, and these blows were painless.

He stopped hitting me and sat on a workbench stool. He breathed in gasps and might have been crying and I continued to weep and settled my cheek against the broken face of my watch.

He said, "You are stronger than me, but I'm meaner. You don't understand what I've lived through. I'll never touch you again. I'm sorry if I've hurt you, but I believe you can handle anything, especially some soft punches from your old father."

He walked out of the garage and into the house and I heard him tell my mother not to worry about what he had done with his son. The front door opened and closed, and his car door opened and closed, and he started his car and it idled in the driveway for ten or fifteen minutes, while I remained on the floor of the garage, in the same spot where I'd once folded my newspapers, and eventually he drove away.

***

At the age of seventeen and a half, I signed the enlistment contract myself, though the credit went to a new recruiter, because the recruiter who'd failed with my parents had been transferred to a different station. My new recruiter was Staff Sergeant Erikson, a nice guy who smoked and drank and cursed like a jarhead should and probably hadn't run a 10K in ten years, but still I liked him. He told crude jokes and he too had prostitute stories, and he listed from memory the price of a whore in the Philippines, Guam, Okinawa, Bangkok, Sydney, Hong Kong, and Athens, and on good days, he remembered their names.

Once, when I visited the recruiting station with a pretty girl I was trying to impress—a foolish attempt because what young woman in her right mind in 1988 would've been impressed with a boy joining the Marine Corps?—Erikson pulled me aside and said, "Swofford, I'd drink a gallon of her pee just to see where it came from."

The girl might not have been impressed with Erikson or the Marine Corps, but she became my girlfriend for a short time, and the night before I shipped to boot camp I didn't sleep because we were so busy sweating and fucking in my bed.

The next day my father drove me to the Oakland in-processing station, where northern California men and women joining all of the military services receive a physical prior to basic training. After passing my physical and being sworn in, I'd fly to San Diego to start boot camp. The Marine Corps ran a shuttle from Sacramento to Oakland every afternoon, but my father insisted on taking me himself. On the way toward the Bay Area, we drove through the town of Vacaville, and by the family home at the time of my birth. We also drove past the church where my father and I had both been baptized. We entered Travis Air Force Base, and my father pulled into a parking lot in front of a one-story concrete building. He turned the engine off and we sat for a few minutes in silence. I knew he'd been stationed at Travis after Vietnam, but I didn't know why we'd stopped. It was December, but the sun shone brightly on the closed car, and I felt beads of sweat forming on my forehead and upper lip. I looked at my father as he looked at the sturdy building in front of us.

He patted my knee and said, "I thought you might like to see where you were born. It's not a hospital anymore, it's payroll. But whenever I'm on base, I come up here."

I started to speak, but he blinked hard twice, patted my knee again, and said, "Guess we better get you on the road. There's a drill instructor in San Diego waiting to give you a big wet kiss."

I've never asked my father why he drove us to the place of my birth just hours before I joined the Marine Corps, but I think I know: to remember how he'd once loved our family, to reacquaint himself with his own lost youth and vigor, and also to ask me not to go off and get myself killed.

Falling Through the Earth

DANIELLE TRUSSONI

Prologue

The guide knelt before the tunnel entrance. Old, energetic, and clearly happy with his job, he smiled as he listed the booby traps he had planted to kill American soldiers: the punji sticks and scorpions rigged into bamboo cages, the explosives packed in Coke cans. The Vietcong, he said, made weapons from whatever they could find, old C-ration tins or beer bottles. Matériel was never a problem. The Americans left a lot of trash behind.

Hundreds of entrances survived the war. This one—much wider than the wartime tunnels—had probably been expanded to accommodate Western-sized tourists. The guide motioned for us to kneel next to him, above the gaping hole in the earth. We formed a semicircle, knees upon the hot sun-baked clay, watching him lower himself into the ground, demonstrating various styles of entry. He went in feet first, then head-first, grinning all the while. I got the feeling he would have come to that patch of jungle even if tourists did not. Maybe the tunnels were a kind of haven, a place to retire to. A Vietcong's own private Florida.

My father volunteered to be a tunnel rat in 1968. The job consisted of crawling through webs of tunnels and rooms searching for men like my tour guide, Vietnamese guerrillas hiding out underground. Tunnel exploration was considered one of the most dangerous assignments in Vietnam. The distinction set my father apart from his platoon, bumping him into the Hazardous Duty pay grade and increasing his chances of dying tenfold. Tunneling was a suicide mission, but he chose it. He saw men die underground, and yet he kept going down. It takes that kind of person—two parts stubborn, one part insane—to fight in a tunnel. Dad fit the bill. Only a man determined to see the worst that war had to offer—and to beat it—would volunteer to be a tunnel rat.

Tunneling, my father always said, was the scariest thing on earth. As I stood above the entrance, I knew he was right. I used to think Dad was all balls and no brains, a man caught up in being a cowboy. But perhaps his attraction to the tunnels was more than bravado. Maybe my father looked into the tunnels and saw what I did: a mystery, a test, a challenge hard to walk away from. Perhaps the tunnels called to him with the same rich voice I heard thirty years later, dangerous and seductive. I crouched before the entrance. A jittery adrenaline-rich sensation filled my stomach, and I knew I wanted to go down. I wanted to feel the fear, the heat, the thrill of making it through. At heart, I was my father's daughter.

I followed the guide into the tunnel. A pool of sunlight fell from the entrance shaft and expanded around me, becoming darker by degrees. The tunnel was just as I imagined it would be, a shock of darkness that gave way to a narrow communication shaft. The old man crawled ahead but turned back when he realized that I was not close behind. In the weak light I saw his face, inches from mine. As our eyes locked, I imagined a knife in his hand, its cool blade brushing my neck. *Follow me,* he gestured, and crawled off again, ahead. I let my eyes adjust to the dark and pushed forward.

As I crawled deeper, the tunnel narrowed. The heat thickened; the air thinned. My T-shirt clung to my skin. Deeper, deeper we went. I paused, to scratch a wall with my fingernails, a sensation that sent shivers up my spine, a spidery prickle that asked, *What in the hell are you doing here?* I breathed, slowly. Suddenly, I was alone. Where had the man gone? I saw nothing but dark in front of me, nothing but dark behind. I moved my hand, my knee, my other hand, my other knee, forward, going deeper and deeper.

One

Winter of '85, and we were on the run.

Dad veered the truck into an alley, cut across a parking lot, and merged with traffic running alongside the frozen Mississippi. "Cops don't come down this road," he said, checking the rearview mirror. "If they're here, it's because they followed us." My father was prone to paranoia, but the police were real. We'd been picked up twice for drunk driving that year. After the last arrest, he'd lost his license. We tried to keep a low profile, but the cops knew our truck and where we lived—*Those sons-of-bitches got nothing to do but bother hardworking taxpayers.* Faster, faster we drove. If they caught us again, Dad would go to jail.

Streets expanded before us, eerie and lonesome. Salt and steel-link tire chains had beaten the snow thin. Pawnshops and motels and tattoo parlors fell away as we passed. I unrolled my window. The city was cold and sharp-angled, as if emerging from a block of ice. I couldn't help but wish for spring. If it were warm, we could escape on a riverboat. We could float past Illinois and Missouri, down south to Louisiana. But it was deep winter, the river frozen, and the only hope for a quick getaway was the ironwork bridge that scaled out to Minnesota. I stared at it as we drove past, my vision ribboning its girders. Dad looked over his shoulder, listening for sirens.

My father was running from the police, from his first ex-wife, his creditors, and his dreams. He was running from his second ex-wife (my mother), his illegitimate children, and his past. He was running from himself, and I was right there with him, an eleven-year-old accomplice to his evenings of escape. I had been at his side for the last year, since my mother divorced us. Mom kept the house and my younger sister and brother; Dad kept me. No matter how far or fast we ran, I was there. I was all he had left.

We slowed down before Roscoe's, Dad's favorite bar, and parked near a set of rusty snow-packed railroad tracks. The lot was dim, as if seen through a starlight scope. Bleak electrocuted trees tangled before the buildings' brick façades. A blue boxcar had been abandoned mid-line, a pretty stranded Christmas present, but it wouldn't be long before an engine hooked it and trolled the freight to a warehouse beyond the city limits. Wisconsin winters were fierce. Nothing was left in the cold for long.

Dad locked his truck and walked ahead. Like most tunnel rats, he was a small man—only five feet eight inches and a hundred and fifty pounds—but quick. Impatient by nature, he always moved fast. I tried to match his pace, jogging to keep up. A neon beer sign blinked, sending chills of pink over his face. As he turned his head to light a cigarette, I saw myself in his olive skin, the hint of haughtiness in his profile. His eyes were deep brown, his face thin. He had lost his hair in his twenties, just after returning from Vietnam, a premature baldness that was beginning to look natural only now, as he neared forty. The empty nickel-hard sky bowled overhead, framing my father in a background of gray. He looked at me, his smile boyish, and pulled the door to Roscoe's open. "After you, Danielle-my-belle."

Roscoe's Vogue Bar was a mouthful, an unchewable four syllables. Everyone who was anyone called my father's favorite tavern Roscoe's or The Vogue. I called it Roscoe's. Rigid in this preference, I made fun of those regulars who called it The Vogue, finding it hilarious, with a preteen's sense of ruthless snobbery, that the worst-dressed women in America hung out at a place named after a slick fashion magazine. When I felt contentious (which, at eleven, was all the time), I told the women parked on their bar stools that they were looking *very Vogue*. That afternoon I said, "Barb, those Wranglers are great. Very Vogue." Barb tipped her beer my way and said, "You look beautiful too, smart-ass."

And she was right: I looked fantastic. My father had picked me up from school, and I hadn't had time to change. My uniform was a starched navy-blue skirt, white cotton blouse, and a stiff-necked navy-blue blazer, an ensemble I hated. I'd dressed it up with red knee socks and Doc Martens. I'd smeared on glittery eye shadow and purple lip gloss. My ears had been pierced five times; I'd written lyrics from my favorite songs (by semi-obscure and hundred-percent-depressing British bands) on my arms with red ink. I told myself that I was a post-punk rebel ready to take on the world, and it was true: I was ready to have a go at everyone, single-handedly. If it weren't for my name, people might have thought that Catholic school had done strange things to me. As it was, everyone in town knew I was Dan Trussoni's girl. This pedigree explained a lot.

During happy hour, Roscoe's was crowded. Drinks were cheap and the juke-box plugged with quarters. The way I remember it, Roscoe's was always the same—the barroom was packed (Dad and I had to squeeze onto our stools), the music played too loud, and I was forever a child, quick on my feet and dull to the truth that my father, with all his speed, could never outrun the past.

Dad ordered a round of drinks—brandy and Coke for him, a cherry Coke for me. He stubbed out his cigarette in a black plastic ashtray and lit another. My father had spent most of his adult life (aside from his tour in Vietnam) laying bricks, and his hands proved it; they were tumescent and covered with scars. The knuckles were cracked, as if cement had dried in the creases of his skin, split-ting it. Dad worked harder than anyone else I knew—twelve-hour days in the summer, sometimes fourteen. When I was little, I would wait for him to come home from work and run down the driveway, meeting his truck at a gallop. I was his tag-along daughter, his dark-haired namesake, the shadow girl chasing after him wanting love, love, love. He would throw his tool-box in the garage, slap me on the back, and hit the shower. I would lean my head against the bath-room door, pressing my ear to the wood. He had not showered yet that day, and as we sat at the bar I wanted to take a toothpick from the dispenser and pry the pieces of coagulated concrete from his cuticles. I wanted to free his fingerprints of dirt.

I watched him, assessing his mood. When Dad was in high spirits, he was the most charismatic guy in the place. His buddies would walk by, shake his hand, tell him a joke, and ask how business was going. Drinks would arrive, bought by women we'd never met before. He filled the room with his presence, wher-ever he went. But if my father was stuck thinking of my mother, he would be surly. He met my mother the year he came back from Vietnam, when he was wild and haunted. Maybe she liked that about him—how much he needed her. I've seen pictures of my parents taken the year I was born; they were holding hands and kissing, so in love it appeared nothing in the world could stop them. After Mom left, Dad became unrecognizable. He spent all his time at the bar, drink-ing from early afternoon until late in the night. When Dad got drunk, memo-ries of Vietnam crept back on him. I never knew what had hurt him more, the war or my mother.

The drinks arrived as the jukebox came to life. Patsy Cline's soft voice filled the bar with sound. A row of taxidermy hung above the jukebox: a deer head, a beaver, and a sorry-looking turkey. My father sipped his brandy and Coke in silence, his gaze fixed on the turkey. After the second round, he squinted slightly, scanned the perimeter of the bar, tipping his Stetson to anyone who met his eye. Sometime between the third and fourth drink, he loosened up and began to talk. Not to me, exactly, although I was the only one listening. Dad didn't need me. He always went back to the war alone.

"Have I told you about the Vietcong prostitute and her mother?"

"No, Pop," I said, although I knew that he had.

"We were close to Cambodia, near the Black Virgin Mountain. We walked all day through the jungle, set up a perimeter, and the village girls hung around the concertina, watching as we dug in for the night. Smart little things, those girls were. They'd finish their work and then tell us they were giving the money to the Vietcong. We didn't care, though. They snuck around the concertina and into the perimeter all the time. This one slipped right into camp, slid under my poncho, and started doing her business. Usually, I would've just let her go about it, but I didn't have any cash, not even script, so I pushed her back. I said, *No money*. Them Vietnamese girls didn't know how to talk, but they knew the word *money* all right. The girl said, *No money, this love*, and went right on with what she was doing, which was fine by me. Who am I to argue with a free meal?"

"Not you," I said. By twelve, I thought I had seen and heard it all from Dad.

"*No money, this love*, the girl says, and that was that. It was near morning when we were done. She gets up to go and I see, by the perimeter, an old lady standing by. The girl's mother had been watching us, I guess. I feel creepy all of a sudden, like maybe I shouldn't be screwing her daughter for free. Sure enough, the girl starts asking for her money, making a big to-do. They'd probably planned it this way, because the old one starts in too, screeching like a duck about *money, money, money*. I didn't have a cent on me, so I took that girl and tossed her clear over the concertina, to her mama. The old lady got mad at that. She screamed louder, so I got my M-16 and pointed it right smack between her eyes. That shut her up quick. *This one is for love*, I said. *This one's for love*."

Dad told a lot of war stories, but there were a few he always returned to. When he'd had too much to drink, he would start complaining about the police, or the price of gas, and suddenly he would plummet into the jungles of Vietnam. A shadow would fall over his face, obscuring him from me, and I knew he had disappeared into the past. If I reached for his hand, it was rough and cold. He was no longer there.

When Dad spoke, the bar became quiet. Vines slithered up the bar stools; tunnels opened at our feet. And Tommy Goodman, my father's tunnel-rat friend, a man I had learned to imagine from Dad's war stories, pulled up a seat next to us and rested his head on the glossy surface of the bar. *Glad you could make it*, I imagined myself saying. But Goodman and my father never paid attention to me. Before I knew it, they would be gone, two boys headed out to the war. I trailed behind, mopping up blood with cocktail napkins.

APO 96225

LARRY ROTTMANN

A young man once went off to war
in a far country,
and when he had time, he wrote home and
said, "Sure rains a lot here."

But his mother, reading between the lines,
Wrote back, "We're quite concerned.
Tell us what it's really like."

And the young man responded, "Wow! You ought
to see the funny monkeys!"

To which the mother replied, "Don't
hold back, how is it?"

And the young man wrote, "The sunsets here
are spectacular!"

In her next letter the mother
wrote, "Son, we want you to tell us
everything."

So the next time he wrote,
"Today I killed a man.
Yesterday, I helped drop napalm on women and
children. Tomorrow we are going to use
gas."

And the father wrote right back, "Please don't
write such depressing letters. You're upsetting
your mother."

So, after a while, the young man wrote, "Sure rains a
lot here. . ."

APO 96225, Army Post Office Number 96225—Official address of the 25th Infantry Division
in Vietnam

Section 4

Making Changes

Beyond Good & Evil:
Marshall Rosenberg on Creating
a Nonviolent World

AN INTERVIEW BY D. KILLIAN

I first met Marshall Rosenberg when I was assigned by a local paper to cover one of his "Nonviolent Communication" training seminars. Disturbed by the inequalities in the world and impatient for change, I couldn't imagine what use a communication technique could be in solving problems such as global warming or the debt of developing nations. But I was surprised by the visible effect Rosenberg's work had on individuals and families caught in conflict.

Nonviolent Communication, or NVC, has four steps: observing what is happening in a given situation; identifying what one is feeling; identifying what one is needing; and then making a request for what one would like to see occur. It sounds simple, yet it's more than a technique for resolving conflict. It's a different way of understanding human motivation and behavior.

Rosenberg learned about violence at an early age. Growing up in Detroit in the thirties and forties, he was beaten up for being a Jew and witnessed some of the city's worst race riots, which resulted in more than forty deaths in a matter of days. These experiences drove him to study psychology in an attempt to understand, as he puts it, "what happens to disconnect us from our compassionate nature, and what allows some people to stay connected to their compassionate nature under even the most trying circumstances."

Rosenberg completed his PhD in clinical psychology at the University of Wisconsin in 1961 and afterward went to work with youths at reform schools. The experience led him to conclude that, rather than help people to be more compassionate, clinical psychology actually contributed to the conditions that cause violence, because it categorized people and thus distanced them from each other; doctors were trained to see the diagnosis, not the person. He decided that violence did not arise from pathology, as psychology taught, but from the ways in which we communicate.

Humanist psychotherapist Carl Rogers, creator of "client-centered therapy," was an early influence on Rosenberg's theories, and Rosenberg worked with Rogers for several years before setting out on his own to teach others how to interact in nonaggressive ways. His method became known as Nonviolent Communication.

No longer a practicing psychologist, Rosenberg admits that he has struggled at times with his own method, resorting to familiar behavior or fearing the risks involved in a nonviolent approach. Yet each time he has followed through with Nonviolent Communication, he has been surprised by the results. At times, it has literally saved his life.

On one occasion in the late 1980s, he was asked to teach his method to Palestinian refugees in Bethlehem. He met with about 170 Muslim men at a mosque in the Deheisha Camp. On the way into the camp, he saw several empty tear-gas canisters along the road, each clearly marked "Made in U.S.A." When the men realized their would-be instructor was from the United States, they became angry. Some jumped to their feet and began shouting, "Assassin! Murderer!" One man confronted Rosenberg, screaming in his face, "Child killer!"

Although tempted to make a quick exit, Rosenberg instead focused his questions on what the man was feeling, and a dialogue ensued. By the end of the day, the man who had called Rosenberg a murderer had invited him home to Ramadan dinner.

Rosenberg is founder and director of the nonprofit Center for Nonviolent Communication (www.cnvc.org). He is the author of Nonviolent Communication: A Language of Compassion (PuddleDancer Press) and has just completed a new book, to be released by PuddleDancer in fall 2003, on the application of NVC in education: When Students Love to Learn and Teachers Love to Teach. He is currently working on a third book addressing the social implications of Nonviolent Communication.

A tall, gaunt man, Rosenberg is soft-spoken but becomes animated when describing how Nonviolent Communication has worked for him and others. He has three children and currently lives in Wasserfallenof, Switzerland. Rosenberg is in great demand as a speaker and educator and maintains a relentless schedule. The day we spoke was his first free day in months. Afterward, he would be traveling to Israel, Brazil, Slovenia, Argentina, Poland, and Africa.

Killian: Your method aims to teach compassion, but compassion seems more a way of being than a skill or technique. Can it really be taught?

Rosenberg: I would say it's a natural human trait. Our survival as a species depends on our ability to recognize that our well-being and the well-being of others are, in fact, one and the same. The problem is that we are taught behaviors that disconnect us from this natural awareness. It's not that we have to learn how to be compassionate; we have to unlearn what we've been taught and get back to compassion.

Killian: If violence is learned, when did it start? It seems to have always been a part of human existence.

Rosenberg: Theologian Walter Wink estimates that violence has been the social norm for about eight thousand years. That's when a myth evolved that the world was created by a heroic, virtuous male god who defeated an evil female goddess. From that point on, we've had the image of the good guys killing the bad guys. And that has evolved into "retributive justice," which says that there are those who deserve to be punished and those who deserve to be rewarded. That belief has penetrated deep into our societies. Not every culture has been exposed to it, but, unfortunately, most have.

Killian: You've said that *deserve* is the most dangerous word in the language. Why?

Rosenberg: It's at the basis of retributive justice. For thousands of years, we've been operating under this system that says that people who do bad deeds are evil—indeed, that human beings are basically evil. According to this way of thinking, a few good people have evolved, and it's up to them to be the authorities and control the others. And the way you control people, given that our nature is evil and selfish, is through a system of justice in which people who behave in a good manner get rewarded, while those who are evil are made to suffer. In order to see such a system as fair, one has to believe that both sides deserve what they get.

I used to live in Texas, and when they would execute somebody there, the good Baptist students from the local college would gather outside the prison and have a party. When the word came over the loudspeaker that the convict had been killed, there was loud cheering and so forth—the same kind of cheering that went on in some parts of Palestine when they found out about the September 11 terrorist attacks. When you have a concept of justice based on good and evil, in which people deserve to suffer for what they've done, it makes violence enjoyable.

Killian: But you're not opposed to judgments.

Rosenberg: I'm all for judgments. I don't think we could survive very long without them. We judge which foods will give us what our bodies need. We judge which actions are going to meet our needs. But I differentiate between life-serving judgments, which are about our needs, and moralistic judgments that imply rightness or wrongness.

Killian: You've called instead for "restorative justice." How is that different?

Rosenberg: Restorative justice is based on the question: how do we restore peace? In other words, how do we restore a state in which people care about one another's well-being? Research indicates that perpetrators who go through restorative justice are less likely to repeat the behaviors that led to their incarceration. And it's far more healing for the victim to have peace restored than simply to see the other person punished.

The idea is spreading. I was in England about a year ago to present a keynote speech at the international conference on restorative justice. I expected thirty people might show up. I was delighted to see more than six hundred people at this conference.

Killian: How does restorative justice work?

Rosenberg: I have seen it work, for example, with women who have been raped and the men who raped them. The first step is for the woman to express whatever it is that she wants her attacker to understand. Now, this woman has suffered almost every day for years since the attack, so what comes out is pretty brutal: "You monster! I'd like to kill you!" and so forth.

What I do then is help the prisoner to connect with the pain that is alive in this woman as a result of his actions. Usually what he wants to do is apologize. But I tell him apology is too cheap, too easy. I want him to repeat back what he hears her saying. How has her life been affected? When he can't repeat it, I play his role. I tell her I hear the pain behind all of the screams and shouting. I get him to see that the rage is on the surface, but beneath that lies the despair about whether her life will ever be the same again. And then I get the man to repeat what I've said. It may take three, or four, or five tries, but finally he hears the other person. Already at this point you can see the healing starting to take place—when the victim gets empathy.

Then I ask the man to tell me what's going on inside of him. How does he feel? Usually, again, he wants to apologize. He wants to say, "I'm a rat. I'm dirt." And again I get him to dig deeper. And it's very scary for these men. They're not used to dealing with feelings, let alone experiencing the horror of what it feels like to have caused another human being such pain.

When we've gotten past these first two steps, very often the victim's screams, "How *could* you?" She's hungry to understand what would cause another person to do such a thing. Unfortunately, most of the victims I've worked with have been encouraged from the very beginning by well-meaning people to forgive their attackers. These people explain that the rapist must have been suffering and probably had a bad childhood. And the victim does try to forgive, but this doesn't help much. Forgiveness reached without first taking these other steps is just superficial. It suppresses the pain.

Once the woman has received some empathy, however, she wants to know what was going on in this man when he committed this act. I help the perpetrator go back to the moment of the act and identify what he was feeling, what needs were contributing to his actions.

The last step is to ask whether there is something more the victim would like the perpetrator to do, to bring things back to a state of peace. For example, she may want medical bills to be paid, or she may want some emotional restitution. But once there's empathy on both sides, it's amazing how quickly they start to care about one another's well-being.

Killian: What kinds of "needs" would cause a person to rape another human being?

Rosenberg: It has nothing to do with sex, of course. It has to do with the tenderness that people don't know how to get and often confuse with sex. In almost every case, the rapists themselves have been victims of some sort of sexual aggression or physical abuse, and they want someone else to understand how horrible it feels to be in this passive, weak role. They need empathy, and they've employed a distorted means of getting it: by inflicting similar pain on someone else. But the need is universal. All human beings have the same needs. Thankfully, most of us meet them in ways that are not destructive to other people and ourselves.

Killian: We've long believed in the West that needs must be regulated and denied, but you're suggesting the opposite: that needs must be recognized and fulfilled.

Rosenberg: I'd say we teach people to misrepresent their needs. Rather than educating people to be conscious of their needs, we teach them to become addicted to ineffective strategies for meeting them. Consumerism makes people think that their needs will be met by owning a certain item. We teach people that revenge is a need, when in fact it's a flawed strategy. Retributive justice itself is a poor strategy. Mixed in with all that is a belief in competition, that we can get our needs met only at other people's expense. Not only that, but that it's heroic and joyful to win, to defeat someone else.

So it's very important to differentiate needs from strategies and to get people to see that any strategy that meets your needs at someone else's expense is not meeting *all* your needs. Because anytime you behave in a way that's harmful to others, you end up hurting yourself. As philosopher Elbert Hubbard once said, "We're not punished for our sins, but by them."

Whether I'm working with drug addicts in Bogotá, Colombia, or with alcoholics in the United States, or with sex offenders in prisons, I always start by making it clear to them that I'm not there to make them stop what they're doing. "Others have tried," I say. "You've probably tried yourself, and it hasn't worked." I tell them I'm there to help them get clear about what needs are being met by this behavior. And once we have gotten clear on what their needs are, I teach them to find more effective and less costly ways of meeting those needs.

Killian: Nonviolent Communication seems to focus a lot on feelings. What about the logical, analytic side of things? Does it have a place here?

Rosenberg: Nonviolent Communication focuses on what's alive in us and what would make life more wonderful. What's alive in us are our needs, and I'm talking about the universal needs, the ones all living creatures have. Our feelings are simply a manifestation of what is happening with our needs. If our needs are being fulfilled, we feel pleasure. If our needs are not being fulfilled, we feel pain.

Now, this does not exclude the analytic. We simply differentiate between life-serving analysis and life-alienated analysis. If I say to you, "I'm in a lot of pain over my relationship to my child. I really want him to be healthy, and I see him not eating well and smoking," then you might ask, "Why do you think he's doing this?" You'd be encouraging me to analyze the situation and uncover his needs.

Analysis is a problem only when it gets disconnected from serving life. For example, if I said to you, "I think George Bush is a monster," we could have a long discussion, and we might think it was an interesting discussion, but it wouldn't be connected to life. We wouldn't realize this, though, because maybe neither of us has ever had a conversation that was life-connecting. We get so used to speaking at the analytic level that we can go through life with our needs unmet and not even know it. The comedian Buddy Hackett used to say that it wasn't until he joined the army that he found out you could get up from a meal without having heartburn; he had gotten so used to his mother 's cooking, heartburn had become a way of life. And in middle-class, educated culture in the United States, I think that disconnection is a way of life. When people have needs that they don't know how to deal with directly, they approach them indirectly through intellectual discussions. As a result, the conversation is lifeless.

Killian: If we do agree that Bush is a monster, though, at least we'll connect on the level of values.

Rosenberg: And that's going to meet some needs—certainly more than if I disagree with you or if I ignore what you're saying. But imagine what the conversation could be like if we learned to hear what's alive behind the words and ideas, and to connect at that level. Central to NVC training is that all moralistic judgments, whether positive or negative, are tragic expressions of needs. Criticism, analysis, and insults are tragic expressions of unmet needs. Compliments and praise, for their part, are tragic expressions of fulfilled needs.

So why do we get caught up in this dead, violence-provoking language? Why not learn how to live at the level where life is really going on? NVC is not looking at the world through rose-colored glasses. We come closer to the truth when we connect with what's alive in people than when we just listen to what they think.

Killian: How do you discuss world affairs in the language of feelings?

Rosenberg: Somebody reasonably proficient in NVC might say, "I am scared to death when I see what Bush is doing in an attempt to protect us. I don't feel any safer." And then somebody who disagrees might say, "Well, I share your desire for safety, but I'm scared of doing nothing." Already we're not just talking about George Bush, but about the feelings that are alive in both of us.

Killian: And coming closer to thinking about solutions?

Rosenberg: Yes, because we've acknowledged that we both have the same needs. It's only at the level of strategy that we disagree. Remember, all human beings have the same needs. When our consciousness is focused on what's alive in us, we never see an alien being in front of us. Other people may have different strategies for meeting their needs, but they are not aliens.

Killian: In the U.S. right now, there are some people who would have a lot of trouble hearing this. During a memorial for September 11, I heard a policeman say all he wanted was "payback."

Rosenberg: One rule of our training is: empathy before education. I wouldn't expect someone who's been injured to hear what I'm saying until they felt that I had fully understood the depth of their pain. Once they felt empathy from me, then I would introduce my fear that our plan to exact retribution isn't going to make us safer.

Killian: Have you always been a nonviolent revolutionary?

Rosenberg: For many years I wasn't, and I was scaring more people than I was helping. When I was working against racism in the United States, I must confess, I confronted more than a few people with accusations like "That was a racist thing to say!" I said this with deep anger, because I was dehumanizing the other person in my mind. And I was not seeing any of the changes I wanted.

An Iowa feminist group called HERA helped me with that. They asked, "Doesn't it bother you that your work is against violence rather than for life?" And I realized that I was trying to get people to see the mess around them by telling them how they were contributing to it. In doing so, I was just creating more resistance and more hostility. HERA helped me to get past just talking about not judging others, and to move on to what can enrich life and make it more wonderful.

Killian: You have criticized clinical psychology for its focus on pathology. Have you trained any psychotherapists or other mental-health practitioners in NVC?

Rosenberg: Lots of them, but most of the people I train are not doctors or therapists. I agree with theologian Martin Buber, who said that you cannot do psychotherapy as a psychotherapist. People heal from their pain when they have an authentic connection with another human being, and I don't think you can have an authentic connection when one person thinks of him- or herself as the therapist, diagnosing the other. And if patients come in thinking of themselves as sick people who are there to get treatment, then it starts with the assumption that there's something wrong with them, which gets in the way of the healing. So, yes, I teach this to psychotherapists, but I teach it mostly to regular human beings, because we can all engage in an authentic connection with others, and it's out of this authentic connection that healing takes place.

Killian: It seems all religious traditions have some basis in empathy and compassion—the bleeding heart of Christ and the life of Saint Francis are two examples from Christianity. Yet horrible acts of violence have been committed in the name of religion.

Rosenberg: Social psychologist Milton Rokeach did some research on religious practitioners in the seven major religions. He looked at people who very seriously followed their religion and compared them to people in the same population who had no religious orientation at all. He wanted to find out which group was more compassionate. The results were the same in all the major religions: the nonreligious were more compassionate.

Rokeach warned readers to be careful how they interpreted his research, however, because within each religious group, there were two radically different populations: a mainstream group and a mystical minority. If you looked at just the mystical group, you found that they were more compassionate than the general population.

In mainline religion, you have to sacrifice and go through many different procedures to demonstrate your holiness, but the mystical minority see compassion and empathy as part of human nature. We *are* this divine energy, they say. It's not something we have to attain. We just have to realize it, be present to it. Unfortunately, such believers are in the minority and are often persecuted by fundamentalists within their own religions. Chris Rajendrum, a Jesuit priest in Sri Lanka, and Archbishop Simon in Burundi are two men who risk their lives daily in the service of bringing warring parties together. They see Christ's message not as an injunction to tame yourself or to be above this world, but as a confirmation that we *are* this energy of compassion. Nafez Assailez, a Muslim I work with, says it's painful for him to see anyone killing in the name of Islam. It's inconceivable to him.

Killian: The idea that we're evil and must become holy implies moralistic judgment.

Rosenberg: Oh, amazing judgment! Rokeach calls that judgmental group the salvationists. For them, the goal is to be rewarded by going to heaven. So you try to follow your religion's teachings not because you've internalized an awareness of your own divinity and relate to others in a compassionate way, but because these things are "right" and if you do them, you'll be rewarded, and if you don't, you'll be punished,

Killian: And those in the minority, they've had a taste of the divine presence and recognize it in themselves and others?

Rosenberg: Exactly. And they're often the ones who invite me to teach Nonviolent Communication, because they see that our training is helping to bring people back to that consciousness.

Killian: You've written about "domination culture." Is that the same as "salvationism"?

Rosenberg: I started using the term "domination culture" after reading Walter Wink's works, especially his book *Engaging the Powers*. His concept is that we are living under structures in which the few dominate the many. Look at how families are structured here in the United States: the parents claim always to know what's right and set the rules for everybody else's benefit. Look at our schools. Look at our workplaces. Look at our government, our religions. At all levels, you have authorities who impose their will on other people, claiming that it's for everybody's well-being. They use punishment and reward as the basic strategy for getting what they want. That's what I mean by domination culture.

Killian: It seems movements and institutions often start out as transformative but end up as systems of domination.

Rosenberg: Yes, people come along with beautiful messages about how to return to life, but the people they're speaking to have been living with domination for so long that they interpret the message in a way that supports the domination structures.

When I was in Israel, one of the men on our team was an Orthodox rabbi. One evening, I read him a couple of passages from the Bible, which I had been perusing in his house after the Sabbath dinner. I read him a passage that said something like "Dear God, give us the power to pluck out the eyes of our enemies," and I said, "David, really, how do you find beauty in a passage like this?" And he said, "Well, Marshall, if you hear just what's on the face of it, of course it's as ugly as can be. What you have to do is try to hear what is behind that message."

So I sat down with those passages to try to hear what the speaker might have said, had he known how to put it in terms of feelings and needs. It was fascinating, because what was ugly on the surface could be quite different if you sensed the feelings and needs of the speaker. I think the author of that passage was really saying, "Dear God, please protect us from people who might hurt us, and give us a way of making sure that this doesn't happen."

Killian: You've commented that, among the different forms of violence—physical, psychological, and institutional—physical violence is the least destructive. Why?

Rosenberg: Physical violence is always a secondary result. I've talked to people in prison who've committed violent crimes, and they say: "He deserved it. The guy was an asshole." It's their thinking that frightens me, how they dehumanize their victims, saying that they deserved to suffer. The fact that the man went out and shot another person scares me, too, but I'm more scared by the thinking that led to it, because it's so deeply ingrained in such a large portion of humanity.

When I worked with the Israeli police, for example, they would ask, "What do you do when someone is shooting at you already?" And I'd say, "Let's look at the last five times somebody shot at you. In these five situations, when you arrived on the scene, was the other person already shooting?" No. Not in one of the five. In each case, there were at least three verbal exchanges before any shooting started. The police re-created the dialogue for me, and I could have predicted there would be violence after the first couple of exchanges.

Killian: You have said, though, that physical force is sometimes necessary. Would you include capital punishment?

Rosenberg. No. When we do restorative justice, I want the perpetrators to stay in prison until we are finished. And I am for using whatever physical force is necessary to get them off the streets. But I don't see prison as a punitive place. I see it as a place to keep dangerous individuals until we can do the necessary restoration work. I've worked with some pretty scary folks, even serial killers. But when I stayed with it and forgot about the psychiatric point of view that some people are too damaged ever to change, I saw improvement.

Once, when I was working with prisoners in Sweden, the administrator told me about a man who'd killed five people, maybe more. "You'll know him right away," he said. "He's a monster." When I walked into the room, there he was—a big man, tattoos all over his arms. The first day, he just stared at me, didn't say a word. The second day, he just stared at me. I was growing annoyed at this administrator: *Why the hell did he put this psychopath in my group?* Already, I'd started falling back on clinical diagnosis.

Then, on the third morning, one of my colleagues said, "Marshall, I notice you haven't talked to him." And I realized that I hadn't approached that frightening inmate, because just the thought of opening up to him scared me to death. So I went in and said to the killer, "I've heard some of the things that you did to get into this prison, and when you just sit there and stare at me each day and don't say anything, I feel scared. I would like to know what's going on for you."

And he said, "What do you want to hear?" And he started to talk.

If I just sit back and diagnose people, thinking that they can't be reached, I won't reach them. But when I put in the time and energy and take a risk, I always get somewhere.

Depending on the damage that's been done to somebody, it may take three, four, five *years* of daily investment of energy to restore peace. And most systems are not set up to do that. If we're not in a position to give somebody what he or she needs to change, then my second choice would be for that person to be in prison. But I wouldn't kill anyone.

Killian: For horrendous acts, don't we need strong consequences? Just making restitution might seem a light sentence for some.

Rosenberg: Well, it depends on what we want. We know from our correctional system that if two people commit the same violent crime, and one goes to prison while the other, for whatever reason, does not, there is a much higher likelihood of continued violence on the part of the person who goes to prison. The last time I was in Twin Rivers Prison in Washington State, there was a young man who had been in three times for sexually molesting children. Clearly, attempts to change his behavior by punishing him hadn't worked. Our present system does not work. In contrast, research done in Minnesota and Canada shows that if you go through a process of restorative justice, a perpetrator is much less likely to act violently again.

As I've said, prisoners just want to apologize—which they know how to do all too well. But when I pull them by the ears and make them really look at the enormity of the suffering this other person has experienced as a result of their actions, and when I require the criminals to go inside themselves and tell me what *they* were feeling when they did it, it's a very frightening experience for them. Many say, "Please, beat me, kill me, but don't make me do this."

Killian: You speak about a protective use of force. Would you consider strikes or boycotts a protective use of force?

Rosenberg: They could be. The person who has really spent a lot of time on this is Gene Sharp. He's written books on the subject and has a wonderful article on the Internet called "168 Applications of Nonviolent Force." He shows how, throughout history, nonviolence has been used to prevent violence and to protect, not to punish.

I was working in San Francisco with a group of minority parents who were very concerned about the principal at their children's school. They said he was destroying the students' spirit. So I trained them in how to communicate with the principal. They tried to talk to him, but he said, "Get out of here. Nobody is going to tell me how to run my school." Next I explained to them the concept of protective use of force, and one of them came up with the idea of a strike: they would keep their kids out of school and picket with signs that let everyone know what kind of man this principal was. I told them they were getting protective use of force mixed up with punitive force: it sounded like they wanted to punish this man. The only way protective use of force could work, I said, was if they communicated clearly that their intent was to protect their children and not to bad-mouth or dehumanize the principal. I suggested signs that stated their needs: "We want to communicate. We want our children in school."

And the strike was very successful, but not in the way we'd imagined. When the school board heard about some of the things this principal was doing, they fired him.

Killian: But demonstrations, strikes, and rallies are often presented as aggressive by the media.

Rosenberg: Yes, we've seen protesters cross the line in some of the antiglobalization demonstrations. Some people, while trying to show how terrible corporations are, take some pretty violent actions under the guise of protective use of force.

There are two things that distinguish truly nonviolent actions from violent actions. First, there is no enemy in the nonviolent point of view. You don't see an enemy. Your thinking is clearly focused on protecting your needs. And second, your intention is not to make the other side suffer.

Killian: It seems the U.S. government has trouble differentiating between the two. It tries to make war sound acceptable by appealing to our need for safety, and then it acts aggressively.

Rosenberg: Well, we do need to protect ourselves. But you're right, there is so much else mixed up with that. When the population has been educated in retributive justice, there is nothing they want more than to see someone suffer. Most of the time, when we end up using force, it could have been prevented by using different ways of negotiating. I have no doubt this could have been the case if we'd been listening to the messages coming to us from the Arab world for so many years. This was not a new situation. This pain of theirs had been expressed over and over in many ways, and we hadn't responded with any empathy or understanding. And when we don't hear people's pain, it keeps coming out in ways that make empathy even harder.

Now, when I say this, people often think I'm justifying what the terrorists did on September 11. And of course I'm not. I'm saying that the real answer is to look at how we could have prevented it to begin with.

Killian: Some in the U.S. think that bombing Iraq is a protective use of force.

Rosenberg: I would ask them, What is your objective? Is it protection? Certain kinds of negotiations, which have never been attempted, would be more protective than any use of force. Our only option is communication of a radically different sort. We're getting to the point now where no army is able to prevent terrorists from poisoning our streams or fouling the air. We are getting to a point where our best protection is to communicate with the people we're most afraid of. Nothing else will work.

Three Wondrous Answers
from *The Miracle of Mindfulness*

THICH NHAT HANH

Let me retell a short story of Tolstoy's, the story of the Emperor's three questions. Tolstoy did not know the emperor's name . . .

One day it occurred to a certain emperor that if he only knew the answers to three questions, he would never stray in any matter.

What is the best time to do each thing?

Who are the most important people to work with?

What is the most important thing to do at all times?

The emperor issued a decree throughout his kingdom announcing that whoever could answer the questions would receive a great reward. Many who read the decree made their way to the palace at once, each person with a different answer.

In reply to the first question, one person advised that the emperor make up a thorough time schedule, consecrating every hour, day, month, and year for certain tasks and then follow the schedule to the letter. Only then could he hope to do every task at the right time.

Another person replied that it was impossible to plan in advance and that the emperor should put all vain amusements aside and remain attentive to everything in order to know what to do at what time.

Someone else insisted that, by himself, the emperor could never hope to have all the foresight and competence necessary to decide when to do each and every task and what he really needed was to set up a Council of the Wise and then to act according to their advice.

Someone else said that certain matters required immediate decision and could not wait for consultation, but if he wanted to know in advance what was going to happen he should consult magicians and soothsayers.

The responses to the second question also lacked accord.

One person said that the emperor needed to place all his trust in administrators, another urged reliance on priests and monks, while others recommended physicians. Still others put their faith in warriors.

The third question drew a similar variety of answers.

Some said science was the most important pursuit. Others insisted on religion. Yet others claimed the most important thing was military skill.

The emperor was not pleased with any of the answers and no reward was given.

After several nights of reflection, the emperor resolved to visit a hermit who lived up on the mountain and was said to be an enlightened man. The emperor wished to find the hermit to ask him the three questions, though he knew the hermit never left the mountains and was known to receive only the poor, refusing to have anything to do with persons of wealth or power. So the emperor disguised himself as a simple peasant and ordered his attendants to wait for him at the foot of the mountain while he climbed the slope alone to seek the hermit.

Reaching the holy man's dwelling place, the emperor found the hermit digging a garden in front of his hut. When the hermit saw the stranger, he nodded his head in greeting and continued to dig. The labor was obviously hard on him. He was an old man, and each time he thrust his spade into the ground to turn the earth, he heaved heavily.

The emperor approached him and said, "I have come here to ask your help with three questions: When is the best time to do each thing? Who are the most important people to work with? What is the most important thing to do at all times?"

The hermit listened attentively but only patted the emperor on the shoulder and continued digging. The emperor said, "You must be tired. Here, let me give you a hand with that." The hermit thanked him, handed the emperor the spade, and then sat down on the ground to rest.

After he had dug two rows, the emperor stopped and turned to the hermit and repeated his three questions. The hermit still did not answer, but instead stood up and pointed to the spade and said, "Why don't you rest now? I can take over again." But the emperor continued to dig. One hour passed, then two. Finally the sun began to set behind the mountain. The emperor put down the spade and said to the hermit, "I came here to ask if you could answer my three questions. But if you can't give me any answer, please let me know so that I can get on my way home."

The hermit lifted his head and asked the emperor, "Do you hear someone running over there?" The emperor turned his head. They both saw a man with a long white beard emerge from the woods. He ran wildly, pressing his hands against a bloody wound in his stomach. The man ran toward the emperor before falling unconscious to the ground, where he lay groaning. Opening the man's clothing, the emperor and hermit saw that the man had received a deep gash. The emperor cleaned the wound thoroughly and then used his own shirt to bandage it, but the blood completely soaked it within minutes. He rinsed the shirt out and bandaged the wound a second time and continued to do so until the flow of blood had stopped.

At last the wounded man regained consciousness and asked for a drink of water. The emperor ran down to the stream and brought back a jug of fresh water. Meanwhile, the sun had disappeared and the night air had begun to turn cold. The hermit gave the emperor a hand in carrying the man into the hut where they laid him down on the hermit's bed. The man closed his eyes and lay quietly. The emperor was worn out from a long day of climbing the mountain and digging the garden. Leaning against the doorway, he fell asleep. When he rose, the sun had already risen over the mountain. For a moment he forgot where he was and what he had come here for. He looked over to the bed and saw the wounded man also looking around him in confusion. When he saw the emperor, he stared at him intently and then said in a faint whisper, "Please forgive me."

"But what have you done that I should forgive you?" the emperor asked.

"You do not know me, your majesty, but I know you. I was your sworn enemy, and I had vowed to take vengeance on you, for during the last war you killed my brother and seized my property. When I learned that you were coming alone to the mountain to meet the hermit, I resolved to surprise you on your way back and kill you. But after waiting a long time there was still no sign of you, and so I left my ambush in order to seek you out. But instead of finding you, I came across your attendants, who recognized me, giving me this wound. Luckily, I escaped and ran here. If I hadn't met you I would surely be dead by now. I had intended to kill you, but instead you saved my life! I am ashamed and grateful beyond words. If I live, I vow to be your servant for the rest of my life, and I will bid my children and grandchildren to do the same. Please grant me your forgiveness."

The emperor was overjoyed to see that he was so easily reconciled with a former enemy. He not only forgave the man but promised to return all the man's property and to send his own physician and servants to wait on the man until he was completely healed. After ordering his attendants to take the man home, the emperor returned to see the hermit. Before returning to the palace the emperor wanted to repeat his three questions one last time. He found the hermit sowing seeds in the earth they had dug the day before.

The hermit stood up and looked at the emperor. "But your questions have already been answered."

"How's that?" the emperor asked, puzzled.

"Yesterday, if you had not taken pity on my age and given me a hand with digging these beds, you would have been attacked by that man on your way home. Then you would have deeply regretted not staying with me. Therefore the most important time was the time you were digging in the beds, the most important person was myself, and the most important pursuit was to help me. Later, when the wounded man ran up here, the most important time was the time you spent dressing his wound, for if you had not cared for him he would have died and you would have lost the chance to be reconciled with him. Likewise, he was the most important person, and the most important pursuit was taking care of his wound. Remember that there is only one important time and that is now. The present moment is the only time over which we have dominion. The most important person is always the person you are with, who is right before you, for who knows if you will have dealings with any other person in the future? The most important pursuit is making the person standing at your side happy, for that alone is the pursuit of life."

Tolstoy's story is like a story out of scripture: it doesn't fall short of any sacred text. We talk about social service, service to the people, service to humanity, service for others who are far away, helping to bring peace to the world—but often we forget that it is the very people around us that we must live for first of all. If you cannot serve your wife or husband or child or parent—how are you going to serve society? If you cannot make your own child happy, how do you expect to be able to make anyone else happy? If all our friends in the peace movement or of service communities of any kind do not love and help one another, whom can we love and help? Are we working for other humans, or are we just working for the name of an organization?

Service

The service of peace. The service of any person in need. The word service is so immense. Let's return first to a more modest scale: our families, our classmates, our friends, our own community. We must live for them—for if we cannot live for them, whom else do we think we are living for?

Tolstoy is a saint—what we Buddhists would call a Bodhisattva. But was the emperor himself able to see the meaning and direction of life? How can we live in the present moment, live right now with the people around us, helping to lessen their suffering and making their lives happier? How? The answer is this: We must practice mindfulness. The principle that Tolstoy gives appears easy. But if we want to put it into practice we must use the methods of mindfulness in order to seek and find the way.

I've written these pages for our friends to use. There are many people who have written about these things without having lived them, but I've only written down those things which I have lived and experienced myself. I hope you and your friends will find these things at least a little helpful along the path of our seeking: the path of our return.

Tough Love

CELESTE FREMON

Celeste Fremon is an award-winning journalist and author of Father Greg & the Homeboys. *"Tough Love" first appeared in* The Los Angeles Times Magazine, *October 15, 1995.*

At 8:15 on a summer evening, 64 mothers, most of them Latinas, walk in a procession into the parking lot of a tiny stucco church in the poorest part of East Los Angeles. The women shield their white candles from the evening wind and sing hymns in Spanish as they walk: "I have faith that the men will sing. I have faith that this song will be a song of universal love." In the rectory, five more mothers are completing a meeting with members of the street gang known as The Mob Crew—TMC for short. A few days earlier, the mothers met with Cuatro Flats, a rival gang that claims territory two blocks east. The gangs' enmity is particularly tragic because the members grew up together; they even share a set of brothers.

A week before, this war claimed the lives of two young boys: a 12-year-old Cuatro kid named Johnny and a 13-year-old named Joseph, who was mistaken for his 16-year-old TMC brother. The deaths spurred the mothers to organize these marches and meetings with the hope of hammering out a lasting truce, complete with a kind of multigang United Nations peacekeeping commission to mediate future disputes.

The peace gathering in the rectory is just breaking up as the mothers form a huge circle in the parking lot. The women motion for the gang members to join the circle. At first, the homeboys look unsure in the face of this formidable bloc of feminine energy.

"C'mon now!" One of the mothers, a smallish woman named Pamela McDuffie, bustles out of the rectory, her long magenta fingernails fluttering behind the reluctant young men she herds toward the circle.

"In their hearts they want this peace," Pam whispers to me, nodding toward the gang members, who have by now each taken a mother's hand. "You can see it in their faces."

343

Pam and the other mothers live in the twin housing projects of Pico Gardens and Aliso Village, which combine to form the largest public housing complex west of the Mississippi. Pico/Aliso is the poorest parish in the Roman Catholic Archdiocese of Los Angeles. According to statistics compiled by the Los Angeles Police Department, Pico/Aliso is also one of the city's most violent neighborhoods. Last year, the highest concentration of gang activity in Los Angeles occurred in the Hollenbeck division—and the highest concentration of gang activity in Hollenbeck was in the mile-square-plus Pico/Aliso housing projects. If life in Los Angeles is harsh and scary, it's scariest in Pico/Aliso.

I began visiting Pico/Aliso in the fall of 1990 to research a book on Latino gang members and the celebrated priest who works with them, Father Greg Boyle. In the beginning, I spent most of my time observing the homeboys who grabbed the headlines. It took a while for me to notice the community's women—and Pam.

I first observed her and the Pico/Aliso women in action in January 1991, when they decided to have a showdown with the police department. For years certain officers had been beating up neighborhood kids, and no amount of official complaints or community protests could stop the abuse. The mothers had set up a telephone tree and called one another whenever the police had a kid "hemmed up"—street parlance for spread-eagled, hands against the wall. The idea was that if there were witnesses, the police would behave appropriately. But the technique seemed only to inflame the officers, who shouted the women back inside with threats of arrest and beat on the boys anyway.

So the mothers invited Captain Bob Medina, then head of the Hollenbeck division, to attend a packed-to-the-rafters meeting at Dolores Mission, the local Catholic church. Mother after mother shared anecdotes and demanded respect. Most of the women in the room hadn't finished high school. Many couldn't read. Nonetheless, they looked the officers in the eyes and said, "If you cannot treat us and our kids as human beings, we'll do whatever it takes to get you fired."

The police got the point; the violence diminished for a while.

I live in upscale Topanga, which prides itself on its activism, yet I doubted that my neighbors and I could have confronted the police so effectively. A week later, I became curious about the crowd of adult males I saw gathering in the church parking lot each evening around 6:00. I was told that every night, in rotating shifts, Pam and the other women of the projects make dinner for 125 or so homeless men who sleep in the church. Every weekend, the same women walk the streets of the community in what had come to be called Love Walks, telling the gang members by their words and presence, "You are all our sons. We love you. We don't want you to kill each other." I began to think that the real story in East L.A. wasn't the gang members at all. It was the women.

The roots of the women's activism can be traced to Father Boyle, a Jesuit schooled in liberation theology, a philosophy that marries spirituality with social justice.

In Latin America, liberation theology had sprung from the *comunidades de base*, base communities, which were, in essence, Gospel study groups.

When Boyle was assigned to Dolores Mission in 1986, he decided to rebuild the base communities started by the previous pastor. Under Boyle's influence, they grew from three anemic gatherings to ten energetic groups of mostly women who met weekly to discuss ways to reshape themselves and their surroundings.

Traditionally, base communities are designed around three simple tenets: 1. *Ver:* See your reality. Look at what's going on around you. Are the neighborhood kids shooting at each other every night? Are the local cops behaving badly? Is one of the neighbors beating his wife and children? 2. *Analizar:* Analyze the situation in terms of the Gospel. What does the Gospel say about such problems? Would the Bible suggest hating the gang members or regarding them as kids in need of help? 3. *Actuar:* Act. What action should be taken? *Qué haría Jesús?* What would Jesus do in this situation?

The comforting abstractions of organized religion have always made me nervous. But when the women of Pico/Aliso asked themselves "Qué haría Jesús?" they were not looking for easy answers. It requires a level of commitment and action that goes well beyond what is considered sensible elsewhere. By asking "Qué haría Jesús?" the women of Pico/Aliso not only taught themselves how to face the community's problems, they also found the confidence to see the solutions that lay within reach of their own hearts and hands.

While the rest of America was talking about the importance of personal responsibility, these women were walking the talk. In Pico/Aliso, drug use and drug dealing are rampant. Small craters pock the walls of stores and apartment buildings, reminders of the time this boy was shot, that one killed. Yet for each of the community's tragic aspects, the women seem to have started a program, usually with Father Boyle's help. There is a community owned and operated day-care center (built by a construction crew of local gang members); a women's leadership training program; a mentor program for Pico/Aliso's junior high— and high school-age women; and Comíté Pro Paz en el Barrío, the women's organization struggling to keep peace in their barrio.

Certainly there are other such programs elsewhere in the country, but this profusion in a single impoverished neighborhood struck me as remarkable. In the economic and political climate of the '90s, generosity is at a premium. Yet the mothers of Pico/Aliso seemed to approach life from a different perspective, more as one would in a village, where it's understood that the fates of all the residents are intricately intertwined.

For reasons as much personal as professional, I wanted to know these women.

For a long time, I attended community social events, even bringing my son on many occasions, but I did so as an outsider. Most Pico/Aliso community events are mother-organized potlucks. Yet in the beginning, I never brought any food.

It was clear that no one expected me to bring anything, and I didn't offer. Eventually, I asked what I could contribute. Correctly assessing that my skills as a chicken *mole* chef were somewhat lacking, the women assigned me safe items to bring, like soft drinks and paper plates. Then I was invited to yet another event, and I asked Pam McDuffie what she was bringing: "I always bring my barbecued chicken," she said. "That seems to go over good."

"Do you think it'd be OK if I brought a salad?" I asked.

"I think that'd be just fine, honey," she said. "They'll be honored you made the effort."

I was going to make a nice, boring green salad. But I decided instead to use those fancy, prewashed baby greens you can get at upscale supermarkets. Plus, I added feta cheese to the usual fare of tomatoes, cucumbers, avocados, and carrots. I didn't go overboard; there was no raspberry vinegar or goat cheese. But it was a step more Westside than any salad I'd seen during my year in the projects.

That salad was a turning point. For the first hour after I set the bowl on the food table, people just walked by and stared at it. Some even gave it an experimental poke with a fork. Nobody tried it. I know this because I kept going back and checking the salad. It remained inviolate. I felt stupid.

Pam broke the spell. She had arrived late, bringing her chicken as promised. "Is this your salad?" she asked, heaping herself a plate of the rejected greens. "Delicious, girl!" she pronounced it. "I like that salty white stuff, what d'you call it?" After Pam's foray, the other women gathered around the salad for the rest of the afternoon, chatting and taking helpings until the whole bowl was gone.

At the next party, Pam asked me to bring the salad. By the third party she said, "I told them you'd bring your famous salad." Now all the women say it. "You're bringing your famous salad, aren't you?" It became my calling card. It made me an equal. Because of the salad, I was no longer an outsider. I was a girlfriend.

Pam McDuffie and I aren't the likeliest of companions. Pam wears high-heeled Spring-O-Lators with everything, including shorts. She's a white woman in her 40s, like me. But I'm an ex-USC cheerleader, ex-New York fashion editor, current DAR daughter. Pam is an ex-welfare mother who was born in, raised in, and never left the housing projects of East L.A. I wear low-key clothes in blacks and neutrals, and little more than lipstick. In addition to her manicure, Pam paints on a full face of makeup, including perfect Clara Bow lips, every day of her life, wears neon tones cut down to there and up to there, and struts all of it with panache.

I feel stressed raising one child on my own. Pam is raising a boy my son's age, as well as a drug-addicted girl whose blood mother died locked up in the Los Angeles County jail, plus her own four grand-babies. These children of her eldest daughter descend on her almost nightly, like little birds for a feeding. Joseph, her godchild, was the 13-year-old just killed in the gang war. It was Pam, with the support of the community women, who raised the money to bury him.

Pam calls everybody "honey," including Vice President Al Gore when he came on a fact-finding swing through her barrio. "C'mon, honey, give me a hug!" purred Pam, sweeping past the horrified Secret Service agents with arms outstretched. Gore obediently gave her the hug. Pam used to be the local VISTA volunteer. Now, as the official gang consultant for the city's Housing Authority, she is finally being paid for her community work. She is the first mother on the street when anything happens: a gang fight, a shooting, a minor riot.

When the mothers accepted me, so did the girls of the community. Since I have no daughters, I warmed quickly to these new relationships. Unlike those of a real mother or a real aunt, however, my responsibilities were temporary. At least that's what I thought until a girl named Grace taught me otherwise.

Grace Campos has the soft, pliable beauty of a Modigliani Madonna. She tests in the highly gifted range and wants to be a doctor. When I met her, she was still attending Bravo, a medical magnet high school in Los Angeles. But she had just become pregnant by a gang member named Stranger. On Halloween eve of 1991 I drove Grace to the hospital, where she gave birth to a daughter, Beatriz. She was not yet 16.

Four months after Beatriz was born, the harsh reality of her situation slammed Grace in the face. She was a teenage dropout with a baby, stuck in a dingy apartment with Stranger, who was spending most of his time on the street. A year later he was convicted of murder and sentenced to life without the possibility of parole. Grace talked about killing herself.

In the midst of this, Grace asked me to be her *comadre*—godmother to her daughter. When she first asked me to help baptize her baby, I was flattered, viewing my role as akin to being the maid of honor at a wedding. I understood that certain things were expected. I would buy the baby her baptism outfit and arrange for the cake at the party. That was about it. Grace and I went to Penney's department store, where she'd determined we would find the best selection of baptism dresses. As Grace leafed through a rack of lacy white garments, she chatted absently about why she had chosen me as godmother. "I think you'll be a good person for Beatriz to lean her head to when she's growing up," she said. I suddenly got the picture: Grace was asking me to make a commitment to this baby—for the rest of my life.

My first reaction was to frantically calculate how I could weasel out of my obligation. Then I took a long, hard look at the situation. I can't exactly say that I asked "Qué haría Jesús?" But here was Grace, trying to make a decent future for her daughter in the face of long odds. And she was offering me the privilege of being a part of that future. How could I possibly turn her down?

So I became godmother to a beautiful little girl and got a ringside seat to watch as Grace turned her life around. (She is now married and working as a kindergarten teacher.) As I did so, my commitment to the community underwent a change. These women, even the young women, take their friendships seriously. And if I wanted to be a girlfriend or an auntie or a *comadre*, it was clear I'd better get serious, too.

❧

In the summer of 1992 Father Boyle left Pico/Aliso for a year's sabbatical. In his absence, a war broke out between two of the project's main gangs. By then I, like Pam, could no longer ignore my responsibilities to these kids. I knew them too well and understood too vividly the high cost of doing nothing.

To plug the hole in the dike created by Boyle's departure, Pam and I formed our own informal mother posse of two. I would drive to the projects every weekend and pick Pam up, then we would walk the neighborhoods, stopping to talk to kids in the various gangs. If nothing bad happened, I would go home around midnight. If there was trouble, we would stay on the street, perhaps going to the hospital or rushing to intervene when we felt our presence could do some good.

One night we saw a group of armed gang members walking toward the territory where we knew another gang was waiting. We got between the two opposing forces, shouting them apart like mother cats hissing at bad kittens. On other nights, we cajoled armed boys off the street and into my car to take them home when we knew the situation was about to turn catastrophic.

When I told my Westside friends the stories of our mishaps, they would lecture me sternly. "You have a child to raise," they would begin. I tried to explain that my own child did always, would always, come first. But I am committed to these other kids, too. Surely one shouldn't have to sacrifice the one for the other.

I don't mean to give the wrong impression. The Pico/Aliso women can be gossipy and petty. And members of my home community of Topanga are capable of great courage and generosity when the situation demands it—most notably during the fires, floods, and other natural disasters that descend on our canyon. Perhaps the main difference is that the community makes demands on the women of Pico/Aliso with a staggering frequency, and the demands are so often unbearable. Such was the case of a woman named Marta Sosa.

Marta lives in a third-story apartment with two bedrooms and no phone. Her husband is serving time in prison, convicted of a drug-related theft. Marta had three children. Her eldest, Brenda, has grown up and moved away. Osmin, the youngest, recently turned 15. The middle child, Edgar, was 18 when he was killed in a gang-related shooting two years ago, shot by boys he had known all his life.

Edgar was known on the street as Triste—Sad Boy. He had a face dusted with freckles, a slow, cherubic smile, and sad-clown eyes that always appeared to be on the verge of tears. He had just bought a soda and was standing at the corner of Third and Clarence Streets when a flatbed truck drove by. Kids lying down in the back, Cuatro Flats gang members, opened fire. It took the paramedics 20 minutes to arrive. Edgar died at USC Medical Center.

Edgar was killed on May 15, the birthday of Stranger, the father of Grace's baby, my godchild. Pam's sister was inside the market when Edgar was shot. It was she who screamed for someone to call the ambulance. Pam and the other mothers organized the food sales to raise money for the funeral.

In years past, Marta had been *blandita*—passive—but Edgar's death transformed her. Instead of rejecting Edgar's homeboys, she befriended them. She began walking the streets with the Comité Pro Paz mothers, even walking into

Pico Gardens, where the members of Cuatro Flats hang out. The Cuatro-boys would watch her, unsure how to react. Their expressions would swing from angry defensiveness to awe and back again as they stared at the luminous face of this woman who came to pray with them.

In a matter of months, Marta went from speaking only Spanish to commanding enough English to give talks in public. The other mothers, recognizing an emerging talent, handed her the microphone when they needed a spokesperson. By the summer of 1994 she had been elected president of the Comité Pro Paz. This past spring, she left the presidency to help other L.A. communities ignite their own mother-based activism.

I got to know Marta only after Edgar's death. I had been following Edgar for my book, and his death stunned me, a peripheral adult in his life. I could hardly imagine how Marta must have felt. A psychologist might have suggested that she was submerging her grief beneath all this intense activity and that there would be hell to pay later. Yet any fool could see that her pain never went away, and her activism was the thing that kept her standing upright.

Last spring I was blindsided by some pain of my own. My father was hospitalized for two weeks and, in my heart, I knew he was dying. During those weeks, the only times I left the hospital were to be with my son or to go to the projects. I needed to be around my Pico/Aliso girlfriends even more than with other friends of much longer standing. One night I slipped away from the hospital to attend a party for a photo/video portrait of Pico/Aliso that had been created by Grace and some other teenagers from the projects. At some point during the video presentation, an image of Edgar's face flickered briefly across the screen. Marta and I clutched each other's hands and cried—her about Edgar, me about my father.

When my father died a week later, Pam and several carloads of women from the projects came to his funeral. I knew Pam was coming, but I was surprised by the presence of the other women, some of whom I barely knew. Very few of my Westside friends had come. When some asked if I wanted them there, I told them no, I was OK. The women of Pico/Aliso never asked. They just came. I had shared their grief; now they came to share mine.

A few months ago, I gathered with the women of Pico/Aliso to bury yet another of their young men. The night of the funeral, Pam sang in the choir. Other mothers circulated through the crowd, collecting money for the family. Marta was among the mourners. When the casket was opened, Marta and I went to say a prayer over the boy, a 19-year-old named Erick Rivera who, unable to imagine a future for himself, had shot himself in the head four nights before.

After we passed the casket, Marta began crying. "Who's next? Who's next?!" she sobbed. I had been asking myself the same question. Each death here calls up all the others.

349

Suddenly Marta's sobs became more extreme, as if the wound from Edgar's death had broken open anew. "I don't want to live anymore," she sobbed. "I don't want to live anymore. I don't care about nothing. I just want to see Edgar again. I don't care about nothing."

Osmin, her younger son, came up and stood beside her, panic-stricken. Immediately, Pam and a few other mothers gathered, whispering instructions to one another. One walked outside with Osmin; the rest of us tried to comfort Marta. As the night wore on, Marta needed more help than we could provide, and by midnight, four of us—Marta, Pam, Maria Teixeira (another woman who works in the neighborhood) and I—were sitting in the emergency room of White Memorial Hospital.

After three hours of bureaucratic tangles, the wait had become excruciating. To ease the tension, Pam told dark and funny stories about her impending separation from her husband. "Did I tell you about the insurance policy he took out on me? Girl! You're not going to believe this one. I get this call from Sears. This woman calls and says they're having a special and that we can double our life insurance for a tiny little fee more per month. And I tell her we don't have any life insurance. And she tells me that we do; that my husband's taken out a policy on me. That man planning to kill me! I tell you after that, girl, I'm sleeping with one eye open like this!" And she demonstrates. "I tell every one'a my friends. If something happens to me, he did it. Don't give him any'a my money. Burn it before you give it to him!"

Soon we were all laughing—even Marta. To have told this story about herself—exaggerated though it was—was an act of love on Pam's part.

Next I told a story about my divorce. Then Maria told a story. It was as if we were pooling our sadness and making a poultice to draw the sorrow out of Marta—if only for that moment. This is what girlfriends do, I kept thinking.

As terrible as the night had been, I drove home feeling peaceful. Nothing had been solved exactly. We couldn't bring Edgar back. What we could do is tell Marta by our presence, "Look: We're all in this together. This time it's your grief. Next time it could be ours."

❧

The grief continues. A week after the June meeting of mothers and gangs there was another shooting death, and the peace process was derailed again. When I found Pam late in the afternoon after the shooting, she had been on the street all day, talking with homeboys of both sides, calming things down.

"Doesn't it sometimes seem hopeless?" I blurted when I finally reached her.

"Well," she said, "on the day I spent four and a half hours in the mall, shopping for a suit to bury Joseph"—her 13-year-old godson—"I did feel hopeless. I had planned on buying him the suit for his eighth-grade graduation. But instead, there I am trying to find a suit for his funeral." Her voice cracked for a moment. "That day, I felt real hopeless. I was so filled with anger and rage that I couldn't even hug my own kids 'cause I didn't want them to feel what I was feeling, it was so terrible. And the other mothers are the same as me. They're hurting and they're angry. [For the] community, these deaths are like an earthquake that has shattered us down to ground level."

She paused to steady herself. "But we can't stay that way, you know what I'm saying? Because if we do, it means we are hopeless and our children are hopeless. No. We are going to make this peace work."

Give and Grow

ANNIE CAMPBELL

I grew up in the small town of Dunedin in New Zealand. From a very early age, I understood I should help people. This was what one did, child or adult, if one were physically able. My mother would say, "Annie, help Mrs. Irwin with her garden" or "Please darn Mr. Herrick's socks" or "Please carry the groceries for Mrs. Brown; she's got a bad back." Probably, this was my prelude to volunteer service.

After moving to Santa Fe, I started volunteering for Santa Fe Cares and provided three hours of service weekly to clients who were HIV positive or had AIDS. Here was a place I could apply what I had learned in my childhood and determine what I really wanted to do in life. I know now that I wish to be involved in similar work when I graduate from acupuncture college. Quite simply, I am a person who is willing to help as much as I can. Helping makes me feel good about myself, and I like it.

My current volunteer work involves massaging clients who are HIV positive or have AIDS. Through these weekly interactions with clients, I have learned firsthand about the problems experienced by the clients and the anguish they feel. Many clients no longer are responding to the "cocktail" drugs. They are suffering very difficult side effects from the numbers and dosages of drugs they ingest daily. Many know they are facing death, since the drugs are no longer able to hold the virus in check.

My volunteer work at Santa Fe Cares has helped me become aware of some of the issues and problems that go along with dying. I can now recognize and identify some of the stages of grief and the physical and emotional processes of dying. This experience has made me go through a gamut of emotions. It is difficult to watch the blank stares of individuals who are very medicated and to work around the smells that seem to be a part of the process of dying. There were times I wanted to escape the terrible sadness, panic, and anxiety sometimes present in patients and their families. But this experience has also been a strong catalyst in pushing me to explore my own thoughts about death and one's right to choose how and when to die. I have learned also how the disease affects one's life, attitudes, health, expectations and dreams. Being close to death has taught me much about life.

Some people turn their anguish into service. The clients who volunteer to go into the high schools amaze me. What courage they have to stand up and tell their stories in order to educate the public, hoping to prevent more people from becoming victims of this virus. One of my clients goes before Congress in Washington, D.C. to advocate for more funding and research. He also speaks to our local government bodies, though he is rarely in even moderate health.

There are three different kinds of volunteer work. Each type is suited to different personalities and physical capabilities.

- ☞ Direct Service: This is the kind of volunteer work that requires a direct, hands-on approach and necessitates personal contact with people. It can be a very gratifying experience to receive an instant smile, a thank you, or a hug from a person using this direct style of service.

- ☞ Indirect Service: This is slightly different from direct service, but no less important because it provides essential services without the direct contact with people. It is a behind-the-scenes sort of volunteer work and is often a style of service in which younger children can participate. They can collect food for the homeless, garden to beautify an area or have a class bake sale to raise money for a cause.

- ☞ Advocacy Service: This is vital volunteer work because these are the voices, fighters and agitators for change. These are the brave people with AIDS who go into the schools and tell young people what it's *really* like to have AIDS. They speak before Congress and the public to raise the public's awareness of issues and tribulations resultant from living with AIDS or HIV.

The beauty of volunteer work is it links people and groups to communities. As a result, it helps break down stereotypes we may have about groups or races and teaches people about what we have in common. We need to begin early to teach our children to volunteer and to help them understand the social and community value of this type of work. In turn, this will help young adults be prepared better for the real world.

Volunteering is not just for the young. It is for people of all ages. Recently I read an article about the "untapped force of seniors" in the United States. The article explained how seniors could provide much needed volunteer work for services and agencies in the community. In return, these seniors would gain a heightened sense of contributing, and they would begin to be valued more in our society. This concept could change the American perception of our elderly. To me this seems an exciting possibility that could bring about social change. I hope I can be someone who plays a part in making the change by telling people how much volunteering has meant to me.

By volunteering, we learn from the training we receive and the work that follows. We also learn by reflecting on what this work means to us, what it teaches us, how it changes us, and what we feel about life. Whether we learn in a classroom and take our skills out into the world or learn the skills in life and bring them into the classroom, each learning situation is a valid way to learn about service, gain knowledge, and develop our skills and talents. Performing hospice volunteer work has helped me to know this is the area in which I would like to focus my attention when I graduate from acupuncture school. Volunteering can help us find out if we are really interested in a cause or like a particular path of work.

Volunteering for Santa Fe Cares has taught me about the indomitable spirit of people who live through one of life's most trying circumstances. I have discovered there are many individuals who will reach out to lend a helping hand. It has promoted my personal and intellectual growth. From this growth, I have developed a sense of civic responsibility, which is exciting to me and exhilarating.